Studies in the History of Medieval Religion
VOLUME LII

MEDIEVAL WOMEN RELIGIOUS
c. 800–c. 1500

From the *Vita beatae Hedwigis*, Poland 1353, "Saint Hedwig and the New Convent". Ms. Ludwig XI 7 (83.MN.126), fol. 56. Courtesy of the Getty's Open Content Program.

MEDIEVAL WOMEN RELIGIOUS

c. 800–c. 1500

NEW PERSPECTIVES

Edited by

KIMM CURRAN AND JANET BURTON

THE BOYDELL PRESS

First published 2023
The Boydell Press, Woodbridge

ISBN 978-1-83765-029-3

The Boydell Press is an imprint of Boydell & Brewer Ltd
PO Box 9, Woodbridge, Suffolk IP12 3DF, UK
and of Boydell & Brewer Inc.
668 Mt Hope Avenue, Rochester, NY 14620-2731, USA
website: www.boydellandbrewer.com

A CIP catalogue record for this book is available from the British Library

The publisher has no responsibility for the continued existence or accuracy of URLs for
external or third-party internet websites referred to in this book, and does not guarantee that
any content on such websites is, or will remain, accurate or appropriate

This publication is printed on acid-free paper

Contents

Illustrations

Contributors

Janet Burton is Professor of Medieval History at University of Wales Trinity Saint David, Lampeter. She is the author of many books and articles on monastic history. With Karen Stöber she is a general editor of the *Journal of Medieval Monastic Studies* and its associated book series, *Medieval Monastic Studies* (Brepols).

Sara Charles is an editor at the Institute of Historical Research, working for the journal *Historical Research*. She researches female literacy in the post-Conquest period.

Tracy Collins was a founding director of Aegis Archaeology, a heritage consultancy firm based in Ireland. She has a special research interest in medieval women's monasticism and her publications include varied aspects of archaeology and women religious. She is currently a state archaeologist with the National Monuments Service.

Kimm Curran is an independent researcher based in Scotland. She has published on medieval women monastic superiors, women religious in Scotland, monastic education, and experiential approaches to landscapes of women's religious communities. Her research explores the landscapes and places of medieval women's religious communities in northern Europe, 1200–1600 and their heritage legacies.

Rachel M. Delman is the Heritage Partnerships Coordinator at The Oxford Research Centre in the Humanities, University of Oxford. Her research explores the relationship between gender, power, and the built environment in late medieval Britain. She has published in various scholarly journals, including the *Journal of Medieval History*, *Urban History*, *Viator*, and the *Royal Studies Journal*.

Diana Denissen is a Lecturer in Medieval English Language and Literature at the University of Lausanne (Switzerland). She works on late medieval spiritual life writing, female author- and readership, and devotional compilations. She is the author of *Middle English Devotional Compilations. Composing Imaginative Variations in Late Medieval England* (2019).

Cate Gunn is an independent researcher with a focus on medieval English literature, religious literature, and medieval devotional culture. She has written on *Ancrene Wisse* and related works, anchoritism, and Edmund of Abingdon.

She has taught occasionally for the University of Essex. She is the co-editor, with Catherine Innes-Parker, of *Texts and Traditions of Medieval Pastoral Care* (2009) and co-editor with Liz Herbert McAvoy, of *Medieval Anchorites in Their Communities* (2017).

Elizabeth A. Lehfeldt is Professor of History and Mandel Professor in Humanities at Cleveland State University. She is the author of *Religious Women in Golden Age Spain* (2005). Her work has appeared in various scholarly journals including *Renaissance Quarterly* and *Sixteenth Century Journal.*

Alison More is Associate Professor of Medieval Studies at the University of St Michael's College, University of Toronto. Her research investigates the intersections between social and religious culture in northern Europe. She is the author of *Fictive Orders and Feminine Religious Identities, 1200–1600* (2018).

Mercedes Pérez Vidal is the Ramon y Cajal senior researcher and lecturer at the Autonomous University of Madrid – UAM. She holds a PhD in Art History and her recent publications include *Arte y liturgia en los monasterios de Dominicas en Castilla: Desde los orígenes hasta la reforma observante (1218–1506)* (2021). She is the editor of *Women Religious Between the Cloister and the World: Nunneries in Europe and the Americas, ca. 1200–1700.*

Laura Richmond completed her PhD on vowesses of late medieval England in 2017. She works on gender and religion in England in the fourteenth, fifteenth and sixteenth centuries and is a regular contributor and an advisory editor at the Oxford Dictionary of National Biography.

Yvonne Seale is Associate Professor of History at the State University of New York, Geneseo. Her research focuses on the history of Premonstratensian women in medieval France, and she is the co-editor, with Heather Wacha, of a forthcoming edition of the thirteenth-century cartulary of the abbey of Prémontré.

Katharine Sykes is Associate Professor in Early Medieval History at the University of Birmingham. Her research interests include monastic legislation, mixed-sex communities, and the relationships between monastic and secular households. Her publications include *Inventing Sempringham* (2011).

Steven Vanderputten is a Full Professor of Medieval History at Ghent University. He is the author of numerous articles, book chapters, edited volumes, and monographs on monastic history. His principal publications include *Monastic Reform as Process* (2013), *Dark Age Nunneries* (2018), *Medieval Monasticisms* (2020), and *Dismantling the Medieval* (2022).

Preface

The idea for this book was first conceived during many lively discussions at the International Medieval Congress at Leeds over the years and a proposal was submitted to Boydell and Brewer in the late summer of 2019. When we agreed a submission date no-one had any idea of how all our lives would be changed later that year and as we passed into 2020. As with so many publications this book grew to life in the challenging circumstances of a pandemic, details of which do not need to be repeated here. However, this makes it more than ever necessary for us to express our sincere thanks to our authors, who have come through lockdowns, lack of access to their offices, to libraries and archives, and through illness, caring for others, and volunteering in emergency foodbanks. All our contributors will have individuals and institutions they would like to acknowledge. Our thanks go out to them for sticking with us and producing their chapters and answering our queries with remarkable good cheer. We are grateful as well to Caroline Palmer and all her colleagues at Boydell and Brewer for their utmost patience and allowing us extra time to submit the manuscript. Any academic endeavour is dependent on domestic goodwill and encouragement: Kimm would like to thank Brian and Max, and Janet, as ever, thanks William.

Kimm Curran, Glasgow
Janet Burton, Lampeter and Oxford
December 2021

Abbreviations

AASS	*Acta Sanctorum*
AFH	*Archivum Franciscanum Historicum*
AFP	*Archivum Fratrum Praedicatorum*
Anchoritic Traditions	Liz Herbert McAvoy (ed.), *Anchoritic Traditions of Medieval Europe* (Woodbridge, 2010)
AW	Bella Millett (ed.), *Ancrene Wisse: A Corrected Edition of the Text in Cambridge, Corpus Christi College, MS 402, with variants from other manuscripts*, 2 vols, vol. 1 EETS, OS, 325 (Oxford, 2005)
AW Guide	Bella Millett (trans.), *Ancrene Wisse: Guide for Anchoresses* (Exeter, 2009)
BAR	British Archaeology Reports
Berman, *White Nuns*	Constance H. Berman, *The White Nuns: Cistercian Abbeys for Women in Medieval France* (Philadelphia, 2018)
Berman, *Cistercian Evolution*	Constance H. Berman, *The Cistercian Evolution: The Invention of a Religious Order in Twelfth-Century Europe* (Philadelphia, 2000)
BL	British Library, London
Burton and Stöber, *Monasteries and Society*	Janet Burton and Karen Stöber (eds), *Monasteries and Society in the British Isles in the Later Middle Ages* (Woodbridge, 2008)
CCO	Birkedal Bruun, Mette (ed.), *The Cambridge Companion to the Cistercian Order* (Cambridge, 2012)
CH	*Church History*
CHMM	Alison I. Beach and Isabelle Cochelin (eds), *The Cambridge History of Medieval Monasticism in the Latin West*, vols 1 and 2 (Cambridge, 2020)

Cîteaux	*Cîteaux Commentarii Cistercienses*
Constable, *Reformation*	Giles Constable, *The Reformation of the Twelfth Century* (Cambridge, 1996)
CPL	*Calendar of Entries in the Papal Registers Relating to Great Britain and Ireland: Papal Letters*
EETS	Early English Text Society
EETS, ES	Early English Text Society, Extra Series
EETS, OS	Early English Text Society, Original Series
Elkins, *Holy Women*	Sharon K. Elkins, *Holy Women of Twelfth-Century England* (Chapel Hill, NC, 1985)
EME	*Early Medieval Europe*
Female vita religiosa	Gert Melville and Anne Müller (eds), *Female Vita Religiosa Between Late Antiquity and the High Middle Ages: Structures, Developments and Spatial Contexts* (Berlin, 2011)
Foot, *Veiled Women*	Sarah Foot, *Veiled Women: Volume I: The Disappearance of Nuns from Anglo Saxon England* (Aldershot, 2000)
FS	*Franciscan Studies*
GH	*Gender and History*
GMC	Roberta Gilchrist, *Gender and Material Culture: The Archaeology of Religious Women* (London, 1994)
Golding, *Gilbert*	Brian Golding, *Gilbert of Sempringham and the Gilbertine Order, c. 1130–c. 1300* (Oxford, 1995)
Griffiths, *Garden of Delights*	Fiona J. Griffiths, *The Garden of Delights: Reform and Renaissance for Women in the Twelfth Century* (Philadelphia, 2007)
Hall, *Women and the Church*	Dianne Hall, *Women and the Church in Medieval Ireland, c. 1140–1540* (Dublin, 2003)
Hamburger, *Nuns as Artists*	Jeffrey F. Hamburger, *Nuns as Artists: The Visual Culture of a Medieval Convent* (Berkeley, 1997)
HR	*Historical Research*
JEH	*Journal of Ecclesiastical History*

JMH	*Journal of Medieval History*
JMModS	*Journal of Medieval and Early Modern Studies*
JMMS	*Journal of Medieval Monastic Studies*
Johnson, *Equal*	Penelope Johnson, *Equal in Monastic Profession: Religious Women in Medieval France* (Chicago, 1991)
JRSAI	*Journal of the Royal Society of Antiquaries of Ireland*
Kerr, *Religious Life*	Berenice M. Kerr, *Religious Life for Women, c. 1100–c. 1350: Fontevraud in England* (Oxford, 1999)
KNOB	*Bulletin van de Koninklijke Nederlandse oudheidkundige bond*
Lehfeldt, *Golden Age Spain*	Elizabeth A. Lehfeldt, *Religious Women in Golden Age Spain: The Permeable Cloister* (Burlington, 2005)
Lester, *Creating Cistercian Nuns*	Anne E. Lester, *Creating Cistercian Nuns: The Women's Religious Movement and its Reform in Thirteenth-Century Champagne* (Ithaca, 2011)
MA	*Medieval Archaeology*
Makowski, *Periculoso*	Elizabeth Makowski, *Canon Law and Cloistered Women: Periculoso and Its Commentators, 1298–1545* (Washington, DC, 1997)
Medieval Anchorites	Cate Gunn and Liz Herbert McAvoy (eds), *Medieval Anchorites in their Communities* (Cambridge, 2017)
Medieval Feminist Forum	*Medieval Feminist Forum: A Journal of Gender and Sexuality*
MGH	Monumenta Germaniae Historica
NQ	*Notes and Queries*
Nuns' Literacies: Antwerp	V. Blanton, V. O'Mara, and P. Stoop (eds), *Nuns' Literacies in Medieval Europe: The Antwerp Dialogue* (Turnhout, 2017)
Nuns' Literacies: Hull	V. Blanton, V. O'Mara, and P. Stoop (eds), *Nuns' Literacies in Medieval Europe: The Hull Dialogue* (Turnhout, 2013)

Nuns' Literacies: Kansas	V. Blanton, V. O'Mara, and P. Stoop (eds), *Nuns' Literacies in Medieval Europe: The Kansas City Dialogue* (Turnhout, 2015)
OHCM	Bernice M. Kaczynski (ed.), *The Oxford Handbook of Christian Monasticism* (Oxford, 2020)
OHWG	J. M. Bennett and R. Mazo Karras (eds), *The Oxford Handbook of Women and Gender in Medieval Europe* (Oxford, 2013)
Oliva, *FMN*	Marilyn Oliva, *The Convent and the Community in Late Medieval England: Female Monasteries in the Diocese of Norwich, 1350 to 1540* (Woodbridge, 1998)
PL	J.-P. Migne (ed.), *Patrologia cursus completus, series Latina*, 221 vols (Paris, 1844–64)
P & P	*Past and Present*
Power, *Nunneries*	Eileen Power, *Medieval English Nunneries c. 1275 to 1535* (Cambridge, 1922)
PSAS	*Proceedings of the Society of Antiquaries of Scotland*
RB	*Revue Bénédictine*
RSB	*Rule of St Benedict*
RM	*Revue Mabillon*
SCH	Studies in Church History
Scheepsma, *MRW Low Countries*	Wybren Scheepsma, *Medieval Religious Women in the Low Countries: The 'Modern Devotion', the Canonesses of Windesheim, and Their Writings*, trans. by D. S. Johnson (Woodbridge, 2004)
Schulenburg, *Forgetful of their Sex*	Jane Tibbetts Schulenburg, *Forgetful of their Sex: Female Sanctity and Society, ca. 500–1100* (Chicago, 1998)
Spear, *Leadership*	Valerie Spear, *Leadership in Medieval English Nunneries* (Woodbridge, 2005)
TEAMS	Teaching Association for Medieval Studies
TELAS	*Transactions of the East Lothian Antiquarian and Field Naturalists' Society*

Thompson, *Women Religious*	Sally Thompson, *Women Religious: The Founding of English Nunneries After the Norman Conquest* (Oxford, 1991)
TNA	The National Archives, London
TRHS	*Transactions of the Royal Historical Society*
Vanderputten, *DAN*	Steven Vanderputten, *Dark Age Nunneries: The Ambiguous Identity of Female Monasticism, 800–1050* (Ithaca, 2018)
Venarde, *Women's Monasticism*	B. L. Venarde, *Women's Monasticism and Medieval Society: Nunneries in France and England, 890–1215* (New York, 1997)
VCH	Victoria County History
Warren, *Spiritual Economies*	Nancy Bradley Warren, *Spiritual Economies: Female Monasticism in Later Medieval England* (Philadelphia, 2001)
WMMW	Janet Burton and Karen Stöber (eds), *Women in the Medieval Monastic World* (Turnhout, 2015)
Yorke, *Anglo-Saxon*	Barbara Yorke, *Nunneries and the Anglo-Saxon Royal Houses* (London, 2003)

Introduction

KIMM CURRAN AND JANET BURTON

THIS book addresses varied aspects of the lives and communities of medieval women religious in western Europe. These lives and communities were complex and often transcended boundaries of what was expected of medieval women more generally: they might exhibit more in the way of agency, authority, and autonomy than previous scholarship has allowed – and certainly more in the way of ambiguity and fluidity in their ways of life. The complexity of defining women religious as one thing or another – enclosed religious, canoness, anchorite – or their role in medieval society, is found in the example of St Hedwig of Silesia (1174–†1243), duchess of Poland. Hedwig was educated in a women's religious community in her early years, a member of a well-connected family, considered pious, and participated in works of charity, especially for women.[1] She was the founder of the women's community at Trebnitz, Poland – its construction and introduction of the community of women is pictured on the cover of this volume – and after the death of her husband, she moved into the community, where her daughter, Gertrude, was abbess, and resided there as a lay sister until her death.[2]

Whilst her life may seem an exception to the norm, it serves as starting point in thinking about the perception of medieval women religious, how they are often defined or categorised, and compared with the lives and experiences of male religious. Indeed, St Hedwig is often viewed through the lens of her hagiography, the manuscript culture and production of the *Vita*, and late medieval art and devotional texts[3] rather than in the context of late medieval monastic life, the

---

[1] See for example, Getty Museum, *Vita beatae Hedwigis*, MS. Ludwig XI 7 (83.MN.126), fos 18, 30, 38v, 46, 56v, 59.

[2] St Hedwig did not take vows to enter religious life, and the absence of the habit can be seen in the manuscript where she is pictured next to enclosed women religious, *Vita beatae Hedwigis*, fos. 70r, 70v. For the construction of the community at Trebnitz, see *Vita beatae Hedwigis*, fo. 56.

[3] See for example, Jeffrey F. Hamburger, *The Visual and the Visionary: Art and Female Spirituality in Late Medieval Germany* (New York, 1998), pp. 437–40; *Nuns as Artists*, pp. 173–4.

varied religious experiences for women at the time, and her contribution to the regional identity of women religious more generally. This demonstrates that the lives of women religious and communities were diverse, not based solely on a life imagined or embodied in one text, and deserve further investigation.

Women Religious and Their Communities: A Survey of Historical Approaches

Despite the many recent studies of women religious,[4] the dominant discourse still manages to make them footnotes, or separate categories, rather than placing them within wider monastic movements, and include them in the broad canvas of women's history of the Middle Ages.[5] The many scattered references in general monastic histories or histories of monastic orders, for example, indicate how challenging it is to incorporate or place women religious within the wider context of orders and movements. On the one hand, excluding them could suggest belittling the experience of women religious within wider religious orders, but including them also presents further issues of identity and ensuring that all nuances of women's religious life are incorporated – which brings challenges of gender, lived experience, and authority.

Women religious and their communities have often been overshadowed by comparing them to the religious experiences and lives of men – whether that be institutionally (orders), organisation, and leadership, or neglecting them altogether. The reason often cited is lack of sources – documentary and material – or being 'too different' because they do not fit into neat institutional boxes used to study male religious. Historians have been quick to draw attention to the dearth of archival and documentary evidence (which is not always the case, however) and the need to rely on sparse references and negative historiography. The lack of material remains (archaeology and material culture) for many women religious also makes understanding the lives and communities of these women more demanding. Regardless of these challenges, those who undertake the study of the lives and communities of women religious have debunked these ideas regarding the lack of evidence and found creative ways to examine the rich, diverse sources – both written and material – demonstrating that these lives are worthy of further examination. This volume and the wealth of references just in the footnotes to this book are witness to this welcome scholarly attention.

---

[4]   The studies are too numerous to cite but examples may be found in the select bibliography to this volume.

[5]   There are some exceptions. See for example Steven Vanderputten, *Medieval Monasticisms: Forms and Experiences of the Monastic Life in the Latin West* (Munich, 2020).

Over the last twenty or thirty years, there has been an explosion of books, papers, and articles, on women religious.[6] Historians have explored the nature of women's religious communities at certain periods of time or regions, in relation to individual establishments, and thematically. A vibrant and sometimes contentious scholarship has addressed the relationship between women's communities and the various monastic orders, notably the Cistercian, as well as mendicant women. Other scholars have considered aspects of female leadership, relations between religious men and religious women, literacy, and patronage of art and literature. The list has grown apace. What follows is a brief summary of some of the main trends in scholarship spanning the last three decades or so, which provide a context for this collection; references are perforce selective.[7]

It is notable that in the last few years scholars have begun to add an 's' to the word 'monasticism', to convey a sense that there was no one medieval 'monasticism': it was a diverse movement, which did not develop lineally or uniformly.[8] Consider the issue of 'reform'. Traditional accounts have seen monasticism as a series of phases, of highs and lows, decline and resurgence, reform and renewal, followed by more decline. This assumes a teleological view and ignores both chronological and regional or local patterns and diversities. A major landmark at the beginning of the period covered by this book is the series of reforming councils of the second decade of the ninth century. These accounts are traditionally said to have produced a female monastic landscape in which woman's houses were either 'Benedictinised', with their enclosed women following the Rule of St Benedict, or undertook a more outward-facing lifestyle as secular canonesses. Vanderputten and others have questioned this neat paradigm and have demonstrated that daily observances and practice within both types of community were 'ambiguous'.[9] Indeed, Vanderputten argues that the Aachen decrees were not intended to be normative but rather 'written reference points' that allowed for experimentation.[10] Moreover, contrary to the discourse of traditional scholarship, women did not allow themselves to be categorised, by male church leaders, as

---

[6]   See for example, select bibliography to this volume.

[7]   This is largely an anglophone historiography and reflects much wider scholarship in other languages. This is a focus which aligns with the intention of this book, namely to open this field to students and new researchers.

[8]   Vanderputten, *Medieval Monasticisms*, pp. 1–4; see also Gert Melville, *The World of Medieval Monasticism: Its History and Forms of Life*, trans. by James Mixson (Collegeville, 2016).

[9]   Vanderputten, *Medieval Monasticisms*, pp. 164–5. Vanderputten expands on the themes of ambiguity and 'enduring diversity', below, pp. 22–42.

[10]   Vanderputten, *DAN*, p. 9.

'nuns' or 'canonesses'. On the contrary, women's communities are now seen as active agents in determining their own identity.

Sarah Foot has argued that women religious in England between the late ninth century and the coming of the Normans were active in setting their own lifestyle, which was marked by diversity: some entered cloistered communities, others lived in less formal groups. This is reflected in the variety of vocabulary employed to describe religious women. Her recognition of the more flexible definition of 'religious women' has permitted the identification of more women's communities than a 'rigid Benedictine interpretation' had previously allowed.[11] Moreover, Foot argues, this diversity continued into the tenth century: there is no evidence, as has been traditionally accepted, to suggest that the majority of women's houses – still less the smaller communities – were involved in the monastic revival that led to the adoption of the Rule of St Benedict found in houses for men.[12] Barbara Yorke, too, suggests that although women's communities in England were affected in some ways by the tenth-century reform, in other respects they lived in ways that were 'contrary to the Benedictine Rule, but were relevant to their roles as dynastic foundations including retention of private wealth and the ability of their members to leave in order to be married'.[13]

One way in which women religious sought to determine their self-identity was through the commissioning and production of hagiographies providing them with a past, a history that allowed them to assert their independence to decide. Jirki Thibault, for instance, draws on the written life of Hathumoda, abbess of the Saxon monastery of Gandesheim, to demonstrate how women constructed an identity for themselves, and hence a distinct place, within what she calls 'an increasingly dense and dynamic monastic environment'.[14] This theme also emerges in Steven Vanderputten's study of Remiremont, in which he argues that the hagiographies composed at the community were part of a strategy, on the part of its women, not only to recast the origin myth of their house, but also to align their community with heads of neighbouring male houses, and to use memories of abbatial authority and communal identity to secure its independence.[15]

---

[11] Sarah Foot, *Veiled Women I*; vol. II *Female Religious Communities in England, 871–1066* (Aldershot, 2000), vol. 1, pp. 2, 26–30, 86, 96–104, at p. 86. Foot detects that *mynecenu* often refers to a cloistered woman, and *nunne* to a vowess who continued to live within the world.

[12] Foot, *Veiled Women*, I, pp. 87–96.

[13] Yorke, *Anglo-Saxon*, p. 192.

[14] Jirki Thibault, 'Female Abbatial Leadership and the Shaping of Communal Identity in Ninth-Century Saxony: The *Life* of Hathumoda of Gandesheim', *JMMS*, 7 (2018), 21–45, at p. 23.

[15] Steven Vanderputten, '"Against the Custom": Hagiographical Rewriting and Female Abbatial Leadership at Mid-Eleventh Century Remiremont', *JMMS*, 10 (2021), 41–66.

It is not only in the abbeys of Saxony that women superiors demonstrated strong leadership. In a study that ranges over nine centuries at Sainte-Croix of Poitiers Jennifer Edwards has demonstrated ways in which women superiors wielded considerable authority and took on challenges from elite families, kings, and popes, and indeed the male community of canons on their own doorstep: they did this by conscious use of their archive, and their visual culture.[16] Like the women of Gandesheim and Remiremont, they delved into the past to reinforce their present and protect their future.

An important theme in Edwards's *Superior Women* is how the heads of Sainte-Croix drew on the memory of their founder, the Frankish queen Radegund, to sustain their own authority, which was reinforced by the powerful support network garnered by Radegund herself. Houses of women religious were not regarded as second best, or inferior but rather the houses over which they ruled might be regarded as prestigious institutions, and their intercessions and com-memorations were highly prized. Another women's community whose prestige, property, and wealth were demonstrably forged and sustained by networks of power and patronage was S. Salvatore (later S. Giulia) di Brescia. Annamaria Pazienza and Veronica West-Harling interrogate the ninth-century *Liber vitae* of this community to demonstrate the ways networks of patronage endowed the house with deep roots in the social and political landscape of Lombardy and acted as a bridge between the older aristocracy and the new Frankish imperial officials.[17]

This leads us to another important strand in recent scholarship: the place of women in the 'new orders' that emerged in the late eleventh and twelfth centu-ries. Twenty years ago, it was common to read of an inbuilt hostility within the Cistercian Order to the acceptance of women. That women religious held a full and rightful place in the Cistercian Order has been championed by Constance Berman for two decades, beginning with her controversial re-evaluation of the origins and development of the Cistercian Order (2000), and continuing in such publications as *Women and Monasticism in Medieval Europe: Sisters and Patrons of the Cistercian Reform* (2002).[18] More recently Berman has attributed tradi-tional views of Cistercian hostility to what she perceives as misogynist attitudes, not among medieval Cistercian monks, but among generations of historians.[19]

---

[16] Jennifer Edwards, *Superior Women: Medieval Female Authority in Poitiers' Abbey of Sainte-Croix* (Oxford, 2019).

[17] Annamaria Pazienza and Veronica West-Harling, 'Networking Nuns: Imperial Power and Family Alliances at S. Salvatore di Brescia (*c.* 837–61)', *JMMS*, 10 (2021), 9–39.

[18] Berman, *The Cistercian Evolution*; and see also her rather earlier 'Were there Twelfth-Century Cistercian Nuns?', *CH*, 68 (1999), 824–64; *Women and Monasticism in Medieval Europe: Sisters and Patrons of Cistercian Reform* (Kalamazoo, MI, 2002).

[19] Berman, *White Nuns*.

While not necessarily agreeing with her in all respects, other historians have patiently examined the documentary and literary evidence to confirm that there were, indeed, Cistercian women religious: Anne Lester for Champagne,[20] Guido Cariboni for Italy,[21] Brian Patrick McGuire for Denmark and Sweden;[22] Carmen Florea for Transylvania;[23] Erin Jordan for the Low Countries,[24] Elizabeth Freeman for England, and Janet Burton for England and Wales.[25] Yet it is important not to homogenise women's Cistercian experience. Looking at chronologies of expansion demonstrates that it was quicker in some places and slower in others; some regions enjoyed a spread of women's communities in the twelfth century; in others it did not appear until the thirteenth – and later. In some countries, Cistercian houses of women were deemed to be abbeys, in others they were priories. These regional diversities are yet to be explored to the full, but studies of individual houses and areas, such as those mentioned above, are moving us towards a more complete picture.[26]

Although the Cistercian Order continues to dominate studies, other emergent orders of the twelfth century have attracted attention. Brian Golding's 1995 study of the development of the Gilbertine Order stands now as a classic account of the emergence and shaping of the only monastic order to have its origins in England, and of the foundation and endowment of individual houses – the latter aspect now enhanced by Jill Redford's edition of the Alvingham cartulary.[27] Further to this, Katharine Sykes has explored the development of the role of the master within

---

[20] Lester, *Creating Cistercian Nuns;* see also Bernadette Barrière and Marie-Elizabeth Henneau (eds), *Cîteaux et les femmes* (Paris, 2001).

[21] Guido Cariboni, 'Cistercian Nuns in Northern Italy: Varieties of Foundations and Construction of an Identity', in *WMMW*, pp. 53–74.

[22] Brian Patrick McGuire, 'Cistercian Nuns in Twelfth- and Thirteenth-Century Denmark and Sweden: Far from the Madding Crowd', in *WMMW*, pp. 167–84.

[23] Carmen Florea, '"For They Wanted Us to Serve Them": Female Monasticism in Medieval Transylvania', in *WMMW*, pp. 211–27.

[24] Erin Jordan, '*Pro remedio anime sue:* Cistercian Nuns and Space in the Low Countries', in *WMMW*, pp. 279–98; 'Gender Concerns: Monks, Nuns, and Patronage of the Cistercian Order in Thirteenth-Century Flanders and Hainault', *Speculum*, 87 (2012), 62–94; *Women, Power and Religious Patronage in the Middle Ages* (Basingstoke and New York, 2006).

[25] Elizabeth Freeman, 'Cistercian Nuns in Medieval England: Unofficial meets Official', *SCH*, 42 (2006), 110–19; Janet Burton, '*Moniales* and *Ordo Cisterciensis* in Medieval England and Wales', in *Female vita religiosa*, pp. 375–89.

[26] See, for instance, Anne E. Lester, 'A Shared Imitation: Cistercian Convents and Crusader Families in Thirteenth-Century Champagne', *JMH*, 35:4 (2009), 353–70, in which she argues that women were drawn to Cistercian spirituality as a way of participating in Christ's passion that was a feature of crusading fervour.

[27] Golding, *Gilbert*; Jill Redford (ed.), *The Cartulary of Alvingham Priory* (Lincoln, 2018).

the order and the innovatory nature of Gilbertine organisation.[28] Sykes has also written effectively on how monastic legislators and founders of new communities provided for the spiritual care of women religious (*cura monialium*) and reconciled the integrity of communities with physical separation within them. Her study extends from the Gilbertines to the Dominican house of St Sisto in Rome.[29] Relations between women and men within a religious order are also considered in connection with Fontevraud, an abbey and an order in which women ruled men (unlike Sempringham, in which men ruled over women), with Constant Mews detecting early uncertainty about gender roles in this community.[30] Discussion has moved on from the constitutional aspects of the 'double houses' of these orders to more developed questions of gender and the body.[31] Women religious and their interactions with men of the Premonstratensian Order are also getting further attention regarding their status, identity, and recruitment.[32] Other themes currently being explored are the development of the order, the collaboration between men and women religious, as well as the ambiguous nature of communities.[33]

Houses of women following the Rule of St Augustine have not figured to any great extent in recent scholarship, though there are notable exceptions. Research into the situation in Ireland has demonstrated the preponderance of houses of Augustinian canonesses among religious houses for women. The majority of these were associated with the Order of Arrouaise. Edel Bhreathnach treats houses of canons and canonesses together, seeing the important dynamic as the widespread adoption of the Rule of St Augustine.[34] Christy Cunniffe explores the foundations

---

[28] Katharine Sykes, *Inventing Sempringham: Gilbert of Sempringham and the Origins of the Role of the Master* (Berlin, 2011).

[29] Katharine Sykes, 'Rewriting the Rules: Gender, Bodies, and Monastic Legislation in the Twelfth and Thirteenth Centuries', *JMMS*, 9 (2020), 107–45.

[30] On Fontevraud: Bruce L. Venarde, 'Robert of Arbrissel and Women's *vita religiosa*', in *Female vita religiosa*, pp. 329–40; Jacques Dalarun's 1986 monograph, published in French, is now available in English translation: *Robert of Arbrissel: Sex, Sin, and Salvation in the Middle Ages,* trans. by Bruce L. Venarde (Washington, DC, 2006); See also Constant J. Mews, 'Negotiating the Boundaries of Gender in Religious Life: Robert of Arbrissel and Hersende, Abelard and Heloise', *Viator*, 37 (2006), 113–48. On Sempringham, Fontevraud, and the Paraclete, see Katherine Sykes, below, pp. 44–50.

[31] See Alison I. Beach and Isabelle Cochelin, 'The Double Monastery as a Historiographical Problem (Fourth to Twelfth Century)', in *CHMM*, pp. 561–78, which stresses diversity.

[32] Shelley Wolbrink, 'Women in the Premonstratensian Order of Northwestern Germany, 1120–1250', *Catholic Historical Review*, 89 (2003), 387–408.

[33] See Sykes, below, pp. 50–5.

[34] 'The *Vita Apostolica* and the origin of the Augustinian Canons and Canonesses in Medieval Ireland', in Martin Brown OSB and Colmán Ó Clabaigh OSB (eds), *Households of God: The Regular Canons and Canonesses of Saint Augustine and of Prémontré in Medieval Ireland* (Dublin, 2019), pp. 1–27.

at Clonfert, arguing that what began as a double or co-located house for men and women became two separate establishments by the thirteenth century, while Tracy Collins examines the archaeologies of female houses of the Augustinian Order and the affiliation of Arrouaise.[35] More regional studies such as these would further our understanding of the distinctiveness of the life and observance of these women.

It has been common to ignore or marginalise the role of women in the military orders that emerged in the twelfth century – very likely because it was assumed that they had no place in military enterprises. Myra M. Born has demonstrated that these orders did indeed admit women, as full sisters and as donats or members of a confraternity. They were valued for the spirituality and their prayers and contributed to the care of the sick. Her study moves beyond the well-known orders of the Knights Templar and Hospitaller to the Teutonic Order, the Orders of Santiago, St Lazarus, and St Thomas of Acre.[36] As she so rightly states, however, we should not assume that women's participation was limited to caring functions: 'The fact that the order welcomed these women, made the effort to accommodate them and expressed the value of their prayers mean that they took the religious life of these women and that in return these women should be considered in the history of the order in earnest'.[37] The essays in a collection edited by Anthony Luttrell and Helen Nicholson, which range from chronological studies, to discussions of particular regions and houses, also stress that Hospitaller women fulfilled diverse functions, that they were accommodated in a variety of ways, and followed different ways of life: there was no 'one rule' for them.[38]

Questioning of traditional narratives has also informed recent work on mendicant women, which has stressed the malleability and multiplicity of forms of life 'particularly evident in documentation for women'.[39] The research of Alison More has cut through the 'fictive' histories that were constructed to create the illusion that women were from the early years incorporated within the formal

---

[35] Christy Cunniffe, 'The Canons and Canonesses of St Augustine at Clonfert', in Brown and Ó Clabaigh (eds), *Households of God*, pp. 103–23; Tracy Collins, 'An archaeology of Augustinian Nuns in Later Medieval Ireland', in Brown and Ó Clabaigh (eds), *Households of God*, pp. 87–102.

[36] Myra M. Born, *Women in the Military Orders of the Crusades* (New York, 2012).

[37] Born, *Women in the Military Orders*, p. 4.

[38] See A. Luttrell and H. J. Nicolson (eds), *Hospitaller Women in the Middle Ages* (Aldershot, 2006). For a local study see also H. J. Nicholson, 'The Sisters' House at Minwear, Pembrokeshire: Analysis of the Documentary and Archaeological Evidence', *Archaeologia Cambrensis*, 151 (2002), 109–38.

[39] Frances Andrews, 'The Early Mendicants', in *OHCM*, pp. 264–84, at p. 276, referencing B. Roest, *Order and Disorder: The Poor Clares between Foundation and Reform* (Leiden, 2013).

male structures of the mendicants, obscuring their origins in informal groups of pious women who wished to live within the world.[40] The struggle against ecclesiastical efforts to reconstruct women's mendicant origins is also highlighted by Catherine Mooney in relation to Clare's foundation of the Order of San Damiano (the Poor Clares).[41] Similar issues are highlighted by Joan Mueller and Lezlie Knox.[42] Further to this, Sean Field's work on Isabelle of Longchamp reiterates the need to look at variations on Franciscan life for women. The development of the *sorores minores* of Longchamp indicates how women exercised agency, and authority, and negotiated institutional forms of power within the dominant Franciscan Order.[43] Dominican scholarship has ranged from the development of formal legislation for Dominican women, to the foundation of individual houses, and female spirituality, to the reception of the writings of Catherine of Siena and her wider role in Italian public life.[44]

Important in all these studies is the relationship between religious men and women. Traditional scholarship has stressed the complete dependence of religious women on men. Rooted in medieval commonplaces (pace: the author of the Life

---

[40] Alison More, *Fictive Orders and Feminine Religious Identities, 1200–1600* (Oxford, 2018); 'Dynamics of Regulation, Innovation, and Invention', in James D. Mixson and Bert Roest (eds), *A Companion to Observant Reform in the Late Middle Ages and Beyond* (Leiden, 2015), pp. 85–110; 'Between Charity and Controversy: The Grey Sisters, Liminality, and the Religious Life', in Jennifer Kolpacoff Deane and Anne E. Lester (eds), *Between Orders and Heresy: Rethinking Medieval Religious Movements* (Toronto, 2022), pp. 242–62. Alison More expands of some of these themes, below, pp. 61–75.

[41] Catherine M. Mooney, *Clare of Assisi and the Thirteenth-Century Church: Religious Women, Rules, and Resistance* (Philadelphia, 2016).

[42] Joan Mueller, *The Privilege of Poverty: Clare of Assisi, Agnes of Prague, and the Struggle for a Franciscan Rule for Women* (Philadelphia, 2006), and *A Companion to Clare of Assisi: Life, Writings, and Spirituality* (Leiden, 2010); Lezlie Knox, *Creating Clare of Assisi: Female Franciscan Identities in Later Medieval Italy* (Leiden, 2008). See also Roest, *Order and Disorder* (above, note 40).

[43] Sean L. Field, *Isabelle of France: Capetian Sanctity and Franciscan Identity in the Thirteenth Century* (Notre Dame, 2006).

[44] Julie Anne Smith, 'Prouille, Madrid, Rome: the evolution of the earliest Dominican Instituta', *JMH*, 35:4 (2009), 340–52; Maria Pia Alberzoni, 'Jordan of Saxony and the Monastery of St Agnese in Bologna', *FS*, 68 (2010), 1–19; Paul Lee, *Nunneries, Learning and Spirituality in Late Medieval English Society: The Dominican Priory of Dartford* (York, 2001); Claire Taylor Jones, *Ruling the Spirit: Women, Liturgy, and Dominican Reform in Late Medieval Germany* (Philadelphia, 2018); Jennifer N. Brown, *Fruit of the Orchard: Reading Catherine of Siena in Late Medieval and Early Modern England* (Toronto, 2019); Gabriella Zarri, 'Catherine of Siena and the Italian Public', in Jeffrey F. Hamburger and Gabriela Signori (eds), *Catherine of Siena: The Creation of a Cult* (Turnhout, 2013), pp. 69–79.

of Gilbert of Sempringham, that a male presence was necessary 'because women's efforts achieve little without help from men'),[45] the need for women's communities to secure male assistance for the giving of the sacraments and other priestly and authoritative functions produced scholarship that viewed women as inferior. Recent publications have nuanced, indeed reversed, this view and argue that women as office holders were more than capable not just of ruling their houses, but of exercising pastoral functions. Using the methodologies of palaeographical and codicological analysis of surviving liturgical books from women's houses, for instance, Katie Ann-Marie Bugyis argues that the women as office holders of English communities from the early tenth to the early thirteenth centuries (abbesses, prioresses, cantors, and sacristans) were liturgically active. (Re) discovering the activities and creativity of women as scribes has asserted their agency in caring for themselves and others.[46] Through her work, we are able to picture women as cantors and sacristans (such as Eadburgh of Nunnaminster, Wulfruna-Judith of Barking), as liturgical leaders, playing an important role in the Eucharist, guardians of shrines, and scribes and authors.[47] Bugyis's work complements an earlier study, by Anne Yardley, of the offices of abbess, *cantrix*, and sacristan in women's communities, which is based both on normative texts (rules and customaries), and evidence of musical and liturgical activities from a range of sources from Benedictine, Bridgettine, Franciscan, and Dominican houses.[48] Jennifer Edwards highlighted the active and effective leadership of the abbesses of Sainte-Croix, and in an English context Valerie Spear has discussed the wide-ranging functions of women superiors, thus laying to rest the ghost of Eileen Power's incompetent abbesses and prioresses.[49] The theme of abbatial authority is taken up here by Elizabeth Lehfeldt.[50]

---

[45] Raymonde Foreville and Gillian Keir (eds), *The Book of St Gilbert* (Oxford, 1987), p. 37, when talking of Gilbert introducing lay brethren into Sempringham.

[46] Katie A.-M. Bugyis, *The Care of Nuns: The Ministries of Benedictine Women in England during the Central Middle Ages* (Oxford, 2019). For discussion of literacy, scribal activity, and cultural production, see introduction below, pp. 13–14.

[47] Katie A.-M. Bugyis, 'Female Monastic Cantors and Sacristans in Central Medieval England: Four Sketches', in Katie A.-M. Bugyis, A. B. Kraebel, and Margot E. Fassler (eds), *Medieval Cantors and their Craft: Music, Liturgy, and the Shaping of History, 800–1500* (York, 2017), pp. 151–69.

[48] Anne Bagnall Yardley, *Performing Piety: Musical Culture in Medieval English Nunneries* (Basingstoke and New York, 2006).

[49] Edwards, *Superior Women*; Spear, *Leadership*; see also Kimm Curran, '"Quhat say ye now, my lady priores? How have ye usit your office, can ye ges?": Politics, Power and Realities of the Office of a Prioress in her Community in Late Medieval Scotland', in Burton and Stöber, *Monasteries and Society*, pp. 124–41; Power, *Nunneries*.

[50] See below, pp. 105–20.

Recognising the authority and autonomy exercised by women religious does not deny the realities of male assistance but clarifies the relationship to women religious. In *Nuns' Priests' Tales* Fiona Griffiths argues that although women religious did indeed depend on male clerical support for the provision of the sacraments and the hearing of confession, this did not imply that their status was inferior to that of men.[51] Such a perception has arisen from the attitudes of scholars. Rather, she demonstrates that nuns' priests had a high regard for women's spirituality and intercession and, moreover, felt that their own spiritual life was enhanced by their engagement with monastic women. Male/female cooperation is also addressed in an edited collection *Partners in Spirit*, which explores institutional arrangements and less formal interactions between the sexes in diverse regions.[52] An example of how male religious could develop their relationship with religious women, and shape their communities, can be seen in St Albans, where the abbots of that great Benedictine monastery established what was at first a leper hospital for women, and then, in the fourteenth century, transformed it into a Benedictine cell.[53] For an earlier period Helen Foxhall Forbes addresses the various ways in which the three communities of tenth- and eleventh-century Winchester, two male and one female, cooperated and interacted within their urban space and liturgical context.[54]

An important addition to scholarship on the literacy of medieval women religious has been the series of books under the title *Nuns' Literacies* that are the written legacy of conferences held at Antwerp, Hull, and Kansas City. It is not possible to list all the contents here, but the reader is directed to this series for wide-ranging essays on Latin and vernacular texts read by women religious, written by women religious, and exchanged among them, taking into account reading practices in individual houses or orders, and across diverse geographical contexts.[55] Fundamental are the debates concerning how literacy was defined in particular regions and orders; how it was affected by social class or status; how far religious profession provided access to literacy; the degree of literacy enjoyed by women religious in Latin, and how they used Latin and vernacular texts.[56]

[51] Fiona J. Griffiths, *Nuns' Priests' Tales: Men and Salvation in Medieval Women's Monastic Life* (Philadelphia, 2018).

[52] Fiona J. Griffiths and Julie Hotchin (eds), *Partners in Spirit: Women, Men, and Religious Life in Germany, 1100–1500* (Turnhout, 2014).

[53] Philippa Byrne, 'Making Space for Leprous Nuns: Matthew Paris and the Foundation of St Mary de Pré, St Albans', in Victoria Blud, Diane Heath, and Elnat Klafter (eds), *Gender in Medieval Places, Spaces, and Thresholds* (London, 2019), pp. 45–60.

[54] Helen Foxhall Forbes, 'Squabbling Siblings: Gender and Monastic Life in Late Anglo-Saxon Winchester', *GH*, 23:3 (2011), 653–84.

[55] *Nuns' Literacies: Hull; Nuns' Literacies: Kansas; Nuns' Literacies: Antwerp.*

[56] *Nuns' Literacies: Hull*, pp. xvii–xviii.

The wide-ranging debates about literacy and learning have been enriched by regional and local studies. Sara Charles has explored the issue of literacy among religious women in England in the early thirteenth century, making use of BL MS Claudius D. iii, which contains the earliest known intact bilingual version of the Rule of St Benedict (in Latin and English) and adapted for female use.[57] In medieval England the importance of Barking Abbey as a centre for literacy and learning has been investigated, and the role of its abbesses as the patrons and commissioners of Latin texts.[58] Susan Powell has produced valuable studies of the Bridgettine abbey of Syon.[59] Further studies have enriched our understanding of the experiences of women religious at Chelles (France) and in Italy, noticeably at Monteluce.[60]

More widely, regional studies allow us to see women religious in diverse settings both within and outside the cloister, in relation to their broader communities and families, and appreciate their varied experiences, influences, and importance. Women's religious communities participated in confraternities, patronage of the arts, as well as looking after hospitals for pilgrims and caring for the sick. In addition, prosopographical studies of individual religious, as well as 'long' histories, breaking down traditional periodisations, are starting to view the importance of these broader communities and networks, to religious women within their own worlds, to the legacies of the past, and of transformation through time.[61] We can now envisage Cistercian women engaged in care for the sick,[62] confraternities in medieval and early modern Barcelona using conventual spaces for their ceremonies, providing a glimpse of the interaction between religious women and civic

---

[57] Sara Charles, 'The Literacy of English Nuns in the Early Thirteenth Century: Evidence from London, British Library, Cotton MS Claudius D. iii', *JMMS*, 6 (2017), 77–107.

[58] Jennifer N. Brown and Donna Alfano Bussell (eds), *Barking Abbey and Medieval Literary Culture: Authorship and Authority in a Female Community* (York, 2012).

[59] Susan Powell, *The Birgittines of Syon Abbey. Preaching and Print* (Turnhout, 2017).

[60] Cf. Ugolino Nicolini, *Memoriale di Monteluce: cronaca del monastero delle clarisse di Perugia dal 1448 al 1838* (Porziuncola, 1983); Helene Scheck, 'Future Perfect: Reading Temporalities at the Royal Women's Monastery at Chelles, ca. 660–1050', *Mediaevalia*, 36–37 (2015/16), 9–50; Julie Beckers, 'Invisible Presence: The Poor Clares of Central Italy: Families, Veil, and Art Patronage, c. 1350–1550' (Unpublished Ph.D. dissertation, KU-Leuven, 2017). See also, Marilyn Dunn, 'Convent Creativity', in Jane Couchman and Allyson M. Poska (eds), *The Ashgate Research Companion to Women and Gender in Early Modern Europe* (Farnham, 2016), pp. 71–92.

[61] Steven Vanderputten, *Dismantling the Medieval: Early Modern Perceptions of a Female Convent's Past* (Turnhout, 2021).

[62] Anne E. Lester, 'Cares beyond the Walls: Cistercian Nuns and the Care of Lepers in Twelfth- and Thirteenth-Century Northern France', in Emilia Jamroziak and Janet Burton (eds), *Religious and Laity in Western Europe, 1000–1400: Interactions, Negotiation, and Power* (Turnhout, 2006), pp. 197–224.

organisations,[63] and the place of the diverse communities of Bologna in civic life.[64] Kimm Curran presents us with a view of the opportunities offered by prosopography to uncover the lives of medieval women religious.[65]

Attention has also been given to cloistered women, the visual arts, and cultural production.[66] Significant contributions over the last few decades have addressed literacy and manuscript culture, and align with current studies on women religious, literacy, and agency. Rosamund McKitterick, for example, has detailed the book production in the scriptorium where women religious copied and wrote manuscripts at the community of Chelles, noting that this kind of activity was not the exception but rather the norm.[67] Expanding the subject to Bavaria is Alison Beach's investigation of the activities of women religious as scribes and copyists which revealed a long tradition of women's participation in manuscript production.[68] The visual arts – both art made for women religious and made *by* them – was once a long-neglected subject. Jeffrey Hamburger and Robert Suckale have drawn attention to women religious as commissioners and producers of artistic endeavours such as devotional objects; Hamburger has also highlighted women's artistic achievements at St Walburg, Eichstätt, indicating a strong visual culture present in the community.[69] Fiona J. Griffiths's investigation of the (no longer extant) manuscript of the *Hortus Deliciarum*, commissioned by Herrad, abbess of Hohenburg and produced within the house, reveals the intellectual vitality of this Augustinian community in the late twelfth century.[70] Griffith's study resonates

[63] Ascensión Mazuela-Anguita, 'Confraternities as an Interface between Citizens and Convent: Musical Ceremonial in Sixteenth-Century Barcelona', *Confraternitas*, 31:2 (2020), 14–35.

[64] Sherri Franks Johnson, *Monastic Women and Religious Orders in Late Medieval Bologna* (Cambridge, 2014).

[65] Kimm Curran, 'Looking for Medieval Female Religious in Britain and Ireland', in Karen Stöber, Julie Kerr, and Emilia Jamroziak (eds), *Monastic Life in the Medieval British Isles: Essays in Honour of Janet Burton* (Cardiff, 2018), pp. 161–72; 'Looking for Nuns: A Prosopographical Study of Scottish Nuns in the later Middle Ages', *Scottish Church History*, 35:1 (2005), 28–67.

[66] Some of these themes are taken up in this volume by Mercedes Pérez Vidal, pp. 202–20.

[67] Rosamund McKitterick, 'Nuns' Scriptoria in England and Francia in the Eighth Century', *Francia*, 19:1 (1992), 1–35.

[68] Alison I. Beach, *Women as Scribes: Book Production and Monastic Reform in Twelfth-Century Bavaria* (Cambridge, 2004).

[69] Jeffrey F. Hamburger and Robert Suckale, 'The Art of Religious Women in the Middle Ages', in Jeffrey E. Hamburger and Susan Marti (eds), *Crown and Veil: Female Monasticism from the Fifth to the Fifteenth Century* (New York, 2008); pp. 76–108; Jeffrey F. Hamburger, *Nuns as Artists*; see also *The Vision and the Visionary: Art and Female Spirituality in Late Medieval Germany* (New York, 1998).

[70] Griffiths, *Garden of Delights*. On Herrad see below, Sykes, pp. 56–7 and Denissen, p. 141.

with others: women religious and their communities were actively engaged in cultural production on a scale that we have yet to fully uncover.

Closely aligned to the visual culture of medieval women's communities is their architectures and the study of space. An important and pioneering study is Gilchrist's integration of historical and archaeological evidence with theories of space.[71] Studies of architecture include both general studies,[72] and those relating to women mendicants, such as Caroline Bruzelius's study of Clarissan and Carola Jäggi's of Clarissan and Dominican architecture.[73] Anne Müller has investigated symbolism in women's monastic space, arguing for a holistic approach to women's spaces which encompasses 'social behaviour, rituals, religious practice, art, and decoration [...] as well as atmospheric qualities'.[74] Joan Barclay Lloyd has made a thorough study of the architecture of several houses for Dominican women and her case study of the community of San Sisto, Rome, has shown the social context of the building and paintings, and how architecture and the placement of paintings in particular contribute to the devotional life of women religious.[75] June Mecham's study of six female communities in Lower Saxony links their art and architecture to what she calls the 'creation of ritual environment', blending local customs, social protocol, and gender.[76]

---

[71] GMC.

[72] For instance, Carola Jäggi and Uwe Lobbedey, 'Church and Cloister: The Architecture of Female Monasticism in the Middle Ages', in Hamburger and Marti (eds), *Crown and Veil*, pp. 109–31.

[73] Caroline A. Bruzelius, 'Hearing is Believing: Clarissan Architecture, c. 1213–1340', *Gesta*, 31 (1992), 83–91; Carola Jäggi, *Frauenklöster im Spätmittelalter: die Kirchen fer Klarissen und Dominikanerinnen im 13. und 14. Jahrhundert: Studien zur internationalen Archiektur- und Kunst-geschichte* (Petersberg, 2006).

[74] Anne Müller, 'Symbolic Meanings of Space in Female Monastic Tradition', in *WMMW*, pp. 299–325, at p. 319. See also Gisela Muschiol, 'Time and Space; Liturgy and Rite in Female Monasteries of the Middle Ages', in Hamburger and Marti (eds), *Crown and Veil*, pp. 191–206, who argues that female monasticism is not traditionally incorporated into studies of liturgy.

[75] Joan Barclay Lloyd, 'The Architectural Planning of Pope Innocent III's Nunnery of S. Sisto in Rome', in Andrea Sommerlechner (ed.), *Innocenzo III: Urbs et Orbis: atti del congresso internazionale, Roma, 9–15 settembre 1998* (Rome, 2003), pp. 1292–1311; Joan Barclay Lloyd, 'Paintings for Dominican Nuns: A New Look at the Images of Saints, Scenes from the New Testament and Apocrypha, and Episodes from the Life of Saint Catherine of Siena in the Medieval Apse of San Sisto Vecchio in Rome', *Papers of the British School at Rome*, 80 (2012), 189–232. See also her forthcoming study *Dominicans and Franciscans in Medieval Rome: History, Architecture, and Art*, Medieval Monastic Studies, 6 (Turnhout, 2022).

[76] June Metcham, *Sacred Communities, Shared Devotions: Gender, Material Culture, and Monasticism in Late Medieval Germany* (Turnhout, 2014). On themes of women's spaces in religious and devout secular households, see below, Delman, pp. 121–36.

Linked closely to architecture and space are studies addressing the landscape and environs of women religious and their communities. Archaeology and multi-disciplinary approaches have allowed scholars to explore and understand daily life, the sacred and spiritual spaces, as well as the development of communities over time. Tracy Collins, for example, has contributed a valuable regional study of the archaeology of women's monasticism within an Irish context.[77] The impact of monastic communities on the environment and vice versa has also led to further discoveries of community economies, the industry of women religious, and influences of nature and health on women religious – especially where documentary evidence may be scarce.[78] Kimm Curran explores new methodologies to uncover and explore the landscapes of medieval women religious and their place within modern landscapes.[79] Experiential approaches such as phenomenology and psychogeography (used primarily by prehistorians and modern walking practitioners) have allowed for the places of women religious – that often go unnoticed due to ruination or negative historiography – to be experienced and understood in new ways. These new approaches in landscape and archaeology are opening new avenues for placing women religious and their communities within wider local heritage contexts.[80]

The term 'women religious' encompasses a whole range of lived experience. Studies discussed so far have dealt within institutions or orders, but there were others whose lives were spent – in diverse ways – outside the confines of a monastery, and scholarship has increasingly turned to the anchorites and hermits, beguines, vowesses, mystics, secular canonesses, and those serving hospitals. As Sigrid Hirbodian has pointed out, the description of such women as 'semi-religious' is problematic, and her rather longer description of 'women who, in terms

---

[77] Tracy Collins, *Female Monasticism in Medieval Ireland: An Archaeology* (Cork, 2021). See also her 'Archaeologies of Female Monasticism in Late Medieval Ireland', in Blud et al. (eds), *Gender in Medieval Places*, pp. 25–44, and below, pp. 182–201. For the presence, or places, of religious women within the landscape, see the contribution by Seale, below, pp. 166–81.

[78] See, for example, Erin Jordan, 'Transforming the Landscape: Cistercian Nuns and the Environment in the Medieval Low Countries', *JMH*, 44:2 (2018), 187–201; András Vadas, 'Long-Term Perspectives on River Floods: The Dominican Nunnery on Margaret Island (Budapest) and the Danube River', *Interdisciplinaria Archaeologica*, 4 (2013), 73–82; Mallory A. Ruyman, 'Nuns as Gardeners: Using and Making Enclosed Gardens', *Athanor*, 35 (2017), 41–8.

[79] Kimm Curran, '"Shadows of Ghosts": Rediscovering the Special Places of Medieval Monasteries through Experiential Approaches to Landscape', in Edel Bhreathnach, Malgorzata Krasnodębska-D'Aughton, and Keith Smith (eds), *Monastic Europe: Medieval Communities, Landscapes, and Settlement* (Turnhout, 2019), pp. 523–44.

[80] Cf. Roberta Gilchrist, *Sacred Heritage: Monastic Archaeology, Identities, Beliefs* (Cambridge, 2020), *passim*.

of Church law, belonged somewhere between the secular and the religious, but who thought of themselves as leading religious lives' is more apt.[81] Or, as Walter Simons has put it, an 'important group of people who defy easy categorisation yet were all were loosely associated with the religious life [...] straddling the border between the lay and the monastic (or religious) categories of society'.[82] Stress is being laid on the permeable boundaries between cloistered women and those living the religious life in different, less formal and less rigid ways, for instance, those who formed part of the *Devotio moderna* movement in the Low Countries in the fourteenth and fifteenth centuries.[83] The ambivalent legal status of such women has been discussed by Elizabeth Makowski.[84]

The literature on anchorites has been enriched by the work of scholars such as Liz Herbert McAvoy and Anneke Mulder-Bakker.[85] They and others have foregrounded not only the role of medieval recluses but also the 'multiple nature of medieval reclusion'.[86] E. A. Jones offers readers access to a range of primary sources both for enclosed anchorites and wandering hermits in medieval England, and the relationship between them.[87] The vibrancy of study of anchorites in all their diversity is illustrated in particular by two collections of essays that are the product of international conferences, integrating exciting research in an English context into wider findings within a continental context.[88] A seemingly minor –

---

[81] Sigrid Hirbodian, 'Religious Women: Secular Canonesses and Beguines', in *OHCM*, pp. 285–99, at p. 285. For studies of women recluses across Europe, see Frances Andrews and Eleonora Rava (eds), *Ripensare le reclusione volontaria nell'Europa medievale*, 2 vols, Quaderni di storia religiosa medievale, 24:1–2 (2021).

[82] Walter Simons, 'On the Margins of Religious Life: Hermits and Recluses, Penitents and Tertiaries, Beguines and Beghards', in Miri Rubin and Walter Simons (eds), *The Cambridge History of Christianity*, vol. 4: *Christianity in Western Europe, c. 1110–c. 1500* (Cambridge, 2009), pp. 311–23, at p. 311.

[83] John Van Engen, *Sisters and Brothers of the Common Life: The Devotio Moderna and the World of the Later Middle Ages* (Philadelphia, 2008). On learning and literacy among late medieval religious women, with a focus on Alijt Bake of Ghent, a house of the Windesheim congregation, see the contribution by Diana Denissen in this collection, below, pp. 144–50.

[84] See also Elizabeth Makowski, *"A Pernicious Sort of Woman": Quasi-Religious Women in the Later Middle Ages* (Washington, DC, 2005); Elizabeth Makowski, *English Nuns and the Law in the Middle Ages: Cloistered Nuns and Their Lawyers, 1293–1540* (Woodbridge, 2011).

[85] *Anchoritic Traditions* contains essays on the anchoritic experience in several geographical regions; Anneke B. Mulder-Bakker, *Lives of the Anchoresses: The Rise of the Urban Recluse in Medieval Europe* (Philadelphia, 2005).

[86] *Anchoritic Traditions*, p. 2.

[87] E. A. Jones, *Hermits and Anchorites in England 1200–1550* (Manchester, 2019).

[88] Liz Herbert McAvoy and Mari Hughes-Edwards (eds), *Anchorites, Wombs and Tombs: Intersections of Gender and Enclosure in the Middle Ages* (Cardiff, 2005); Liz Herbert

but significant – corrective suggested by Liz Herbert McAvoy has been the rejection of the English term 'anchoress' – a gendered noun that is found in historical scholarship, but not in Middle English before the fifteenth century.[89] Attention has also focussed on the physical and symbolic spaces occupied by anchorites and their material culture.[90] Such issues, including anchoritic spirituality, are discussed in this volume by Cate Gunn.[91]

Beguines and canonesses – placed by Hirbodian and others firmly in their social, spiritual and secular environments – offered opportunities for women of the elite, commercial and urban classes to participate in lives of varying degrees of dependence on and interaction with the world.[92] Scholarship has stressed the difference: secular canonesses tended to occupy old and often wealthy churches and were both religious and secular; beguinages might be located in cities, small towns, as well as rural settlements, and, in eschewing enclosure they seemed to break all the rules – which made them subject to attack.[93] Scholars have discussed the problems of nomenclature – the labels that were used to describe the women who followed a range of lifestyles in very different settings in different parts of Europe. The sheer diversity of experience has been uncovered by regional studies of beguines, notably the Low Countries, Paris, Prague, and Strasbourg.[94]

Finally, visionary women religious continue to be explored in detail in relation to themes of literary and writing, spirituality, and embodied experiences.[95] Studies

---

McAvoy (ed.), *Rhetoric of the Anchorhold: Space, Place and Body within the Discourses of Enclosure* (Cardiff, 2008).

[89] *Anchoritic Traditions*, pp. 11–12, though as she admits it is modern usage that endows the -ess suffix with a negative or diminutive quality.

[90] See, for instance, Michelle M. Sauer and Jenny C. Bledsoe (eds), *The Materiality of Middle English Anchoritic Devotion* (Leeds, 2001).

[91] Below, pp. 76–89.

[92] Sigrid Hirbodian, 'Religious Women: Secular Canonesses and Beguines', in *OHCM*, pp. 285–97.

[93] On beguines see, for instance, Letha J. Böhringer et al., *Labels and Libels: Naming Beguines in Northern Medieval Europe* (Turnhout, 2014).

[94] Walter Simons, *Cities of Ladies: Beguine Communities in the Medieval Low Countries, 1200–1565* (Philadelphia, PA, 2001); Tanya Stabler Miller, *The Beguines of Medieval Paris: Gender, Patronage, and Spiritual Authority* (Philadelphia, 2014); Jana Grollová, 'The "Clever Girls" of Prague: Beguines, Preachers, and Late Medieval Bohemian Religion', in Jennifer Kolpacoff Deane and Anne E. Lester (eds), *Between Orders and Heresy: Rethinking Medieval Religious Movements* (Toronto, 2022), pp. 306–36.

[95] Sarah Alison Miller, *Medieval Monstrosity and the Female Body* (London, 2010); Alastair Minnis and Rosalynn Voaden (eds), *Medieval Holy Women in the Christian Tradition, c. 1100–c. 1500* (Turnhout, 2010); Elizabeth A. Petroff, 'Women and Mysticism in the Medieval World', in Nahir I. Otaño Gracia and Daniel Armenti (eds), *Women's Lives: Self-Representation, Reception and Appropriation in the Middle Ages* (Cardiff, 2022), pp. 13–33.

have revealed the writings and experiences of beguine mystics – Mechthild of Magdeburg, Hadewijch of Antwerp, for example – and their writings on Godly love and experiences of divine passion, as well as the relationship of women religious and communal authorship where mystics resided (Helfta, for instance) and individual mystics.[96] More recently, mystics such as Julian of Norwich, Bridget of Sweden, and Margery Kempe, for instance, have encountered further investigation in relation to how they fit within women's mystical experience, gender, and women's spiritual friendships.[97]

The Scope of this Book:
New Questions, Approaches, and Perspectives

So why do we need another book? First, this volume takes an interdisciplinary approach, bringing together historians, archaeologists, literary scholars, and specialists in visual and material culture, to explore a series of interlocking themes. Second, it is distinctive in that it is not solely about nuns and nunneries, that is, cloistered women and their monasteries. Indeed, 'nun' and 'nunneries' are words that our authors have consciously avoided. It is about the whole range of medieval women religious, those who followed a variety of vocations in a variety of settings. It moves beyond the confines – literally – of the enclosed monastic community to embrace not just those women who lived their lives according to a monastic or religious rule, but also those who chose the solitary existence of the anchorhold or hermitage, as well as those who took vows to remain celibate and who moved between the secular world and the monastic sphere. The chapters in this volume argue cogently for reasons why we need to look at the nuances of women's religious experience – within or outside the 'orders' – not placing defining labels on them. We challenge ideas of women religious and where they belong within the current discourse of monastic studies, how we can understand their experiences more widely by resisting the temptation to pigeonhole them into traditional

[96] Anna Harrison, 'The Nuns of Helfta', in Julia A. Lamm (ed.), *The Wiley-Blackwell Companion to Christian Mysticism* (Oxford, 2013), pp. 297–310; J. Tar, 'Angela of Foligno as a Model for Franciscan Women Mystics and Visionaries in Early Modern Spain', *Magistra*, 11:1 (2005), 83–105. See also the essay by Denissen, below, pp. 140–3.

[97] See, for example, Laura Saetveit Miles, 'Queer Touch Between Holy Women: Julian of Norwich, Margery Kempe, Birgitta of Sweden, and the Visitation', in David Carrillo-Rangel, Delfi I. Nieto-Isabel, and Pablo Acosta-Garcia (eds), *Touching, Devotional Practices, and Visionary Experience in the Late Middle Ages* (Cambridge, 2019), pp. 203–35; Liam Peter Temple, 'Returning the English "Mystics" to their Medieval Milieu: Julian of Norwich, Margery Kempe and Bridget of Sweden', *Women's Writing*, 23:2 (2016), 141–58.

religious orders, whilst at the same time placing them within wider contexts of these orders more generally.

Some explanation is needed of the chronological span. Why 800–1500? The stories of women religious and their communities does not begin or end neatly. However, as a starting point, the early ninth century is highly appropriate, since the Councils of Aachen between 816 and 819 have been seen as monuments in the development of monastic and religious life, which, very pertinently for this collection, sought to define and delineate various terms used to describe the female religious experience.[98] In the opening essay, Steven Vanderputten reinterrogates the sources and argues against the rigidness of these parameters and the neat historiographical pattern of reform. This sets the tone for our questioning of traditional chronological arcs frequently used by historians. Katharine Sykes explores the 'experimentation, ambivalence and tradition' that exemplified the long twelfth century, when three communities – Fontevraud, the Paraclete, and Sempringham – were, in different ways with different results, affected by their relationship with male founders and mentors. Alison More moves our story into the thirteenth and fourteenth centuries, unravels the complexities of female interaction with the mendicant orders, and how these traditional and 'fictive' orders need to be challenged and understood more broadly, particularly after the Fourth Lateran Council (1215) and the papal bull *Periculoso* (1298).

These chapters celebrate the experimentation characteristic of women's groups and raise important questions about their subsequent institutionalisation, and the relationship between women religious and the established male monastic orders.[99] They provide a deeper understanding of where women fit in the wider historiography. The end date – *c.* 1500 – is in one sense arbitrary. As with beginnings, so with endings: there were regional, political, geographical differences that influenced the influx and foundation of monastic communities as well as the decline, secularisation, and removal of these institutions from the religious landscape. In England and Wales monastic – though not religious – life came to an official end between 1536 and 1540, but the geographical range of this collection is cast much wider – to Ireland, to France, Italy, Iberia, the Netherlands, and beyond, where change was felt sometimes sooner, sometimes later.

Subsequent chapters look more broadly at the experiences of women within religious life, the role of a women's monastic house within its local and regional setting, and the influence it had on the secular community of which it was a part. Cate Gunn, in her revisiting of the nature of anchoritic life for women, argues that although anchorites might be liminal both physically (at the edges of settlement)

---

[98] See, above, introduction, pp. 3–4.
[99] See, above, pp. 5–8.

and symbolically (between earth and heaven, life and death) they were in fact central to medieval society as intercessors. The concept of liminality is also investigated by Laura Richmond in relation to vowesses, who moved between the world and the cloister; she argues that they might be more integrated into women's monastic communities than previous scholarship has allowed. Again, we see the fluidity and varied opportunities for medieval women.[100] Elizabeth Lehfeldt contributes to the growing body of scholarship on the authority of the heads of women's monastic houses, drawing on a body of material from England, France, and Spain. In the case of the first of these, the shadow cast by Eileen Power – one hundred years ago – has until recently remained remarkably persistent, leaving us with the traditional view that women superiors were at worst incompetent and at best highly dependent on the assistance of men.[101] Lehfeldt argues, conversely, for the importance of recognising their agency within the community and without. Like Lehfeldt, Rachel Delman uses the term 'monastic household', and her exploration of 'crossing boundaries' highlights the similarities between the role of the head of the monastic household and that of an elite secular one. Effective comparisons emerge in relation to physical layout of the houses, reception of visitors, models of leadership, use of space, visual culture. These chapters show women as active agents, not passive ones, and as influencers of their supporters and patrons.

As noted above, much scholarly attention has been given in recent years to the question of the literacy of religious women. As Diana Denissen reminds us, the word 'literacy' in the singular is a catch-all phrase and we need to think about different levels of literacies within women's religious experience, as well as acknowledge regional diversities. She provides a discussion of the broad context before focussing on the fifteenth-century case of Alijt Bake and the links between literacy (reading and writing) and spiritual progress, revealing some of the tensions this caused within the church hierarchy. This emphasises the extent to which literacy, books, and religious movements such as the *Devotio moderna* were part of women's religious experience in medieval Europe. Books were also, as highlighted by Sara Charles, a feature of patronage networks; her exploration of giving and bequeathing of books to named women religious or their communities might be a practical gesture but might also be charged with emotional weight and with memory, a reminder of family and patronal networks.

The experience of women religious is not just about documentary evidence. Landscape studies, archaeology, and material culture play large roles in our

---

[100] It may be noted that some groups, notably beguines and mystics, do not here have discrete chapters, but they are introduced into the discussion by several of our authors, see, for instance, More, pp. 68–9, Denissen, pp. 138–9, 143.

[101] Power, *Nunneries*.

awareness of the experience and legacy of monastic communities, and women religious. Landscape, and the use of the landscape, is not just a discussion of the economic exploitation of the estates of a monastic house, but, as discussed by Yvonne Seale, has much to tell us about the impact of the presence of women religious on the world around them. Tracy Collins takes up the question of materiality and archaeology; she both discusses the state of current research and scholarship and points the way for future developments. In our final chapter, Mercedes Pérez Vidal explores the ways in which women religious expressed memory – individual, familial, and collective – in the use of space and in the material culture of their communities.

The editors have brought together a team of scholars, both established and early career, from across Europe, the United States, and the United Kingdom, to offer readers new and fresh ideas about identities, authority, materiality, landscape, and memory. The contributions show just how vast the subject of women religious and their communities and their impact on the medieval world are continually developing and emerging. What we hope to have produced is a collection that will allow readers to find their way into these compelling discussions about women religious and the varied aspects of their lives and activities, the influence and importance they exuded, and one that will give a new sense of purpose and determination to the study of women religious for the future.

CHAPTER 1

Reform, Change, and Renewal:
Women Religious in the Central Middle Ages,
800–1050

STEVEN VANDERPUTTEN

IN the final years of the fourteenth century, the Franciscan friar and chronicler Jacques de Guise recorded an account of a heated dispute between a group of early ninth-century Church reformers and the heads of several women's monastic communities in present-day Belgium and Germany.[1] A major Church council had decreed that all communities of women religious would henceforth strictly observe the Rule of St Benedict and the message was relayed to all the convents in the area; however, the leaders of these places quickly agreed to appeal jointly against the reform. After much diplomatic wrangling involving the pope and Emperor Louis the Pious, a decision was made to hold a synod at the royal abbey of Nivelles to discuss the issue further. Bishop Walcand of Liège opened the meeting by reiterating the council's precepts. But once he had finished speaking the heads of these women's communities rejected his call and responded with one voice:

> First, we protest with God and all of those listening, that we have never vowed to the Rule of St Benedict. Second, we promise to remain chaste, but we will not let ourselves be forced to accept the veil. Third, we are prepared to vow ourselves to obedience to our abbesses and an honest life. Fourth, if this response is not enough, we are prepared to lodge further appeals.[2]

These words sent shockwaves through the meeting. When Walcand sternly reminded the women of their duty to comply with the reform all remained silent, except for Abbess Doda of Sainte-Waudru in Mons. She, according to the chronicler, 'spoke inappropriately'. The organisers hastily dissolved the synod and

---

[1]   Jacques de Guise, *Annales Hannoniae*, ed. E. Sackur, MGH *Scriptores*, 30:1 (Hannover, 1896), pp. 162–3.

[2]   Jacques de Guise, *Annales Hannoniae*, p. 163; translation, Vanderputten, *DAN*, p. 174.

subsequently convened with a number of prominent clerical and lay lords to work out 'a short instruction for an honest life without any vows, except for that of any Christian', in order to give the women at least some written guidelines. This text they then sent to the heads of these women's monastic communities. They added that henceforth the heads of these women's monasteries and their subjects would be known as 'secular religious' instead of 'nuns'. The account closes with the ominous statement that Walcand ended by deposing many of the heads of these women's communities as a token of their eternal punishment, and that he installed in their place noblemen as secular abbots.

De Guise's text (which claims to be based on a now-lost *Life of Walcand*) contains several anachronisms that make it suspect as an authentic account of early ninth-century events. These include the claim that post-reform, the term 'nun' (*sanctimonialis*) was used strictly to refer to Benedictine women religious, and also that the written 'instructions' for a cohort of 'secular religious' had originated as a result of a dispute with a group of superiors of women's monastic communities in the southern Low Countries.[3] But his testimony remains valuable because it helps us document the continuity in commentaries from the mid-eleventh century onwards about the objectives and failure of the reform. Furthermore, it reveals the remarkable stability since that time of a perception of the Central Middle Ages as a 'dark age' for women's monasticism.[4] The resistance of religious to the reforms; rulers and church leaders' inability to impose the Rule of St Benedict as a unified and unifying observance; secular encroachment by lay agents; political instability from the mid-ninth century onwards, and foreign invasions: all these things, it was argued, had triggered a process of decline on multiple (institutional, disciplinary, and spiritual) fronts, and rapidly turned women's monasticism into a mere shadow of its vibrant, diverse, and influential early medieval self.[5] Tenth- and early eleventh-century reformers in various parts of the Latin West sought to reverse the downward trend by restoring buildings and lost estates, getting rid of lay superiors, and imposing on the women a strict Benedictine observance: but their impact was limited. In the optic of these commentators, it would take until the paradigm-shifting and male-led reforms of the mid-eleventh century onwards before women's monasticism regained its former attraction to those who wished

---

[3] For example, Schulenberg, *Forgetful of Their Sex,* pp. 112–15.
[4] On conceptualisations of the Central Middle Ages as a 'dark age' for women's monasticism, see Vanderputten, *DAN,* pp. 1–10.
[5] On pre-800 forms and experiences of the religious life for women, see Anne-Marie Helvétius, 'Le monachisme féminin en Occident de l'antiquité tardive au haut moyen age', in *Monachesimi d'oriente e d'occidente nell'alto medioevo: Spoleto, 31 marzo–6 aprile 2016,* vol. 2 (Spoleto, 2017), pp. 193–230.

to pursue a life of ascetic self-abnegation, and before it was able to achieve the same with credibility to outsiders.

Since the 1990s this account of decline, attempted rebirth, and dramatic renaissance has been subject to considerable nuancing. In one strand of research, scholars began to take notice of the biased nature of contemporary and later reports of the institutional and spiritual status of women's monasticism in the Central Middle Ages.[6] In another, they started critically to review assumptions in the older scholarship regarding the purpose of rules and other normative commentaries; the objectives of various reform interventions over the course of this period; the nature of secular agents' involvement in monastic governance; and the '(ir)regularity' of monastic forms and experiences.[7] In addition, scholars also expanded the range of their source material, shifting the focus of their investigations from normative texts and (often biased) narrative commentaries, to written, material, and archaeological sources. These revealed something about the concrete situation of women religious, including their embedding in the secular environment, experience of space, recruitment patterns, reading culture and spirituality, and so on.[8] And finally, they also became interested in testing the claims in a (primarily Anglophone) strand of late twentieth-century scholarship that conceptualised women religious as disempowered victims of a clerical campaign to extinguish their influence in the Church.[9]

While all these trends in research are now documented in a large body of scholarship, unfortunately it is still common to see studies on earlier and later periods rehearsing outdated views. Partly this is because the representation of the Central Middle Ages as a 'dark' era for women's monasticism remains an attractive (if somewhat facile) narrative device by which to argue for (1) the dynamic

---

[6] For example, Ulrich Andermann, 'Die unsittlichen und disziplinlosen Kanonissen. Ein Topos und seine Hintergründe, aufgezeigt an Beispielen sächsischer Frauenstifte (11.–13. Jahrhundert)', *Westfälische Zeitschrift*, 146 (1996), 39–63.

[7] Anne-Marie Helvétius, 'Normes et pratiques de la vie monastique en Gaule avant 1050: présentation des sources écrites', in O. Delouis and M. Mossakowska Gaubert (eds), *La vie quotidienne des moines en Orient et en Occident (IVe–Xe siècle). Vol. 1, L'état des sources* (Cairo, 2015), pp. 371–86.

[8] For example, Yorke, *Anglo-Saxon;* Gordon Blennemann, *Die Metzer Benediktinerinnen im Mittelalter. Studien zu den Handlungsspielräumen geistlicher Frauen* (Husum, 2011).

[9] For example, Mary Skinner, 'Benedictine Life for Women in Central France, 850–1100: A Feminist Revival', in J. A. Nichols and L. T. Shank (eds), *Medieval Religious Women: Volume One, Distant Echoes* (Kalamazoo, 1984), pp. 87–114; Jo Ann Kay McNamara, *Sisters in Arms: Catholic Nuns Through Two Millennia* (Cambridge, MA, 1996), pp. 148–201; and Julia A. Smith, *Ordering Women's Lives: Penitentials and Nunnery Rules in the Early Medieval West* (Aldershot, 2001), pp. 142–5. Also (and more nuanced) Suzanne Fonay Wemple, *Women in Frankish Society: Marriage and the Cloister, 500 to 900* (Philadelphia, 1981), pp. 165–74.

and diverse nature of pre-800 forms and experiences and (2) the revolutionary implications of the eleventh- and twelfth-century reforms. But partly it is also because a number of late twentieth-century scholars have identified the period as emblematic of women's oppression by a male-dominated Catholic Church and are reluctant to allow for a more nuanced reading of historical realities. Alongside these factors, we must also consider that the research is highly fragmented across methodological, linguistic, and national boundaries. The purpose, then, of this chapter is briefly to introduce the reader to former and more recent perspectives on women's monasticism between c. 800 and 1050. The first of four parts outlines the traditional view on the Carolingian reforms and their aftermath in the tenth and early eleventh centuries. The second looks at new interpretations of the reforms, their objectives, and their written output, and at the implications of these for the study of monastic forms and experiences in the ninth century. The third part deals with new interpretations of tenth- and eleventh-century reform, its background, purpose, and outcomes. And the final section considers the enduring diversity of monastic forms and experiences in the wake of the first and second 'wave' of reforms.

Traditional Narratives

All traditional narratives of women's monasticism in the Central Middle Ages consistently begin with a statement about the paradigm-shifting impact of a series of reform councils held in Aachen during the years 816–19.[10] Prior to those fateful meetings, they claim, organised community life for religious women had been extremely diverse, loosely regulated, and mostly private. But shortly after the installation of Louis the Pious as sole ruler of the Frankish empire in 814, houses of women religious were swept up in a massive effort to 'correct' the Frankish Church and integrate its institutions in the Carolingian state and the exercise of sovereign rule. Alongside taking legislative measures to establish two internally homogeneous forms of community life for men (one of Benedictine monks and the other of clerics), the reformers also decided to regulate women's monasticism.

---

[10] The classic thesis first appeared in K. H. Schäfer, *Die Kanonissenstifter im deutschen Mittelalter* (Stuttgart, 1907) and subsequently influenced a century-long strand of scholarship. See, for example, Raymund Kottje, 'Claustra sine armario?: Zum Unterschied von Kloster und Stift im Mittelalter', in J. F. Angerer and J. Lenzenweger (eds), *Consuetudines monasticae. Festgabe für Kassius Hallinger* (Rome, 1982), pp. 125–44; Michel Parisse, *Les nonnes au moyen âge* (Le Puy, 1983), pp. 24–8; Jane T. Schulenburg, 'Strict Active Enclosure and Its Effects on the Female Monastic Experience, ca. 500–1100', in Nichols and Shank (eds), *Medieval Religious Women*, pp. 51–86; and I. Crusius (ed.), *Studien zum Kanonissenstift* (Göttingen, 2001).

In addition to barring women religious from pastoral roles and participation in ecclesiastical governance, they decided that all should follow the Rule of St Benedict: strict claustration, individual poverty, and prayer service were the three pillars on which the reformers' vision rested.

However, it soon became apparent that there was much resistance to wide-spread application of the Rule's stringent asceticism. Some of it came from within the monasteries, where the members objected on practical grounds and out of principle.[11] And some of it came from the aristocracy, who objected to the idea of depriving their kin who had entered the convent of a comfortable lifestyle. In response, the reformers calibrated their expectations and created a second cohort of secular women religious (or canonesses) alongside that of Benedictine women religious: to make this possible they issued a text known as the *Institutio sanctimonialium*.[12] Among other things, this newly conceived rule allowed the members of the new cohort to own private property and to leave it to their heirs. They were permitted to receive an individual allowance (also known as a prebend) from a community's estate and could also leave the monastic life to get married or to pursue their way in the secular world. The reforms allowed Emperor Louis in particular to establish, alongside a small elite cluster of Benedictine convents, an empire-wide network of 'secular' monastic institutions where the Frankish aristocracy would send their unmarried and widowed relatives. Communities of women religious rapidly emerged as hubs of imperial power, functioning as relays between the court and local society and as representative institutions where the members spent most of their time praying for the welfare of the state and the sovereign. They also provided essential support to the exercise of imperial power, for instance by subsidising troops and by putting their infrastructures at the disposal of royal visitors, messengers, and other associates.[13]

Nineteenth- and twentieth-century studies saw mostly positive short-term effects of these developments. Many formerly private institutions that had been struggling to survive now benefited from considerable investment. In turn, this made it possible to launch extensive building campaigns, raised the profile for

---

[11] For instance, in the ninth- or tenth-century *Life of Odilia* of Hohenbourg in Alsace; *Vita Odiliae abbatissae Hohenburgensis*, ed. W. Levison, MGH, *Scriptores Rerum Merovingicarum*, 6 (Hannover, 1913), p. 46.

[12] Thomas Schilp, *Norm und Wirklichkeit religiöser Frauengemeinschaften im frühen Mittelalter* (Göttingen, 1998).

[13] Jean Verdon, 'Notes sur le rôle économique des monastères féminins en France dans la seconde moitié du IXe et au début du Xe siècle', *RM*, 58 (1975), 329–44 and idem, 'Recherches sur les monastères féminins dans la France du nord aux IXe–XIe siècles', *RM*, 59 (1976), 49–96; Heinrich Wagner, 'Zur Notitia de servitio monasteriorum von 819', *Deutsches Archiv für Erforschung des Mittelalters*, 55 (1999), 417–38.

new recruits, and invited extensive privileges, liberties, and protections from the emperor. But beginning in the early 1980s, feminist historians began to focus on what they saw as indications that women's monastic life at this point stopped being 'shaped by its practitioners'. In their understanding, the reformers' focus on strict enclosure and mindless prayer service, as well as the fact that women were barred from exercising sacramental roles (such as taking confession, preaching, and ordaining women), catastrophically impacted on the 'aura of heroic sanctity' these monasteries had formerly enjoyed.[14] Among other things it caused the monastic experience to lose its attraction to women who were sincerely drawn to the religious life. And it also fundamentally altered former lay perceptions of women's monasteries as centres of spiritual reflection, pastoral and charitable support, and cultural production.[15] As a combined result of these developments, there were practically no new foundations of new monasteries for women.[16] The one exception was recently conquered Saxony, where newly established monasteries for women became critical building stones of Carolingian power and were instrumental in anchoring newly emerged aristocratic networks.[17]

Yet this difference in scholarly perspective on short-term effects did not prevent a consensus on long-term ones. Because of the concessions lawmakers had made to the aristocracy, scholars indicated, a process was set in motion whereby life in many of these places was increasingly tailored to reflect that secular elite's interests. Meanwhile, lay involvement in monastic governance, which was already strong from the time of Louis' reign due to his appointment of superiors and other lay officers, only increased over time. Especially when royal power declined in the decades after the death of Louis the Pious, women's monastic communities increasingly became a pawn in a geopolitical game that opposed royal agents

[14] McNamara, *Sisters in Arms*, p. 148.

[15] See the literature cited above, n. 9.

[16] Jane Tibbets Schulenburg, 'Women's Monastic Communities, 500–1100: Patterns of Expansion and Decline', *Signs: Journal of Women in Culture and Society*, 14 (1989), 261–92; Suzanne Fonay Wemple, 'Female Monasticism in Italy and its Comparison with France and Germany From the Ninth Through the Eleventh Century', in U. Vorwerk and W. Affeldt (eds), *Frauen in Spätantike und Frühmittelalter. Lebensbedingungen Lebensnormen – Lebensformen* (Sigmaringen, 1990), pp. 291–310; Venarde, *Women's Monasticism*.

[17] M. Hoernes and H. Röckelein (eds), *Gandersheim und Essen Vergleichende Untersuchungen zu sächsischen frauenstiften* (Essen, 2006); Hedwig Röckelein, 'Bairische, sächsische und mainfränkische Klostergründungen im Vergleich (8. Jahrhundert bis 1100)', in E. Schlotheuber (ed.), *Nonnen, Kanonissen und Mystikerinnen. Religiöse Frauengemeinschaften in Süddeutschland* (Göttingen, 2008), pp. 23–55; Michel Parisse, 'Les monastères de femmes en Saxe des Carolingiens aux Saliens', in M. Parisse, *Religieux et religieuses en Empire du Xe au XIIe siècle* (Paris, 2011), pp. 141–72.

(including a number of queens and princesses),[18] bishops, and members of the regional elites. Foreign invasions by Magyars, Vikings, and Muslims, as well as domestic instability in the decades on either side of the year 900, made women's communities even more vulnerable than before to being deprived of property and income, or being turned into a secular estate.

Historians viewed the outcomes of these processes and dynamics as mixed. Some institutions in the Carolingian realms and in other regions such as England and northern Spain (where similar dynamics were thought to have influence on women's monasticism's status) ceased to exist. Either they were abandoned or were transferred as a subsidiary institution to another monastery. Some were adapted to another use – turned into a secular estate, a parish church served perhaps by a handful of clerics, or a farm.[19] Others struggled on in obscurity, bogged down by decades of social isolation and dwindling or ineffective royal support, financially crippled by disrupted trade routes, theft of property, lack of donations, and faltering recruitment rates. Eventually, such institutions were dissolved, transferred, or otherwise ceased to exist as women's monasteries. But still others thrived. Thanks to the support of mighty patrons, they continued to be a strong and influential presence.

But at the same time these places reified women's monasticism's tenth-century insertion into aristocratic and territorial politics, as well as its descent into redundancy as a religious phenomenon. In the words of one scholar, women's monasteries quickly turned into little else than 'shelter, a prison, an old-age home' and 'a source of income for princesses and queens'.[20] They and a number of newly founded institutions retained or achieved great fame and influence, not because they were highly regarded as spiritual centres but because they were wealthy, strategically important, and highly elitist institutions, and because extremely well-connected heads of women's monastic houses led them.[21] Any artistic, literary, architectural, or other achievements were attributed to these factors and to the sheer concentration of human, social, and cultural capital in these places.[22] Members enjoyed a cloistered environment that replicated the domestic comfort of aristocratic households, and

[18] Cristina La Rocca, 'Monachesimo femminile e poteri delle regine tra VIII e IX secolo', in G. Spinelli (ed.), *Il monachesimo italiano dall'età longobarda all'età ottoniana (secc. VIII–X)* (Cesena, 2006), pp. 119–43; Simon Maclean, 'Queenship, Nunneries and Royal Widowhood in Carolingian Europe', *P & P*, 178 (2003), 3–38.
[19] For example, Foot, *Veiled Women.*
[20] Wemple, *Women in Frankish Society*, p. 172.
[21] Gerd Althoff, 'Gandersheim und Quedlinburg: Ottonische Frauenkloster als Herrschafts- und Überlieferungszentren, *Frühmittelalterliche Studien*, 25 (1991), 123–44.
[22] A selection of such achievements is presented in the exhibition catalogue *Krone und Schleier. Kunst aus mittelalterlichen Frauenklöstern*, J. Frings and J. Gerchow (eds) (Bonn, 2005).

were not particularly encouraged (possibly even actively discouraged, so as not to interfere with prayer service or disturb internal peace) to pursue an ascetic life or delve deeply into questions about spiritual identity.

Beginning in the early tenth century, multiple regional waves of Benedictine reform and foundations of new Benedictine communities (particularly in Lorraine, southern England, and again Saxony) helped fill some of the gaps that had arisen in Europe's women's monastic landscape and presumably reinjected elements of ascetic rigour into women's experiences.[23] But overall the impact of these interventions was limited, due to the restricted geographical scope of the reforms, the fact that monasteries remained deeply embedded in an aristocratic logic of power, and the fact that the Rule's stringent precepts proved difficult to uphold in the long term. Meanwhile communities of 'secular' religious still vastly outnumbered Benedictine houses and, over time, several of the latter slipped into a 'secular' observance too. Frustrated at the lack of progress, churchmen began to call for a drastic intervention. At a 1059 synod in Rome, Hildebrand, the future Pope Gregory VII, complained that there were exceedingly few women's monastic communities in Europe that were truly Benedictine monasteries and harangued 'secular' women religious for being nothing but fat, bloated matrons.[24] This dramatic speech closely followed the first foundation of a truly cloistered convent, that of Marcigny, by Abbot Hugo of Cluny.[25] These events were the kick-start, so scholars long asserted, of women's monasticism's dramatic revival in the later eleventh and twelfth centuries.

Rules and Experiments

Former accounts of women's monasticism's status in the Central Middle Ages all hinged on the notion that the Aachen councils marked the point at which the diverse and barely regulated world of early medieval women's monasticism abruptly transitioned into two strictly regulated and easily distinguishable cohorts of Benedictine women religious and 'secular' canonesses. Over time, interpretations of the origins and outcomes of that transition shifted. In 1059, Hildebrand

---

[23] For Lotharingia, see the classic essay by Michel Parisse, 'Der Anteil der Lothringischen Benediktinerinnen an der monastischen Bewegung des 10. und 11. Jahrhunderts', in Peter Dinzelbacher (ed.), *Religiöse Frauenbewegung und mystische Frömmigkeit im Mittelalter* (Cologne, 1988), pp. 83–98. Also refer to the general discussion in Hedwig Röckelein, 'Frauen im Umkreis der benediktinischen Reformen des 10. bis 12. Jahrhunderts. Gorze, Cluny, Hirsau, St. Blasien und Siegburg', *Female vita religiosa*, pp. 275–328.

[24] *Die Konzilien Deutschlands und Reichsitaliens 1023–1059*, D. Jasper (ed.), MGH, *Concilia 8. Concilia aevi Saxonici et Salici* (Hannover, 2010), pp. 396–8.

[25] Else M. Wischermann, *Marcigny-Sur-Loire. Gründungs- u. Frühgeschichte des 1. Cluniacenserinnenpriorates (1055–1150)* (Munich, 1986).

argued that lay ruler Louis the Pious had 'audaciously' and 'stupidly' interfered with ecclesiastical custom to create a lifestyle for secular religious that flew against a tradition of the ascetic life for women that went all the way back to apostolic times. Three and a half centuries later, Jacques de Guise argued that the creation of the *Institutio* was in fact a compromise solution arising from a failed attempt to turn all women's monasteries into Benedictine houses. Finally, nineteenth- and twentieth-century historians were inclined to say that the compromise was actually programmed into the reform and derived from the awareness of Louis and his fellow reformers of a need to create a mode of life for women religious that matched the aristocracy's interests. But beginning in the 1990s this long-lasting narrative of abrupt transition started to unravel, thanks to a number of publications that showed how each of these interpretations is based on anachronistic assumptions. These studies revealed a need to reassess what the reformers of the early ninth century had tried to achieve, what the purpose was of the various decrees they issued, and the degree to which the Rule and *Institutio* had subsequently shaped forms and experiences of the religious life for women.

We can learn a great deal about the reformers' intentions by looking at how they handled their legislative project. Louis stated that he wanted all religious communities in the empire to follow their respective rule to the letter, but any materials he and other lawmakers submitted for use for women's religious communities were poorly designed for that purpose. Contrary to what they did for Benedictine monks, he and his fellow reformers made no effort to establish an authoritative version of the Rule for women: all the known manuscript versions from the ninth to early eleventh centuries are local productions.[26] And while they published a detailed account of the life in clerical communities in a document known as the *Institutio canonicorum*, the women's counterpart of that text is a far less accomplished document. With the exception of the prologue, the *Institutio sanctimonialium* is a barely coherent assemblage of patristic and conciliar excerpts and hardly qualifies as a foundational document for a new cohort of secular religious. Furthermore, the text features many passages that align with the contents and message of the Rule of St Benedict.[27]

Comparisons with earlier attitudes and perceptions help us further to deconstruct the notion that these decrees were paradigm shifting. Core dispositions of

---

[26]   Katrinette Bodarwé, 'Eine Männerregel für Frauen. Die Adaption der Benediktsregel im 9. und 10. Jahrhundert', in *Female vita religiosa*, pp. 235–74. On the dispositions for Benedictine monks, see Josef Semmler, 'Benedictus II: una regula – una consuetudo', in W. Lourdaux and D. Verhelst (eds), *Benedictine Culture 750–1050* (Leuven, 1983), pp. 1–49; Michèle Gaillard, *D'une réforme à l'autre (816–934): Les communautés religieuses en Lorraine à l'époque Carolingienne* (Paris, 2006), pp. 123–47.

[27]   Schilp, *Norm* and Gaillard, *D'une réforme*.

the *Institutio* closely match those in an edict issued by Louis's father Charlemagne and a group of bishops at the council of Chalon-sur-Saône (813). This text had been addressed to 'women religious who call themselves canonesses'. It revealed that lawmakers expected these women essentially to adopt the same lifestyle as Benedictine religious by observing strict enclosure, living chastely under the direction of a mother superior, and performing a tightly choreographed prayer service. One of just two fundamental differences between the two cohorts – Benedictine 'nuns' and other women religious – was that the 813 decree and the *Institutio* both foresaw that each community of 'secular' women had the option to choose between systems of property-holding: one of communal property, one of use of personal properties brought in by the members and received from the community's estate under the guidance of a lay officer, or one of free personal use of these resources. The other was (we have already seen) that the women were in principle free to leave the monastery to get married.[28]

The reformers' lack of interest in creating and strictly regulating two distinct cohorts of Benedictine nuns and secular canonesses can be inferred from other indicators too. To begin with, the terminology used to describe women religious remained as vague as it had been before the reform.[29] Furthermore, rites for the admission of women religious and the ordination of heads of women's monastic communities also remained notably similar to those in the earlier period.[30] And in royal law texts and in conciliar decrees from after 819, references to two distinct cohorts of Benedictine women religious and 'secular religious' almost completely disappear.[31] Based on these observations, specialists concluded that the purpose of the Aachen councils' accounts of monastic life for women had been three-fold: first, to demonstrate the comprehensive nature of the reformers' project to 'correct' the Frankish Church;[32] second, to instruct monastics, bishops, and lay lords on what were the four priorities regarding women's observance: namely, enclosure, chastity, prayer service, and symbolic and material support to the sovereign; and third, to indicate to local stakeholders in monastic houses where

---

[28] Regarding the above, see now Vanderputten, *DAN*, pp. 16–17.

[29] Franz Felten, 'Auf dem Weg zu Kanonissen und Kanonissenstift. Ordnungskonzepte der weiblichen vita religiosa bis ins 9. Jahrhundert', in I. Crusius (ed.), *Vita religiosa sanctimonialium: Norm und Praxis des weiblichen religiösen Lebens vom 6. bis zum 13. Jahrhundert* (Korb, 2005), pp. 71–92.

[30] For example, Steven Vanderputten and Charles West, 'Inscribing Property, Rituals, and Royal Alliances: The "Theutberga Gospels" and the Abbey of Remiremont', *Mitteilungen des Instituts für Österreichische Geschichtsforschung*, 124 (2016), 296–321.

[31] Vanderputten, *DAN*, pp. 22–3.

[32] Rutger Kramer, *Rethinking Authority in the Carolingian Empire: Ideals and Expectations During the Reign of Louis the Pious (813–828)* (Amsterdam, 2019).

lay the boundaries of legitimate experimentation in the organisation of religious community life for women.[33]

And experimentation there certainly was. The publication of the Rule and *Institutio*; the insertion of women's monasteries into institutional and personal networks controlled by the ruler and his associates;[34] and patronage by powerful aristocrats and bishops:[35] all these things undoubtedly fostered a certain degree of integration. But it would be wrong to overlook the many subtle and not-so-subtle variations in the organisation and observance of women's monasteries that emerge from the primary evidence. These tell us that representatives of the court and local stakeholders worked together to reconcile four things: (1) the reformers' objectives, (2) the expectations of the convent members and of the secular environment, (3) local constraints such as a convent's geophysical location, size, and recruitment profile, and (finally) a monastery's distinctive historical legacy.[36] For instance, although the community of Remiremont in Lorraine self-identified as Benedictine from the 820s onwards it retained core elements of the convent's pre-reform rituals, in particular the perpetual prayer service for which it was widely known: Abbess Thiathildis even advertised its intercessory power to prominent reform agents at the Carolingian court.[37] And we also have references to women religious who had found ways to remain involved, be it directly or indirectly, in the running of hospices and hospitals.[38] To this and other negotiated forms and experiences we must also add the ones that derived from a renewed interest in the comparative study of rules, commentaries, and other accounts of women's ascetic spirituality.[39] Examples include houses that self-

---

[33] Albrecht Diem, 'The Gender of the Religious: Wo/men and the Invention of Monasticism', in *OHWG*, p. 443.

[34] Katrinette Bodarwé, 'Ein Spinnennetz von Frauenklöstern: Kommunikation und Filiation zwischen sächsischen Frauenklöstern im frühmittelalter', in G. Signori (ed.), *Lesen, Schreiben, Sticken und Erinnern: Beiträge zur Kultur- und Sozialgeschichte mittelalterlicher Frauenklöster* (Bielefeld, 2000), pp. 27–52.

[35] E.g. Giancarlo Andenna, 'San Salvatore di Brescia e la scelta religiosa delle donne aristocratiche tra eta langobarda ed eta franca (VIII–IX secolo)', in *Female vita religiosa*, pp. 209–33.

[36] Veronica West-Harling (ed.), *Female Monasticism in Italy in the Early Middle Ages: New Questions, New Debates* (Florence, 2019).

[37] Eva-Maria Butz and Alfons Zettler, 'Two Early Necrologies: The Examples of Remiremont (c. 820) and Verona (c. 810)', in J.-L. Dueffic (ed.), *Texte, liturgie et mémoire dans l'église du moyen âge* (Turnhout, 2012), pp. 197–242.

[38] For example, Vanderputten, *DAN*, p. 62.

[39] Steven Stofferahn, 'Changing Views of Carolingian Women's Literary Culture: The Evidence from Essen', *EME*, 8 (1999), 69–97; Katrinette Bodarwé, *Sanctimoniales litteratae. Schriftlichkeit und Bildung in den ottonischen Frauenkommunitäten Gandersheim, Essen und Quedlinburg* (Münster, 2004); and Steven Vanderputten, 'Debating

described as 'Benedictine' yet gave prebends to their members; so-called 'houses of canonesses' where the lifestyle of members was far stricter than the one described in the *Institutio*; and finally also communities where groups of convent members lived according to different interpretations of the monastic ideal.[40] Sources from early tenth-century Rome and Lotharingia further attest to the involvement of the inmates of certain houses in sacramental tasks and possibly even in preaching.[41]

Early ninth-century women monastics, their male associates, and other stakeholders had been mentally prepared for these processes of negotiation and experimentation. As a number of studies have recently argued, the reforms of the early ninth century bookended, not started, a phase of intense transformation in monastic life for women. Indeed, as far back as the late seventh century, clerical and lay rulers had insisted on the need for communities to observe a rule, live according to a cloistered regime, and specialise in prayer service. Since that time, many former aristocratic foundations had come under the influence of Merovingian and (later) Carolingian royalty, a transition that required considerable adjustment of the identity of monasteries and their relationship with the secular environment. Finally, we also see that the growing role of the clergy in the eighth century had already drastically impacted on the status and societal role of (especially women's) religious communities with a contemplative focus. All three of these processes had compelled extensive negotiation, adaptation, and experimentation across the Latin West, long before there was any talk of a global reform project like the one proclaimed at the Aachen synod.[42]

Tenth- and Early Eleventh-Century Reform

Early ninth-century reform shifted the goalposts of what was considered acceptable conduct for women religious, but it did so much less drastically than former commentators had assumed. Furthermore, it did not fundamentally alter early medieval attitudes to rules and other normative texts as being inspirational

Reform in Tenth- and Early Eleventh-Century Female Monasticism', *Zeitschrift für Kirchengeschichte*, 125 (2014), 289–306.

[40] For Saxony, see now Jirki Thibaut, 'De ambigue observantie en heterogene identiteit van vrouwengemeenschappen in Saksen, ca. 800–1050' (Unpublished Ph.D. dissertation, Ghent University – KU Leuven, 2020).

[41] Mary M. Schaefer, *Women in Pastoral Office. The Story of Santa Prassede, Rome* (Oxford, 2013) and Gordon Blennemann, 'Die Darstellung und Deutung des räumlichen im hagiographischen Dossier der Hl. Glodesindis, Äbtissin in Metz (BHL 3562–3564)', in D. R. Bauer, K. Herbers, H. Röckelein, and F. Schmieder (eds), *Heilige – Liturgie – Raum* (Stuttgart, 2010), pp. 157–74.

[42] Michèle Gaillard, 'Les fondations d'abbayes féminines dans le nord et l'est de la Gaule à la fin du VIe siècle', *Revue d'histoire de l'église de France*, 76 (1990), 6–20.

documents rather than prescriptive law texts. These fundamental observations allow us to correct the former narrative in a number of ways. First, a binary approach (Benedictine *versus* canonical) to forms and experiences of women's monastic life in the ninth to early eleventh centuries is no longer tenable. Second, it is wrong for modern observers to rely on written rules as an objective means to reconstruct monastic forms and experiences. Rather, we should see variations (between institutions, but also between generations in the same institution) as the norm rather than the exception. Finally, we should not see indications of an 'ambiguous' observance (in which the women of a particular house practised a mix of several lifestyles for women religious as described in rules) as evidence of a state of institutional or spiritual decline.

A further corollary of these findings is that they have also complicated scholars' understanding of tenth- and early eleventh-century reform. The earliest testimonies regarding a need drastically to intervene in women's monasticism date back to the 870s, when a number of lay rulers and clerical authors relied on a language of reform to postulate a need to 'restore' the institutions and properties of women's monastic communities. These statements, in charters, conciliar decrees, and narrative texts, indicate that abuse of power by lay officers, depredations by secular agents, and the violence of foreign invaders had devastated the ability of religious communities to pursue their cloistered lifestyle and focus on their spiritual pursuits. Yet, while older studies used to read these commentaries as overall reliable accounts, the current reading is a good deal more nuanced. To begin with, it is now clear that such commentaries often functioned as a political tool in the hands of clerical and lay rules who sought to self-style (using much the same arguments as their predecessors had done in the 810s and 820s) as 'correctors' of the Church and 'restorers' of its properties and must be read in light of intense aristocratic competition over the resources of religious institutions.[43] Furthermore studies on the agency of lay superiors and other secular agents in the governance of ninth- and tenth-century women's monastic communities have also adjusted the view of these people as predatory agents who bled dry conventual resources and deprived communities of a spiritual director.[44] Finally, even the accounts of violent destruction, pillage, and rape at the hands of invaders

---

[43] Julia S. Barrow, 'Developing Definitions of Reform in the Church in the Ninth and Tenth Centuries', in R. Balzaretti, J. Barrow, and P. Skinner (eds), *Italy and Early Medieval Europe: Papers for Chris Wickham* (Oxford, 2018), pp. 504–7.

[44] Anne-Marie Helvétius, 'L'abbatiat laïque comme relais du pouvoir royal aux frontières du royaume: Le cas du nord de la Neustrie au IXe siècle', in R. Le Jan (ed.), *La royauté et les élites dans l'Europe carolingienne (du début du IXe aux environs de 920)* (Villeneuve d'Ascq, 1998), pp. 285–99 and Gaëlle Calvet-Marcadé, 'L'abbé spoliateur de biens monastiques (Francie du Nord, IXe siècle)', in P. Depreux, F. Bougard, and R. Le Jan

deserve to be treated with caution, as the real short- and long-term impact on specific houses, their membership, staff, and estates are often impossible to gauge, and as their description is often couched in literary tropes. What we do know for certain is that a significant number of women's monastic communities continued to be operational as spiritual centres in the decades on either side of the year 900, drawing both mighty patrons and pilgrims to their sanctuaries, and functioning as political, economic, and cultural hubs. Quite a few also enjoyed the active support of secular and clerical lords, who often sought to turn these places into personal and dynastic sanctuaries. In return these aristocrats restored lost goods, made new donations, and protected the religious. Later commentators either glossed over or completely erased the memories of these mutually beneficial relationships.[45]

A few decades into the tenth century this discourse of restoration mutated into another one that insisted on the need for a 'renewal' (*renovatio*) of monastic life, which commentators argued could be achieved by 'restoring' lost properties and adding new ones if necessary, removing all secular interference in governance, and imposing strict observance of the Rule of St Benedict under the direction of a regular mother superior. We find a typical example of this blend of arguments in a 945 charter by Bishop Adalbero of Metz for the urban monastery of Saint-Pierre-aux-Nonnains. In it, the prelate justified his intervention at this institution by stating that it had recently been 'defamed by bad actions'. Although he declined to specify these 'bad actions', he did suggest that institutional and spiritual decline were closely linked: domestic warfare, he stated, 'the inundation of the violence of tyrants', and incompetent leadership had all depleted the monastery's resources, with catastrophic consequences for the members' conduct and reputation.[46] Along with numerous other commentaries of reform, this document established a long-standing perception that a 'secular' observance (or any other 'ambiguous' interpretation of the monastic ideal) by definition implied an inferior institutional and spiritual performance. It was held to expose these communities more than Benedictine ones to all kinds of external risks, including the erosion of estates, interference in governance, and meddling by lay agents, even as to the women's observance. And finally, the inmates of these places were not to be trusted to come up with a model for community life for women that shielded them from these external and internal risks and that was true to the original ascetic and contemplative identity of their monasteries.

(eds), *Compétition et sacré au haut moyen âge: Entre médiation et exclusion* (Turnhout, 2015), pp. 313–27.

[45] Vanderputten, *DAN*, pp. 78–9 and 81–3.

[46] Georg Wolfram, 'Die Urkunde Ludwigs des Deutschen für das Glossindenkloster', *Mitteilungen des Instituts für Österreichische Geschichtsforschung*, 11 (1890), 17.

Foundation charters of new houses, particularly from Lotharingia and Saxony, echoed this discourse of Benedictine reform and the need for clerical oversight. When in 938 Bishop Gozelin of Toul turned a private settlement of women anchoresses at Bouxières into a Benedictine community, he made no mention of the site's former ascetic identity or of its residents, except to say that there had been 'some women religious who were wandering like sheep but looking for the pasture of eternal life, fervent in the love of God and wishing to serve Him in a remote location'.[47] Another example dates from half a century later, when a monk named Constantin of Saint-Symphorien commemorated the foundation of Saint-Marie-aux-Nonnains in Metz, on the former site of a hospice run by 'handmaidens of God'. Of that hospice, he merely stated that it was 'very poor and very vile' and had no redeeming features except that it was dedicated to the Holy Virgin. But the bishop of Metz, Adalbero II, had 'restored the splendour of its buildings, assembled material wealth, and ordained that women religious should perpetually celebrate the Creator of all'.[48]

Reform discourse further influenced two shifts. Beginning in the middle of the tenth century, scribes working on ritual handbooks for use by bishops created distinct rites for the ordination of a range of different groups: of virgins taking the veil while entering the cloistered life, virgins taking the veil but opting for a life in their own home, deaconesses, widows taking the veil, monastic superiors ruling over houses of canonesses, and Benedictine heads of houses. Over time these new rites anchored in the public consciousness a fundamental difference between Benedictine women religious and these other cohorts. In a second shift, authors also began using specific terms to refer to Benedictine women religious (*monachae, nonnae, sanctimoniales*) and to 'secular' religious (*canonissae*), something that they had rarely (and then only very inconsistently) done up to that point. Agents of Benedictine reform widened this conceptual and terminological split by giving it a qualitative dimension. They insisted on the notion that only the women who strictly observed the Rule (in particular its principles of chastity, stability, and individual poverty) and rejected any roles except that of prayer service and commemoration truly deserved to be called *sanctimoniales* ('women religious') or *monachae* ('nuns'). These terms, and *canonissae* or 'canonesses', were increasingly weaponised in the struggle for control over the destinies of women's monastic communities. *Canonissae* in particular

---

[47] Klaus Oschema, 'Zur Gründung des Benediktinerinnenklosters Notre-Dame de Bouxières. Eine wiedergefundene Urkunde des 10. Jahrhunderts', *Mitteilungen des Instituts für Österreichische Geschichtsforschung*, 110 (2002), 182–90 at p. 188.

[48] Constantin of Saint-Symphorien, *Vita Adalberonis II Mettensis episcopi*, ed. G. H. Pertz, MGH, *Scriptores*, 4 (Hannover, 1841), p. 662.

became a derogatory expression, which, in the propaganda of those who advocated a Benedictine reform, stood for the perversion of women's monasticism's origins as an ascetic movement. Such reformists also publicly attacked those institutions whose lifestyle did not fit their expectations. Communities were accused of not maintaining sufficient distance from the lay world, of compromising the status of sanctuaries as unpolluted sites of interaction with the divine, and of allegedly corrupting their Benedictine origins.[49]

The concessions that women's monastic communities were forced into making arguably had a far greater impact than those their predecessors had made in the early ninth century. Admittedly it is tempting to focus exclusively on the triumphant accounts of restoration and renewal by apologetic commentators and on the evidence regarding the production of manuscripts, the construction of new buildings, and other achievements in the context of a Benedictine reform. Yet the overall picture as it emerges from recent studies is undoubtedly mixed. Reformist propaganda underplayed or even outright dismissed the commitment of 'secular' religious to the monastic life, erasing in the process memories of vibrant pre-reform cultures of intellectual and spiritual reflection. As we already saw for Bouxières and Sainte-Marie-aux-Nonnains, clerical reformers also suppressed a broad range of lifestyles that had shaped the lay perception of the diverse role in society played by women religious, including those that combined community life with eremitical practices, pastoral work, education, and the management of hospitals. Some institutions even lost their identity as women's monastic communities, when the inmates were evicted or transferred to other houses, to be replaced by groups of (Benedictine) monks or clerics.[50] Recent studies have also nuanced the 'liberties' that were awarded to reformed houses, particularly the freedom to elect a regular monastic superior. In these places, reformist bishops and lay rulers remained firmly in control of governance decisions, the appointment of the head of house and other key offices, and the community's social network.[51] And while some prominent heads of monastic houses managed to establish themselves as major lords in their own right, interacting with their aristocratic peers on an equal

---

[49] Towards the end of the tenth century the women at the abbey of Pfalzel in Trier responded to that trend, defiantly stating that their recently deceased Abbess Ruothildis, although she had been veiled as a canoness, had actually lived and died as a true *monacha*: Vanderputten, *DAN*, pp. 136–43.

[50] For the example of Homblières in the 940s, see Steven Vanderputten, 'The Dignity of Our Bodies and the Salvation of Our Souls. Scandal, Purity, and the Pursuit of Unity in Late Tenth-Century Monasticism', in Stefan Esders, Sarah Greer, and Alice Hicklin (eds), *Using and Not Using the Past after the Carolingian Empire, c. 900–c. 1050* (Abingdon, 2019), p. 267.

[51] Vanderputten, *DAN*, pp. 89–110.

footing, a look at the background of these women reveals that most of these individuals had been well connected in the first place and had been manoeuvred into their leading position for political and representative purposes.[52]

Reform sometimes also put monasteries at risk financially. While reformers usually did (as they claimed) restore lost properties and bring new wealth and patronage, there was also a tendency among some of them to be selective with these transfers (keeping some lost estates for their own use), and the estates they 'restored' or donated were not necessarily picked regarding the convent's advantage. As a result of this, the monastic superiors of a number of reformed women's houses faced the immense task of managing a much-dispersed estate, struggled to generate the funds to maintain a functioning religious community, and generally remained dependent on their reformer's assistance and benevolence. Some of their colleagues in newly created institutions had to make do with a small and fractured estate that set them the same challenges: several such institutions in Lotharingia (where there had been a flurry of new foundations between c. 930 and the late tenth century) by the turn of the millennium were struggling to provide for their members.[53] Inclusion of these places within the sphere of influence of a reformist lord also brought with it considerable long-term risks. While a number of late ninth- and early tenth-century monasteries had managed to diversify their patronage network and attract new donations from pilgrims,[54] reform once again linked their fate to the political destiny of a particular individual or group of individuals. For instance, following the death of founder Gozelin of Toul the abbey of Bouxières saw its network of patrons collapse as a result of the disintegration of Gozelin's aristocratic network. And when aristocratic inheritance policies in the German empire shifted in the early eleventh century to the disadvantage of (unmarried) noblewomen, several monastic houses (including those that were reformed in earlier decades) faced a dramatic downturn in new recruits and income.[55]

Enduring Diversity

The outcome of all these processes and arguments was that women's monasticism became institutionally fragile, was reduced in terms of the different roles it had formerly played in society and was tarnished as a result of vicious clerical

[52] Jirki Thibaut, 'Intermediary Leadership. The Agency of Abbesses in Ottonian Saxony', in S. Vanderputten (ed.), *Abbots and Abbesses as a Human Resource in the Ninth to Twelfth-Century West* (Zürich, 2018), pp. 39–56.
[53] Vanderputten, *DAN*, pp. 112–18.
[54] Blennemann, 'Die darstellung'.
[55] Karl J. Leyser, *Rule and Conflict in an Early Medieval Society: Ottonian Saxony* (London, 1979).

criticism. But against the background of these tenth- and early eleventh-century criticisms, interventions, and other challenges, it retained notable elements of its former diversity. Within the landscape of reformed houses, we find that monastic identities and practices were still rooted in local traditions, circumstances, and perceptions. Hagiographic, liturgical, archival, and material evidence reveals countless minor and more substantial variations in how the Benedictine model was applied and subsequently observed across the Latin West. To some extent the variation was due to differing structural circumstances, such as the size of the community, its embedding in the physical and social landscape, relations with the secular environment, and so on. But some communities also tried to retain key elements of a former identity – whether pastoral, caritative, or educational – by employing male agents as proxies, financing institutions run on a day-to-day basis by men, or through similar means. In some Benedictine institutions in England, women might have found a way to remain personally involved in pastoral duties, possibly even taking confession.[56] And, as in earlier decades, the libraries of at least some communities also continued to hold multiple rules and other normative commentaries, which, along with several patristic texts, conciliar and canon law books, and various penitentials, formed a basis for in-house reflection and debate. Even in newly reformed houses, there still was room for women religious to shape at least some aspects of their spiritual identity.

Meanwhile institutions of 'secular' religious (or more accurately those pursuing a lifestyle that was 'ambiguously' situated between written templates) by no means diminished into a fringe phenomenon. Admittedly some did struggle in the face of clerical attacks and a downturn in patronage and new recruits. But others continued to prosper under the protection of mighty patrons who, for a variety of reasons, saw no need to dismantle the identity narrative and societal role of these places. One such example is that of the community of Nivelles, whose members in the late tenth and early eleventh centuries enjoyed vigorous support from the Ottonian rulers. While clerical critics in other regions of the Latin West were pummelling 'secular' women religious into submission, the Nivelles sisters obtained market, toll, and minting rights and initiated a massive building campaign.[57] Further examples from Saxony, Lotharingia, and Italy are legion. And so are those from England, where aristocratic and royal support helped women's monasteries of various types to thrive.[58] But these places did more than nurture or

---

[56] Katie A.-M. Bugyis, *The Care of Nuns: The Ministries of Benedictine Women in England during the Central Middle Ages* (Oxford, 2019).

[57] Vanderputten, *DAN*, pp. 124–5.

[58] Julia Crick, 'The Wealth, Patronage, and Connections of Women's Houses in Late Anglo-Saxon England', *RB*, 109 (1999), 154–84.

look to renew privileged associations with high-placed patrons. Across the Latin West, 'unreformed' communities relied on similar strategies to the ones some of their predecessors had deployed roughly a century earlier, to generate new income, popularity, and prestige. These strategies included promoting new saints' cults and pilgrimages; adjusting existing saint's cults to appeal to a new audience; networking with prominent men's and women's communities; and even the development of new economic activities.[59] To what extent these strategies were successful depended on the context and the interventionist attitudes of clerical and lay stakeholders.

It would be wrong to see the diversity of women's monasticism as something that played out strictly *between* institutions. Within certain communities, too, there was room for members to experience their status as a veiled individual differently. To begin with, we must remember that convents often consisted of a heterogenous membership, with very different life trajectories, training, and even social backgrounds: the monastic world of the ninth to eleventh centuries far from the homogeneously aristocratic one it was once made out to be. Furthermore, we have indications that in some communities at least there was room for reflection and debate on just how the physical appearance and conduct of religious was to reflect the moral purity of the religious. Tenth- and eleventh-century commentators also occasionally refer to individuals who adopted a lifestyle that set them apart from the rest of their community. In the 920s or 930s the head of the community of Saint-Pierre-aux-Nonnains in Metz and her young niece Geisa apparently practised a lifestyle that was far stricter than that of the other women there.[60] Two generations later Abbess Adelheidis of Vilich took to wearing a hair shirt on her naked skin, eating only those things allowed in the Rule, and caring for the poor and the sick, apparently with a view to inspiring her subjects to emulation.[61] Lest we forget them, anchoresses and recluses also amplified the diversity of religious experiences in and around some religious institutions.[62] In the late ninth-century biography of Liutbirg (d. *c*. 865), a walled-in recluse near the monastery of Wendhausen, much is made of how she developed a deep relationship with the cloistered women of that place. Among other things, she taught girls of noble origin how to sing the psalms and perform certain manual tasks,

---

[59]   Vanderputten, *DAN*, pp. 144–50 and Thibaut, 'De ambigue observantie'.

[60]   John of Saint-Arnoul, *Vita Johannis Gorziensis*, ed./trans. P. C. Jacobsen, *Die Geschichte vom Leben des Johannes, Abt des Klosters Gorze* (Wiesbaden, 2016), pp. 192–8.

[61]   *Vita sanctae Adelheidis*, ed. O. Holder-Egger, MGH, *Scriptores*, 15/2 (Hannover, 1888), p. 759.

[62]   Gabriela Signori, 'Anchorites in German-speaking Regions', in *Anchoritic Traditions*, pp. 43–61 and Tom Licence, *Hermits and Recluses in English Society, 950–1200* (Oxford, 2011); see Gunn, below, pp. 76–89.

interacted closely with the women religious and with the clerics who served them, and provided spiritual counsel to members of the laity who paid her a visit.[63] Such interactions must have had a strong appeal for these ascetics, since they created a stable environment in which they could concentrate on their ascetic goals, independently manage their (financial) resources,[64] and engage in different ways with the secular environment, while at the same time forging a mutually beneficial bond with the members of a religious community. The same was true for the inmates of these monasteries, as it allowed them to witness first-hand (and presumably also find inspiration in) how anchoresses pursued their penitential lifestyle and how they offered pastoral, caritative, and even sacramental services to visitors and fellow anchoresses.[65]

This variance of lifestyles inside and around women's monasteries enriched the spirituality and self-understanding of all those who frequented these places, including the girls who were sent there to receive an education, the noblewomen who visited them for spiritual or other reasons, and those who withdrew there in widowhood. Many pilgrims and casual visitors also found comfort in entering the sanctuaries of these places: they might pay their respects to a saint's grave, hear the sisters' chants, say confession to a cleric or possibly even a veiled woman, or simply attend office. All these and other encounters must have rendered both insiders' and outsiders' experience of women's spirituality significantly more complex – and also significantly less anchored in a specific status in life – than nineteenth- and twentieth-century historians used to imagine. Hagiographies and biographies lift the veil on a broad range of ascetic lifestyles for women, the very individual nature of which made them difficult to capture in permanent record: scholars are only beginning to recognise the full significance of these testimonies.[66]

[63] Valerie L Garver, 'Learned Women? Liutberga and the Instruction of Carolingian Women', in P. Wormald and J. L. Nelson (eds), *Lay Intellectuals in the Carolingian World* (Cambridge, 2007), pp. 121–38.

[64] An early tenth-century widow named Wendilgarth became a recluse at St Gall because she did not want to remarry. According to the chronicler Ekkehard, she lived off the income of her estate and used her wealth to support the poor: Ekkehard of Sankt Gallen, *Casuum S. Galli continuatio*, ed. H. F. Haefele, *Ekkehardi IV.Casuum S. Galli continuatio/St. Galler Klostergeschichten* (Darmstadt, 2013), p. 170.

[65] Bärbel Stocker, 'Die Opfergeräte der heiligen Wiborada von St. Gallen – Eine Frau als Zelebrantin der Eucharistie?', *Freiburger Diöcezan-Archiv*, 111 (1991), 405–19.

[66] Anne-Marie Helvétius, 'La passio de sainte Maxellende et la réforme d'une communauté féminine en Cambrésis', in M.-C. Isaïa and T. Garnier (eds), *Normes et hagiographie dans l'Occident (VIe–XVIe siècle)* (Turnhout, 2014), pp. 167–81.

Conclusions

The purpose with this chapter was to show that sweeping notions of reform and decline do not apply to the complex realities that emerge from the primary evidence regarding women's monasticism in the Central Middle Ages. We must therefore also be careful to avoid anachronistically projecting later institutional realities and conceptualisations of rules and other normative documents onto a period in which forms and experiences of the religious life for women were still very much in a state of flux. As such, the period is revealed to us as one that had many challenges and numerous setbacks, but also many creative solutions. And above all things, it was a period of enduring diversity, on a collective and on an individual level. This paradigmatic shift compels us to revisit, on a massive scale, the written and material evidence from this ill-understood phase in the history of women's religious life.

CHAPTER 2

New Movements of the Twelfth Century: Diversity, Belonging, and Order(s)

KATHARINE SYKES

THIS chapter explores the revolutions in religious life that took place during the long twelfth century, that is, between the foundation of the community of Fontevraud *c.* 1100 and the promulgation of the decrees of the Fourth Lateran Council of 1215, which forbade the foundation of new religious orders.[1] As other chapters of this book make clear, the decrees of the Fourth Lateran Council did not bring about the end of religious experimentation; they did, however, curtail the sorts of experimentation that were possible in earlier periods, and removed some of the ambiguities surrounding groups of women who were affiliated with – but not fully incorporated into – the new orders that had arisen in a century of rapid monastic growth.[2]

The following discussion focuses on three different patterns grouped under the loose headings of experimentation, ambivalence, and tradition. Experimental responses have attracted the most attention, especially when they were institutionalised: a community with a rule, charters, and endowments is more visible to both contemporaries and subsequent generations of historians than one without. Ambivalent responses generated occasional comment – and occasional controversy – among contemporaries; they have attracted considerable attention from historians, who have sought to explain why they did not conform to trajectories and trends that may be more visible with the benefit of hindsight. Finally, the impact of the new monasticism on more traditional forms of life has attracted less scrutiny, but this does not mean that they were unmoved by the broader currents of innovation and reform.

[1] See canon 13 in Norman P. Tanner (ed.), *Decrees of the Ecumenical Councils* (London, 1990), p. 242.

[2] See Vanderputten, pp. 22–43 and More, pp. 61–75.

Experimentation: Fontevraud, the Paraclete, and Sempringham

In discussions of the place of women within the new movements of the twelfth century, three communities in particular – Fontevraud, the Paraclete, and Sempringham – are singled out for discussion and comparison.[3] Of these, Fontevraud was the earliest to take institutional form and has attracted the most attention, in part because of the celebrity – and notoriety – of its founder, Robert of Arbrissel.[4] Towards the end of the eleventh century, Robert, a charismatic preacher and occasional hermit, began to organise the followers who had flocked to hear him preaching in and around the forest of Craon (dept. Mayenne). First, he founded a community for canons at La Roë; soon after (1101) he established a mixed community for women religious and canons at Fontevraud (dept. Maine-et-Loire). Thereafter, Robert continued with his itinerant preaching, returning at intervals to Fontevraud and La Roë to offer spiritual guidance. By the time Robert died in 1116, these original communities were supplemented by further founda-tions within the Loire valley and beyond, which came under the oversight of the superior of Fontevraud;[5] following Robert's death, a small number of additional houses would be founded in England.[6]

Throughout his career, Robert attracted considerable attention, both positive and negative: he was driven out of Rennes after the death of his patron, Bishop Sylvester, and faced virulent attacks from Sylvester's successor, Marbod.[7] One particularly controversial aspect of Robert's career were the allegations that he

[3] Penny S. Gold, *The Lady and the Virgin: Image, Attitude, and Experience in Twelfth Century France* (Chicago, 1985), p. 109; Venarde, *Women's Monasticism*, pp. 79–80; Kerr, *Religious Life*, pp. 58–9; Brian Golding, 'Authority and Discipline at the Paraclete, Fontevraud and Sempringham', in Gert Melville and Anne Müller (eds), *Mittelalterliche Orden und Klöster im Vergleich: Methodische Ansätze und Perspektiven* (Munster, 2007), pp. 87–114; Constant Mews, 'Negotiating the Boundaries of Gender in Religious Life: Robert of Arbrissel and Hersende, Abelard and Heloise', *Viator*, 37 (2006), 113–48; Fiona J. Griffiths, *Nuns' Priests' Tales: Men and Salvation in Medieval Women's Monastic Life* (Philadelphia, 2018), pp. 30, 35, 49.
[4] For Robert, see Jacques Dalarun, *Robert d'Arbrissel: fondateur de Fontevraud* (Paris, 1986); Bruce L. Venarde (trans.), *Robert of Arbrissel: Sex, Sin and Salvation in the Middle Ages* (Washington, DC, 2006); Jacques Dalarun (ed.), *Robert d'Arbrissel et la vie réli-gieuse dans l'Ouest de la France: Actes du colloque de Fontevraud, 13–16 décembre 2001* (Turnhout, 2004).
[5] Dalarun, *Robert of Arbrissel*, pp. 34–7, 59–76, 119–60; Gold, *Lady and the Virgin*, pp. 93–115; Venarde, *Women's Monasticism*, pp. 57–63; Kerr, *Religious Life*, pp. 15–63.
[6] Elkins, *Holy Women*, pp. 146–7; Kerr, *Religious Life*, pp. 64–100; Venarde, *Women's Monasticism*, pp. 155–6.
[7] Marbod's letter is translated in Bruce L. Venarde (ed.), *Robert of Arbrissel: A Medieval Life* (Washington, DC, 2003), pp. 88–100, at pp. 92–100.

practised syneisactism – that is, mortifying the flesh through close contact with his female followers.[8] These allegations may well have had no substance – similar accusations of sexual impropriety would dog other mixed communities – but they certainly represented a challenge for Robert's hagiographers and for his successor. Here, Robert made a choice that was not widely replicated: he handed over control of his communities to Petronilla, prioress of Fontevraud, who became superior of the mother house and Robert's designated successor as head of the fledgling order.[9]

The place of women within the communities of Fontevraud was set out in early legislation, most of which appears to have been composed before Robert's death.[10] Here, the explicit preference was for rule by *conversae* – at Fontevraud, this meant adult, often formerly-married or penitent women – rather than choir sisters who were raised within the community.[11] Analysis of charters and administrative documents provides historians with new insights into day-to-day life with the communities of Fontevraud.[12] Robert of Arbrissel appears frequently as both a recipient and witness in early charters, challenging his long-established reputation as a hands-off, charismatic preacher who took little interest in his communities after their initial foundation.[13] Charters and letters also point to the importance of Robert's successor, Petronilla, in ensuring the longevity of his vision: she played an active role in increasing the endowments of the order, in revising its statutes, and in commissioning the lives of the founder.[14]

Robert's foundation at Fontevraud, as previously noted, is often compared with the slightly later foundations of the Paraclete and Sempringham; a more instructive parallel, as Penny S. Gold has noted, is found in the foundations of

[8] Constable, *Reformation*, pp. 26, 68; Dalarun, *Robert of Arbrissel*, pp. 42–56; Griffiths, *Nuns' Priests' Tales*, pp. 37, 40, 46.

[9] The process is described in the second *Vita*, edited and translated in Venarde, *Robert of Arbrissel*, pp. 22–67, at pp. 27–31. For contrasting interpretations of Petronilla's career see Dalarun, *Robert of Arbrissel*, pp. 123–60, 163–8; Kerr, *Religious Life*, pp. 29, 46–52.

[10] Two versions of the statutes are printed in *PL* 162, cols 1079–86; for discussion, see Gold, *Lady and the Virgin*, pp. 98–102, 111–13; Kerr, *Religious Life*, pp. 47–8, 52–60; Bruce L. Venarde, 'Robert of Arbrissel and Women's *vita religiosa*', in *Female vita religiosa*, pp. 329–40, at pp. 336–8.

[11] Dalarun, *Robert of Arbrissel*, pp. 64–76; Venarde, *Women's Monasticism*, pp. 96–7, 99–100, 116–19; Kerr, *Religious Life*, pp. 41–2, 44–5. For *conversae* at Premonstratensian houses, see below, pp. 53–4.

[12] E.g., Venarde, *Women's Monasticism*, pp. 100–2, 111–12, 144–5.

[13] J.-M. Bienvenu (ed.), *Grande cartulaire de Fontevraud*, 2 vols (Poitiers, 2000–05). For discussion see Gold, *Lady and the Virgin*, pp. 102–8; Venarde, *Women's Monasticism*, pp. 104–10, 144–5.

[14] Venarde, *Women's Monasticism*, pp. 116–20; idem, 'Making History at Fontevraud: Abbess Petronilla and Practical Literacy', in *Nuns' Literacies: Hull*, pp. 19–31, at pp. 22, 24–6.

Norbert of Xanten.[15] Here, early and explicit legislation regarding the position of women has long been recognised as a key factor in determining whether a group remained mixed, or whether it would be segregated into single-sex communities; at Fontevraud, early codification of the order's legislation ensured that women continued to play a dominant role – and perhaps increasingly dominant role – after the founder's death.[16] In many respects, however, after an initial experimental phase during Robert's lifetime, the communities of Fontevraud may not have looked very different from other wealthy, aristocratic women's monastic communities, at least to outsiders.[17]

Some similar patterns of experimentation and routinisation are found at the second case study, the order of the Paraclete. Like Fontevraud, its history is linked with the history of its celebrated – even notorious – founder figures, Abelard and Heloise.[18] In contrast with Robert of Arbrissel's earliest communities, growing out of his preaching and teaching of the *vita apostolica*, the Paraclete was, initially, a thought experiment that emerged from the ashes of Abelard and Heloise's disastrous relationship. In a series of letters, they worked through the implications of living under a rule as a female, formerly-married adult convert: Abelard drafted a working document, composed of a selection of material from well-known sources; Heloise edited and honed it into something of her own.[19] Like the communities of Fontevraud, the experimental phase at the Paraclete was relatively short-lived:

[15] On which see below, pp. 52–4; Gold, *Lady and the Virgin*, pp. 94, 109; see also Venarde, *Women's Monasticism*, pp. 79–80.

[16] Gold, *Lady and the Virgin*, pp. 111–13; Dalarun, *Robert of Arbrissel*, pp. 125–6, 152–7, 163–8.

[17] Gold, *Lady and the Virgin*, pp. 102–5; cf. Kerr, *Religious Life*, p. 52.

[18] Bonnie Wheeler (ed.), *Listening to Heloise: The Voice of a Twelfth-Century Woman* (New York, 2000); Michael Clanchy, *Abelard: A Medieval Life* (Oxford, 1997), pp. 9–16, 149–72, 237–63, 277–82; Babette Hellemans (ed.), *Rethinking Abelard: A Collection of Critical Essays* (Leiden, 2014).

[19] Abelard's 'rule' (the *Institutio*) is printed in D. Luscombe (ed.) and B. Radice (trans.), *The Letter Collection of Peter Abelard and Heloise* (Oxford, 2013), pp. 352–517; Heloise's response (*Institutiones Nostrae*): Chrysogonus Waddell (ed., trans.), *The Paraclete Statutes: Institutiones Nostrae* (Trappist, 1987); Constant Mews, 'Imagining Heloise as Abbess of the Paraclete', *Journal of Religious History*, 44 (2020), 422–42, at pp. 440–2. For discussion, see Chrysogonus Waddell, 'Cistercian Influence on the Abbey of the Paraclete', in Terryl Kinder (ed.), *Perspectives for an Architecture of Solitude* (Turnhout, 2004), pp. 329–40; Jacques Dalarun, 'Nouveaux aperçus sur Abélard, Héloïse et le Paraclet', *Francia*, 32 (2005), 19–66; Fiona J. Griffiths, 'Men's Duty to Provide for Women's Needs: Abelard, Heloise, and their Negotiation of the *cura monialium*', *JMH*, 30 (2004), 1–24; Julie Ann Smith, '*Debitum obedientie*: Heloise and Abelard on Governance at the Paraclete', *Parergon*, 25 (2008), 1–23; William Flynn, 'Abelard and Rhetoric: Widows and Virgins at the Paraclete', in Hellemans (ed.), *Rethinking Abelard*, pp. 155–86.

after Heloise's death, it may have been largely indistinguishable, as far as outside observers were concerned, from other elite female communities in the region.[20] But there was clearly still something that set the Paraclete apart from its contemporaries, especially at a regional level: its prestige and appeal were a factor in the relatively slow growth of women's Cistercian communities within the north of France in the twelfth century, which had important but unintended consequences for the place of women within the Cistercian Order.[21] Further afield, Abelard and Heloise's correspondence found an enthusiastic audience at the community of Marbach.[22]

Finally, the question of Cistercian influence brings us to the third of the experimental communities, namely the order of Sempringham or Gilbertines. In contrast with Fontevraud and the Paraclete, the order of Sempringham did not owe its foundation to a celebrated or notorious figure, but to a local priest, the eponymous Gilbert, who supervised the enclosure of a group of women at the parish church of Sempringham (Lincolnshire) in the 1130s.[23] As the community grew, Gilbert took on lay brothers and sisters to serve the needs of the enclosed women; in the late 1140s, as the number of his foundations swelled, Gilbert added canons to provide spiritual services and oversight.[24] By the end of the twelfth century there were around twenty-six Gilbertine foundations, predominantly located within the eastern counties of Yorkshire and Lincolnshire; despite a few abortive attempts in the early thirteenth century to found houses at Dalmilling (Ayrshire), Brachy (dept. Seine-Maritime), and San Sisto in Rome, the Order of Sempringham would remain confined to England until its suppression in the 1530s.[25]

From the 1180s, there was an apparent shift in orientation within the order: only one further mixed community would be founded, while the rest would be single-sex houses of men.[26] This has been read as part of a more general shift away from a charismatic, mixed phase to a more routinised and segregated period, in

---

[20] Venarde, *Women's Monasticism*, pp. 120–2.
[21] See below, pp. 50–5. For the daughter houses see Mews, 'Imagining Heloise', pp. 434–6, 439–40. For relationships between the Paraclete and Cistercian foundations for women, see Lester, *Creating Cistercian Nuns*, p. 160; Berman, *White Nuns*, pp. 223–4, 226–32.
[22] Fiona J. Griffiths, 'Brides and *dominae*: Abelard's *cura monialium* at the Augustinian Monastery of Marbach', *Viator*, 34 (2003), 57–88.
[23] Elkins, *Holy Women*, pp. 78–84, 105–17, 125–44; Golding, *Gilbert*, pp. 7–55, 71–137.
[24] For the foundation narrative, see Raymonde Foreville and Gillian Keir (eds), *The Book of St Gilbert* (Oxford, 1987), pp. 30–57.
[25] Golding, *Gilbert*, pp. 191–262; Brenda Bolton, 'Daughters of Rome: All One in Christ Jesus?', in W. J. Sheils and D. Wood (eds), *Women in the Church*, SCH, 27 (Oxford, 1990), pp. 101–15; Julie Ann Smith, 'Prouille, Madrid, Rome: the Evolution of the Earliest Dominican *Instituta* for Nuns', *JMH*, 35 (2009), 340–52; Katharine Sykes, 'Rewriting the Rules', *JMMS*, 9 (2020), 107–31.
[26] Golding, *Gilbert*, pp. 219–48.

keeping with apparent trends within other new orders of the twelfth century.[27] However, it also reflected a shift in the nature of donations to the order, as it began to attract fewer, substantial, nucleated endowments, and a greater number of smaller, far-flung donations which were not capable of supporting larger communities.[28] Yet in spite of this shift in emphasis – and in contrast with some of the communities that are examined in the next section – the order of Sempringham retained its mixed houses until the order was dissolved in the 1530s.

As with Fontevraud, early and emphatic legislation that enshrined the position of women within the order was key to their continued presence. In their surviving form the statutes of the order of Sempringham (known as the Institutes) show considerable influence of early Cistercian legislation, which was incorporated into a distinctive four-fold framework, and brought canons, sisters, laybrothers, and laysisters under the oversight of the master of the order, the General Chapter, and men and women inspectors (the scrutators and scrutatrices).[29] Some insight into how this complicated framework might have functioned in practice is gleaned from surviving liturgical manuscripts, and from the charters, privileges, and cartularies of individual houses, although important questions relating to the performance of the liturgy and the use of space within the mixed communities remain unresolved.[30]

To summarise, each of these three groups fulfilled some of the defining characteristics of the new monasticism, but to differing degrees. Fontevraud and Sempringham were the offspring of charismatic preachers, but Robert of Arbrissel fits this stereotype much more closely than Gilbert of Sempringham. Abelard was certainly a charismatic teacher but of a very different type, and his role in the foundation of the Paraclete was less pivotal. All three communities appealed to new groups of recruits, most notably married or formerly-married women;

---

[27] Elkins, *Holy Women*, pp. 122–3.

[28] Golding, *Gilbert*, pp. 263–87.

[29] Elkins, *Holy Women*, pp. 134–44; Golding, *Gilbert*, pp. 71–137; Katharine Sykes, *Inventing Sempringham: Gilbert of Sempringham and the Origins of the Role of Master* (Berlin, 2011), pp. 162–205.

[30] For the liturgy, see Janet Sorrentino, 'In Houses of Huns, in Houses of Canons: Liturgical Dimension to Double Monasteries', *JMH*, 28 (2002), 361–72. For the charter material see F. M. Stenton, *Documents Illustrative of the Social and Economic History of the Danelaw* (London, 1920), pp. 2–74, 320–5; idem, *Transcripts of Charters Relating to the Gilbertine Houses of Sixle, Catley, Bullington, and Alvingham* (Horncastle, 1922); Jill Redford (ed.), *The Cartulary of Alvingham Priory* (Lincoln, 2018). For the use of space, based on William St John Hope, 'The Gilbertine Priory of Watton, in the East Riding of Yorkshire', *Yorkshire Archaeological Journal*, 58 (1901), 1–34, see *GMC*, pp. 93–4, 104, 115, 119, 133, 137–8, 163, 166; Elizabeth Freeman, 'Nuns in the Public Sphere: Aelred of Rievaulx's *De Sanctimoniali de Wattun* and the gendering of authority', *Comitatus*, 27 (1996), 55–80, at pp. 61, 70.

here, Fontevraud and the Paraclete were the most visibly and explicitly innovative, at least during the lifetimes of their founders. In terms of their economies,
the granges of the order of Sempringham were closer to the self-sufficient paradigm of the 'new monasticism' than the manors and estates of Fontevraud or the
Paraclete;[31] all three groups, however, took a considerable interest in the management of their assets.[32]

This brings us to the categorisation of these communities as experimental: in
what ways were they experimental, and what sort of challenges and opportunities
were they attempting to address? First, all three of these groups attempted to tackle
a perennial challenge that had received fresh emphasis in the wake of the Second
Lateran Council of 1139: how might men and women religious work together, whilst
remaining apart?[33] While, as is often pointed out, all women's religious communities
required the services of priests, setting out the precise forms that these relationships
should take was something new or, at least, something that had rarely been seen
since the pre-Carolingian era. As I have discussed elsewhere, some contemporaries were aware of the difference between a double monastery (in which canons
or monks formed an integral part of community life) and a community of women
religious (to which priestly services might be supplied in different ways).[34] All three
orders produced statutes or other legislative material that incorporated men and
women into a single unit: this is most true of Fontevraud and Sempringham; at
the Paraclete it appears that Abelard's vision of a women's community under the
oversight of an abbot was never fully implemented.[35]

It is also worth keeping in mind the nature of experimentation. At Fontevraud
and Sempringham, Robert and Gilbert were attempting to deal with the practical consequences of their preaching; at the Paraclete, Abelard and Heloise were
approaching a *quaestio* (what would a rule for women look like?) in scholastic
fashion.[36] It is assumed or implied there were institutional links between them,
but the evidence for this is far from clear: the earliest Fontevraudine houses in
England date from the 1150s, by which point the order of Sempringham was
already well established.[37] The links between Fontevraud and the Paraclete are
easier to substantiate, but there is relatively little evidence of direct borrowing

---

[31] Gold, *Lady and the Virgin*, pp. 106–7; Kerr, *Religious Life*, pp. 180–236; Golding, *Gilbert*,
    pp. 392–443.
[32] Kerr, *Religious Life*, pp. 180–1.
[33] Lateran II, canon 27 prohibited nuns and canons/monks from singing together in the
    same choir: Tanner (ed.), *Decrees*, p. 203.
[34] Sykes, 'Canonici Albi et Moniales'.
[35] Mews, 'Imagining Heloise', pp. 430–6, 439.
[36] Sykes, 'Rewriting the Rules', p. 110.
[37] Elkins, *Holy Women*, pp. 57–9; Kerr, *Religious Life,* pp. 64–100.

in terms of the legislation of the two groups.[38] In fact, both the Paraclete and Sempringham owed an equal if not greater debt to Cîteaux than they did to Fontevraud, although these Cistercian influences would be woven into very different institutional and liturgical settings.[39] This desire to find links among the three groups owes as much to their nature as mixed communities as it does to any other overarching characteristics: mixed communities are viewed as an aberration in need of explanation. However, mixed communities were much more common than traditional narratives of the twelfth century might suggest.

Ambiguity and Ambivalence: Women and the Cistercian and Premonstratensian Orders

The Cistercians play a central role within the historiography of the new movements of the twelfth century, not least because they were fond of foundation narratives, telling and retelling the story of the origins of their order and of individual houses.[40] In 1098, a group of monks left the monastery at Molesme and set up a new community at Cîteaux, under the leadership of the former abbot of Molesme, Robert. Robert soon returned to Molesme, leaving the community in the care of two of his companions, Alberic and Stephen Harding, who undertook the work of transforming the community into an institution. Under Stephen's leadership new houses were founded, attracting new recruits, including the future abbot of Clairvaux, Bernard; the houses of the order began to draft early versions of the documents that would set out the blueprint for a new type of religious organisation, the monastic order.[41]

Within these Cistercian narratives of the origins of their order there is no mention of the presence of women, who are also overlooked or explicitly excluded in the major legislative developments of the 1130s, 1150s, and 1230s. For this reason, they are often excluded from the historiography of the order; at best, they are included as an addendum to or deviation from the main pattern of development.[42] Yet by the time that Cistercian legislation began to take on a more

---

[38] Dalarun, Robert of Arbrissel, p. 32; Mews, 'Imagining Heloise', pp. 423–4, 431, 439.

[39] Mews, 'Imagining Heloise', pp. 434, 438–40; Clanchy, Abelard, p. 237; Golding, Gilbert, pp. 112–19; Sykes, Inventing Sempringham, pp. 172–89.

[40] For the early legislative texts see Chrysogonus Waddell (ed.), Narrative and Legislative Texts from Early Cîteaux (Nuits-St-Georges, 1999).

[41] I am following the dating of these early documents as given in Waddell, Narrative and Legislative Texts, pp. 139–61, 199–231, 261–73, 371–80; Brian Patrick McGuire, 'Constitutions and General Chapter', in Mette Birkedal Bruun (ed.), The Cambridge Companion to the Cistercian Order (Cambridge, 2012), pp. 87–99, at pp. 87–94. For an alternative timeline see Berman, Cistercian Evolution, passim.

[42] E.g. Louis J. Lekai, The Cistercians: Ideals and Reality (Kent, OH, 1977), pp. 347–63.

defined shape in the 1130s there were already at least two women's communities, Jully-les-Nonnains (dept. Yonne) and Tart (dept. Côte-d'Or), with close connections to Cistercian houses;[43] the community at Tart in particular was well-connected and by the thirteenth century stood at the head of a branch of women's communities.[44] As a result, historians have been unsure about how to deal with the question of Cistercian women religious, referring to them in quotation marks ('Cistercian') or with qualifiers ('quasi-Cistercian').[45] Although it is now widely accepted that there were, indeed, Cistercian women religious, there is still considerable debate surrounding definitions, chronology, distribution, and numbers. In terms of chronology and distribution, it is clear that there were Cistercian women religious from the early years of the twelfth century, but there were not many female Cistercian communities in France, Germany, or the Low Countries until the thirteenth century.[46] In contrast, a considerable percentage of communities for women that were founded in England, Scotland, and Ireland during the twelfth century, especially those in the counties of Lincolnshire and Yorkshire, identified as Cistercian at some point in their history.[47]

This brings us to the question of definitions. Part of the problem of defining and identifying Cistercian women religious is there was little attempt to do so before the thirteenth century and, even then, women Cistercians were much less clearly and consistently defined than their male counterparts. Judging twelfth-century communities by thirteenth-century criteria is like comparing apples and oranges; the experience of being a Cistercian in the twelfth century was more varied than

[43] Jean de la Croix Bouton, *Les moniales cisterciennes*, 4 vols (Grignan, 1986–89); Bernadette Barrière and Marie-Elizabeth Henneau (eds), *Cîteaux et les femmes* (Grane, 2001); N. Bouter, *Unanimité et diversité cisterciennes: filiations – réseaux – relectures du XIIe au XVIIe siècle* (Sainte-Étienne 2000).

[44] Laurent Veyssière, 'Cîteaux et Tart, fondations parallèles', in Barrière and Henneau (eds), *Cîteaux et les femmes*, pp. 179–91.

[45] Earlier work is discussed in Constance H. Berman, 'Were there Cistercian Nuns?', *CH*, 68:4 (1999), 824–64; Elizabeth Freeman, 'Nuns', in Bruun (ed.), *Cambridge Companion to the Cistercian Order*, pp. 100–11; Janet Burton, '*Moniales* and *Ordo Cisterciensis* in Medieval England and Wales', and Franz Felten, 'Abwehr, Zuneigung, Pflichtgefühl: Reaktionen der frühen Zisterzienser auf den Wunsch religiöser Frauen, zisterziensisch zu leben', in *Female vita religiosa*, pp. 375–89 and 391–415; Emilia Jamroziak, *The Cistercian Order in Medieval Europe, 1090–1500* (Abingdon, 2013), pp. 124–55.

[46] Gerd Ahlers, *Weibliches Zisterziensertum im Mittelalter und seine Klöster in Neidersachsen* (Berlin, 2002), esp. pp. 47–121; Erin Jordan, *Women, Power and Religious Patronage in the Middle Ages* (New York, 2006), esp. chapter 3; Lester, *Creating Cistercian Nuns*, pp. 15–44; Berman, *White Nuns*, pp. 18–30.

[47] Elizabeth Freeman, 'Houses of a Peculiar Order: Cistercian Nunneries in Medieval England, with Special Attention to the Fifteenth and Sixteenth Centuries', *Cîteaux*, 55 (2004), 245–87; Burton, '*Moniales* and *Ordo Cisterciensis*', pp. 375–89.

it was in the thirteenth century, and this was perhaps especially true for women. The earliest communities were not dissimilar to women's religious communities associated with earlier reform movements: the community at Jully has perhaps more in common with a house like Marcigny (affiliated with the mother house of an otherwise male family of Cluny) than it did with a house like Las Huelgas (prov. Burgos), a royal foundation with close ties to Castilian kings and queens.[48] The incorporation of the houses of Savigny and Obazine in the middle of the twelfth century brought further variety and complexity;[49] so too did the geographical expansion of the order.[50] There is, therefore, some merit in regional qualifiers: English Cistercian communities for women were not quite the same as German, Spanish, or French communities for women, for example. In the thirteenth century there were some moves towards tightening definitions, not least in the wake of the Fourth Lateran Council and increasing concerns about the development of heterodox religious movements.[51] At the same time, regional differences – whether in terms of patterns of foundation and endowment, or the level of episcopal oversight – continued to vary.[52]

The Premonstratensian Order has received less attention than its Cistercian counterpart, but it provides an instructive comparison: both groups were committed to living out the *vita apostolica*; both groups attracted diverse recruits, which they incorporated into novel legislative and administrative structures.[53] For the Premonstratensians, this took the form of the Augustinian Rule (in preference to the Benedictine Rule), which they supplemented with Cistercian customs; in marked contrast with early Cistercian legislation, however, the earliest Premonstratensian statutes concerned themselves with women as well as men.[54]

[48]   Griffiths, *Nuns' Priests' Tales*, pp. 16, 22, 133–4, 137–8; Ghislain Baury, *Les religieuses de Castille: patronage aristocratique et ordre cistercien XIIe–XIIIe siècles* (Rennes, 2012).
[49]   Bernadette Barrière, 'The Cistercian Convent of Coyroux in the Twelfth and Thirteenth Centuries', *Gesta*, 31 (1992), 76–82; Berman, *White Nuns*, pp. 39–41.
[50]   Freeman, 'Houses of a Peculiar Order', pp. 247–64; Jamroziak, *Cistercian Order*, pp. 126–36.
[51]   Lester, *Creating Cistercian Nuns*, pp. 78–116; Berman, *White Nuns*, pp. 18–30.
[52]   Freeman, 'Houses of a Peculiar Order', pp. 280–2; Jamroziak, *Cistercian Order*, pp. 245–8.
[53]   H. M. Colvin, *The White Canons in England* (Oxford, 1951); Kasper Elm (ed.), *Norbert von Xanten: Adliger, Ordensstifter, Kirchenfürst* (Cologne, 1984).
[54]   R. van Waefelghem, 'Les premiers statuts de l'ordre de Prémontré', *Analectes de l'ordre de Prémontré*, 9 (1913), 1–74. Discussion in Micheline de Fontette, *Les religieuses à l'âge classique du droit canon* (Paris, 1967), pp. 13–25; Thompson, *Women Religious*, pp. 134, 136–9; Yvonne Seale, '"Ten Thousand Women": Gender, Affinity, and the Development of the Premonstratensian Order in France' (Unpublished Ph.D. dissertation, University of Iowa, 2016), pp. 83–93. For Premonstratensian legislative material associated with the Paraclete (which contains the only surviving copy of *the Institutiones Nostrae*), see

In terms of their legislation and early history, the communities of Prémontré also have much in common with the early communities of Fontevraud; and the careers of Norbert of Xanten and Robert of Arbrissel share some significant similarities. Norbert, like Robert, had undergone a profound conversion in his thirties (c. 1115), leading him to give up his life as a secular canon and to embrace a vocation as a wandering preacher and teacher.[55] Like Robert, Norbert soon attracted followers, whom he began to organise into an ascetic community at Prémontré (dept. Aisne) near Laon in the early 1120s. In 1126, he was appointed to the archbishopric of Magdeburg (Saxony-Anhalt), where he embarked on a new phase of preaching and founding religious communities; Norbert's new pastoral responsibilities prompted the appointment of a successor, Hugh of Fosse, to lead Prémontré and its daughter houses, and to a period of organisational development.[56] By the middle of the twelfth century Premonstratensian communities housed considerable numbers of women – Herman of Tournai put their numbers in the thousands – but, from this point onwards, the tide is traditionally thought to have turned against the women of the order: in the 1220s, Jacques de Vitry would attribute the expansion in the numbers of Cistercian communities for women to Premonstratensian reluctance to accept women recruits.[57]

Traditionally, the Premonstratensian General Chapter is thought to have recommended the segregation of men's and women's communities at some point in the late 1130s or early 1140s, culminating in a complete ban on recruiting women in 1198.[58] In recent years, however, historians have challenged this narrative, pointing both to the lack of reliable evidence for this apparent shift, and to the plentiful evidence for the continuation of the recruitment of women, especially in Germany and eastern Europe.[59] Although this recruitment clearly continued,

---

Benton, 'The Paraclete', pp. 411–16; Dalarun, 'Nouveaux aperçus', pp. 28, 31–6; Mews, 'Imagining Heloise', p. 433.

[55] Charles Dereine, 'Les origines de Prémontré', *Revue d'Histoire Ecclésiastique*, 42 (1947), 352–78; Colvin, *White Canons*, pp. 1–25.

[56] Placide Lefèvre, *Les statuts de Prémontré au milieu du XIIe siècle* (Averbode, 1978); Bruno Krings, 'Zum Ordensrecht der Prämonstratenser bis zur Mitte de 12. Jahrhunderts', *Analecta Praemonstratensia*, 6 (2000), 9–28.

[57] Herman of Tournai, 'De miraculis S. Mariae Laudunensis', *PL* 156, cols 962–1018, at cols 996–7; Jacques de Vitry, *Historia Occidentalis: A Critical Edition*, ed. John Hinnebusch (Fribourg, 1972), at p. 117.

[58] A. Erens, 'Les soeurs dans l'ordre de Prémontré, *Analecta Praemonstratensia*, 5 (1929), 5–26, at pp. 8–13; de Fontette, *Les religieuses*, pp. 13–25; Colvin, *White Canons*, pp. 327–8.

[59] Thompson, *Women Religious*, pp. 134–6; Shelley Wolbrink, 'Women in the Premonstratensian Order of Northwestern Germany, 1120–1250', *Catholic Historical Review*, 89 (2003), 387–408, at p. 404; Seale, 'Ten Thousand Women', pp. 38–41, 58–9, 93–5, 113–21.

the status of these women – and the communities within which they lived – is far from clear: were they *conversae* or sisters? If they were *conversae*, what did that imply about their lifestyle and status? Were they central or peripheral to the communities that they inhabited? What was the status of the men who appear alongside them?

To some extent, varied forms of evidence suggest complex answers to these questions: charters and administrative documents, for example, give the impression that Premonstratensian women lived in communities of women which benefited from the services of male religious (rather than mixed communities);[60] liturgical manuscripts, on the other hand, suggest that men and women of the order might work in close collaboration with each other in communities which still looked and functioned like double monasteries, many decades after the apparent order to segregate into single-sex communities.[61] This is further complicated by the divergence between the western and eastern branches of the order, which display different patterns in terms of recruitment. Both branches initially contained mixed communities but by the end of the twelfth century there was a shift away from earlier practices, with the houses of the western branch (comprised predominantly of houses in France, but with additional foundations in England and Ireland) appearing to segregate earlier and more thoroughly than the eastern branch (comprised of foundations within the lands of the empire, Poland, Hungary, and Bohemia).[62] Women are much less visible in the houses of the western branches after 1200, although isolated references suggest that some communities may have housed small groups of women up to the sixteenth century. [63] These differences *within* orders are in many ways as significant as the differences *between* orders, highlighting some of the perils of taxonomy and model-making that has consumed a considerable amount of historical energy; the twelfth century was a period of both continuity and change, marked by considerable regional, chronological, and institutional diversity.

[60] Wolbrink, 'Women in the Premonstratensian Order', pp. 393–405; eadem, 'Necessary Priests and Brothers', in Fiona J. Griffiths and Julie Hotchin (eds), *Partners in Spirit: Women, Men and Religious Life in Germany, 1100–1500* (Turnhout, 2014), pp. 171–212.

[61] Alison I. Beach, *Women as Scribes*, pp. 104–27.

[62] Wolbrink, 'Women in the Premonstratensian Order', p. 393: of twenty-three houses in north western Germany, six 'housed primarily male religious' and seventeen 'housed primarily female religious'.

[63] For the English houses, Thompson, *Women Religious*, pp. 133–45; Elkins, *Holy Women*, pp. 88–9.

Beyond the Orders: Miscellaneous Mulierculae *and* New Trends at Older Communities

Nowhere are these perils more apparent than in the way historians have approached communities of women religious that do not fit within the taxonomy outlined earlier in this chapter, in which belonging to an order was one of the defining characteristics of the 'new monasticism'. This variation was also troubling to twelfth-century observers: in 1139, the Second Lateran Council had taken steps against 'the pernicious and detestable custom' whereby some women claimed to live as women religious whilst failing to adhere to the well-known rules of Augustine, Basil, or Benedict.[64]

The place of women religious within the new orders of the twelfth century was subject to considerable variation; the experience of women religious outside these orders (or on their margins) was just as diverse.[65] Some lived in newly-founded communities that did not generate additional foundations or become affiliated to larger groups; others belonged to long-established communities that picked up on some of the new trends. Some were small-scale and obscure; others were prestigious and wealthy. Within such communities, there is less of a distinction between the period 1100–1200 and the periods that preceded and followed it; the visible spike in activity associated with the international affiliated orders masks long-term cycles of expansion and contraction in religious life for women as well as men.[66]

This variegated pattern is particularly apparent among the older female communities in German-speaking lands, which offer a useful corrective to the dominant paradigms derived from French (and to a lesser extent English) examples.[67] Here, there were successive waves of reform among long-established communities for women, or men and women: some adopted the Benedictine, others the Augustinian rule. At the beginning of the twelfth century some were already mixed; by the end of the twelfth century mixed or double monasteries were thinner on the ground, but they had not disappeared entirely.[68]

---

[64] Lateran II, canon 26: Tanner (ed.), *Decrees*, p. 203.

[65] For more detailed discussion of these variations, see More, pp. 61–7, Gunn, pp. 76–89, and Richmond, pp. 76–89.

[66] For patterns see Venarde, *Women's Monasticism*, pp. 6–16, 54, 138; Steven Vanderputten, *DAN*, pp. 6–10, 155–8, and *passim*, and above, pp. 22–42.

[67] Recent collections of essays include Griffiths and Hotchin (eds), *Partners in Spirit*; Beach (ed.), *Manuscripts and Monastic Culture*.

[68] Elsanne Gilomen-Schenkel, 'Double Monasteries in the Southwestern Empire (1100–1230) and their Women's Communities in Swiss Regions', in Griffiths and Hotchin (eds), *Partners in Spirit*, pp. 47–74; Griffiths, *Nuns' Priests' Tales*, pp. 21–8, 31–2.

The process by which some of these unaffiliated mixed-sex communities were transformed into single-sex houses again offers a corrective to the traditional narrative of Cistercian and Premonstratensian segregation from the middle of twelfth century. In contrast with the implicit distinction between an active male propagation of new communities (the Cistercian system of filiation, for example) and a passive response from women (the segregation of mixed communities, with the transplantation of a women's element to a new, secluded location) in many instances individual women religious – as well as groups of women religious – left to set up new foundations.[69] At Marbach, for example, women remained part of a mixed community for many years until they were sufficient in number and resources to set up a new house;[70] a similar pattern can be observed at Muri in the Aargau, where the women eventually moved out to a new site at Hermetschwil.[71]

The careers of Hildegard of Bingen and Herrad of Hohenbourg also serve as exempla of broader trends.[72] As a child, Hildegard was given as an oblate to the Benedictine community at Disibodenberg, where she joined a small group of women recluses who were housed alongside a larger community of monks.[73] Eventually, Hildegard left to found a new community at Rupertsberg;[74] some years later, some of the Rupertsberg women religious left to found a second community at Eibingen.[75] At Hohenbourg, in contrast, a long-established community for women was restored and reformed by the emperor in the 1150s, adopting the Augustinian Rule.[76] Its second superior in the post-reform period, Herrad, would eventually rule over two subordinate houses of canons, as well as the mother house.[77] Both Rupertsberg and Hohenbourg developed a reputation for learning under their women superiors, at different ends of the twelfth-century educational

[69] A critique is given by Berman, *Cistercian Evolution*, esp. pp. 94–7, 99–110.
[70] Griffiths, 'Brides and Dominae'; Gilomen-Schenkel, 'Double Monasteries', pp. 58–61.
[71] Gilomen-Schenkel, 'Double Monasteries', pp. 55–6, 62–4.
[72] Barbara Newman, *Voice of the Living Light: Hildegard of Bingen and Her World* (Berkeley, 1998); Sabine Flanagan, *Hildegard of Bingen, 1098–1179: A Visionary Life* (London, 1998); Debra Stoudt, George Ferzoco, and Beverly Kienzle (eds), *A Companion to Hildegard of Bingen* (Leiden, 2014).
[73] Franz J. Felten, 'What Do We Know About the Life of Jutta and Hildegard at Disibodenberg and Rupertsberg', in Stoudt et al. (eds), *Companion to Hildegard of Bingen*, pp. 15–38; Constant J. Mews, 'Hildegard of Bingen and the Hirsau Reform in Germany, 1080–1180', in Stoudt et al. (eds), *Companion to Hildegard of Bingen*, pp. 57–83.
[74] Mews, 'Hildegard', pp. 79–82; Fiona J. Griffiths, 'Monks and Nuns at Rupertsberg: Guibert of Gembloux and Hildegard of Bingen', in Griffiths and Hotchin, *Partners in Spirit*, pp. 145–69.
[75] Franz J. Felten, 'What Do We Know?', p. 35.
[76] Griffiths, *Garden of Delights*, pp. 24–48.
[77] Griffiths, *Garden of Delights*, pp. 43–5.

and devotional spectrum: Hildegard's work had a strong visionary and contemplative element;[78] Herrad compiled a handbook of the latest scholastic theology to enable her sisters to test out and discard inadequate priests.[79]

The women's religious communities of the empire were not the only houses of religious women to experience reorganisation and reorientation in the twelfth century, as examples from Ireland demonstrate.[80] Ireland was an important centre of monastic learning and culture in the Early Middle Ages, with a strong tradition of eremitism and asceticism.[81] However, it remained relatively untouched by the reforms of the eighth and ninth century that had prompted a shift towards the adoption (or enforcement) of more uniform, written customs such as the Rule of St Benedict.[82] At the beginning of the twelfth century, therefore, the principal distinctions within women's religious communities – and between one community of women and another – still lay in marital and sexual status – that is, between virgins and widows or penitents – rather than between Benedictine or Augustinian houses, or between sisters and canonesses.[83]

In the twelfth century, the new international orders would establish a strong presence in Ireland, in large part due to the networking activities of Malachy, archbishop of Armagh.[84] Whilst there is little evidence of a woman's presence at any of the new Cistercian or Premonstratensian foundations, numbers of women at houses following some form of the Augustinian rule were considerable.[85] As within the houses of the empire, the Rule of Augustine offered a flexible but orthodox umbrella for existing communities within Ireland that found themselves out of step with the trends of the day; it also offered a framework that could be adopted – or pressed upon – new groups of men and women religious, either on its own or in combination with the customs of Arrouaise, which found

---

[78] Justin A. Stover, 'Hildegard, the Schools and their Critics', in Stoudt et al. (eds), *Companion to Hildegard* (Turnhout, 2014), pp. 109–35.

[79] Griffiths, *Garden of Delights*, pp. 68, 71–2, 81.

[80] Constable, *Reformation*, pp. 309–10; Marie Therese Flanagan, *The Transformation of the Irish Church in the Twelfth and Thirteenth Centuries* (Woodbridge, 2010), esp. pp. 118–68; Tracy E. Collins, 'Space and Place: Archaeologies of Female Monasticism in Later Medieval Ireland', in Vicky Blud, Diane Heath, and Einat Klafter (eds), *Gender in Medieval Places, Spaces, and Thresholds* (London, 2019), pp. 25–44.

[81] Christina Harrington, *Women in a Celtic Church: Ireland 450–1150* (Oxford, 2002); Lisa M. Bitel, *Landscape with Two Saints: How Genovefa of Paris and Brigit of Kildare Built Christianity in Barbarian Europe* (Oxford, 2009).

[82] Harrington, *Women in a Celtic Church*, pp. 191–225. Cf. Flanagan, *Transformation*, p. 161: the Rule of Benedict was known in Ireland from an early period, and its spread on the continent was associated with Columbanus and his followers.

[83] Harrington, *Women in a Celtic Church*, pp. 197–201.

[84] Flanagan, *Transformation*, pp. 118–68.

[85] Collins, 'Space and Place', p. 27, n. 5.

a particularly receptive audience in Ireland.[86] The Arrouaisian Order followed a now familiar pattern of development: a pair of hermits living in the forest near Arras began to attract followers and endowments, which provided the basis for a more institutionalised form of life; in the 1130s a network of houses developed, the majority of which were located in England and Ireland.[87] Some of these communities housed women, and some were mixed, at least initially: one of the earliest of these was Harrold (Bedfordshire), which was founded in 1136x8.[88] Similar foundations followed suit in Ireland: a papal confirmation of 1196 suggests that there were at least thirteen Arrouaisian communities that housed women, the best documented of which is Termonfeckin (Co. Louth).[89] By the end of the twelfth century, the order of Arrouaise again appears to have conformed to a familiar pattern, by segregating mixed communities and restricting the recruitment of female members.[90] But here, as elsewhere, varied types of evidence record and imply different things: charters might suggest something divergent from site plans, and responses to questions about living arrangements might depend on who was asking them.[91]

As indicated at the beginning of this chapter, the Fourth Lateran Council of 1215 marked a significant shift in terms of the regulation and oversight of religious communities, which had particular implications for new communities of women religious that had begun to appear in more urbanised regions in Flanders, along the Rhine valley, and in northern Italy.[92] Some of these had gathered around miscellaneous *mulierculae* – a diminutive or dismissive term, which also had

---

[86] P. J. Dunning, 'The Arroasian Order in Medieval Ireland', *Irish Historical Studies*, 4 (1945), 297–315; Flanagan, *Transformation*, pp. 136–54 (esp. 146–54 for women).

[87] Ludo Milis, *L'Ordre des chanoines réguliers d'Arrouaise*, 2 vols (Bruges, 1969); Thompson, *Women Religious*, pp. 145–50.

[88] Thompson, *Women Religious*, pp. 151–6; Elkins, *Holy Women*, pp. 55–6, 121; Flanagan, *Transformation*, pp. 151–2.

[89] Flanagan, *Transformation*, pp. 150–4. Termonfeckin may well have been the Arrouaisian community that drew Gerald of Wales's criticism in the *Speculum Ecclesiae*: Collins, 'Space and Place', p. 34; for discussion of Ireland and women's monasticism, see below, Collins, pp. 182–201.

[90] Thompson, *Women Religious*, pp. 149–50, 153–5; Flanagan, *Transformation*, pp. 153–4.

[91] Collins, 'Space and Place', pp. 35–8.

[92] John Freed, 'Urban movements and the "*cura monialium*" in Thirteenth-Century Germany', *Viator*, 3 (1972), 311–27; Walter Simons, *Cities of Ladies: Beguine Communities in the Medieval Low Countries, 1200–1565* (Philadelphia, 2001); Kaspar Elm, *Religious Life between Jerusalem, the Desert and the World: Selected Essays by Kaspar Elm* (trans.) by James D. Mixson (Leiden, 2015), esp. pp. 220–54, 277–316; Maria Pia Alberzoni, *Clare of Assisi and the Poor Sisters in the Thirteenth Century* (New York, 2004); Frances Andrews, *The Early Humiliati* (Cambridge, 2009); Tanya Stabler Miller, *The Beguines of Medieval Paris: Gender, Patronage, and Spiritual Authority* (Philadelphia, 2014).

penitential echoes – who gained a reputation for sanctity, whilst others consisted of women who had withdrawn into their own homes to lead lives of quiet contemplation.[93] Over time, these groups were subject to new forces of regulation: some became beguinages;[94] others came under the oversight of nearby Cistercian or Dominican communities;[95] a few were suspected of fostering heretical behaviour and were eradicated.[96] But these developments take us well out of the twelfth century and into the thirteenth, and into new socio-economic and institutional contexts that are beyond the scope of this chapter.

Conclusion

Looking at women's religious communities as an integral part of the new movements of the twelfth century – rather than as an inconvenient afterthought – encourages us to revisit and reformulate some old questions. In terms of chronology and periodisation, the experience of women religious underlines the ways in which some of the trends traditionally associated with the twelfth century – the origins and expansion of the Cistercian Order, for example – are more visible in the thirteenth century. In terms of institutionalisation and routinisation, women religious might be at the centre of developments, as in the communities of Fontevraud, but they might also be on the periphery; within the Premonstratensian Order there was considerable variety, even within the broad division between French-speaking and German-speaking communities. Even as the idea of the order was reaching its zenith at the beginning of the thirteenth century, it was, in many cases, little more than a convenient fiction.

A renewed interest in the study of manuscript and archival resources, coupled with new, less invasive archaeological techniques, is helping to shed light on the diversity of both men's and women's religious experiences, and to qualify earlier assessments of the universality of particular practices and forms questions in terms of future research in this field. Digital editions, for example, can offer new opportunities for the presentation of multiple, variant readings of legislative and liturgical texts, in ways that were more constrained within print. In terms of

[93] Simons, *Cities of Ladies*, pp. 1–34; Dyan Elliott, *Proving Women: Female Spirituality and Inquisitional Culture in the Later Middle Ages* (Princeton, 2004), esp. pp. 47–84; Tanya Stabler Miller, 'What's in a name? Clerical Representations of Parisian Beguines (1200–1328)', *JMH*, 33 (2007), 60–86; Lester, *Creating Cistercian Nuns*, pp. 5, 17–19, 34–9, 79–81, 95, 115.

[94] Simons, *Cities of Ladies*, pp. 35–60; Miller, *Beguines of Medieval Paris*, esp. Chapter 1.

[95] André Simon, *L'Ordre des pénitentes de Ste Marie Madeleine en Allemagne au XIIeme siècle* (Fribourg, 1918); Smith, 'Prouille, Madrid, Rome'; Lester, *Creating Cistercian Nuns*, pp. 87–116.

[96] Simons, *Cities of Ladies*, pp. 12–34; Lester, *Creating Cistercian Nuns*, pp. 78–81.

the material culture and archaeology of women's communities, new such techniques offer less invasive ways of recording their presence within the landscape.[97] Coupled with new research frameworks, these methods and techniques have the potential to shape new narratives about diversity, belonging and order(s) over the course of the long twelfth century.

---

[97]   See below, Collins, pp. 182–201 and Seale, pp. 166–81.

CHAPTER 3

Change and Renewal: Mendicants and Tertiaries in Later Medieval Europe

ALISON MORE

Tʜᴇ story of the mendicants is fundamental to understanding the history of religious life in western Europe during the Later Middle Ages. Focussed on the ideals of poverty, preaching, and presence, these new orders provided both later medieval men and women with examples of the *vita apostolica,* and expressions of popular devotion. Through sermons, charity, and care for the sick, the major mendicant orders – Franciscan, Dominican, and Augustinian – established themselves as mediators between the institutional Church and the laity.[1] Unsurprisingly, those to whom they ministered were not always content to admire their works, and soon sought ways of participating in the forms of devotion modelled by the friars. At first these were unofficial ways of life, but they quickly became subject to a complex (if inconsistent) process of institutionalisation.

The mendicant orders were established by men who became known as friars. The mendicant spirit stretched wider, and reached out to men and women who sought a number of different vocations. Each of these went through their own separate programme of change and renewal. This chapter discusses the development of mendicant life, and its implications for those in its ambit. It first discusses monasticised feminine forms of life connected with the friars before moving to its central focus of the women who came to be known as members of third orders or 'tertiaries'.[2] The stories of mendicants, women religious, and tertiaries are inextricably linked. The various groups emerged from the same spiritual milieu, often had a shared form of devotion, and engaged in mutually beneficial spiritual and social enrichment. At the same time, it is important to remember that each group had its own distinct place in the social, intellectual, and spiritual climate of later medieval Europe.

---

[1] André Vauchez, *The Laity in the Middle Ages: Religious Belief and Devotional Practices,* Daniel Bornstein (ed.) Margery J. Schneider (trans.) (Notre Dame, 1993).

[2] Alison More, 'Dynamics of Regulation, Innovation, and Invention', in James Mixson and Bert Roest (eds), *Observant Reform in the Late Middle Ages and Beyond* (Leiden, 2015), pp. 85–110.

Mendicancy and Mendicant Orders

The idea that the mendicant orders represented a revolutionary new form of religious life is often repeated both in mendicant chronicles and modern scholarship.[3] It is certainly true that their way of life marked a distinct break with traditional monasticism. Rather than attempting to flee the world and find solace in cloistered contemplation, the mendicants took a more practical approach to bringing about Christ's earthly kingdom. To this end, they lived lives of radical poverty. They sought alms, cared for the suffering, and provided education and edification through their preaching. They endeavoured to be the presence of Christ in the world.

Despite its familiarity, this narrative is problematic.[4] The emergence of mendicant orders in the thirteenth century was certainly characteristic of the time. Rather than a flourishing of spiritual growth, however, it should be seen as an ordering of spiritual chaos. The eleventh and twelfth centuries had been a time of significant devotional renewal. Social and spiritual changes caused the complex web of relationships between clergy and laity, monastery and secular Church, and Church and city state to be reimagined. Consequently, many began to wonder whether 'each and every Christian might not be called by the command of the gospels and the example of the apostles to model his or her life on the gospels and apostolic standards'.[5]

At the same time, the growth of cities and rise of literacy inspired a flood of popular religious movements, many of which incorporated the ideals of the *vita apostolica*. Living piously, practising chastity and charity, and preaching God's word were acts no longer exclusively the preserve of those who had taken monastic vows. Instead, lay and quasi-religious men and women joined other religious in their desire to bring about God's kingdom on earth.[6] Groups that shared this ideal were united by a common desire to live the gospel life and imitate Jesus and his apostles, but there was little uniformity in how this was done. The resulting

[3]   Félix Vernet, *Les ordres mendiants* (Paris, 1933), pp. 10–14. On the prevalence and implications of this myth, see Augustine Thompson, 'The Origins of Religious Mendicancy in Medieval Europe', in Donald Prudlo (ed.), *The Origin, Development, and Refinement of Medieval Religious Mendicancies* (Leiden, 2011), pp. 3–4.
[4]   Thompson, 'Origins of Religious Mendicancy', pp. 3–30.
[5]   Herbert Grundmann, *Religious Movements in the Middle Ages: The Historical Links Between Heresy, the Mendicant Orders, and the Women's Religious Movement in the Twelfth and Thirteenth Centuries*, trans. Steven Rowan (Notre Dame, 2005), pp. 1–2.
[6]   Daniel E. Bornstein, 'Relics, Ascetics, Living Saints', in Daniel E. Bornstein (ed.), *A People's History of Christianity* (Minneapolis, 2009), 75–106, at p. 102.

forms of religious or quasi-religious life were as rich as the climate from which
they had sprung.

These new forms of life were welcomed as they brought a certain religious vitality
to western Europe, but the disorder they brought to the Church was a source of
canonical consternation.[7] Gregorian reform had created a new emphasis on order
that made defining a clear and official role for visible movements something of an
imperative.[8] Certain lay, pauperistic, and penitential movements were encouraged
to take on the appearance and structures of traditional religious orders. Groups
of men who lived an apostolic life, enjoyed canonical support, and were willing to
adopt some hallmarks of an institutional identity were granted official recognition as
mendicant orders. Groups such as the Franciscans, Dominicans, and Augustinians
were steered towards increased clericalism, internal unity, and structures that were
clearly recognisable to the existing canonical framework.[9] There were, however,
some differences, and the term 'mendicant order' became a recognised category
connected with, but not precisely the same as, the early idealism of mendicancy.[10]
Nevertheless, they were a successful new category within the Church.

Female Sanctity and Mendicant Monastics:
Clarissans and Dominican Women Religious

The situation for women is more problematic. On one level, the idea of increased
gender equality is part of the mendicant mythology. For instance, early Franciscan
texts speak of a close relationship between Francis and a woman known as Clare of
Assisi, who is often discussed as the 'foundress of the Order of St. Clare', or even
the 'cofounder of the Franciscans'.[11] As is discussed below, Clare's contributions to
the Church were certainly significant; however, neither she nor her early spiritual
daughters can be truly described as 'mendicant' in any technical sense. The same is
true for the women generally hailed as Dominican women religious. While there
were always women associated with the order, they were more monastic than mendicant. Both Clarissan and Dominican women had a separate history of institutionalisation that more closely resembled traditional monastic institutions.[12]

---

[7] Elizabeth Makowski, 'A Pernicious Sort of Woman': Quasi-Religious Women in the Later
     Middle Ages (Washington, DC, 2005).
[8] Constable, Reformation, pp. 157–9.
[9] Thompson, 'Origins of Religious Mendicancy', pp. 3–30.
[10] Thompson, 'Origins of Religious Mendicancy', pp. 3–4.
[11] Cf. Lezlie Knox, Creating Clare of Assisi: Female Franciscan Identities in Later Medieval
     Italy (Leiden, 2008), pp. 4–8.
[12] For the early institutionalisation of the Clares, see Maria Pia Alberzoni, 'Sorores
     Minores e autorità ecclesiastica fino al pontificato di Urbano IV', in Giancarlo Andenna
     and Benedetto Vetere (eds), Chiara e la diffusione delle clarisse del secolo XIII (Galatina,

The fictive early history of the women associated with Clare of Assisi features a small group of women associated whom Jacques de Vitry refers to as the *sorores minores*.[13] These women are often discussed as 'early female mendicants' and associated with Clare and her sisters before the institutional Church steered her towards a more monastic lifestyle. There is little evidence to support this position, and it would seem that even Clare herself lived a vocation that was more monastic than mendicant. Clare of Assisi, or Chiara di Faverone, was born around 1194 to the noble Offreduccio family.[14] In keeping with the customs of the minor nobility, or *maiores*, of Assisi, Clare was well educated and brought up in a pious manner. Clare and the female members of her household regularly distributed alms to the poor and developed a concern for helping the needy independently of, though in conjunction with, the radical Francis.[15] Around 1212, Clare left her family and endeavoured to join Francis in his mendicant vocation.

While a spirituality of wandering, serving, and begging was radical for men, it was always controversial and completely unacceptable in central Italy for a woman to adopt such a lifestyle. Francis accepted Clare's profession to religious life. She possibly spent some time living with him as a hermit, but soon went to the Benedictine community of San Paolo delle Abbadesse, where she lived before being given permission to found a religious community in the house of San Damiano.[16] Here, Clare and her companions followed the Rule of St Benedict, and were placed under the care of the cardinal protector of the Franciscans, Hugolino of Ostia (Gregory IX after 1227).

A talented canonist, Cardinal Hugolino turned his attention to creating a way of life for the women under his care. He gave them constitutions to supplement the Rule of St Benedict and differentiate their identity from traditional

---

1998). The implications of this and the later development of Clarissan orders is outlined in Bert Roest, *Order and Disorder* (Leiden, 2013).

[13] Jacques de Vitry, Letter 1, in *Lettres de Jacques de Vitry, 1160/1170–1240, évêque de Saint-Jean d'Acre*, ed. R. B. C. Huygens (Leiden, 1960), pp. 70–2. Cf. Catherine M. Mooney, 'The "Lesser Sisters" in Jacques de Vitry's 1216 Letter', *FS*, 69 (2011), 1–29. Cf. Catherine M. Mooney, *Clare of Assisi and the Thirteenth-Century Church* (Philadelphia, 2016), pp. 36–48.

[14] Clare's first *Legenda* is often attributed to Thomas of Celano. However, this is questioned. See Stefano Brufani, 'Le "legendae" agiografiche di Chiara d'Assisi del secolo XIII', in Enrico Menestò (ed.), *Chiara di Assisi* (Spoleto, 1993), pp. 327–40.

[15] Roest, *Order and Disorder*, pp. 11–15.

[16] For a discussion of the monastery, see Marino Bigaroni, 'I monasteri benedettini femminili di S. Paolo delle Abbadesse, di S. Apolinare in Assisi e S. Maria di Paradiso prima del Concilio di Trento', in Francesco Santucci (ed.), *Aspetti di vita benedettina nella storia di Assisi*, Atti Accademia Properziana del Subiaso, ser. 6, n. 5 (Assisi, 1981), pp. 171–231. Cf. Roest, *Order and Disorder*, pp. 13–16.

monastics. They were known as the Order of San Damiano. After becoming pope in 1227, he granted the community the 'privilege of poverty', which further distanced them from their traditional Benedictine sisters. While new and spiritually inclined toward poverty and suffering, the Order of San Damiano still observed the ideals of community and enclosure, and did not endeavour to be 'mendicant' in any literal sense. This emphasis on maintaining traditional ideals is seen in later 'Feminine Franciscan' rules written by Innocent IV, Isabelle of France, and Clare's own Rule of 1253.[17]

In 1263, eight years after Clare's death, Pope Urban VI attempted to bring unity by suppressing all existing rules concerning the Damianites and replacing them with a single rule for the 'Order of St Clare'. His concerns were not heterodoxy or mendicancy, but a plurality of rules governing what, in his mind, should be a unified form of religious life. Here, naturally, Clare of Assisi was held up as a model of ideal feminine Franciscan virtue. Like Francis and Dominic, the hagiographical and mythical elements of her mendicancy have had a rich afterlife. In particular, her image was used by the Observant reform movement, who were intent on restoring religious orders to the original intent of their founders and Christianity to a form of purity that, in their minds, had existed in the early Church. Observant chronicles and much traditional scholarship praise Clare as a founder of the order, and the incarnation of Franciscan feminine ideals.

The situation is equally complex for the Dominicans. Although Dominic had close ties with certain women who were active in his spiritual circles, there was no early attempt to make them a part of his order. The earliest house under Dominican *cura* was Prouille in southern France. Rather than a house of mendicant women, it was set up as an institute for Cathar women who were in the process of returning to the Catholic Church.[18] Around 1220, the house of San Sisto was placed under official Dominican *cura*. Rather than a house of Dominican women religious, however, San Sisto was an existing community that adhered to the idea that universal *coenobium,* or a movement towards general spiritual care, rather than affiliation with a particular order might provide an answer to the increasingly problematic *cura monialium.*[19] A third house, San' Agnese, in Bologna, seems more recognisably Dominican, but certainly not mendicant. One woman from this house, Diana d'Andolò, appears

[17] For a discussion of the various Clarissan orders and their institutional histories, see Roest, *Order and Disorder, passim.*

[18] Julia Ann Smith, 'Prouille, Madrid, Rome: The Evolution of the Earliest Dominican *Instituta* for Nuns', *JMH,* 35 (2009), 340–52, at pp. 342–3.

[19] Cf. Brenda Bolton, 'Daughters of Rome: All One in Christ Jesus', in W. J. Sheils and D. Woods (eds), *Women in the Church: Papers Read at the 1989 Summer Meeting and the 1990 Winter Meeting of the Ecclesiastical History Society* (Oxford, 1990), pp. 101–15.

to have had close links with the friars.[20] Like Clare, Diana was struck after an encounter with the enigmatic Dominic, escaped a noble home, and lived for a time in a house of penitents before finding a suitable monastic house. Following Dominic's death in 1221, his successor, Jordan of Saxony, took personal responsibility for the care of Diana and the small community of women who were attracted to her way of life, but this was not to last, and the house never had an institutional link with the friars.[21] In 1252, Innocent IV released Dominicans from their duties of *cura monialium*. The Dominican General Chapter of 1257 ruled that no women religious could be received under the order's care without the explicit approval of the chapter, except those houses which had been under the order's *cura* in the past.[22]

Unlike the friars and Clarissans, the Dominican women religious did not have a female saintly figure who was designated as founder for this order. This position was later occupied by the saintly laywoman, Catherine of Siena, who is often hailed as a Dominican 'sister' or 'tertiary' (although neither status existed canonically during her lifetime). While their later institutional history is familiar, recognising the interplay between history and mythology is integral to understanding the beginnings and identities of various groups.

Transitioning to Tertiaries

Just as it is an oversimplification to equate all women associated with the Franciscans and Dominicans as 'tertiary women', it would be a mistake to assume that they all became enclosed mendicants. The area of non-cloistered or unofficial women religious is difficult to study. Prior to the eleventh century, house ascetics or pious lay women under simple vows were not treated differently from cloistered women religious.[23] As this way of life became increasingly prevalent, it also became both increasingly problematic and increasingly visible. From the earliest days, mendicant friars had a significant lay following, comprised of both men and women. Strengthened by popular preaching and social concern, this continued, particularly in the case of the Franciscans, well after Francis's death in 1226.

---

[20] Maria Pia Alberzoni, 'Giordano di Sassonia e il monastero di S. Agnese di Bologna', in Franz J. Felten, Annette Kehnel, and Stefan Weinfurter (eds), *Institution und Charisma. Festschrift für Gert Melville* (Cologne, 2009), pp. 513–28.

[21] Alberzoni, 'Giordano', pp. 513–28.

[22] Simon Tugwell, 'Were the Magdalen Nuns Really Turned into Dominicans in 1287?', *AFP*, 76 (2006), 39–77, at p. 44.

[23] Eliana Magnani, 'Female House Ascetics from the Fourth to the Twelfth Century', *CHMM*, vol. 1 (Cambridge, 2020), pp. 213–31.

Particularly in the case of women, the early haphazard programme of pastoral care and informal association soon grew into something more official. As 'Daughters of Eve', women were thought to be more open to deception than their male contemporaries. This left them open to suspicions of heterodoxy or even outright heresy, as well as the obvious dangers of sexual immorality. To protect pious lay women, particularly those who wished to dedicate their lives to serving God in the secular world, those responsible for their spiritual care developed ways these pious lay women could be identified as orthodox. The resulting programme of institutionalisation was to create semi-official statuses that were to have implications first for the ways pious lay women interacted with their societies, and now how they are thought of in the modern world.

In the first half of thirteenth century institutionalisation generally took the form of mandates from local bishops demanding that groups of laywomen associate themselves with recognised male religious orders, and bishops frequently appointed mendicant groups to this role. The documents that were part of this trend are included in Giles Gérard Meersseman's *Dossier de l'ordre de la pénitence*.[24] In large part, these documents prescribe adopting the hallmarks of a religious life, including a recognisable habit, structure of leadership, and affiliation with a religious order. Due to their visibility and popularity, these affiliations were often with groups of mendicant friars.[25]

The most elegant solution was the invention of fictive tertiary orders. While they had no historical institutional link with the mendicants, they provided a framework for pastoral care.[26] At first, these groups had no standing in canon law and official histories that state otherwise are largely later fabrications. None of the major mendicant founders had direct links with a tertiary order.[27] In the earliest phases of regularisation, they were overwhelmingly women dependent on pastoral and personal relationships. While the official stories of their saintly founders and desire to become canonical religious (or *moniales*) are often later creations, early women known as tertiaries and the mendicants who provided their spiritual care both seem to have had a sincere desire to serve God and society. Both groups

---

[24] Giles Gérard Meersseman, *Dossier de l'ordre de la pénitence au XIIIe siècle* (Fribourg, 1961), *passim*.

[25] For the Dominicans see, Maiju Lehmijoki-Gardner, 'Writing Religious Rules as an Interactive Process: Dominican Penitent Women and the Making of Their "Regula"', *Speculum*, 79 (2004), 660–87. Cf. Maiju Lehmijoki-Gardner, *Worldly Saints: Social Interaction of Dominican Penitent Women* (Helsinki, 1999). For Franciscan examples see, Alison More, 'Institutionalizing Penitential Life in Later Medieval and Early Modern Europe: Third Orders, Rules and Canonical Legitimacy', *CH*, 83 (2014), 297–323. For the Augustinians see Alison More, *Fictive Orders and Feminine Religious Identities* (Oxford, 2018), *passim*.

[26] More, 'Dynamics of Regulation', pp. 85–110.

[27] More, 'Dynamics of Regulation', pp. 85–110.

had a shared ethos, spirituality, and desire to live as religious while remaining in the secular world. Looking at the interaction between these groups allows a glimpse into the spiritual climate from which they emerged.

Institutionalisation and Order

In 1289, Pope Nicholas IV issued the bull *Supra montem*, which claimed to provide a 'new rule' for the order that Francis of Assisi had founded.[28] A papally approved rule was more official than local directives and would appear to give some legitimacy to the order. Nevertheless, it is important to keep in mind that there is no record of Francis founding a canonical tertiary order. Instead, this rule was simply an optional identity marker for individual communities who sought some protection. The bull itself neither created an order, nor mandated links between the friars and the women under their care. If it had not been for subsequent canonical developments, *Supra montem* would likely have been simply another component of the regulatory material that had sought to bind friars and laywomen throughout the thirteenth century.[29]

Less than a decade later, Nicholas's successor Boniface VIII issued the decretal *Periculoso* (1298), which demanded that all *moniales*, that is women who were recognised as religious by canon law, were obliged to be enclosed.[30] There was, however, considerable disagreement about who, precisely, was affected by this decretal. Arguments surrounding its meaning became even more important at the beginning of the fourteenth century. In 1311, the Council of Vienne condemned 'beguines': a term that, at this point, had no official meaning and was used to refer to a number of non-enclosed religious women.[31]

The conciliar document, *Cum de quibusdam* condemned women commonly known as 'beguines' who neither promised obedience nor professed a canonical rule. Jacqueline Tarrant argues, however, that this should not be taken to mean that all non-monastic women were condemned. Instead, the council made an explicit exception for faithful women, 'whether or not they promise chastity who lived honestly in their own dwellings, doing penance, and serving the Lord in a spirit of humility, this being allowed to them as the Lord inspires them'.[32]

---

[28] Meersseman, *Dossier*, p. 75.

[29] Meersseman, *Dossier*, pp. 7–8.

[30] Makowski, *Periculoso*, pp. 65–6.

[31] Jacqueline Tarrant, 'The Clementine Decrees on the Beguines: Conciliar and Papal Versions', *Archivum Historiae Pontificae*, 12 (1974), 300–8. Elizabeth Makowski also raises questions about the precise dating and authorship of these documents. See, Makowski, 'A Pernicious Sort', pp. 23–50, at pp. 24–5.

[32] Makowski, 'A Pernicious Sort', pp. 22–8, at p. 24.

Several canonists argued that pious lay women, or at least tertiaries who professed the 1289 Rule, were exempt. The same argument was also often put forward for 'tertiaries' who followed the Augustinian Rule. Consequently, the two rules came to serve as identity markers for 'membership' in one of two tertiary orders, the Franciscan or Dominican (as Dominicans followed the Rule of St Augustine). The reality, however, was more complex. While there were many houses of women known as 'tertiaries' who had close relationships with friars, there were others who adopted the rules as markers of orthodoxy but had no such connection. Due to the informal nature of pastoral care, it was often impossible to distinguish tertiaries with mendicant links from those who simply followed one of the associated rules. To bring some clarity to the situation, several churchmen turned their attention to the creation of cohesive and coherent tertiary order identities.[33]

Because there was no single canonical category or even clearly defined rubric under which 'religious women who were not *moniales*' could be discussed, this proved insurmountable. Instead of portraying the diversity among beguine communities and supporting those women who lived a pious lifestyle, Vienne's decrees made all communities of non-monastic women look equally suspect. In an attempt to restore order, John XXII issued a bull *Etsi apostolicae* in 1319, which explicitly granted members of the 'Tertium Ordinem Poenitentium seu Continentium S. Francisci', or women who professed the 1289 Rule, an exemption from the enclosure required by Vienne's decretals.[34] While a solution for women in the Franciscan ambit, this created numerous problems for other communities of pious women who were either independent or affiliated with a different group.

The 1289 Rule did not require any institutional link with the Franciscan friars. It had, however, become enough of an identity marker to cause discomfort among groups tied to the Augustinian or Dominican friars.[35] The Dominican master general, Munio of Zamora, assisted communities in northern or central Italy with adjustments that would help them fit into the new milieu, but remain under Dominican *cura* and profess different rules, either the Augustinian or his own rule written in 1285.[36]

---

[33] More, 'Dynamics of Regulation', 85–110.

[34] John XXII, '*Etsi apostolicum*', in *Bullarium Franciscanum*, t. V, no. 354, pp. 163–4.

[35] Augustine Thompson, *Cities of God: The Religion of the Italian Communes, 1125–1325* (Ithaca, 2005), p. 78.

[36] Maiju Lehmijoki-Gardner has convincingly argued that this is not the case. See Maiju Lehmijoki-Garner, 'Writing Rules as an Interactive Process: Dominican Penitent Women and the Making of their "Regula"', *Speculum*, 79 (2004), 660–87.

Identity, Connections, and Lay Women

One prominent means of creating a group or unified identity was providing saintly models. Pious laywomen throughout Europe, notably Elisabeth of Hungary, Umiliana of Cerchi, and Angela of Foligno, found themselves posthumously enrolled in the Franciscan third order. The Dominicans were to develop a similar canon of saints, but this came later.[37] Augustinians and Dominicans involved in the *cura* of 'tertiaries' often used the same women, with no order affiliation, or drew on examples such as the biblical Martha to promote the lifestyle of their women.[38] The various hagiographic and sermon accounts of women known as tertiaries often include examples of ordinary concerns or ordinary service, including domestic tasks. The *vitae* of Elisabeth of Hungary, for instance, recount instances of cooking and serving food. Other ordinary tasks are similarly praised in sermons in her honour.[39] The *vitae* of these women, who generally only had tenuous links with the order, repeatedly stressed their devotion to the order in question as well as their engagement with the secular world.

There is certainly evidence that women who were described as tertiaries had a particular appeal to the laity. In 1310, a woman named Fina, the wife of Ricuccio from Antria, made an oath in the church of St Francis in Cortona.[40] In the presence of her husband, local nobility, and certain Franciscan friars, Fina recounted the anguish she had experienced when giving birth. According to her testimony, Fina's agony had resulted in her losing her sight and, one year later, Fina walked barefoot to the tomb of Margaret of Cortona to beg for its return. When she reached the saint's tomb, her sight was immediately restored. Fina's account in the church was both to express her gratitude for Margaret's intercession and bear public witness to a miracle obtained through her intercession. It appears that Fina was not unique in this regard, and that Margaret had an interest in helping those in distress. Together with accounts of liberation from despair, raising the dead, freeing the possessed, and restoring sight, speech, and hearing, the eleventh chapter of, or, more accurately, 'addendum to', Margaret's *Legenda* presents the acts of a woman both concerned and familiar with the secular world.[41]

---

[37]   More, *Fictive Orders*, pp. 8–12.

[38]   Alison More and Anneke Mulder-Bakker, 'Striving for Religious Perfection in the Lay World of Nothern Europe', *CHMM*, vol. 2, pp. 2057–73.

[39]   This text is edited in Ottó Gecser, *The Feast and the Pulpit: Preachers, Sermons, and the Cult of St Elizabeth of Hungary, 1235–ca. 1500* (Spoleto, 2012), pp. 326–9.

[40]   Giunta Bevegnati, *Legenda de vita et miraculis Beatae Margaritae de Cortona*, ed. Fortunato Iozzelli (Rome, 1997), c. XI.

[41]   Bevegnati, *Legenda*, c. XI. Cf. Fortunato Iozzelli, 'I miracoli nella "Legenda" di santa Margherita da Cortona', *AFH*, 86 (1993), 217–76.

As well as providing evidence of Margaret's apparent *fama sanctitatis*, Giunta's appendix may have had another purpose. The *Legenda* first recounts that the friars' initial reluctance to form official ties with Margaret stemmed from her early life as a concubine and her possible heretical associations.[42] While these were almost certainly a factor, it is also important to keep in mind that the idea of a third order was not universally popular.[43] There were certain friars who saw creating or providing care to the laity as a valuable pursuit. Around the middle of the thirteenth century, a Florentine woman from a prominent family, Umiliana of Cerchi, became a model for this way of life, which it seems her hagiographer was interested in promoting to others. A young pious, and wealthy widow, Umiliana came to the attention of the Franciscan Vito of Cortona who presented a version of her life that championed socially relevant acts of piety in the secular world.[44] To Vito, Umiliana was a perfect model of chastity, charity, and service. Through the guidance of the friars, she was able to create a model of lay piety that was an acceptable and orthodox path to holiness and ultimately contemplation.

At the same time, there were many who rejected associations with tertiaries entirely. Around 1268, the pseudo-Bonaventurean document, 'Why the friars ought not to promote the order of penitents' warned of the dangers involved in caring for unenclosed women.[45] In particular, it stressed that the temptations and potential scandals, most especially of a sexual nature, arising from regular contact with unenclosed women, would damage the orders' reputation.[46] This was not unlike the controversies inherent in the ongoing struggles between the Franciscan friars and the women associated with Clare of Assisi and her legacy.[47]

Perhaps with these concerns in mind, Giunta's text repeatedly depicts Christ making it clear that Margaret was a gift to the Franciscan Order. In one instance, he recounts a vision in which Christ spoke to Margaret saying: 'You [Margaret] are the third light given to the Order of my blessed Francis. The first light is in the Order of the Friars Minor. The second is in the Order of the sisters of the blessed Clare. The third is you, in the Order of penitents'.[48] Throughout the *vita*, Giunta emphasises the ways in which Margaret and the friars complement each other.

---

[42] Iozzelli, 'Introduzione', in, *Legenda*, pp. 149–69. Cf. Mary Harvey Doyno, 'The Creation of a Franciscan Lay Saint: Margaret of Cortona and her Legenda', *P & P*, 228 (2015), 57–91.

[43] More, 'Institutionalizing', 297–323.

[44] Vito of Cortona, 'Vita beata Humilianae de Cerchis', in *AASS*, May IV, pp. 385–400.

[45] Meersseman, *Dossier*, pp. 123–5.

[46] Bonaventure, 'Justification par S. Bonaventure de la réserve des Mineurs envers les Pénitents (1266–68)', in Meersseman, *Dossier*, p. 124.

[47] For struggles between the friars and the so-called 'second order' see, Roest, *Order and Disorder*.

[48] Bevegnati, *Legenda*, p. 285 and p. 442.

In his account, a close spiritual relationship between the friars and tertiaries was part of Christ's plan: the friars offered guidance; the tertiaries were guided to be models of Franciscan spirituality in the world. At the same time, Margaret's fame and reputation for sanctity attracted pilgrims to Cortona who also sought guidance from the Franciscan Order.

Order and Observance

The process of steering pious laywomen towards an ordered identity intensified as the Middle Ages progressed. In particular, the Observant reform movement that was to take hold at the end of the fourteenth century gave a new focus towards turning tertiary groups into tertiary orders. The Observant movement had developed from a desire to return to an age before disorder and corruption had entered Christianity. As a result of the reforms, mendicants and tertiaries had an official framework in which to operate within the Church.[49] In reality, this new model was only a single option. Instead of replacing the existing canonical chaos, it came to co-exist with the irregular and extra-regular vocations that had persisted for centuries. Nevertheless, the Observants wrote official histories that stated otherwise. These were widely circulated and eventually came to be the official versions of the story.

The Franciscans drew their fragmentary history from the long tradition of unofficial ties between the friars and laywomen, isolated hagiographical references to a third order, and a fabricated (but consistent) rota of saints.[50] In 1440, Giovanni da Capistrano wrote a *Defensorium tertii ordinis*. This document both legitimised the Franciscan tertiary order and gave specific criteria for membership.[51] Capistrano's defence of tertiaries made it clear that the order's acceptance did not extend to any extra-regular community (or even those communities that professed the 1289 Rule). Instead, this status should only be recognised for those 'tertiary' communities that had ties with the Franciscan Order, wore recognisable habits, and observed enclosure. Despite not being universally accepted, it provided the external structures that provided the 'order' with some legitimacy. Capistrano's account and the catalogues of Franciscan *beati/ae* were often featured in later chronicles.[52]

The Dominicans had an equally pressing need for an ordered tertiary framework, but less quasi-official regulation to draw upon. While penitent women

[49] More, 'Dynamics of Regulation', 85–110.
[50] Chiara Mercuri, *Santità e propaganda: Il terz'ordine francescano nell'agiografia*, Bibliotheca Seraphico-Capuccina 59 (Rome, 1999).
[51] Giovanni da Capistrano, *Defensorium tertium ordinis* (Venice, 1580). Cf. More, *Fictive Orders*, p. 67.
[52] More, *Fictive Orders*, pp. 158–9.

had been affiliated with the Dominican Order since the thirteenth century, their ties had initially been unofficial.[53] The situation changed after the death of one such lay *beata,* Catherine of Siena.[54] Catherine's active charity, renowned visionary abilities, and public role were famed in her lifetime. While influenced by various quasi-religious communities in Siena, she did not become an official member of any such group until after 1368 and was certainly never canonically a Dominican.[55] A series of miracles after Catherine's death ensured the endurance of her saintly legacy and Dominican hagiographers ensured she was remembered as a tertiary.

Shortly after Catherine's death, the Dominican Order tried to regulate penitents. The Observant Thomas Caffarini (Thomas of Siena, †1434) praised Catherine's life, but placed her in a Dominican third order rather than a lay community.[56] The 'order' in question was largely the work of Thomas's imagination. His account wove the tales of pious laywomen who has some sort of affiliation with the Dominicans into a fictive but coherent order. Despite its historical inaccuracies, Thomas's efforts created the framework for the Dominican Order of Penitence, which was given both canonical recognition and a separate rule in 1405.[57] The Order of Penitents was closely tied to the Dominican Observance and spread widely throughout Europe. Many of these communities were indistinguishable from Dominican *moniales,* in so far as many Observant tertiaries increasingly observed enclosure.[58] There were, however, still many communities with unofficial ties to the Dominicans to whom this recognition did not apply.

Influential Observants campaigned to have their orders given some sort of official canonical recognition. This occurred for the Augustinian tertiaries in 1399 and Dominican tertiaries in 1405. The Franciscan case had a few iterations but was generally settled by 1447.[59] This official framework should have settled the question of tertiaries and tertiary identity. The categories and appearance of order was a victory for the Observants. However, as they could not ensure all communities

---

[53] Lehmijoki-Gardner, *Worldly Saints,* pp. 11–91.

[54] Raymond of Capua, *Vita s. Catherina Senensis, AASS,* April III, pp. 853–959.

[55] F. Thomas Luongo, *The Saintly Politics of Catherine of Siena* (Ithaca, 2006), pp. 34–40.

[56] Carolyn Muessig, 'Catherine of Siena in late Medieval Sermons', in George Ferzoco, Beverly Kienzle, and Carolyn Muessig (eds), *A Companion to Catherine of Siena* (Leiden, 2012), pp. 203–26. Cf. Lehmijoki-Gardner, 'Writing Religious Rules', 678–9.

[57] Meersseman, *Dossier,* pp. 143–56; cf. Lehmijoki-Gardner, 'Writing Religious Rules', 682.

[58] This was both imposed responsible for the *cura* of such communities such as Girolamo Savonarola (†1498) and requested by women such as Colomba Guadagnoli of Rieti (†1501) and Lucia Brocadelli da Narni (†1544). Cf. Tamar Herzig, *Savonarola's Women: Visions and Reforms in Renaissance Italy* (Chicago, 2007), pp. 44 and 89–90.

[59] More, *Fictive Orders,* pp. 70–6.

claiming informal affiliations would adhere to the new guidelines, arguments about identity markers such as rules and enclosure as well as the nature of vows lasted well into the early modern period.[60]

Order Identity and Pastoralia

When examining the portrayal of these groups, the history seems either one of hagiography or propaganda. There was, however, certainly more to the situation. The complex story of relations between mendicants and tertiaries is the tale of individuals rather than institutions. Both men and women associated with the mendicants were interested in spiritual growth, spiritual exchange, and shared ministry. This is particularly evident in an examination of *pastoralia*. Mendicants appear to have felt some responsibility for tertiaries under their care, regardless of official affiliation.[61]

Compilations, miscellania, and *rapiaria* from houses of what can be thought of as tertiaries from throughout Europe contain sermons, short theological explanations of sacraments, and treatises on spiritual growth and norms for living as a devout woman, such as the *Speculum virginum*.[62] These were generally written in a combination of Latin and various vernaculars. Order identity is often cultivated or enhanced with images of saints in the habits of particular orders, prayers, references to a shared spiritual heritage, or order-specific liturgies.[63] The importance of this seems to have varied between communities. It is fair to say, however, that the rigid categorisations in canon law were far from hegemonic.

There were several women involved in the Observant reform movement and they often worked closely with friars to establish models of *pastoralia,* discussion points, or teaching opportunities for their convents. There are numerous examples of women preaching and teaching in the Italian context as well as in northern Europe.[64] Although the parameters of the interaction had certainly changed, there

---

[60]   Cf. Raymond Creytens, 'La Riforma del Monasteri Femminile dopo i Decreti Tridentini', in *Il Concilio de Trento e la Riforma Tridentina,* vol. 1 (Rome, 1963) pp. 62–77.

[61]   More, *Fictive Orders*, pp. 87–108.

[62]   See Sabrina Corbellini, 'Een oude spiegel voor nieuw maagden: het gebruik van het "Speculum virginum" in gemeenschappen van tertiarisse', *Ons Geestelijk Erf* 80 (2009), pp. 171–98.

[63]   Anna Welch, *Liturgy, Books and Franciscan Identity* (Leiden, 2015), *passim*.

[64]   Eliana Corbari, *Vernacular Theology: Dominican Sermons and Audience in Late Medieval Italy* (Berlin, 2013); Carolyn Muessig, 'Communities of Discourse: Religious Authority and the Role of Holy Women in the Later Middle Ages', in Anneke Mulder-Bakker (ed.), *Women and Experience in Later Medieval Writing* (New York, 2009), pp. 65–82; Anne Winston-Allen, *Convent Chronicles: Women Writing about Women and Reform in the Late Middle Ages* (University Park, 2004).

was still no single model for the interaction between mendicants and tertiaries. Recognising the plurality inherent in this way of life allows for explorations to be taken in new directions.

Conclusions and Implications

Both the mendicant and tertiary vocation sprung from a period of rapid growth and spiritual innovation that renewed the Church but threatened the idea of universal order. They, largely, retained both their relational character and diversity. Rather than classifying tertiaries as belonging to a single order or looking at women connected to the mendicants as a uniform group, current scholarship has moved towards more elaborate and constructed models, and variable strands that make up the identities of various communities. Ideas about what makes up an 'order' or even what is a 'religious' have been called into question.[65] Instead of complicating the picture, this has allowed for an exploration of how friars, women religious, and sisters worked together to adapt to the changing spiritual needs of their day. By recognising the complexities and relationships involved in mendicant and tertiary relations, it is possible to move past hegemonic categories of 'order' and 'tertiary' and free scholarship from the inherent assumptions of an ordered society. Further investigations into the relationships between friars, women religious, and sisters would allow us to gain a wider understanding of issues related to gender and authority, as well as women's contributions to mendicant programmes of education and formation. It is evident these groups had many close interactions and saw themselves as participating in the same salvific work. At the same time, looking more closely at canonical identity and conflation of various vocations lived by women religious will enable scholars to ask new questions about the roles of tertiary women in the secular world.

---

[65] Alison I. Beach and Isabelle Cochelin, 'Introduction', *CHMM*, vol. 1, pp. 1–16.

CHAPTER 4

On the Fringes: Anchorites

CATE GUNN

ANCHORITES, solitaries who were enclosed for life in cells usually attached to a church, were found throughout medieval Europe. Documentary and archaeological evidence, as well as anchoritic guidance texts – which together provide information about and insight into the lives of female anchorites – is abundant and accessible for medieval England, often building on the foundational work over a century ago of Rotha Mary Clay.[1] In contrast, P. L'Hermite-Leclercq has commented on the situation in France: 'No rule (or "guide" as they tend to be referred to within the English tradition) for anchorites has survived from France'.[2] While anchorites can be men or women, women who became recluses are often referred to as 'anchoresses': 'the anchoress' is constructed in Anglo-American scholarship as a liminal figure, by virtue of her gender as well as her vocation. Writing of men as well as women, E. A. Jones claims that 'Followers of 'semi-religious' vocations, including hermits and anchorites – who fall in the gaps between clergy and laity, monastic and secular – are liminal in the sense of 'betwixt and between';[3] he also explores the role of the anchorite in liminal events,

---

[1] Rotha Mary Clay, *The Hermits and Anchorites of England* (London, 1914), available at http://www.historyfish.net/anchorites/clay_anchorites.html [accessed 3 Oct. 2019].

[2] P. L'Hermite-Leclercq, 'Anchoritism in Medieval France', in McEvoy (ed.), *Anchoritic Traditions*, pp. 112–30, at p. 123. It is only fairly recently that the secular tradition (with which this chapter is primarily concerned) has begun to be studied in Italy; see M. Sensi, 'Anchorites in the Italian Tradition', in *Anchoritic Traditions*, pp. 62–90. A notable exception is the work of Anneke Mulder-Bakker on urban recluses in the Low Countries which has been translated into English; however, her *Lives of the Anchoresses: The Rise of the Urban Recluse in Medieval Europe*, trans. Myra Heerspink Scholz (Philadelphia, 2005) focuses on the lives of five exceptional women (pp. 8–9). In the Introduction to *Anchoritic Traditions*, McAvoy acknowledges the lack of cross-fertilisation between continental and anglophone research in the area (p. 2) though that volume goes some way to rectifying this: it includes Anneke Mulder-Bakker, 'Anchorites in the Low Countries', pp. 22–42.

[3] E. A. Jones, '"O Sely Ankir!"', in Cate Gunn and Liz Herbert McAvoy (eds), *Medieval Anchorites in their Communities* (Cambridge, 2017), pp. 13–34 refers (p. 23) to Victor Turner, *The Ritual Process: Structure and Anti-Structure* (Ithaca, 1969), p. 95, and his

such as the visit of Henry V to an anchorite on the death of his father, Henry IV.[4] On the threshold between heaven and earth, God and people, anchorites occupied a liminal position, able to intercede and mediate; Liz Herbert McAvoy sees the desert that becomes an allegorical space for the anchoress as itself liminal.[5] This does not mean, however, that she was necessarily marginal: the evidence suggests that anchoresses played a central role in the devotional and social life of the Middle Ages.[6] Anneke Mulder-Bakker claims, with reference to the urban anchoresses of the Low Countries, that 'The anchoritic experience actually approached that of a parish priest'.[7] How far, then, or in what sense, could the lives of anchoresses be considered 'on the fringes'?

Anchoresses were withdrawn from life, belonging neither to the rigid institutions of the church or the secular world. In addition, being women meant they were marginal to the power structures of medieval society. The reasons they entered the anchorhold rather than a monastery are debatable; while they may have felt called to an austere vocation at a time when there was a rise in women's spiritual expression and devotion,[8] it is also possible that there were simply no places available (or affordable) in any suitable women's religious communities.[9] Advised to consider themselves dead to the world, anchoresses existed in a twilight zone between death and life. Their life embodied their liminal nature: they took vows of obedience, chastity, and stability of abode, but were not professed

---

definition of liminal entities as 'betwixt and between the positions assigned and arrayed by law, custom, convention and ceremonial'. Hermits, who unlike anchorites did not take vows of stability of abode and strict enclosure, were usually men. There are exceptions in the early English period, such as Pega who became a recluse in the fens, at a place now named after her, Peakirk in Lincolnshire: Clay, *Hermits and Anchorites*, p. 14.

[4]   Jones, "'O Sely Ankir'", pp. 31–2.

[5]   As in the introduction to *Medieval Anchoritisms: Gender, Space and the Solitary Life* (Cambridge, 2011), when she makes an analogy between the anchoritic experience and Gertrude Bell's experience of the desert, which McAvoy describes as 'liminal to the world' (p. 1), and in a reference to the anchorhold of Emma Stapleton as the 'liminal desert … which John the Baptist traditionally inhabited', p. 159.

[6]   Jones implies the distinction between 'liminal' and 'marginal' when he points out that liminality is sometimes used as 'no more than a loose synonym for "marginality"': "O Sely Ankir'", p. 23.

[7]   Mulder-Bakker, *Lives of the Anchoresses*, p. 13. Further on the central role of the anchoress in society see pp. 81 and 174.

[8]   The classic description of this is found in Herbert Grundmann, *Religious Movements in the Middle Ages*, Steven Rowan (trans.) (Notre Dame, 1995).

[9]   The reasons the *Ancrene Wisse* was written may have been pragmatic since there were not many places available in convents in the part of England where these anchoresses lived: Cate Gunn, *Ancrene Wisse: From Pastoral Literature to Vernacular Spirituality* (Cardiff, 2008), p. 48.

women religious; enclosed, they were not part of daily society but nevertheless remained dependent upon it for sustenance and support. Their vocation fell between established categories.[10] *Ancrene Wisse*, an English guidance text from the early thirteenth century, which describes the life of solitary enclosure for women who had entered the anchorhold from the world rather than a woman from a monastic community,[11] acknowledged the anxiety they felt when asked to what order they belonged.[12] We first find the English word *ancre* used in *Ancrene Wisse*; the popularity of this work in the centuries following its composition led to the term 'anchoress' being associated with the increasing number of women undertaking such an arduous life.[13] It is these women, who entered the anchorhold in England as an alternative to becoming enclosed women religious, cherishing their solitude and enclosure as penance, that this chapter explores.

Geographical Boundaries

Men and women anchorites were to be found throughout Europe: there was a strong women's eremitical movement in Italy at the very heart of western Christendom and even in Prussia then 'at the north-eastern margin of Christianity', Dorothy of Montau was enclosed as a widow at a cell at the cathedral of Marienwerder in 1393.[14] Tom Licence has written of recluses occupying cells 'through the German empire, Flanders, France, and along the North Sea littoral',[15] on the northern fringes of Europe, while Anneke Mulder-Bakker identifies an area of the Low Countries, 'the delta region between the Seine and the Elbe' as being the place of origination of both the Beguine movement and the Modern Devotion (*Devotio moderna*) as well as being the location for the anchoresses she studies.[16] Across the North Sea in England is the county of Norfolk, where the second highest

---

[10]   E. A. Jones, *Hermits and Anchorites in England* (Manchester, 2019), pp. 5–6, suggests that solitary lives are 'best understood … as part of the range of semi religious or non-regular vocations'.

[11]   The definition of anchorite is vexed, as Liz Herbert McAvoy and I acknowledge in the Introduction to *Medieval Anchorites in their Communities*, p. 5; see also Tom Licence, *Hermits and Recluses in English Society, 950–1200* (Oxford, 2011), p. 73.

[12]   *AW; AW Guide*, p. 3 [page numbers in both are the same, so henceforth only one reference will be given].

[13]   Licence, *Hermits and Recluses*, p. 15.

[14]   Sieglinde Hartmann, 'Bridal Mysticism and the Politics of the Anchorhold: Dorothy of Montau', in Catherine Innes-Parker and Naoë Kukita Yoshikawa (eds), *Anchoritism in the Middle Ages: Texts and Traditions* (Cardiff, 2013), pp. 101–13, at p. 101.

[15]   Licence, *Hermits and Recluses*, p. 72.

[16]   Anneke B. Mulder-Bakker, 'Anchorites in the Low Countries', in *Anchoritic Traditions*, pp. 22–42, at p. 22, and see also *Lives of the Anchoresses*, p. 21, where Mulder-Bakker confirms that 'Brabant and Liège' 'form the core' of her study.

number of recorded anchorites was to be found between the twelfth and sixteenth centuries;[17] this includes some in King's Lynn on the north west coast of Norfolk. The highest number of anchorites was to be found in Yorkshire, where many anchorholds appear on the edge of the land, with high concentrations around the Humber estuary.[18] If we were to take as the centre of a map not a land-mass but the North Sea, a map similar to one showing trading links between Norwich and the Continent in the Middle Ages,[19] we would see that the Humber, Norwich and King's Lynn, Brabant and Liège are at the centre of such a map. Rather than existing on the borders of the country, many medieval anchoresses are found in busy places connected through trade and travel with the continent.

Norfolk is described as 'very much a place apart from the rest of the country; it's a place you don't go through to get anywhere else',[20] yet in the Middle Ages King's Lynn was an important port trading with the Low Countries. It may be hard, therefore, to grasp how important, economically and spiritually, Norfolk and, in particular, King's Lynn and Norwich, were in the High Middle Ages. There was economic stagnation, but by the 1520s Norwich was England's second city not only in economic terms but also as 'Europe's *most* religious city', based not only on the number of religious institutions (churches, religious houses, and even England's only beguinage) but also because of the enthusiasm for late medieval religion.[21] This intensity of religious fervour must have been due in large part to the number of anchorites and hermits: Tanner claims that 'Norwich contained the largest number of hermits and anchorites known to have lived in any English city after 1370, including London, namely 40 or so',[22] while Jones claims with reference to Norwich that between 'the end of the fourteenth century and the dissolution of the monasteries in the sixteenth, at least thirty-five and perhaps as many as forty-seven solitaries appear in the record'.[23] Neither Tanner nor Jones makes the distinction between men and women anchorites (or anchorites and

---

[17] Ann K. Warren, *Anchorites and their Patrons in Medieval England* (Berkeley, 1985), Appendix 1, pp. 292–3.

[18] Andrew W. Taubman, 'Clergy and Commoners: Interactions between Medieval Clergy and Laity in a Regional Context' (Unpublished Ph.D. dissertation, University of York, 2009), p. 143.

[19] Carole Rawcliffe and Richard Wilson (eds), *Medieval Norwich* (London, 2004), map 12, p. 180.

[20] https://www.visitnorfolk.co.uk/VN-about-Norfolk.aspx [accessed 27 April 2021].

[21] Carole Rawcliffe, Introduction to *Medieval Norwich*, pp. xix–xxxvii, at p. xxxvi; Norman Tanner, 'Religious Practice', in *Medieval Norwich*, pp. 137–56, at p. 137.

[22] Norman Tanner, *Ages of Faith: Popular Religion in Late Medieval England and Western Europe* (London, 2009), pp. 44–5. See also, Carole Hill, *Medieval Women and Religion in Late Medieval Norwich* (Woodbridge, 2017).

[23] Jones, *Hermits and Anchorites*, p. 8.

hermits) but the data Warren provides suggest at least equal numbers of men and women anchorites in Norfolk throughout the Middle Ages.[24] These figures include women enclosed at the Carmelite and Dominican friaries and at Carrow Abbey (a community of women religious) as well as church anchoresses, the most famous of whom is Julian of Norwich who now occupies a central place in our appreciation of medieval spirituality.[25]

On the other side of the country, the sisters for whom *Ancrene Wisse* was initially written were enclosed in cells in the Welsh Marches, an area on the very boundaries of England. Christopher Cannon argues that the landscape, political and geographical, of the Marches resembles the conditions represented by the group of texts which includes *Ancrene Wisse* and that are connected by their West Midlands dialect.[26] Liz Herbert McAvoy has picked up Cannon's argument and suggests 'that it was more specifically the marginality and eccentricity of the Marcher lands that helped to nurture an anchoritic impulse which was to spread rapidly throughout England during the Later Middle Ages'.[27] But if anchoritism was a popular vocation, in what sense were the anchorites themselves marginal or eccentric? Prior to 1200, England was 'liberally populated by recluses', some of whom were women, in the eleventh century.[28] However, specific information on the lives of these women is based largely on accounts of exceptional women such as Christina of Markyate and Eve of Wilton. It was only after *c.* 1200 that anchorites had to be licensed by a bishop, their enclosure henceforward appearing in bishops' registers. There are also more extant wills from the Later Middle Ages that may mention bequests to anchorites; Ann Warren has collected this kind of documentary evidence to allow her to paint a broad picture of anchoritism in England in the High Middle Ages when, as she comments: 'Medieval English

---

[24] Warren, *Anchorites and their Patrons*, Appendix 1, p. 293.

[25] We now know Julian through her visionary writing; it is not clear how widespread her works ('A Vision Showed to a Devout Woman' and the later, fuller 'A Revelation of Love') were in her lifetime and soon afterwards; see Nicholas Watson and Jacqueline Jenkins (eds), *The Writings of Julian of Norwich* (University Park, 2006) pp. 10–12; her fame is attested by Margery Kempe who visited her, probably in 1413, *The Book of Margery Kempe*, ed. by Barry Windeatt (Harlow, 2000), pp. 119–23.

[26] Cannon revives Eric Dobson's claim (in *The Origins of Ancrene Wisse*) that *Ancrene Wisse* was originally written for three sisters living in the 'Deerfold' near Wigmore: Christopher Cannon, *The Grounds of English Literature* (Oxford, 2004), p. 142. Sally Thompson has pointed out that this attribution is due to a misreading of *fratres* as *sorores*, see *Women Religious*, p. 34, n. 126; and see Bella Millett, 'The Origins of *Ancrene Wisse*: New Answers, New Questions', *Medium Aevum*, 61 (1992), 206–28 for more on authorship of *Ancrene Wisse*. Nevertheless, the association of the text with this area of the West Midlands stands.

[27] McAvoy, *Medieval Anchoritisms*, p. 149.

[28] Licence, *Hermits and Recluses*, p. 84.

anchoritism was extraordinary in its endurance, in its high degree of stability, in its success in gaining and keeping the support of large numbers of the broad community from the King down to the parishioner of modest means'.[29]

On the Edge of Society

Recluses may have originally been found in remote areas but as towns grew and the number of anchorites increased so 'by the sixteenth century urban anchorites were in the majority'.[30] Their cells were usually positioned on the outside wall of the church – a window allowing a view through to the altar – or in the cemetery among the dead.[31] The small cell (probably of an anchoress) excavated during an archaeological dig at Colne Priory (Essex) was attached to the cold northern side of the church and was a temporary structure, confirming the marginal existence of its occupant within a male monastic community.[32] While the size of the anchor-hold varied, it was rarely large, representing as it did the grave, since the anchoress was to consider herself dead to the world; indeed in *Ancrene Wisse* the anchor-esses are told to scrape the earth floor of their cell to dig the grave 'þet ha schulen rotien in' ['in which they will rot'].[33] This appears to emphasise the liminality of the anchorite: on the threshold between death and life, they considered them-selves dead to the world; yet the church was often at the heart of the community. This is typical of the paradoxes that permeate anchoritism.[34]

Anchorites, observing vows of chastity and stability of abode, should be demure and obedient, but their solitude and lack of direct control could be sub-versive; their enclosure, from *c.* 1200, had to be approved by the diocesan bishop, but there was not necessarily any day-to-day control, and anchoresses could cause problems for those nominally in charge of them. Isolda de Heaton, for example, was enclosed in the churchyard at Whalley. The male monastic community who held the advowson were responsible for her maintenance and appear to have objected to 'the intrusion of women'. Isolda ran away and the endowment was redirected to pay for chantry priests.[35]

[29] Warren, *Anchorites and their Patrons*, p. 289.
[30] Jones, *Hermits and Anchorites*, p. 11.
[31] Licence, *Hermits and Recluses*, p. 125, demonstrates that prior to 1200 many cells were 'set within cemeteries, causing their occupants to live among the dead'.
[32] Cate Gunn, 'Was there an anchoress at Colne Priory?', *The Essex Society for Archaeology and History*, 2 (2011), 117–23, at p. 117. For further 'Archaeological insights' see Licence, *Hermits and Recluses*, pp. 87–9.
[33] *AW*, Pt 2, p. 46.
[34] The essays in *Medieval Anchorites in their Communities*, for example, examine the sociability of solitaries.
[35] British History Online, 'The parish of Whalley', *A History of the County of Lancaster:*

Ann Warren has pointed out that 'English society was successful in preserving, under cautious controls, a potentially disruptive way of life'.[36] Such disruption is portrayed in the fictional film *Anchoress* based on the account of a real anchoress, Christina Carpenter, who was enclosed in a cell attached to the church of St James in Shere, Surrey.[37] The process for admission to an anchorhold was highly controlled by ecclesiastical and civic authorities: Christina's enclosure was approved by the bishop of Winchester and her enclosure performed according to the procedures of the church.[38] When she escaped from the cell, she placed herself outside the church, in effect an outlaw, and in danger of excommunication. The film, however, portrays her decision to enter the anchorhold as itself aberrant: she is removing herself from the village society and her place within it and claiming for herself a status and autonomy that, it is suggested, were not warranted.

Christina Carpenter's surname suggests that she came from an artisan family, but most anchorites probably came from a middle class which was increasing in numbers and becoming increasingly literate. It was also this burgeoning middle class that supported anchorites financially; members of the merchant class included anchorites among their general bequests as an expression of a general sense of public responsibility.[39] This was a pattern found throughout Europe; in Siena women hermits were often located at gates and by the walls of the city but were still very much at the heart of civic life.[40] Siena had more women than men hermits but in English towns the hermits living at the edge of the city (and often

    Volume 6 (1911), https://www.british-history.ac.uk/vch/lancs/vol6/pp349-360 [accessed 27 Jan. 2020].

[36] Warren, *Anchorites and their Patrons*, p. 280.

[37] Liz Herbert McAvoy, 'Christina Carpenter', *ODNB*, http://www.oxforddnb.com/view/article/105610; doi: 10.1093/ref:odnb/105610 [accessed 25 Nov. 2019]. On the film, see Miri Rubin, 'An English Anchorite: The Making, Unmaking and Remaking of Christine Carpenter', in Rosemary Horrox and Sarah Rees Jones (eds), *Pragmatic Utopias: Ideals and Communities, 1200–1630* (Cambridge, 2001), pp. 204–23.

[38] Christina could only be enclosed after her father, the rector of the parish and 'a number of named men within the village and beyond' had vouched for 'her devoutness' and her virginity: McAvoy, 'Christina Carpenter'. See also the admission of the anchoress Isolda of Kneesall for which she had to prove both religious vocation and financial support: Jones, *Hermits and Anchorites*, pp. 27–8.

[39] Warren, *Anchorites and their Patrons*, p. 284.

[40] Allison Clark, 'Spaces of Reclusion: Notarial Records of Urban Eremiticism in Medieval Siena', in Liz Herbert McAvoy (ed.), *Rhetoric of the Anchorhold: Space, Place, and Body within the Discourses of Enclosure* (Cardiff, 2008), pp. 17–33. These women seemed to have had a looser form of life than the English anchoresses and tended not to be strictly enclosed or necessarily to be solitary.

with responsibilities for gates and bridges) were men,[41] reflecting the anxiety over the control of women and their bodies.

The control over women's bodies and lives crossed class boundaries; aristocratic women were particularly prey to male control. Liz Herbert McAvoy suggests that women in the powerful Marcher families were viewed as 'valuable commodities';[42] one such woman was Katharine de Audley who faced a long battle to withdraw into reclusion. Even in death Katharine was the pawn of men's imaginations since her legend was written and rewritten as preconceptions were projected onto her life, including by Wordsworth, who used her legend as the subject of his sonnet 'St Catherine of Ledbury'.[43] Better known are two sisters, also members of a powerful Marcher family, Annora and Loretta de Braose; both were enclosed in the first part of the thirteenth century as widows and possibly seeking 'political sanctuary' since their father had died in exile in France and their mother and brother had starved to death while captives of King John.[44] In Loretta's case, King John retained control over her, and she was unable to enter an anchorhold without his permission.[45] Nevertheless, Loretta was able to exert some power and influence from within the anchorhold and played an important role in the establishment of the Franciscans in England. Thomas of Eccleston, writing of the first Franciscans to come to Canterbury, noted that the 'noble countess, the lady anchoress of Hackington' was among those – the great and the good of the church in Canterbury – who promoted their cause and that she in particular 'cherished them in all things as a mother would her sons'.[46]

Women such as the de Braose sisters also played a role in the copying, revision and dissemination of anchoritic and related texts.[47] These texts were often circu-

---

[41] Jones, *Hermits and Anchorites*, p. 8.

[42] Liz Herbert McAvoy, 'Uncovering the "Saintly Anchoress": Myths of Medieval Anchoritism and the Reclusion of Katharine de Audley', *Women's History Review*, 2013, http://dx.doi.org/10.1080/09612025.2013.769380 [accessed 21 Dec. 2019], p. 2.

[43] McAvoy, 'Katharine de Audley', p. 7.

[44] Catherine Innes-Parker, 'Medieval Widowhood and Textual Guidance: The Corpus Revisions of *Ancrene Wisse* and the de Braose Anchoresses', *Florilegium*, 28 (2011), 95–124, at p. 101, https://journals.lib.unb.ca/index.php/flor/article/view/21563/25050 [accessed 20 Feb. 2021].

[45] Frederick M. Powicke, 'Loretta, Countess of Leicester', in J. G. Edwards et al. (eds), *Historical Essays in Honour of James Tait* (Manchester, 1933), pp. 247–71; Hilary Pearson, *The Recluse of Iftele: Annora de Briouze. The Life and Times of an Anchoress in Medieval England* (Iffley, 2019).

[46] 'Nobilisque comitissa, domina inclusa de Hakyngton, quae, sicut mater filios, sic fovit eos in omnibus', in A. G. Little (ed.), *Fratris Thomae vulgo dicti de Eccleston Tractus de Adventu Fratrum Minorum in Angliam*, (Manchester, 1951), p. 20. Other supporters included Simon Langton, archdeacon of Canterbury and brother of the archbishop.

[47] See Catherine Innes-Parker, 'The Legacy of *Ancrene Wisse*', in Yoko Wada (ed.), *A*

lated through reading circles of aristocratic women, 'some of them patronesses of anchorites and religious communities':[48] the anchoritic life and its associated literature was at the heart of the expansion of vernacular theology in the High Middle Ages.[49] The texts commissioned and read by anchoresses and their patrons and correspondents reached out through medieval society and across time; the spirituality they expressed also transcends the walls of the anchorhold.

Liminal Spirituality

The spirituality of anchorites seems extreme and yet anchorites and the guides written for them, rather than being exclusive or at the extreme edge of acceptable religious practice, reflected contemporary spirituality while also being instrumental in constructing that spirituality. They were often 'role models of orthodox spirituality'.[50] The author of *Ancrene Wisse* was able to claim that heresy was not prevalent in England,[51] but by the time Richard Rolle and Walter Hilton were writing in the later fourteenth century Lollardy was a developing threat to church unity. Hilton, an Augustinian canon who spent at least part of his life as a solitary, wrote a guide to the contemplative life in which he is concerned 'to defend orthodox belief'.[52]

Religious faith was the accepted norm in society, but anchorites lived out a spiritual vocation that was not possible for most people. *Ancrene Wisse* reminds the anchoresses that they should be not only dead to the world but rejoice in 'beon ahonget sariliche ant scheomeliche wið Iesu on his rode' ['being hanged painfully and shamefully with Jesus on the cross'];[53] it was through a life of privation that an anchoress could imitate Christ. Death is the final frontier: anchoresses are 'poised on the brink of infinity'.[54] The hagiographical Lives of anchoresses tend to construct the asceticism as a form of martyrdom, which

Companion to Ancrene Wisse (Cambridge, 2003), pp. 145–73, at p. 150.
[48] Catherine Innes-Parker, 'Anchoritic Textual Communities and the Wooing Group Prayers', in *Medieval Anchorites in their Communities*, pp. 167–82, at p. 179.
[49] The term 'vernacular theology' was defined by Nicholas Watson in 'Censorship and Cultural Change in Late-Medieval England: Vernacular Theology, the Oxford Translation Debate and Arundel's Constitutions of 1409', *Speculum*, 70 (1995), 822–64, at pp. 823–4.
[50] Mari Hughes-Edwards, *Reading Medieval Anchoritism: Ideology and Spiritual Practices* (Cardiff, 2012), p. 109.
[51] *AW*, Pt 2, p. 33.
[52] Introduction to Walter Hilton, *The Scale of Perfection*, ed. Thomas H. Bestul, TEAMS (Kalamazoo, 2000), p. 1.
[53] *AW*, Pt 6, p. 134. (I have made a slight alteration to Millett's translation).
[54] McAvoy, 'Uncovering the "Saintly Anchoress"', p. 13.

could frequently include severe self-inflicted wounds.[55] Nevertheless, the teaching of the guides must have had a wider appeal. Some anchoritic guides reached out to a wider audience, including people in the world. Sections of *Ancrene Wisse* are deliberately targeted at readers others than the anchoresses:[56] part 5 on Confession, for example, 'limpeð to alle men iliche' ['is relevant to everybody alike'][57] and, apart from a short final section, is not directly addressed to the anchoresses. Similarly, not all the material in Richard Rolle's *The Form of Living*, ostensibly written for an anchoress, Margaret Kirkeby, 'seems relevant to an anchoress'.[58] Material about confession, an essential part of Christianity as it was understood in the Middle Ages, was in demand by lay people and, in particular, by preachers.[59] This was advice that must have percolated down to the wider public, all of whom were expected, once they reached the age of discretion, to take communion once a year, having first made their confession to their own parish priest.[60]

[55] See, for example, Johannes von Marienwerder, *The Life of Dorothy of Montau* quoted by Hartmann, 'Dorothy of Montau', *passim*; Marie d'Oigny lived a life of extreme privation and denial, even once cutting a piece of flesh out of her side but then burying it out of shame: James of Vitry, *Vita Mariae Oigniacensis*, sec. 22, in *Acta Sanctorum*, ed. D. Papebrochius (Antwerp, 1707), vol. 4, p. 641.

[56] And here too, listeners, as the anchoresses are told to read the relevant part of *Ancrene Wisse* to their maidservants once a week: *AW*, Pt 8, p. 163.

[57] *AW*, Pt 5, p. 129.

[58] Nicholas Watson, *Richard Rolle and the Invention of Authority* (Cambridge, 1991), p. 251.

[59] *Ancrene Wisse* was clearly influenced by the preaching manuals produced in the twelfth and thirteenth centuries; see Gunn, *Ancrene Wisse*, pp. 99–109 and Bella Millett, '*Ancrene Wisse* and the Conditions of Confession', *English Studies*, 80 (1999), 193–215. Andrew Reeves points out the emphasis put on teaching elements of the faith to lay people in the thirteenth century and that 'Lay ownership of religious books shows a demand that existed in answer to the supply of this religious instruction provided by the English clergy': 'Teaching the Creed and Articles of Faith in England: Lateran IV to *Ignoratia Sacerdotum*' (Unpublished Ph.D. dissertation, University of Toronto, 2009), p. 201; the multiple versions of *Ancrene Wisse* were also responding to this demand.

[60] 'Omnis utriusque sexus fidelis, postquam ad annos discretionis pervenerit, omni sua solus peccata confiteatur fideliter, saltem semel in anno proprio sacerdoti', 'Constitutio 21', *Concilium Lateranense IV* (1215) in *Conciliorum Oecumenicorum Decreta*, ed. J. Alberigo et al. (Bologna, 1973), pp. 227–71, p. 245. Leonard Boyle has pointed out that 'confession and preaching went hand in hand': 'The Fourth Lateran Council and Manuals of Popular Theology', in Thomas J. Heffernan (ed.), *The Popular Literature of Medieval England* (Knoxville, 1985), pp. 30–43, at p. 33. See also Andrew Reeves, 'Teaching the Creed and Articles of Faith in England: 1215–1281', in Ronald J. Stansbury (ed.), *A Companion to Pastoral Care in the Late Middle Ages (1200–1500)* (Leiden, 2010), pp. 41–2.

Later anchoritic writers placed more emphasis on contemplation,[61] which also required a life that was removed from the demands of the world, and yet contemplative works addressed initially to an anchorite gained popularity in the wider community. The works of Richard Rolle, for example, were 'more widely read than those of any other vernacular writer'.[62] Rolle describes contemplation as 'a wonderful ioy of Goddis loue, þe which ioy is a praysynge of God þat may nat be told'.[63] While the burning joy of the love of God on earth that could be achieved through contemplation was something attained only by a few, the hope that after death, and after the purgation of all sins either in this world or the next, one may come into the presence of God is at the heart of Christianity as it was understood in the Middle Ages and an idea that sustained those following the active life.

Rolle appears a transgressive character and his spiritual programme was radical,[64] but it was this very radicalness that led to Rolle's work being widely copied and disseminated so that Margaret Kirkeby 'deserves to be seen as a key figure in the development of English spirituality'.[65] Also in the late fourteenth century, Julian of Norwich wrote of Jesus as mother. Far from being a radical reinterpretation of the nature of divinity, however, she was reconceiving a tradition that stretched back to the Church fathers and was most significantly used by St Anselm in eleventh-century England: 'And you, Jesus, are you not also a mother? Are you not the mother who, like a hen, gathers her chickens under her wings?'.[66] In her visionary writing Julian adapted this image for a new, vernacular readership influenced by the affective spirituality of the High Middle Ages; she was able to reduce difficult trinitarian theology to the accessible image of a loving family:

[61] This distinction forms the organising structure of Hughes-Edwards, *Reading Medieval Anchoritism*.

[62] Jonathan Hughes claims that Rolle's works 'survive in some 470 manuscripts written between 1390 and 1500, and in ten sixteenth- and early seventeenth-century printed editions': 'Richard Rolle', in *ODNB* (2008), https://doi.org/10.1093/ref:odnb/24024 [accessed 27 Jan. 2020].

[63] Richard Rolle, *The Form of Living* in *Richard Rolle: Prose and Verse*, ed. S. J. Ogilvie Thomson, EETS, OS, 293 (Oxford, 1988), pp. 3–25, at p. 24.

[64] He was famous for using a gown of his sister as an improvised habit, and as a hermit he was outside the strict hierarchical structures of the church.

[65] Watson, *Richard Rolle*, p. 242.

[66] Jennifer P. Heimmel, *'God is our Mother': Julian of Norwich and the Medieval Image of Christian Feminine Divinity* (Salzburg, 1982), p. 25, quoting Anselm of Canterbury's Prayer to Paul: 'Sed et tu IESU, bone domine, nonne et tu mater? An non est mater, qui tamquam gallina congregat sub alas pullos suos?': Anselm of Canterbury, *Orationes siue meditationes* vol. 3, oratio 10, p. 40. My thanks to Margaret Healy-Varley for assistance in identifying this quotation; further on Anselm's influence on Julian's theology see Margaret Healy-Varley, 'Wounds Shall Be Worships: Anselm in Julian of Norwich's *Revelation of Love*', *Journal of English and Germanic Philology*, 115 (2016), 186–212.

'And thus in our making God almighty is oure kindly fader, and God alle wisdom is oure kindly mother, with the love and the goodnes of the holy gost, which is alle one God, one lorde'.[67]

The possibility of accessing some of the spiritual benefits previously thought of as the province only of dedicated religious was taking hold, especially as increasing literacy among a growing middle class was fuelling the demand from lay readers for works of spiritual value. Increased leisure time as well as literacy meant that educated members of the middle and gentry classes could participate to some extent in the devotions followed by the dedicated religious. *Ancrene Wisse* makes use, not of the full Office or Opus Dei that members of religious houses used daily, but of the shorter 'Little Hours' of the Virgin Mary, anticipating 'in many respects the devotional routine of the later Books of Hours produced for a lay readership'.[68] Hilton wrote an 'Epistle on the Mixed Life' in which we see the appeal to a lay reader of a way of life that was in many ways similar to the daily routine of the anchorite: as well as doing active works of charity, the day is to be bound by prayer: 'In nyghtes aftir thi slepe, yif thou wolt rise for to praie and serve thi Lord, thou schalt feele thisilf first fleschli, hevy, and sumtyme lusti. Than schalt thou dispose thee for to praie or for to thenke sum gode thought, for to quickene thyn herte to God'.[69] The reader of the 'Epistle of Mixed Life' would no doubt have been using a Book of Hours; the use of the Hours of the Virgin Mary and the praying of the Ave Maria, both of which are advocated in anchoritic guides, are expressions of a Marian devotion that was increasingly popular in the High Middle Ages.

Devotion to Mary, the human mother of Jesus, is one aspect of the incarnational spirituality at the heart of high medieval devotions. Attending Mass, when God was made flesh in the host as he had been incarnated in the person of Jesus Christ, was the essential religious observation for all Christians and central to the anchoritic life. The anchoresses for whom *Ancrene Wisse* was written are told that at the moment that the priest communicates 'þer forȝeoteð al þe world, þer beoð al ut of bodi, þer in sperclinde luue bicluppeð ower leofmon, þe into ower breostes bur is iliht of heouene' ['there forget all the world, there be quite out of the body, there in burning love embrace your lover, who has descended from heaven into the chamber of your breast'],[70] linking eucharistic devotion to bridal mysticism.

[67] Julian of Norwich, 'A Revelation of Love', in *The Writings of Julian of Norwich*, p. 307.
[68] Bella Millett, '*Ancrene Wisse* and the Book of Hours', in Denis Renevey and Christiania Whitehead (eds), *Writing Religious Women: Female Spiritual and Textual Practices in Late Medieval England* (Cardiff, 2000), pp. 21–40, at p. 32.
[69] Walter Hilton, 'Epistle on the Mixed Life', in Barry Windeatt (ed.), *English Mystics of the Middle Ages* (Cambridge, 1994), pp. 108–30, at p. 124.
[70] *AW*, Pt. 1, p. 13.

Devotion to the consecrated host also became popular among the wider congregation of lay people as the mass became 'a focus for lay participation'[71] and devout people made extraordinary efforts to witness its elevation; Caroline Walker Bynum recounts that 'By the thirteenth century we find stories of people attending mass only for the moment of elevation, racing from church to church to see as many consecrations as possible, and shouting at the priest to hold the host up higher'.[72] When the screen obstructed the view of the altar and the elevation, holes were sometimes made in the screen; similarly the defining feature of an anchorhold is the window or squint angled to allow the occupant of the cell to witness the consecration and elevation of the host at the altar. Corpus Christi as an annual feast to celebrate the eucharist was established in the thirteenth century at the instigation of Juliana of Cornillon, one of five women Mulder-Bakker takes as examples in *Lives of the Anchoresses*. Juliana clearly had a yearning for the reclusive life, but after a turbulent career only achieved this towards the very end of her life.[73]

Conclusion

Anchoritism is an area of multi-disciplinary study and, as such, the cross-over of disciplines is constantly opening new areas to investigate while also encouraging feminist and inter-sectional approaches. Ideas of queer identity are being used as a theoretical basis for the exploration of anchoritism and this, as well as the idea of silence as a spiritual practice, are areas where the relevance of medieval anchoritism to modern life can be more fully explored.[74] Anchoresses, living a life centred on the Hours of the Virgin, through which they expressed their devotion to the Virgin Mary, and on witnessing the daily celebration of the eucharist, were

---

[71]   Miri Rubin, *Corpus Christi: The Eucharist in Late Medieval Culture* (Cambridge, 1991), p. 172.

[72]   Caroline Walker Bynum, *Holy Feast and Holy Fast: The Religious Significance of Food to Medieval Women* (Berkeley, 1987), p. 55.

[73]   Mulder-Bakker claims that Juliana, having been a prioress of a leper colony, withdrew into the reclusive life: *Lives of the Anchoresses*, p. 9. Barbara Newman points out that Juliana was forced to seek refuge in a Cistercian convent, only being found a cell when she became seriously ill and where 'she was able to live out the few remaining days of her life', ending them 'like her beloved friend Eve, as a recluse': Introduction to *The Life of Blessed Juliana of Mont Cornillon*, Barbara Newman (trans.) (Toronto, 1988) and reprinted in *Vox Benedictina: Journal of Translations from Monastic Sources*, 5 (1988). The Eve referred to is Eve of St Martin, who was enclosed at the chapter church of St Martin in Liège.

[74]   See for example, Cate Gunn, "'Þis seli stilðe": Silence and Stillness in the Anchorhold: Lessons for the Modern World?', in Cate Gunn, Liz Herbert McAvoy, and Naoë Kukita Yoshikawa (eds), *Women, Words and Devotional Literature in the Later Middle Ages: Giving Voice to Silence* (Cambridge, forthcoming).

participating in this incarnational spirituality that was interwoven into popular religion, forming the essential fabric of its daily expression. Indeed, anchoritism can be viewed as a synecdoche for medieval Christianity, representing its essence as an affective and incarnational religion, requiring devotion not to an abstract God but to a suffering and human one who could be depicted as a baby in the arms of Mary and dying on the cross, as well as a lover in the marriage bed of the chaste anchoress. Far from being 'on the fringes', anchorites were found through-out Europe, often in the centre of towns and villages, and their very liminal status on the threshold between heaven and earth allowed them to intercede and pray for people, therefore occupying a central and important place in medieval society. With new archaeological surveys and studies of church architecture, for example, evidence of anchorites may be unearthed that could expand our knowledge of their lived experiences within the anchorhold – such as age, background, disa-bility – as well as their locations within towns, cities, and the countryside. When Mulder-Bakker suggests that anchoresses could play a similar role to that of the priest, she adds that rather than being a father figure, however, they were the mother: 'always at home'.[75]

---

[75]   Mulder-Bakker, *Lives of the Anchoresses*, p. 14.

CHAPTER 5

'Quasi-religious': Vowesses

LAURA RICHMOND

A LTHOUGH vowesses might now be considered comparatively obscure, the vocation was once not only well-known, but indeed fundamental to the social and spiritual fabric of medieval England. A vowess was a woman who had taken a vow of chastity without the accompanying monastic vows of poverty and obedience. These women were almost always widows, although married women did occasionally take the vow if their husbands also embarked on a chaste life. Such vows seem to have been fairly common, especially in the Later Middle Ages, and vowesses were often described as widows who had 'taken the mantle and the ring' – an allusion to the ring and mantle bestowed, usually by a bishop, at the vowing ceremony.[1] Allusions to the ring and mantle are peppered throughout medieval English literature, from *The Book of Margery Kempe* to John Gower's *Mirour de l'Omme* to Chaucer's 'Squire of Low Degree'.[2] By at least the fourteenth century, the ring and mantle had become part of the English cultural milieu.

Vowesses interacted with monastic communities and with other women religious in different ways. Some vowesses seem to have seldom gone near a religious house, while others were fully integrated into convent communities. For those who did choose to participate in monastic life, their quasi-religious status has interesting implications for how they were accommodated within these spaces. This chapter will provide a brief introduction to how women were vowed, the complexities around vowing, and the consequences for how vowesses have been

---

[1] This chapter offers only a brief introduction and cannot encompass the nuances and complexities around veiled widowhood. For more, see Laura M. Wood, 'In Search of the Mantle and Ring: Prosopographical Study of the Vowess in Late Medieval England', *Medieval Prosopography*, 34 (2019), 175–205.

[2] Lynn Staley (ed.), *The Book of Margery Kempe*, TEAMS *Middle English Texts*, 1996, http://d.lib.rochester.edu/teams/publication/staley-the-book-of-margery-kempe/ [accessed 15 Jan. 2017], i, 773–83; Marie-Françoise Alamichel, *Widows in Anglo-Saxon and Medieval Britain* (Bern, 2008), p. 194; Erik Kooper (ed.), *The Squire of Low Degree*, TEAMS, *Middle English Texts*, 2005, https://d.lib.rochester.edu/teams/text/kooper-sentimental-and-humorous-romances-squire-of-low-degree/ [accessed 14 May 2021].

remembered and researched ever since. It will go on to consider vowesses within the context of women's religious life in England during the Later Middle Ages, using individual case studies to illustrate ways in which vowed women participated in convent communities.

Vowing Ceremonies

The tradition of veiled widowhood has its origins in the early Church, but the benediction ceremonies at which widows became vowesses appear to have been a peculiarly English phenomenon. Other manifestations of widowed or quasi-monastic religious life, such as beguines and Franciscan tertiaries, ran in parallel across the European Continent and beyond, with different vocations flourishing in different centuries over the course of the Middle Ages. English vowing ceremonies date back to at least the seventh century, continuing into the 1530s with a decline that ran parallel to the dissolution of the monasteries. There seems to have been a 'peak' in the popularity of widows' vows in the 1480s, falling away gradually after 1500: the rise of cults such as that of St Anne and the influence of royal vowed women such as Lady Margaret Beaufort, mother of Henry VII, and Cecily Neville, duchess of York, may have been contributing factors.[3] Although it is not clear to what extent the 'peak' may be a trick of inconsistent record keeping and document survival, more vows are recorded for the late fifteenth century than any other time.

A woman who wished to become a vowess would issue a request to a bishop or archbishop, who would establish both that she was of good reputation and that she had the financial means to be self-sufficient. If satisfied, the bishop or archbishop would send a commission, a letter of recommendation sometimes known as a certification or a licence, to another bishop, usually her diocesan, requesting that he perform the vowing ceremony. Mary C. Erler has described the proceedings of such an event, as outlined in an early sixteenth-century pontifical.[4] Before the gospel was read at Mass, the woman, in her ordinary clothes but carrying dark clothing over her left arm, led by two male family members, approached the seated bishop. She knelt, placed the paper with her vow written on it at the bishop's feet, and recited or read the vow aloud.

---

[3] Patricia Cullum, 'Vowesses and Veiled Widows: Medieval Female Piety in the Province of York', *Northern History*, 32 (1996), 21–41, at p. 41.

[4] Mary C. Erler, 'Three Fifteenth-Century Vowesses', in Caroline M. Barron and Anne F. Sutton (eds), *Medieval London Widows, 1300–1500* (London, 1994), pp. 165–84, at pp. 165–6. The pontifical cited is reproduced in F. C. Eeles, 'Two Sixteenth-Century Pontificals Formerly Used in England', *Transactions of the St Paul's Ecclesiological Society*, 7 (1911–5), 69–90. This chapter builds on Erler's seminal work on vowesses.

Numerous examples of these vows have survived as they were sometimes copied into episcopal registers, such as that of John Stanberry, bishop of Hereford (1453–74), which records the vow of Joan Sergeant on 6 March 1461:

> I, Johanne Sergeant, now late wyfe of Thomas Sergeant, whose soul God assoyle, of my free will and good deliberacion, vow and promitte to our Lord God and his moder, seynt Mary and all the seyntes of hevyn, in to your holy hands, my gostly fadur, John, by the grace of God bysshop of Hereford, from this day forward to my lyves end to kepe and observe clene chastite and continence of my body of trew wydewhode from all men ertheley, and in trew signe, tokene, and confirmacion hereof, I signe with myne owne hand this byll of my profession and vow with this holy + [5]

Such vows are quite formulaic, although there is some variation amongst them, and they seem to have used the individual phrasing of the woman herself or of someone composing the vow on her behalf. They usually explicitly state that the widow is free to make this promise on account of the death of her husband. Some also refer to 'the rule of St Paul', presumably referring to his teaching on widowhood in 1 Timothy 5, and subsequently the fact that widows have had a unique role in the Church from its earliest beginnings.

After Joan Sergeant spoke these words, she would have marked the document with a cross on the bishop's knee and given him the paper. The bishop would have blessed her and asperged her new clothes and ring with holy water. After this came the offertory of the Eucharist, and then Joan would have received the bishop's blessing once more and kissed his ring. The new clothing often included a veil and a hood, but most important symbolically seems to have been the profession mantle: not only were vowesses often referred to as those who had 'taken the mantle and the ring', profession mantles were sometimes bequeathed in women's wills.

Identifying Vowed Women

Some women may have styled themselves as vowesses without taking a formal vow in a benediction ceremony. Susan Steuer describes this as 'tacit profession': just as novices could live as women religious for a year and then continue legitimately without the need for a ceremony, widows may have similarly substituted a trial period for a formal vow and still been recognised as vowesses.[6] The bound-

---

[5]   Joseph H. Parry and Arthur Thomas Bannister (eds), *Registrum Johannis Stanbury, Episcopi Herefordensis A.D. 1443–74* (London, 1919), pp. 68–9.

[6]   Susan Steuer, 'Identifying Chaste Widows: Documenting a Religious Vocation', in L. E. Mitchell, K. L. French, and D. L. Biggs (eds), *The Ties that Bind: Essays in Medieval*

ary between vowesses and widows who informally pursued a semi-religious life is blurred and indistinct: written record of many women's vows has been lost to time, some vowing ceremonies may have been conducted but not necessarily recorded, and it is impossible to identify women who vowed privately.

This renders the work of studying vowesses collectively rather complicated. Patricia Cullum has speculated that vowesses' quasi-religious state is the reason that they have so far received little scholarly attention: their vow excludes them from research into lay piety and yet nor are they typically included in studies of women religious.[7] Another consideration is the varied and disparate nature of the historical sources in which these women are to be found. Women are sometimes named as vowed in their wills, using the term 'vowess' but also 'avowess', 'advowess', and 'widow professed'. They are occasionally identified as such in others' wills. Some vowesses' wills include a ring, a mantle, or, more rarely, a hood, of profession. Legal records, property records, and papal records also sometimes identify a woman as a vowess. Inscriptions on monumental brasses occasionally name a woman as a vowess or refer to a vow. Episcopal registers include commissions and vows, but these were recorded sporadically: it seems that many went wholly undocumented, and survival of the registers is patchy at best.

While the fluidity and flexibility of the vocation of a vowess may prove tricky for historians, these methodological difficulties reflect the remarkable variety among vowed women's lives. Being quasi-religious, vowesses were free to select their own position on the continuum between enclosure and integration, between contemplative and active piety. Vowesses could own property, live where they chose, and dictate their own patterns of religious observance. The chastity vow could lend women an unusual degree of autonomy in a patriarchal system, and vowed lifestyles varied considerably. Some vowesses were active businesswomen; some were leading ladies in their parishes; some were great patronesses; some founded schools; some ran large estates. Some seem to have been deeply devout and others rather less so. Some vowed when they were old and others while still in their twenties. There was no 'typical' vowess. Case studies of individual vowed women illustrate this variety, and they also shed light upon ways in which vowesses could participate in convent communities.

British History in Honor of Barbara Hanawalt (Burlington, VT, 2011), pp. 87–105, at pp. 95–6.

[7]   Cullum, 'Vowesses and Veiled Widows', p. 21.

Alice Hampton

Alice Hampton (†1516) was a remarkable vowess, notable not only for being the only known unmarried woman to have vowed in this way but also because she forged close links not just with one convent, but with three.[8] In a sense, she embodied the quasi-religious nature of her vocation rather neatly in that she spent most of her life semi-enclosed. Surviving evidence outlines her living arrangements in considerable, and unusual, detail. In the 1480s, Alice had unexpectedly inherited her family's Gloucestershire estates and the wealth of her uncle, who was mayor of London, after her father and brothers died. A papal privilege, dated 1484 and issued in response to a petition made by Alice, states that:

> she, who is of noble family, took a vow of perpetual chastity before the local ordinary, in accordance with a certain custom still observed in the kingdom of England, and so that she might more conveniently hear and approach to hear divine offices from there, at her own expense built a certain oratory near the monastery of Dartford... at which oratory she lives at present... on account of the fasts and various abstinences which she has so far observed, she has incurred various physical infirmities, due to which she can no longer safely observe the fasts to which she has bound herself, nor attend in person at masses and other offices in the church of the said friars.[9]

The privilege goes on to grant that Alice may have Mass and other divine offices celebrated in her oratory, by her own or another suitable priest. She was also free to choose her own confessor to commute her fasts into other works of piety. In this way, Alice's purpose-built oratory was sanctified for the celebration of eucharistic liturgy and became an extension of the convent itself. Her vow was cited as justification for this decision. The location of Alice's oratory, and its proximity to the convent's cloister, are unclear, but the papal privilege suggests that this was not the typical precinct residence that any well-to-do lady might have. The fact that she had fasted herself into illness suggests that she participated in the severe austerity of the Dartford sisters, who fasted often and, even when not fasting, ate one meagre meal a day and abstained from meat altogether.[10]

Alice's presence at the community at Dartford was originally financed by her uncle and was also connected to one of the sisters there, Anne Bamme. The Hampton and Bamme families were closely linked. Indentures from the prior

[8] For a fuller biography of Alice Hampton, see: 'Hampton, Alice (d. 1516)', *ODNB*, May 2012.
[9] *CPL*, vol. 15 pp. 32–3, no. 60.
[10] Paul Lee, *Nunneries, Learning, and Spirituality in Late Medieval Society: The Dominican Priory of Dartford* (York, 2001), p. 29.

of Holy Trinity, London, to John Bamme, dated 1483, refer to an enfeoffment
of the manor of Charles in Dartford which involved the payment of an annuity
of £15 granted at Bamme's request directly to Alice.[11] Documents relating to this
arrangement and to the lands involved were to be locked in a chest and Bamme
was given a key, should he need it during Alice's lifetime. This enabled Alice to
live as a vowess at Dartford prior to her uncle's death, at which time she inherited
her family's estates.

By 1492, Alice was no longer at Dartford but was living at the community at
Halliwell in Shoreditch.[12] The reasons for the move are unclear, although it may have
be related to the death of Anne Bamme: since she was already a sister at Dartford in
1442, she is likely to have been some decades older than Alice and possibly elderly
by the 1480s.[13] A lease between Alice Hampton and the mother superior at Halliwell,
Elizabeth Prudde, states that she was already 'abyding within the same monastery'
in 1492.[14] The superior granted that Alice might build an 'entree or tresaunce' 21ft
3ins long, at the 'west end of the church', which would go along the common
entrance leading into the hall. Alice was also granted two parcels of empty ground,
one 12ft wide and passing from the common entrance to the side of the church, and
another 28ft 10ins by 23ft on the west side of the common entrance. In addition to
this, she was to have a storehouse, measuring 23ft 8ins by 11ft 3ins, adjoining her
'entree or tresaunce', and two chambers 'over and above' the storehouse.

Alice was also granted permission to make a window in the wall at the west end
of the church, which divided the church from one of her chambers, thus enabling
her to hear Mass and see the Eucharist at the altar without leaving her chamber.
This may have been because she chose to include some element of secluded prayer
in her routine. The lease also grants her 'free entre and issue comyng and goyng
[…] into and from our lady chapell' from 7:00am until 8:00pm and permits her to
'make and sette by' a pew there from which to perform her devotions.

Alice's integration into the community at Halliwell is evident not only because
she had her own seat in the Lady Chapel but also because the lease stipulates her
right to use the mother superior's well and washing house. In addition to this, she
was permitted to construct a locked door, to which she would keep the key, in the
garden beside the convent's entrance, so that she and her servants might 'walke
and take their pleasure'. For these privileges, Alice was to pay the community four
pounds of pepper, twice a year.

[11] The National Archives [TNA], Exchequer [hereafter E] 41/479; E 40/5815; and E 40/5939.
[12] Alice's time at Halliwell was first identified by Mary C. Erler: 'Syon's "Special Benefactors
and Friends"': Some Vowed Women', *Birgittiana*, 2 (1996), 209–22, at pp. 211–17.
[13] Lee, *Nunneries, Learning and Spirituality*, p. 63.
[14] TNA, Office of the Auditors of Land Revenue [hereafter LR] 14/813.

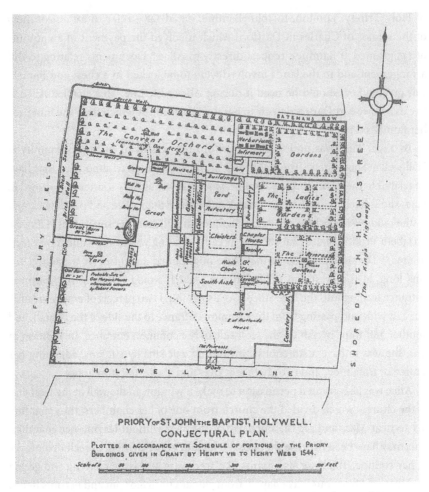

PRIORY of ST JOHN the BAPTIST, HOLYWELL.
CONJECTURAL PLAN.
PLOTTED IN ACCORDANCE WITH SCHEDULE OF PORTIONS OF THE PRIORY
BUILDINGS GIVEN IN GRANT BY HENRY VIII TO HENRY WEBB 1544.

Fig. 5.1. Plan of Halliwell Priory. Cited in: Erler, Mary, *Women, Reading, and Piety in Late Medieval England* (2006), p. 14. Public domain: A 1544 map showing the details of the agreement between Alice Hampton and Elizabeth Prudde concerning the use of Halliwell Priory. *Survey of London: Volume 8, Shoreditch*, ed. James Bird (London, 1922), British History Online, http://www.british-history.ac.uk/survey-london/vol8 [accessed 4 November 2021].

Alice's 'entree or tresaunce' was more than an oratory: it was a cluster of buildings on the north western side of the complex, a residence with everything required for a comfortable life. She was not enclosed, but free to come and go as she wished. She was separated from the sisters by the walls of her dwelling, but she used the facilities and participated in the spiritual life of the convent. She was quite literally at the threshold, not of the convent but of the inner sanctum of the sisters' cloister. She seems to have maintained this home for the rest of her life.

Her will of 1514 requests burial within the conventual church at Halliwell, and both of her executors were based there, as were all the will's beneficiaries.[15]

Whilst laywomen did sometimes have residences in the precincts, Alice's presence at Dartford and at Halliwell is indicative of a much closer connection to these places, one that was facilitated by her status as a vowess. At the same time, she had not relinquished secular society as the sisters of Dartford and Halliwell had done and she maintained links with her original home of Minchinhampton, Gloucestershire. She is recorded as leasing properties there in 1499 and proceedings in the manor court were conducted in her name in 1507.[16] She gave a bell, inscribed with her name and dated 1515, to one of the town's market-houses, and it was later transferred to the parish church.[17] She also set up an almshouse for three poor people, each with an allowance of 1d a day.[18] Her only bequest to the parish church was the ring by which she became a vowess, of greater sentimental than material value, but it seems likely that she made other gifts which disappeared in the mid sixteenth century. Alice and her family are commemorated in brass at Holy Trinity, Minchinhampton, and a brass plate below the effigies describes Alice as 'right beneficiall to this church'.[19]

In 1507, Alice Hampton began the process of signing away all her property, but it did not go to Halliwell, Dartford, or the parish church at Minchinhampton, but to the community of Syon. She placed her estates in the hands of feoffees for fifty years. If the king's licence, under mortmain, could be obtained, the property was to pass to Syon. If not, it was to remain to the feoffees and their heirs.[20] The feoffees in question included Richard Whitford, the religious author who signed himself 'the Wretch of Syon' and whom Alice seems to have known personally. The king's licence was indeed obtained, and the estate was handed over to the community: Syon's valuation of 1534 includes 'rents of lands and tenements lately of the Lady Alicia Hampton' worth £9 4s 5d.[21] This is a surprisingly small sum and leaves much

---

[15] London Metropolitan Archives, Consistory Court 9171/9, fols 5v–6.

[16] TNA, E 210/10318; Special Collections [hereafter SC] 2/175/85.

[17] Arthur Twisden Playne, *A History of the Parishes of Minchinhampton and Avening* (Gloucester, 1915), p. 70.

[18] George James Aungier, *The History and Antiquities of Syon Monastery, the Parish of Isleworth and the Chapelry of Hounslow* (London, 1840), p. 450.

[19] Cecil T. Davis, *The Monumental Brasses of Gloucestershire* (London, 1899; repr. Bath, 1969), pp. 110–13; William Lack, H. Martin Stuchfield, and Philip Whittemore, *The Monumental Brasses of Gloucestershire* (London, 2005), pp. 282–6. For a more detailed discussion of this brass, see Laura Richmond, 'A Survey of Monumental Brasses of Late Medieval Vowesses', *Transactions of the Monumental Brass Society*, 23 (2022).

[20] TNA, E 211/375.

[21] Aungier, *The History and Antiquities of Syon Monastery*, p. 444.

of Alice's wealth unaccounted for. Some of the properties may have been sold, or the estate may have been broken up. Either way, Alice is listed, at the front of Syon's 'Martyrlogue', in an obituary list of 'Special Benefactors and Friends' for whom the sisters at Syon prayed.[22] Alice's relationship with Syon was different to her relationships with Dartford and Halliwell: at Syon she seems to have been primarily a benefactor, rather than an active member of the convent community.

Vowesses at Syon Abbey

Alice Hampton was not the only vowess to inhabit convent space on a longer-term basis, nor was she the only vowess associated with Syon. Unfortunately, descriptions of the specific arrangements for vowesses living at Syon have not survived as they have for Alice Hampton's accommodation at the communities of Dartford and Halliwell, but nonetheless there were vowesses resident at Syon in the decades before its dissolution. Alice's situation at Dartford and Halliwell can help us to speculate in an informed way about what the arrangements might have been.

Vowesses living at the community of Syon in the early decades of the sixteenth century included Joan Marler, the widow of wealthy Coventry grocer and alderman Richard Marler and a great-niece of William Smyth († 1514), bishop of Lincoln.[23] She also had close family links with Syon: her sister, Agnes Smythe, was a professed sister there, and her son from a previous marriage, John Wood, is named in her will as 'father of Syon'.[24] Joan appears in the Syon cellaress's foreign accounts, accompanied by a few of her own servants and at one point her chaplain, from around the time that she was widowed in 1526 until her own death c. 1530. She paid sums for boarding, bread, and ale throughout this time.[25] Evidently her familial ties to Syon were instrumental in her decision to live there as a widow and vowess.

Similarly, vowess Susan Kyngeston appears in the foreign accounts of the cellaress of Syon from her husband's death in 1514 until 1537, two years before the community was dissolved, though the varying amounts entered for board suggest

[22] Exeter University Library, MS. 95, Canon Fletcher's MS, vol. 10. I am indebted to Dr Virginia Bainbridge, who kindly provided a copy of this.
[23] Edward Alexander Jones and Alexandra Walsham (eds), *Syon Abbey and Its Books: Reading, Writing and Religion, c. 1400–1700* (Woodbridge, 2010), p. 90. See also Margaret Bowker, 'Smith [Smyth], William (d. 1514)', *ODNB*, January 2008.
[24] TNA, Prerogative Court of Canterbury [hereafter PCC], unregistered will of Joan Marler.
[25] Mary C. Erler, 'Syon's "Special Benefactors and Friends"', pp. 217–20; TNA, SC 6/HENVIII/2243–47, 2278.

her presence there was not continuous.[26] Like Alice Hampton, she clearly had her own designated space, perhaps purpose-built, on site: a post-Dissolution inventory mentions 'Lady Kyngeston's chamber'.[27] Like Joan Marler, she seems to have been drawn to residence at Syon by extensive family connections.[28] Two of Susan's sisters were also women religious at Syon, Dorothy Coddington and Eleanor Fettyplace, as were two of her nieces, Susan Purefoy and Elizabeth Yate.

In addition to this, her grandmother, Alice Beselles, was living at Syon as a vowess around the same time, first named in the foreign accounts of the cellaress as 'My lady kyngeston her Grauntdame' in 1520–21. She returned in 1523–24 and continued in the accounts for two subsequent years, attended by two servants in a similar manner to Joan Marler.[29] Alice Beselles was also one of seven women whom the catalogue of Syon brothers' library records as book donors: she gave a folio edition of Italian lexicographer Ambrogio Calepino's Latin dictionary.[30] This would have been an expensive gift and corroborates Felicity Riddy's description of a 'textual community [...] inhabited above all by recluses, nuns, vowesses'.[31] This 'feminine cultural space' was embodied in the literal space of the community of Syon, which, like Dartford, was known as a centre of learning and spirituality. By living within that space, a vowess could plant herself firmly in this religious and intellectual community of women.

For vowesses resident at convents, physical and spiritual kinship often overlapped and intertwined. Susan Kyngeston's stepbrother, Thomas Elyot, translated a sermon by St Cyprian, the *Swete and Deuoute Sermon of Mortalitie,* and addressed Susan directly in the prologue:

> which I haue dedicate and sente vnto you for a token: that ye shall perceyue, that I doo not forgeat you: and that I doo vnfaynedly loue you, not onelye for our allyaunce, but also moche more for your perseuerance in vertu & warkes

---

[26] Syon cellaress's foreign accounts: TNA, SC 6/Hen VIII/2214-5 (1514-15) through to SC 6/Hen VIII/2244-5 (1536-7) show yearly board amounts for Susan ranging from 55s (1536-7) to £33 18s 3d. She occasionally paid for others' board.

[27] TNA, LR 1/112.

[28] Mary C. Erler, *Women, Reading, and Piety in Late Medieval England* (Cambridge, 2002), pp. 85–99.

[29] Erler, *Women, Reading and Piety*, pp. 86-7, 179; TNA, SC 6/HENVIII/2224 (1520-1); SC 6/HENVIII/2227 and 2228 (1523-4); SC 6/HENVIII/2229 and 2230 (1524-25); SC 6/HENVIII/2231 and 2232 (1525-6).

[30] Erler, *Women, Reading and Piety*, p. 87.

[31] Felicity Riddy, '"Women Talking About the Things of God": A Late Medieval Sub-Culture', in Carol M. Meale (ed.), *Women and Literature in Britain, 1150-1500* (Cambridge, 1993), pp. 104-27, at pp. 111-12.

of true faith, praieng you to communicate it with our two susters religiouse
Dorothe & Alianour, and to ioyne in your praiers to god for me.[32]

Thomas and Susan's 'allyaunce' of blood was strengthened and enhanced by the
'perseuerance in vertu & warkes of true faith' that they shared, admired in one
another, and encouraged one another to pursue. The same is likely to have been
true of the bond between Susan and her 'susters religiouse', who were both literally
her sisters and were women religious, as well as with her nieces and grandmother.
One can easily imagine a similar sentiment shared by Joan Marler and her sister
and son. This double kinship of blood and spiritual affinity would have naturally
ensured a bond of strong affection and a desire for physical closeness, rendering
the presence of vowesses in and around religious houses entirely natural. In the
case of Alice Hampton, who had no family left by the time she arrived at Halliwell,
her will creates a strong impression that the convent became her family.

As the community at Syon was a Bridgettine foundation – indeed, the women
religious there were the only Bridgettine sisters in England – the influence of
St Bridget of Sweden would have been extremely pervasive. St Bridget was a
fourteenth-century matron-mystic who embraced her religious calling after the
death of her husband. As such, she was naturally a source of inspiration and
validation for vowesses, most of whom had done likewise. It was also for Syon
that St Catherine of Siena's *Dialogue of Divine Revelation* was translated into
English as *The Orchard of Syon*: as a lay member of the Dominican Order, St
Catherine was also a quasi-religious figure with whom vowesses would have felt
an affinity. Vowed women may have gravitated towards Syon because its culture
was informed by the strong influence of saints like Bridget and Catherine, as well
as because of kinship ties.

Vowesses at Norfolk Convents

While the community of Syon housed several vowesses in the Late Middle
Ages, this was not unique, nor was it exclusive to larger, wealthier convents. In
contrast with Syon, the community at Blackborough, founded in the western
fens of Norfolk *c.* 1150, was small and relatively poor. The source material for
Blackborough is far sparser than for Syon and the surviving cartulary contains
no records dating from after the fourteenth century. Yet it seems to have been
a prominent centre of women's spirituality in the county, with several vowesses
resident in the mid to late fifteenth century.[33] Most of what is known about this

---

[32]   Erler, *Women, Reading and Piety*, p. 87.
[33]   London, BL, MS Egerton 3137.

community at Blackborough derives from women's wills and consists of only a few lines here and there, but examples of the accommodation of vowesses at Dartford, Halliwell, and Syon can be employed tentatively to fill in some of the gaps left by a lack of surviving records.

The wills in question can be rather ambiguous, as testators frequently identified a woman as living at Blackborough and implied that she was not a sister there but did not specify that she had taken a vow of chastity in a widow's benediction ceremony. For example, the will of Joan Bardolf, dated 1447, includes Joan Bumpstead 'comoranti in abathia de Blakborough' ['remaining in the abbey of Blackborough']; the will of Katherine Brasyer (1457) leaves 6s 8d to the mother superior at Blackborough, followed by 'lego domina Alicia Branger ib(ide)m expectans iis' ['Item: I bequeath to Dame Alice Branger remaining there 2s']; and the will of Katherine Goodrede (1464) includes a 'vidua domina Emma' ['widow Dame Emma'] amongst her Blackborough bequests.[34] Marilyn Oliva cites these three as examples of vowesses and yet there is no conclusive indication that they had taken vows.[35] This is not an oversight: although it is frequently difficult to ascertain which widows had taken vows of chastity, boundaries were particularly blurred in the Norwich diocese, noted for its 'informality and ambiguity' of women's religious life.[36]

These wills reveal a close-knit community of Norfolk vowesses and possible vowesses. Katherine Goodrede also bequeathed to Alice Branger a black dress and £13 6s 8d. Joan Bardolf was described in her own will as 'in mea pura viduetato' ['in my pure widowhood'], which was often, but not always, a phrase used by vowesses. Katherine Brasyer was described in the same way in her own will, and her bequest to Alice Branger was followed by one to 'domina Emma ibem inter moniales comoranti' ['dame Emma remaining there amongst the sisters']. This is presumably the same Dame Emma as mentioned by Katherine Goodrede. One wonders why Emma's surname was never used and it is particularly telling that she is described as 'amongst' the sisters: this is not suggestive of a precinctual residence, and she may even have lived in the cloister, or perhaps at its threshold like Alice Hampton at the community at Halliwell.

Katherine Brasyer's will also names another likely vowess, Margaret Purdans, as well as a Roger Bumpstead and Margaret, the daughter of Robert Aleyn.[37] The 1497 will of Katherine Kerre, widow of Robert Aleyn, leaves 6s 8d, a kirtle, and a

[34] Norfolk Record Office, Consistory Court of Norwich [hereafter NCC], Wlybey, fols 130–2; Brosyerd, fols 58–9; Brosyerd, fols 329–30. Abbreviations have been expanded.

[35] Oliva, *FMN*, p. 48.

[36] Roberta Gilchrist and Marilyn Oliva, *Religious Women in Medieval East Anglia* (Norwich, 1993), p. 21.

[37] For more about Margaret Purdans, an extremely devout Norwich widow (†1483), see

smock to 'Margaret, vowess there' – 'there' being the community of Crabhouse, about ten miles from Blackborough.[38] Katherine Kerre made a number of further individual bequests to sisters at the community of Carrow, where another Norfolk vowess, Dorothy Curson, held the farm of the anchorhouse in 1520.[39] These religious women, some of whom had taken a formal vow of chastity while others may have not, congregated in and around convent spaces. These places provided a sanctioned venue for these like-minded, quasi-religious women in Norfolk to meet, to connect with one another, and to 'talk about the things of God'.[40] Again, other examples at the communities at Dartford, Halliwell, and Syon suggest that vowess status may have been instrumental in enabling women to enter and inhabit that space 'amongst the sisters'.

Testamentary Evidence

Ties of family and friendship between vowesses and convent sisters were also evidently significant to the ways in which vowesses were embraced by these communities. Many wives of the gentry and upper merchant classes would have had sisters, daughters, aunts, nieces, and friends from childhood who had entered convents, and so it is perhaps not surprising that some of these wives, when widowed, took vows which enabled them to be more easily reunited. Far from sisters having renounced these relationships when they took vows and entered the convent, some were able to welcome in their married relatives and friends after they were widowed and vowed.

Vowesses' wills reveal these close relationships. In 1504 Maud Baker of Bristol bequeathed to her daughter, who was to be professed at the community of Shaftesbury, plate, linen, a feather bed, 10 marks in money, and two sets of rosary beads, to be delivered to her at the day of her profession, and a further 10 marks to pay for her dinner on that day.[41] Maud was evidently keen to participate in her daughter's profession at the prestigious house, even posthumously, and the will suggests that it was a source of personal and family pride. The same year, Alice

---

Carole Hill, *Women and Religion in Late Medieval Norwich* (Woodbridge, 2010): references to Margaret are scattered throughout the book.

[38] Norfolk Record Office, NCC Multon, fols. 90–1.

[39] Mary C. Erler, 'English Vowed Women at the End of the Middle Ages', *Medieval Studies*, 57 (1995), 155–203, at p. 201; Norfolk Record Office, Hare 5955 227xl, cited in Erler, 'English Vowed Women', p. 201. A stained-glass window, depicting Dorothy Curson, nee Clopton, widowed in 1512, survives at Long Melford in Suffolk. The two are likely to be the same woman.

[40] Riddy, 'Women Talking About the Things of God', pp. 104–27.

[41] Clive Burgess (ed.), *The Pre-Reformation Records of All Saints' Church, Bristol*, vol. 3 (Bristol, 2004), pp. 33–9.

Chester of London bequeathed 3s 4d to the abbess of the London Minoresses, before adding: 'To the lady Riche there 3s 4d. To the lady Hobbis 3s 4d. And to every lady there professed 12d. And unto every novice 8d'.[42] These bequests combine the usual giving to a monastic house in return for services of remembrance with specific gifts to family or friends within the convent.

Alice Chester went on to bequeath to 'mistress Staland', named as a sister at St Katherine's, her black hood of profession. This hood, by which Alice became a vowess in her episcopal ceremony, would have been a treasured possession and a gift of great sentimental value. Similarly, the will of Margaret Browne of Stamford, Lincolnshire, dated 1489, reads: 'I geve to the supprioresse of the Nonnes my mantell that I was professed in'.[43] The decision to leave these profession garments to other women religious demonstrates the closeness between the vocations of sister and vowess, and the bond that these women often shared. These close friendships may have predated professions and been maintained, like family links, or equally they may have originated at the convent after women were vowed.

One of the difficulties of reading wills in this way is that it is never clear what has been left out. People planned for their death and commemoration in various ways and usually through several channels, such as chantry foundations, specifications for a tomb or monumental brass, and other documents in which their property was distributed among friends and family as well as for charitable purposes. This means that relationships that are only briefly mentioned or hinted at in wills were sometimes much closer than the will reveals and that wills are therefore often rather ambiguous. For example, vowess Jane Chamberlayne of London requested burial at the community at Kilburn in her will of 1492, and the mother superior at Kilburn acted as a witness when the will was drawn up.[44] This could simply have been Jane making provision for her burial and commemoration after her death or it might have been indicative of a much closer relationship. In the rare cases where community records survive for this period, such as at Syon, these illuminate the presence of vowesses in convents, a presence that would never have been detected from wills alone. The scant surviving evidence nonetheless suggests that many vowesses were more involved at women's religious communities than is now apparent.

[42] TNA, PCC Prob. 11/14/662.
[43] TNA, PCC Prob. 11/8/525.
[44] TNA, PCC Prob. 11/9/115.

Conclusion

Vowesses embodied liminal space between the world and the cloister, spiritually, psychologically, and sometimes physically as well. To be a vowess was to be simultaneously lay and religious, the widow of a man and the bride of Christ, continuing one life while embarking upon another. Each vowed woman navigated this dual life in her own unique way. Therefore, individual vowesses had different relationships with women's monastic houses: some were closer than others, and some were so close that they were fully integrated into these communities. To date, there has been no comprehensive prosopographical analysis of women who were vowed in this way; the variety among their lives has doubtless contributed to the vocation's more recent obscurity and subsequent neglect. Further prosopographical and biographical research in this area would yield other examples of vowesses' being present in and around convent sites, as well as other ways in which vowesses interacted with convent sisters and women religious more generally.

Not only did vowesses sometimes live on convent sites, the arrangements by which they were accommodated there were clearly quite separate to those for the laity who purchased the right to live on monastic property or in precinctual residences during old age as a sort of retirement package.[45] Eileen Power noted that widows as secular borders were discouraged by the Church because 'it brought too much of the world within cloister walls'.[46] Widows who had taken a vow of chastity, especially if they had done so in an episcopal ceremony, would have been less objectionable company for the enclosed sisters of the convent.

Women like Alice Hampton and Susan Kyngeston, having taken one of the three monastic vows, held a privileged position of access to and intimacy with the inner cloister. They were members of the convent community, benefiting from its facilities, liturgy, and spiritual and intellectual opportunities. Ties of family and friendship strengthened the connection between vowesses and convents in many cases, and some vowesses opted to live within religious houses to be close to professed kin. Alice Hampton's case illustrates in detail how a vowess could arrange a home for herself at a convent, where she held a position of influence and maintained her freedom while participating in the social and devotional life of the community. Although we lack such detail for other vowesses, those resident at Syon and Blackborough appear to have been accommodated similarly, and women's wills offer tantalising hints of vowesses' participation in women's monastic life throughout medieval England.

---

[45]   Nicole R. Rice, *Lay Piety and Religious Discipline in Middle English Literature* (Cambridge, 2008), p. 7.

[46]   Power, *Nunneries*, pp. 38–9.

CHAPTER 6

Authority and Agency:
Women as Heads of Religious Houses

ELIZABETH A. LEHFELDT

THE image of medieval women religious that commonly springs to mind are those living in isolated circumstances, dedicating most of their time to prayerful pursuits. But the tendency to analyse medieval women religious through the lens of enclosed and contemplative monasticism risks obscuring significant evidence of their authority and agency. In order to analyse how medieval religious women exercised power and what enabled them to do so, this chapter focuses on the office of the head of house, or superior, other convent officers, and the resulting collective influence of the diverse, women's monastic household. It draws primarily, but not exclusively, on evidence from Spanish, French, and English communities.

Women as Monastic Superiors and Other Convent Personnel

Within the convent the head of the community was the supreme authority in all things spiritual and temporal as they pertained to the maintenance of her community. Although most religious rules (for example, Benedictine, Augustinian) were written with monasteries for men in mind, these were applied to women's religious communities with the understanding that the expectations for men applied equally to heads of women's communities.[1] As the head of the foundation, all the other sisters owed the superior their obedience.

At the same time, the superior was one of the convent's own and, typically, it selected its monastic officers. Although dispensations could be granted, to be

---

[1] Felice Lifshitz, 'Is Mother Superior? Towards a History of Feminine *Amtscharisma*', in John Carmi Parsons and Bonnie Wheeler (eds), *Medieval Mothering* (New York, 1996), pp. 117–38, at p. 11. Curiously, around 1517 Richard Fox, bishop of Winchester, recast the entire Benedictine Rule in the feminine. He said that he had done this at the request of the religious women in his care in his diocese. See Elizabeth A. Lehfeldt, 'Gender, the State, and Episcopal Authority: Hernando de Talavera and Richard Fox on Female Monastic Reform', *JMModS*, 42:3 (Fall, 2012), 615–34.

eligible for the office of head of house, a sister had to be of legitimate birth and twenty-one years or older (some religious orders specified a higher age).[2] Before they could proceed with the internal election process, however, they had to seek permission from the crown (if a royal convent) or the convent's patron and/or the bishop to hold the election. Houses that were exempt from episcopal oversight typically designated another local ecclesiastic man to certify the installation of a new head. The Cistercian convent of Marham, for example, relied upon a local representative of the Cistercian General Chapter to oversee the selection of a new superior.[3] Once the sisters received assent, they proceeded with an election. The Fourth Lateran Council of 1215 had regularised the procedures for choosing a new head of house, to bring them in line with how abbots and bishops were selected.[4]

Perhaps because the position was freighted with such power and significance, the election of a new head of house could be a contentious affair. In 1262 the community of Notre-Dame-aux-Nonnais, France, was unable to settle upon a candidate and ended up appealing their case all the way to the papacy.[5] The contested election of the head of house of Godstow, England, in the late fifteenth century ended up involving two factions of the community, the bishop, the king, and the pope.[6] As the contest at Godstow indicates, it was not unheard of for ecclesiastical men or lay patrons to intervene in these decisions and exert their influence. In the early fourteenth century the archbishop of York refused to accept the resignation of the outgoing superior of Esholt until he had the opportunity to discuss her decision with the convent's patron.[7]

It is worth considering how particular women rose to the attention of their peers as candidates for the headship of a religious house. In some instances, we can trace their ascendancy through the ranks of other offices within the convent.[8] In cases where convents had strong ties to royalty, nobility, or locally prominent families, it was not unusual for these laypeople to push candidates from their families. Jennifer Edwards has documented instances of this at the abbey of Sainte-Croix in Poitiers, France.[9] Being able to claim a relative who held the position of

[2]   Oliva, *FMN*, p. 77.
[3]   Oliva, *FMN*, p. 77.
[4]   Johnson, *Equal*, p. 169. There were three ways to proceed: unanimous vote, deploying 'scrutators' to question those eligible to vote and then putting forward a candidate, and compromise whereby the candidate who received a majority vote was chosen.
[5]   Johnson, *Equal*, pp. 171–2.
[6]   Spear, *Leadership*, p. 21. See also Laura Mellinger, 'Politics in the Convent: The Election of a Fifteenth-Century Abbess', *CH*, 63:4 (Dec. 1994), 529–40.
[7]   Spear, *Leadership*, p. 21.
[8]   Diana K. Coldicott, *Hampshire Nunneries* (Chichester, 1989), p. 47; Oliva, *FMN*, p. 108.
[9]   Jennifer C. Edwards, *Superior Women: Medieval Female Authority in Poitiers' Abbey of Sainte-Croix* (Oxford, 2019), pp. 229–67.

superior of a religious community was a sign of prestige and created proximity to the sacred. The social background of the head of the community varied widely, by geography and chronology. The evidence from France in the Central Middle Ages points towards heads from elite, if not noble, pedigree. The evidence from late medieval England, on the other hand, suggests that even in prominent convents, superiors were not always from the highest ranks of society, indicating that meritocracy might often prevail in the choice.[10] There is also evidence that women rose through the ranks of other convent offices as a path towards becoming the head of house, what Marilyn Oliva has called a 'monastic career ladder'.[11] At Carrow Abbey, England, the woman who served as cellarer for forty-five years was eventually chosen as head in 1485.[12]

The rituals and ceremony surrounding her installation underscored the solemnity of the superior's selection and her authority. She was typically consecrated by the local bishop and might receive the symbol of office, the crozier. The installation ceremony was like that of an abbot and outlined in pontificals.[13] She pledged her obedience to her ecclesiastical superiors and the sisters of the community in turn swore their obedience to her. Her oath could include other features such as promising to administer the estate of the convent responsibly and even taking an oath of loyalty to the king.[14] Once chosen and installed, a new head was the supreme authority within the convent and the community owed her its unswerving obedience.

The scope of the superior's responsibilities, as well as her relative claustration, made it necessary for her to rely on other individuals. Within the convent other convent officers and the broader community assisted her. To begin with, the community assumed a collective responsibility for certain decisions. The choir sisters met with regularity in their chapter meetings. In this setting they made communal decisions about spiritual and financial matters. The extent to which these meetings complemented or overrode the superior's authority varied by place and time.[15]

Heads of women's religious communities were also assisted in their work by a host of convent officers. While titles and duties varied, these might include a

---

[10] Spear, *Leadership*, pp. 30–9.
[11] Oliva, *FMN*, p. 110.
[12] Oliva, *FMN*, p. 108.
[13] Coldicott, *Hampshire Nunneries*, p. 46.
[14] Coldicott, *Hampshire Nunneries*, p. 46.
[15] Penelope Johnson has argued that the absolute authority of the superior eroded from the eleventh to the thirteenth century in France, with the chapter assuming an autonomous role: Johnson, *Equal*, pp. 191–2. The extent to which this can be discerned in other countries and beyond the thirteenth century awaits further investigation.

cellarer, treasurer, chamberer, sacrist, almoner, and infirmarer.[16] These women assisted the head of the community in the management of the convent affairs and were accountable to her for their actions and performance. Even smaller houses usually had at least three or four convent officers in addition to the superior, which bespeaks the complexity of managing the community's affairs. Selection for these positions seems to have been based on seniority and experience.

Depending upon the size and extent of the convent's patrimony, the head of the community was also assisted in her work by lay personnel, many of whom were men. Particularly, if the convent administered a large patrimony, it was necessary to employ others. Bailiffs and stewards could be responsible for collecting rents and other dues. They might also oversee the work done on the convent's estate. These individuals were typically laymen, but they could be clerical. Some French Cistercian communities often relied upon the lay brothers or *conversi* for help in administering their estates.[17]

Heads of women's religious houses also relied on lawyers and other legal professionals to represent their interests in the courts. Elizabeth Makowski argued persuasively that this made them no different from their male counterparts – secular and religious – who also relied on the services of these individuals, especially as legal matters became increasingly complicated and the role of lawyers increasingly professionalised. Superiors of women's communities might have been unable to appear in court, but they were quite capable of directing their legal affairs and making hiring decisions about who would represent them.[18]

Convents used the services of men for other mundane tasks, like creating official documents to certify gifts, property exchanges, and other transactions. Significantly, as Anne Lester notes, such services could expand the 'patronage network' of communities.[19] Overall, the evidence points to close and cooperative interaction between heads of houses and male lay personnel; as Penny S. Gold observes 'what is most striking is the extent to which these men acted in conjunction with' the head of the community and other convent officers.[20] Yet at the same time it is critical to note that these men were in the employ of the convent, and the

---

[16] Oliva, *FMN*, p. 84.
[17] Lester, *Creating Cistercian Nuns*, p. 175.
[18] Elizabeth Makowski, *English Nuns and the Law in the Middle Ages: Cloistered Nuns and Their Lawyers, 1293–1540* (Woodbridge, 2011).
[19] Lester, *Creating Cistercian Nuns*, pp. 179–80.
[20] Penny S. Gold, 'The Charters of Le Ronceray d'Angers: Male/Female Interaction in Monastic Business', in Joel T. Rosenthal (ed.), *Medieval Women and the Sources of Medieval History* (Athens, 1990), pp. 122–32, at p. 125.

mother superior retained 'administrative control'.[21] She remained in charge. She chose these individuals, oversaw their work, and could suspend them, if necessary.

Supporting and Managing the Community

Spiritually, the superior was supposed to set an example and provide guidance. The *Form of Life of Saint Clare*, for example, instructed her 'to preside over the others more by her virtues and holy behavior than by her office [...] so that, moved by her example, the sisters may obey her more out of love than out of fear'.[22] Ideally, hers was also a nurturing guidance. The bishop of Lincoln instructed the head of the religious community of Nun Cotham, England, to behave like a mother would with her children.[23] But she was also entrusted with ensuring the enforcement of the rule and constitutions that governed the convent with the expectation that she would 'admonish and visit her sisters, and humbly and charitably correct them'.[24] The head also ensured that the community followed the rhythm of the daily office and lived in accordance with the required standards for poverty and chastity. This might include enforcing collective dining in the refectory, limiting personal material possessions, and enforcing the physical boundaries of enclosure. The absence of strong spiritual guidance could result in problems. At the convent of Bondeville, France, in the thirteenth century, Archbishop Eudes Rigaud of Rouen noted that the superior's temperament and inability to enforce discipline led to the community to disrespect her.[25]

A question that hangs over the historiography of the superior's spiritual responsibilities is whether they were empowered to hear the confessions of the sisters in their care. There is evidence to suggest that in the early medieval period, when the practice of penance was less regulated, they were able to do this.[26] The *Regula ad virgines* (512) of Caesarius of Arles makes provision for the superior or a senior sister to hear the confessions of the community. It was previously assumed that the practice waned in later centuries. The work of Katie Bugyis, however, has demonstrated persuasively that English Benedictine heads of

---

[21] Gold, 'The Charters of Le Ronceray d'Angers', p. 126.

[22] Regis J. Armstrong (ed. and trans.), *The Lady: Clare of Assisi: Early Documents* (New York, 2006), p. 114. For further discussion on superiors and good guidance, see below, Delman, pp. 124–5.

[23] John A. Nichols, 'The Internal Organisation of English Cistercian Nunneries', *Citeaux*, 30 (1979), 23–40, at p. 27.

[24] Armstrong, *The Lady*, p. 122.

[25] Johnson, *Equal*, p. 131.

[26] Maria Teresa Guerra Medici, 'For a History of Women's Monastic Institutions. The Abbess: Role, Functions and Administration', *Bulletin of Medieval Canon Law*, 23 (1999), 35–65, at pp. 50–1.

women's communities performed this sacerdotal role as late as the eleventh and twelfth centuries. Some of these superiors even extended their penitential reach to include 'male and female penitents' who visited the convent.[27] The superiors of Santa Maria de las Huelgas in Burgos, Spain, also claimed these powers. Ultimately, Innocent III condemned the practice, saying that it was an overreach of a superior's authority, and the Fourth Lateran Council of 1215 sought to regulate the practice of penance within women religious communities even more broadly.[28] Bugyis's work, nonetheless, demonstrates that we need to be attentive to different sorts of sources as we assess the extent to which heads of women's communities performed these functions.

In some instances, the superior of a particularly powerful house had jurisdiction over a congregation or federation of communities of women religious, providing a unique opportunity to assert her authority. The superior of Santa María de las Huelgas in Burgos, for example, oversaw a group of Cistercian convents in Spain. She presided over an annual chapter meeting and attended the election of the heads of these communities.[29] Jurisdictions could include male clerics. The head of house of Sainte-Croix in Poitiers had oversight of the canons in the convent's sister church of Sainte-Radegonde. This authority did not go uncontested by the canons, as Jennifer Edwards has documented, but ultimately the superiors prevailed.[30]

Further, the Middle Ages saw the creation of new religious orders that included double houses of men and women monastics where the head of the women's religious community was the superior of both.[31] Robert Arbrissel's foundation at Fontevraud put women in charge of the community. When King Henry V founded Syon Abbey, England, in 1415, the mother superior was made the head of a community that included sisters, priests, and lay brothers. Though the structure of the community included a male confessor-general, her ultimate authority was clear; she was 'hede and lady of the monastery' and he was to 'feythfully assiste her'.[32] It is important to acknowledge the counter-model of the Gilbertines. This twelfth-century order created by Gilbert of Sempringham crafted communities of religious men and women but put authority in the hands of a male leader. While double monasteries were unusual across the religious landscape of medieval

[27]   Katie A.-M. Bugyis, 'The Practice of Penance in Communities of Benedictine Women Religious in Central Medieval England', *Speculum*, 92: 1 (2017), 36–84, at p. 82.

[28]   Guerra Medici, 'The Abbess', pp. 51–2.

[29]   Lehfeldt, *Golden Age Spain*, p. 113.

[30]   Edwards, *Superior Women*, pp. 201–28.

[31]   See above, Sykes, p. 44.

[32]   From the *Syon Additions for the Sisters*, quoted in Warren, *Spiritual Economies*, p. 11.

Europe, the existence of ones where a woman was the head of the community speaks to a certain level of comfort with women's authority and administration.[33]

The head of the community was also responsible for its material and financial well-being.[34] In smaller convents that did not have extensive patronage or large estates this could be a daunting task. Superiors and convent officers needed to be careful and shrewd administrators of scarce resources. In wealthy convents this management could involve different challenges, including the administration of a sizeable patrimony. Convents owned arable land and urban property. They received revenues and payments in cash and in kind from a variety of sources that could include alms, rents, annuities, and other financial mechanisms. The head of the house also had responsibility for any of the convent's financial obligations and expenses – the cost of goods, upkeep of the physical estate, wages, etc. She might manage these things directly and personally or be assisted in these tasks by bailiffs or stewards.

In the case of large patrimonies, it was not unusual for the superior to act and be recognised as a seigniorial lord. This came with its own rights and responsibilities. The case of Santa María de las Huelgas, provides an illustrative example. As lord of the nearby town of Zaratán the head of house was entitled to the collection of various dues and taxes. She also had the power to name municipal officials such as the magistrate and a clerk. She could appoint appellate justices for cases outside royal jurisdiction and could collect the accompanying fees from these cases. She oversaw the benefices of the local church, but she also had responsibilities such as raising soldiers from the town at the request of the king.[35] Notably, those who were subject to a superior with seigniorial authority did not tend to couch their objections to this power in gendered terms.[36] Heads of women's religious communities who acted as lords might be disliked, but objections to their administration were typically rooted in more generic concerns about abuses of power.

We can document not just the theory but also the practice of this financial management through sources such as account books. Medieval heads of houses

[33] Katharine Sykes's important work on the English Gilbertine communities nuances the concept of a double monastery in productive ways. Though Gilbert of Sempringham founded what were at their heart communities of women, he also embedded canons within these communities to provide direction and governance, thereby creating a different kind of religious community composed of both men and women. See '"Canonici Albi et Moniales": Perceptions of the Twelfth-Century Double House', *JEH*, 60:2 (2009): 233–45; ibid, 'Rewriting the Rules: Gender, Bodies, and Monastic Legislation in the Twelfth and Thirteenth Centuries', *JMMS*, 9 (2020), 107–31.

[34] For further discussion on this topic, see below, Seale, p. 176.

[35] Lehfeldt, *Golden Age Spain*, p. 60.

[36] Lehfeldt, *Golden Age Spain*, p. 65.

in England, for example, probably kept what were referred to as 'lady books', a rough record of sums and goods received, and items leaving the convent. These might eventually be compiled along with other running account books (like the one kept by a cellaress) into a cleaned-up 'final' account book that recorded all the revenues and expenses of an individual house. Marilyn Oliva persuasively argued that some superiors had both the literacy and numeracy skills to compile these.[37] In other instances male personnel may have created them. These records tracked accountability internally, but also provided the records that could be presented to outside visitors, like bishops, when a convent's affairs were examined.

The historiography of women's religious communities has long wrestled with the question of whether or not superiors – and the officers who assisted them – managed their estates poorly or well.[38] This debate can be traced to Eileen Power's contention that 'it cannot be doubted that the nuns themselves, by bad management contributed largely to their own misfortunes'.[39] Power goes so far as to suggest that these failings were due to wilfulness but 'far more often due to sheer incompetence'.[40] While not accepting this characterisation without scrutiny, some scholars have pointed to various types of evidence as proof of bad management. What does it mean, for example, if the convent required various male personnel – stewards, for example – to administer their estates? Rather than a sign of weakness, the employment of such individuals was entirely customary among powerful secular landholders who needed assistance with complex patrimonies. As John Nichols notes, 'the male presence in a nunnery can indicate a busy, intense institutional life which functioned efficiently under the guidance and leadership of the mother superior'.[41] Evidence from convents reveals that heads of communities in other countries and regions relied on the services of such male personnel.[42] More importantly, these men reported to the head of house, not the other way around.

If anything, the evidence of strong, or at least competent, management by medieval women superiors is clearer and much more common. To begin with, many superiors and convent officers would have come from backgrounds where they had received the literacy and numeracy skills that prepared them for estate

[37] Marilyn Oliva, 'Rendering Accounts: The Pragmatic Literacy of Nuns in Late Medieval England', in *Nuns' Literacies: Hull*, pp. 51–68.
[38] For further discussion on this topic, see below, Seale, pp. 176–8.
[39] Power, *Nunneries*, p. 203.
[40] Power, *Nunneries*, p. 203.
[41] Nichols, 'English Cistercian Nunneries', p. 37.
[42] Kimm Perkins-Curran, '"*Quhat say ye now, my lady priores? How have ye usit your office, can ye ges?*" Politics, Power and Realities of the Office of a Prioress in her Community in Late Medieval Scotland', in Burton and Stöber, *Monasteries and Society*, pp. 124–41 at pp. 129–31.

management. Others probably learned on the job, trained by their peers in the community. Male contemporaries expressed faith in the abilities of these same women when they asked them to witness wills and act as executors.[43]

In instances where we can evaluate the acumen of the heads of women's communities against the challenges of the local and regional economy, these women managed their estates well. Anne Lester finds that Cistercian convents in the Champagne region of France in the thirteenth century fared well and correlates at least some of this success to 'the administrative abilities of particularly competent abbesses'.[44] Nancy Warren has argued that between 1350 and 1450 English communities, like secular landowners of the period, adapted to the constraints of the economy and responded by shifting from direct exploitation of their land to leasing it instead.[45] Similar examples are found amongst women religious communities in late medieval Scotland where superiors leased conventual land to meet a variety of financial and administrative needs.[46] Heads of women's communities and their convent officers were clearly shrewd enough to respond to changes in the economy in order to maximise profit. Marilyn Oliva has analysed the accounts of the convents of Norwich in the late medieval period when the combined pressures of rising wages and declining rents and grain prices put significant financial pressure on estate owners. Overall, she found that only three of the eleven convents under examination were in debt in the 1530s; all the others seemed to be doing reasonably well.[47] Some of the success of these communities may have been due to the financial creativity of their heads. Oliva has also documented how various superiors in the diocese of Norwich developed funding strategies; one, for example, got approval to offer indulgences to those who donated to convent building projects.[48]

It is striking that heads of women's communities were praised for their administrative talents. The 1257 eulogy for Euphemia, mother superior of Wherwell, England, notes her piety, as would be expected, but spends even more time praising her care of the estate, which included having decrepit buildings torn down and replaced with new ones, in addition to other improvements to the physical estate, and having a new mill built.[49] Similarly, the spiritual biography of Juana de la Cruz, mother superior of the convent of Cubas, Spain, in the late fifteenth century, extolled her administrative acumen. Her biographer noted that when she

[43] Spear, *Leadership*, p. 94.
[44] Lester, *Creating Cistercian Nuns*, p. 173.
[45] Warren, *Spiritual Economies*, p. 59.
[46] Perkins-Curran, 'Office of a Prioress', pp. 126–9.
[47] Oliva, *FMN*, pp. 90–9.
[48] Oliva, *FMN*, p. 80.
[49] Spear, *Leadership*, pp. 217–18 (a translated text of the eulogy).

first became superior the convent had only a tiny bit of land from which they garnered a 'pittance' (*miseria*) of wheat and collected only the tiniest bit of rent, nine
reales. She had, however, contributed to the convent's growth not just in virtue
and sanctity but also in its 'buildings, and the other things necessary for human
life'. In all, what her biographer noted as her *buen govierno* (good management)
allowed her to add a dormitory to the convent and dramatically increase the
community's income from rents.[50] It is striking that both women were praised for
their agency – taking charge of the material circumstances of their convents and
making specific changes.[51]

Yet this is not to say that all heads of religious houses were great managers.
In the late fourteenth century, the sisters of the community of Arden, England,
complained about their superior's administration during an episcopal visitation.
They accused her of spending the convent's revenues as she pleased, not providing
candles for the altar in the church, and mishandling the corrodies that brought
much-needed provisions for the community. All the sisters questioned asserted
that the house had been in good financial standing when the mother superior took
office but that, during her administration, the buildings had become dilapidated,
she had sold many items without consulting the community, and that, despite
these sales and the receipt of other income, the convent was extremely indebted.[52]

The available sources complicate our ability to assess good or failing management. Account books only tell part of the story. Though they were often
reviewed by superiors these documents themselves would not necessarily reveal
mistakes. Often visitation records and similar documents are simply silent on
the matter of the superior's management of finances and the physical estate,
but poor management is specifically called out. This might mean that we can
read silence on the question of financial management as evidence of competent administration. Whether acting independently or with the counsel of the

---

[50] Antonio Daza, *Historia, vida, y milagros extasis, y revelaciones de la bienaventurada
Virgen Sor Iuana de la Cruz* (Madrid, 1614), 36v–37r.

[51] Anne Lester also makes a significant point by identifying the importance of the survival
of kept records as evidence of sound administration in convents: 'Charters were the very
fabric of a monastic institution's identity', and she sees their survival in large numbers as
evidence of safeguarding the community and its possessions. Lester, *Creating Cistercian
Nuns*, p. 177.

[52] See Janet Burton's discussion of some of the problems that faced small and poor female
houses, in 'Cloistered Women and Male Authority: Power and Authority in Yorkshire
Nunneries in the Late Middle Ages', in Michael Prestwich, Richard Britnell, and Robin
Frame (eds), *Thirteenth Century England*, X (Woodbridge, 2005), pp. 155–65, at p. 164;
British History Online, Victoria County History, 'Yorkshire, A History of the County
of York: Volume 3, Houses of Benedictine Nuns: Priory of Arden' (1974), http://www.
british-history.ac.uk/vch/yorks/vol3/pp112-116 [accessed 28 March 2021].

community, and whether assisted by male personnel or not, heads of women's religious communities had significant administrative and financial responsibilities. And although there were certainly instances where they made poor decisions or managed things irresponsibly, the overwhelming weight of the evidence suggests that heads of religious houses possessed competent and sometimes even outstanding management skills.

It is worth noting that the heads of other types of women's religious communities had similar administrative responsibilities. The medieval period witnessed the flourishing communities of lay religious women who took informal vows – such as beguines and canonesses – and these communities were led by a mistress who, like their counterparts in other monastic institutions, oversaw the spiritual and temporal well-being of the women and institutions in their care. They managed finances, provided spiritual direction, and performed a host of tasks that would have been very similar to that of a monastic superior.[53]

Wielding and Negotiating Power

The power that accrued to the mother superior because of all these spiritual, financial, and institutional responsibilities created for her a role apart from the rest of the community. The administration of their estates fashioned a different set of expectations for heads of women's communities, and they often left the bounds of the cloister to represent the community's interests. Medieval French superiors often travelled to the bishop's palace to negotiate business and pursue litigation.[54] The head of the community of St-Jacques de Vitry, France, appeared before the Parliament of Paris in 1290.[55] Elivira de Rojas, head of Santa María de las Huelgas, mentioned above, visited Zaratán in 1426 to inspect and enforce the boundaries of the town that she believed were being threatened by outsiders.[56] In the mid-twelfth century Agnes of Barbezieux, head of the community of Notre-Dame, Saintes, France, elected to join the convent's provost out in the fields personally to see to the enforcement of a boundary line that separated the convent's property from that of a local lord. A dispute erupted and Agnes was knocked to the ground by the steward of a local lord.[57] The ability to move freely to manage affairs by the women superiors occurred against the backdrop of increasing pressures to enclose religious women more strictly, which reached a certain apogee

[53] Cf. Tanya Stabler Miller, *The Beguines of Medieval Paris: Gender, Patronage, and Spiritual Authority* (Philadelphia, 2014).
[54] Johnson, *Equal*, p. 153.
[55] Lester, *Creating Cistercian Nuns*, p. 171.
[56] Lehfeldt, *Golden Age Spain*, p. 60.
[57] Johnson, *Equal*, p. 168.

with the papal directive *Periculoso* in 1298. Technically, this legislation required strict active claustration of all solemnly professed religious women. That heads of women's communities continued to leave the cloister speaks to the limitation of this directive and its enforcement during the Late Middle Ages.[58]

Financially, it was not unusual in wealthier foundations for the mother superior to control a semi-private income and living quarters. At St Mary Winchester, England, for example, the head of the community had a separate lodging with its own kitchen and other domestic spaces. The superior of Romsey, England, had her own lodging and a separate chapel.[59] These separate households existed at least in part to serve particular needs, such as entertaining guests and providing hospitality. Guests could include kings and bishops; the convent of Wherwell hosted Kings John, Henry III, and Edward I.[60]

The heads of women's religious houses might also deploy these resources for the benefit of the entire convent community. June Meacham's analysis of Katharina von Hoya's creation of a chapel dedicated to St Anne at her convent of Wienhausen, Germany, demonstrates the ways in which she used her resources to contribute to the spiritual life of her community.[61] Deploying her income in these ways enriched the devotional life of the convent while also providing an outlet for her agency as she chose and directed the ways in which the chapel would be decorated and adorned.

For an institution founded on a communal ethos, the separation and privilege of the mother superior could create tensions within the community. Separate revenue streams and privileges could also be a source of friction within the convent community as the superior might enjoy better food and material conditions as a consequence. The heads of Romsey and Wherwell, for example, were chastised by the archbishop for eating after compline.[62] In the fifteenth century, the superior of Nun Monkton, England, was called out in the episcopal registers for entertaining and drinking with a local clerk.[63]

The head of the community could also abuse her power and privilege – an exercise of agency that might affect the convent negatively. One of a superior's most important possessions, for example, was the convent seal. It was first and foremost one of the most significant signs of her office. The seal was used, as all medieval

---

[58] There is a lively secondary literature on the extent to which *Periculoso* changed women's monastic practice; the best starting place for this is Makowski, *Periculoso*.

[59] Coldicott, *Hampshire Nunneries*, p. 46.

[60] Coldicott, *Hampshire Nunneries*, p. 90.

[61] June L. Mecham, *Sacred Communities, Shared Devotions: Gender, Material Culture, and Monasticism in Late Medieval Germany* (Turnhout, 2014), pp. 127–58.

[62] Coldicott, *Hampshire Nunneries*, p. 75.

[63] Spear, *Leadership*, pp. 129–30.

seals were, to certify documents and transactions. Keeping the convent seal under her control was a sign of stable and responsible management. An uncontrolled seal signalled trouble. In the late fourteenth century the head of the community of Arden confessed that she had had the common seal in her private keeping and used it to enter obligations on behalf of the house without the community's approval. Her fellow sisters told an even direr story and accused her of having pawned the seal.[64] At the community of Ankerwyke, England, in the fifteenth century, one of the sisters issued a scathing condemnation of the superior that linked her private keeping of the seal to other failings, including that: 'the house was ruinous, that a barn had been lately burnt down, and that the prioress kept the convent seal in her own hands and disposed of the goods of the priory without consulting her sisters at all'.[65]

Comments such as these would have been reported to ecclesiastical visitors. While she was the immediate authority for the sisters in her care, the head of a community nonetheless reported to the male ecclesiastical hierarchy that governed the wider church. Typically, this hierarchy began with the bishop. We have already seen that bishops had to approve a superior's election. In addition, the superior was subject to the bishop's oversight and discipline. It was customary for a bishop routinely to visit all the monastic foundations in his diocese. He or his chosen representative would gather information, review the community's accounts and records, and conduct interviews with individual sisters. Based on his assessment of the situation he would issue a series of injunctions detailing any changes that needed to be made or problems that needed to be addressed. These ranged over a variety of issues, including the observance of the Divine Office, the material conditions of the physical buildings, compliance with enclosure, and the availability of adequate resources. And the head of the house was key to the enforcement of these expectations. Where we can examine a series of such visitations and measure whether or not the convents complied with the injunctions, the evidence is mixed. In some instances, convents followed the suggestions, whereas in others the offending behaviour continued. Archbishop Eudes Rigaud of Rouen visited the convent of Saint-Saens, France, numerous times in the mid-thirteenth century, censuring the community in no uncertain terms. Yet their poor behaviour, which included violations of chastity and financial mismanagement, continued despite his exhortations.[66]

---

[64] See above n. 52.

[65] British History Online, Victoria County History, 'Buckinghamshire, A History of the County of Buckingham: Volume 1, House of Benedictine Nuns, The priory of Ankerwick' (1905), http://www.british-history.ac.uk/vch/bucks/vol1/pp355-357 [accessed 28 March 2021].

[66] Johnson, *Equal*, pp. 71–2.

Bishops could also be allies. Heads of women's communities could appeal to them to alleviate financial distress or smooth contention within the convent. Bishops could forgive debts and exempt convents from the payment of tithes.[67] They could also remove a disobedient sister and relocate her to a different house.[68] It was also potentially beneficial for bishops to have the support of mother superiors and their convents. A bishop's power was measured, at least in part, by the number of institutions that were loyal to him. These ties could be cemented through gifts. For example, Bishop Edyngton (d. 1366) of Winchester bequeathed a ruby ring to the mother superior of Romsey.[69] A particularly dramatic example of the potential power of such ties between the bishop and the head of a house was the ceremony observed in Florence, Italy, where the installation and consecration rites surrounding a new bishop included his fictive 'marriage' to the superior of one of the city's most powerful convents, S. Pier Maggiore, a long-standing Benedictine community.[70]

Some convents were exempt from episcopal oversight, and instead answered directly to Rome.[71] This undoubtedly fostered a degree of autonomy for these communities, perhaps enhancing their mother superior's power. It was also, not surprisingly, a source of friction between these convents and the local bishops, who sought to bring them under their control. Penelope Johnson recounts the case of the community of Montivilliers in Normandy that had enjoyed various exemptions from episcopal oversight for almost two centuries. The rise of the powerful Archbishop Eudes Rigaud, however, created a standoff in which he eventually prevailed and began to intervene more directly in the convent's affairs.[72]

Sometimes other male ecclesiastics visited the convents to review their affairs. These interactions often went beyond the routine visits of bishops. Typically, such visitations included an effort to introduce reforms into the convent. As a consequence, these were often contentious encounters, and the heads of houses were at the forefront of them. Even well-intentioned reform could be disruptive to the convent community. In 1494, for example, the superior of Santa Clara of Barcelona, Spain, confronted the demands of two male ecclesiastical visitors, neither of whom were of the communities' religious order. The visitors had mandated various alterations, such as covering, blocking, or putting grilles on windows to attempt to limit the visual access the convent had to the outside

[67]   Spear, *Leadership*, pp. 49–50; Oliva, *FMN*, p. 167.
[68]   Spear, *Leadership*, p. 50.
[69]   Oliva, *FMN*, p. 167.
[70]   Sharon Strocchia, 'When the Bishop Married the Abbess: Masculinity and Power in Florentine Episcopal Entry Rites, 1300–1600', *GH*, 19:2 (Aug. 2007), 346–68.
[71]   Guerra Medici, 'The Abbess', pp. 55–6.
[72]   Johnson, *Equal*, pp. 81–5.

world. They also instructed the sisters to limit the access that secular women had to the cloister. The superior asserted her agency, speaking for them, and refused to comply, arguing that these changes were not consistent with the 'use, practice, and custom' of the convent.[73] Tensions continued to escalate and ultimately the visitors removed her from office and forced the community to elect a new leader. If anything, removing the head of the community underscored the significance of her agency and authority. Successful reform required amenable or at least compliant leadership.

As evidenced through interactions with a host of individuals both inside and outside the cloister, the heads of women's religious communities had enormous responsibilities. And they were expected to perform these indefinitely. Technically, the heads of houses were appointed for life. Sometimes, however, age or infirmity prompted them to step down.[74] Typically, these 'retired' superiors received a pension from the convent, which may or may not have been tied to the properties and income that they oversaw during their time in office.[75]

Heads of religious houses were sometimes removed for other reasons such as old age, ill health, or inappropriate behaviour. For example, the mother superior of Ronceray, France, decided to step down and according to the cartulary she did so 'not for moral fault but because of ill health and old age'.[76] The fifteenth-century superior of Romsey Abbey, Elizabeth Brooke, confessed to adultery and inappropriate relationships with at least two male stewards of the convent.[77] Despite various attempts to remove her from office she remained in that position until her death in 1502. Overall, however, as in other matters of administration, the majority of heads of religious houses served without drama or disruption and would have done so until death removed them from office. Their passing, then, would have prompted the selection process outlined at the beginning of this chapter.

Conclusion

In conclusion, the scholarship of the last twenty or so years has clearly established that the women who directed religious communities had extensive authority and agency. What awaits further investigation is a sense of how that power waxed and waned over time. Jennifer Edwards's work on the superiors of Sainte-Croix is an excellent example of a longitudinal study, but we need more of these to

---

[73] Real Biblioteca del Monasterio de San Lorenzo de El Escorial, *Acta visitationis*, Ms. V.II. 14, 7.

[74] Johnson, *Equal*, p. 172.

[75] Johnson, *Equal*, p. 172.

[76] Johnson, *Equal*, p. 172.

[77] Coldicott, *Hampshire Nunneries*, p. 103.

understand better the forces that shaped the exercise of this kind of authority by women religious.[78] Another priority is to explore fully the gendered dimensions of this exercise of power. To what extent did their status as women shape the contours of how the heads of female houses wielded their authority and influence? Here, comparative studies that included the roles and responsibilities of heads of male houses could be instructive.

The perspective presented in this chapter is a relative snapshot of the authority and agency of medieval heads of women's religious communities and prompts important conclusions and highlights areas for further research. First, the office provided meaningful opportunities for women to assume leadership roles. From directing the liturgical obligations of their communities to managing complex patrimonies, these women were entrusted with – and mostly successfully executed – significant responsibilities. Many of these challenged existing gender norms. That mother superiors heard confessions, left the cloister, and supervised male clerics, should force a reconsideration of the extent to which these norms were observed and enforced. Second, they performed these tasks and managed these communities with the assistance of a diverse range of individuals. Other conventual officers, bishops, secular lawyers, bailiffs, and stewards, all had a hand in supporting and aiding the head of the community in her work. Therefore, her responsibilities allowed her to create strong networks and communities. Finally, all this evidence should encourage a further consideration of the convent as a site of significant power and influence for medieval women. The women's monastic household provided striking opportunities for women both individually and collectively to exercise influence and assert their agency in ways that were not readily available to most women in secular society.

[78] Edwards, *Superior Women.*

CHAPTER 7

Women Religious, Secular Households: The Outside World and Crossing Boundaries in the Later Middle Ages

RACHEL M. DELMAN

I N her *Treasure of the City of Ladies* (1405), Christine de Pizan writes that 'in all things the wise princess will keep her women in order just as the good and prudent abbess does her convent so that bad reports about [her household] may not circulate in the town, in distant regions or anywhere else'.[1] In calling for the princess to configure her authority in a manner akin to the monastic superior, de Pizan promotes monastic governance as an exemplary model of household leadership, thus encouraging a culture of cross-over and exchange between the court and monastic community. De Pizan's statement is also revealing of the wider implications that women's governance of both lay and monastic households could have on the reputation of their establishments in the world beyond their walls.

This chapter takes Christine de Pizan's advice to the model princess as a starting point for an exploration of points of overlap, contact, and exchange between the monastic superior and her lay counterpart, specifically in relation to domestic governance. Through a comparative analysis of the monastic superior and noblewomen who headed their own households in the Later Middle Ages, this chapter argues that there were shared cultural expectations in the ways in which women were required to articulate their domestic authority in monastic and secular contexts. Of particular interest for the discussion is the lay head of household's exercise of spiritual leadership. As the figureheads of religious communities, the monastic superior and her lay counterpart held responsibility for the spiritual well-being of their households. Outward displays of piety, discipline, and chastity were thus essential ingredients of women's exemplary household governance across lay and monastic settings. This chapter elucidates the ways in which the lay head of household articulated her devout domestic governance through her role models, her daily

---

[1] Christine de Pizan, *The Treasure of the City of Ladies*, Sarah Lawson (ed.) (London, 2003), p. 52.

routines, her interactions with servants, her learned piety, and through the medium of gift exchange. It argues that monastic and lay women's performances of spiritual leadership in the monastic establishment and the noble household not only closely resembled, but also actively shaped, one another.

Connections Between Lay and Religious Women

Despite their physical enclosure, women religious had a considerable impact on the world outside the cloister in both tangible and symbolic ways.[2] Recent scholarship has elucidated the existence of a rich culture of contact and exchange between lay and religious women across Europe. Laywomen frequently encountered women's monastic communities in their capacity as the mothers, sisters, aunts, cousins, and friends of women religious, as pilgrims and visitors to monastic churches, as temporary and long-term residents in monastic precincts, as patrons and founders of monastic communities, and as members of wide-reaching spiritual and cultural networks. Scholars have also drawn attention to the considerable overlap in the environment of monastic and lay households, emphasising the domesticity of sacred space and the sacrality of the lay home.[3]

The material culture of women's monastic communities also shared much in common with the houses inhabited by non-professed women from the upper echelons of medieval society. Roberta Gilchrist and Marilyn Oliva have shown that the physical space of East Anglian women's monastic communities closely resembled the houses of the gentry, the social group from which most religious women in that region were drawn.[4] Laywomen's bequests to religious houses, as recorded in their wills, have shed further light on the ways in which moveable goods from secular households shaped the material environment of women's monastic communities.[5] Despite the relative scarcity of wills by women religious, a handful of surviving wills and deathbed dispositions from Scotland show

---

[2]   The works in this area are far too numerous to list here. See, for example, Sharon T. Strocchia, *Nuns and Nunneries in Renaissance Florence* (Baltimore, 2009), esp. chapter 2; Burton and Stöber, *Monasteries and Society*; Kimm Curran, 'Religious Women and their Communities in Late Medieval Scotland' (Unpublished Ph.D. dissertation, University of Glasgow, 2005); Lehfeldt, *Golden Age Spain*; Hall, *Women and the Church*.

[3]   For a discussion of scholarship in this area see, Jennifer Kolpacoff Deane, 'Medieval Domestic Devotion', *History Compass*, 11:1 (2013), 65–76.

[4]   Roberta Gilchrist and Marilyn Oliva, *Religious Women in Medieval East Anglia*, Studies in East Anglian History, 1 (Norwich, 1993), pp. 19–20; Marilyn Oliva, 'Nuns at Home: The Domesticity of Sacred Space', in Maryanne Kowaleski and P. J. P. Goldberg (eds), *Medieval Domesticity: Home, Housing and Household in Medieval England* (Cambridge, 2008), pp. 145–61.

[5]   Spear, *Leadership*, pp. 159–64.

that such relationships could be reciprocal, with monastic superiors bequeathing money, domestic goods, and clothing to surviving (female) relatives and kin.[6] Books also held an important place in the cultivation and maintenance of female alliances across lay and monastic boundaries: literary scholars have drawn attention to the dense and overlapping networks that were cultivated and celebrated through women's exchanges of manuscripts and printed texts.[7]

Some of Europe's wealthiest and most influential noblewomen were present in women's monastic houses as patrons, visitors, or temporary inhabitants. In Italy, many noblewomen, including members of the renowned d'Este family, 'colonized religious communities as extensions of aristocratic living spaces, taking shelter there from unhappy or abusive marriages and transforming these institutions into focal points of artistic and political patronage'.[8] The practice was by no means exclusive to Italy. In the Low Countries, Isabel of Portugal, duchess of Burgundy (†1471) founded several women's religious communities.[9] In 1459, the infanta Beatriz of Portugal (†1506) founded a community of Poor Clares along with her husband, which stood next to couple's residence at Beja. The foundation later held an important place in the cultivation of Beatriz's reputation as a pious widow.[10] In late medieval England, many high-status women, particularly vowesses and pious widows, took up residence at the Bridgettine community of Syon in Middlesex, including Margaret, duchess of Clarence (†1439), the sister-in-law of the founder

[6]   See, for example, Alexander Montgomerie, 'The Deathbed Dispositions of Elizabeth Prioress of the Abbey of Haddington, 1563', *TELAS*, 6 (Haddington, 1955), 1–5; Will of Dame Eufame Leslie, Prioress of Elcho, 1570, National Records of Scotland (hereafter NRS), Edinburgh Commissary Court, CC8/8/2; Will of Elizabeth Home, Prioress of St Bathans, 1628, NRS, Edinburgh Commissary Court, CC8/8/54. I am grateful to Kimm Curran for these references.

[7]   The works in this area are far too numerous to list in full here. See, for example, Mary C. Erler, *Women, Reading, and Piety in Late Medieval England* (Cambridge, 2002), esp. chapters 1 and 4; Felicity Riddy, '"Women Talking about the Things of God": A Late Medieval Sub-Culture', in Carol M. Meale (ed.), *Women and Literature in Britain, 1150–1500* (Cambridge, 1996), pp. 104–27; Anne Marie Dutton, 'Women's Use of Religious Literature in Late Medieval England' (Unpublished D.Phil. dissertation, University of York, 1995). For further discussion on the topic of women's exchanges of books and book ownership see Charles, pp. 152–65.

[8]   Strocchia, *Nuns and Nunneries*, p. 9.

[9]   Francesca Canadé Sautman, 'Building Women's Community through Patronage in Late Fifteenth-Century Burgundy', *The Scholar & Feminist Online*, 15:1 (2018), online at http://sfonline.barnard.edu/women-and-community-in-early-modern-europe-approaches-and-perspectives/building-womens-community-through-patronage-in-late-fifteenth-century-burgundy/ [accessed 23 Aug. 2021].

[10] Nicole Martins, 'Convento da Conceição de Beja: Arquitectura num período de transição (séculos XV e XVI)' (Unpublished Ph.D. dissertation, University of Lisbon, 2019).

of the house, Henry V. Margaret resided in the abbey precinct and obtained special dispensation from the pope, so that members of the house could leave the cloister to visit her.[11] In the sixteenth century, Margaret Beaufort (†1509) had a room reserved for her use at Syon, where she was a regular visitor. Margaret in turn hosted women religious at her principal residence at Collyweston in Northamptonshire, including a sister from the monastic house of Minster in Sheppey (Kent), who stayed at Collyweston for two weeks preceding the enclosure of her sister, an anchoress, at Stamford in Lincolnshire.[12]

The presence of laywomen in monastic houses was mutually beneficial. Just as women religious gained the financial and material support from wealthy patrons, so laywomen accrued spiritual privileges and knowledge from their visits. The example of Lady Margaret Hungerford (†1478), who temporarily resided at Syon after falling out of favour with Edward IV, is illustrative of the ways a residential stay in a monastic community could profoundly affect the spiritual direction of women's lives. Following her departure from Syon, Margaret continued to demonstrate a keen interest in the Marian piety of the women religious at Syon, adopting elements of the Syon office of compline in her mortuary chapel and requesting the burial of her heart at the house.[13] Domestic governance was thus one of a great many ways in which the lives of laywomen and women religious, both implicitly and explicitly, intersected and shaped one another.

Models of Domestic Leadership in Monastic and Lay Households

The leadership of the woman monastic superior was characterised, somewhat paradoxically, by a dual model of authority and submission: on the one hand she was expected to exercise sovereignty over her household, while on the other she needed to demonstrate servanthood and humility as a 'loving mother' to her flock.[14] Such qualities also define idealised portrayals of noblewomen's governance in secular households. Posthumous recollections of Margaret Beaufort's household as penned by her confessor, Bishop Fisher, and her cupbearer, Henry

[11] George R. Keiser, 'Patronage and Piety in Fifteenth-Century England: Margaret, Duchess of Clarence, Symon Wynter and Beinecke MS 317', *The Yale University Library Gazette*, 60:1/2 (October 1985), 32–46, at 37.

[12] See Rachel M Delman, 'The Vowesses, the Anchoresses, and the Aldermen's Wives: Lady Margaret Beaufort and the Devout Society of Late Medieval Stamford', *Urban History*, 48:1 (2021), 1–17.

[13] Malcolm Hicks, 'The Piety of Margaret Lady Hungerford', *JEH*, 38:1 (1987), 19–38.

[14] Spear, *Leadership*, pp. 8–10; see, above, Lehfeldt, p. 105.

Parker, Lord Morley, praised the countess's motherly and kingly qualities in equal measure.[15] When presiding over her feasts, Margaret is said to have been served like a king, yet she is also represented as a caring mother to the members of her household and to the students of her educational foundations.

The interplay of sovereignty and maternal humility to which the exemplary head of household aspired found no better expression than in the figure of the Virgin Mary, whom the monastic superior and her lay counterpart represented and embodied within the home. In the Bridgettine Rule, the monastic superior is described as occupying the position of the Virgin, placing her on an equal level with the bishop, a representative of Christ.[16] At Syon the Virgin Mary was 'absolutely paramount to the […] practice of [the sisters'] faith. The whole of their liturgy was dedicated to praising Mary, and the whole of their earthly existence was meant to model hers'.[17] Assisting the Syon sisters in their imitation of Mary was a devotional treatise known as *The Myroure of Oure Ladye*, which set out the daily offices used by the women religious and emphasised their privileged relationship to the mother of God. According to *The Myroure*, 'Mary was the most pious and blessed human being, man or woman, to have ever lived. Her obedience to God was so perfect that she was set above all other people as the mother of Christ'.[18] Didactic texts aimed at a secular readership similarly promoted the Virgin as the ideal lay head of household. Christine de Pizan, for example, conceptualised her City of Ladies as a household headed by the Virgin Mary, while in the fifteenth-century dream vision, the *Assembly of Ladies*, the author imagined the head of the establishment, Lady Loyalty, as a Marian-like figure presiding over a secular household entirely populated by women.

Representing the Virgin
in Monastic and Lay Households

The lay head of household's proximity to the Virgin was expressed through the material, spatial, and social environment of the home. Images of the Virgin, as displayed on devotional objects and furnishings and large-scale imagery such

---

[15] John Fisher, 'Mornynge Remembraunce had at the moneth mynde of the Noble Prynces Margarete Countesse of Richmonde and Darbye, emprynted by Wynkyn de Worde', in J. E. B. Mayor (ed.), *The English Works of John Fisher, p. I.*, EETS, ES, 27 (1876), pp. 289–310; Henry Parker, Lord Morley, 'The Account of the Miracles of the Sacrament', in M. Axton and J. P. Carley (eds), *Triumphs of English: Henry Parker, Lord Morley, Translator to the Tudor Court* (London, 2000), pp. 253–70.

[16] Warren, *Spiritual Economies*, p. 23.

[17] Laura Roberts, 'The Spiritual Singularity of Syon Abbey and its Sisters', *Ezra's Archives*, 5:1 (Spring, 2015), 65–83, at 78.

[18] Roberts, 'The Spiritual Singularity of Syon Abbey', 78.

as wall paintings and tapestries, provided focal points for devotion as well as a didactic model for the head of household to follow. The choir of the church of the women's monastic house of Minster in Sheppey contained alabaster and painted images of the Virgin. At Syon, a woodcut of the Coronation of the Virgin Mary accompanied the Masses of the women religious.[19]

Mary's relationship to the Trinity was a central and recurrent theme in the devotional practices of the women religious at Syon and was very likely a repeated motif in the iconography of the house. Surviving contemporary images of the Coronation of the Virgin depict Mary in the act of being crowned by the Trinity. In the fifteenth-century wall painting cycle of Pickering parish church in north Yorkshire, the Virgin is shown haloed and crowned, with God the father and Christ on her right and left respectively. The holy spirit, which takes the form of a dove, hovers above her in a downwards-facing position, its beak touching the tip of her crown. In *The Myroure*, Mary's womb is described as containing 'the union of the Trinity in all ways undeparted'.[20] For the Syon sisters, it was Mary's maternal body that made her powerful, because it was through that very body that man was able to obtain salvation.

The dedication shown by the Syon sisters to the Virgin Mary and the Trinity appears to have informed the devotional and visual culture of the residences of laywomen with close links to the house. The Virgin's relationship to the Trinity was certainly a recurrent theme in Margaret Hungerford's devotions following her departure from Syon. Both Margaret Beaufort and Margaret Pole also commissioned large-scale wall paintings of the Virgin Mary and the Trinity in the household chapels of their principal residences at Collyweston and Warblington (Hants), respectively.[21] Margaret Pole spent several years living at Syon with her daughter Ursula before she established her chief seat at Warblington, during which time Margaret Beaufort regularly visited the pair and supported their upkeep.[22] The emphasis on Mary as Queen of Heaven and as the linchpin of the holy family in such imagery fittingly encapsulated the carefully balanced interplay of sovereignty and motherhood that was central to the expression of domestic authority by both religious and lay women. The display of such images within the

[19]   GMC, p. 141.

[20]   Thomas Gascoigne, *The Myroure of oure Ladye: Containing a Devotional Treatise on Divine Service, with a translation of the offices used by the sisters of the Bridgettine monastery of Sion, at Isleworth, during the fifteenth and sixteenth centuries*, ed. J. H. Blount, EETS, ES, 19 (London, 1998).

[21]   St John's College, Cambridge (hereafter SJC) D91.14, p. 109 (Beaufort); TNA, State Papers 1/139, ff. 72–84 (Pole).

[22]   Sue Powell, 'Margaret Pole and Syon Abbey', *Historical Research*, 78 (2005), 563–7.

home both reflected and authorised the women's gendered performances of their authority in the monastic establishment and the great household.

Marian imagery also popularly featured on the seals of women's monastic houses and those of noblewomen. As objects used to authenticate documents, seals not only represented, but also actualised, the authority of the bearer and their establishment.[23] The choice of iconography was therefore an important means through which women could project specific messages regarding their power and status to others. In a sample of 136 seals from women's monastic houses identified by Roberta Gilchrist, over half depict Marian iconography, including the crowned Virgin in a standing posture, the Coronation of the Virgin and the standing Virgin holding the Christ Child.[24] Surviving seals from the larger monastic houses of Syon and Lacock in Wiltshire both feature the enthroned Virgin and Child. Beyond the cloister, Margaret Hungerford adopted Marian imagery on her seal. Margaret's seal shows a seated female figure with an open book on her knees. Foliage surrounds the figure, and above her head is a label bearing Margaret's personal motto, 'myne trouth assured'. Margaret's seal deploys what Carol Meale describes as imagery reminiscent of the Virgin of Humility, in which Mary occupies a *hortus conclusus*.[25] The seal of Matilda of Wallingford, which dates to the first half of the twelfth century, shows a standing female figure holding a lily, a widely recognised symbol of the Virgin Mary. The surviving seals of Scottish noblewomen also frequently recall the iconography of the Marian *hortus conclusus* through horticultural imagery, to communicate messages of lineage, fertility, and motherhood.[26]

Women were cognisant of the ways in which the imagery displayed on their seals could communicate highly stylised messages regarding their power and status.[27] The use of Marian and Marian-inspired imagery on seal matrices was by no means exclusive to women, yet in the case of the monastic superior and the lay head of household, they took on a heightened gendered significance, with representations of the Virgin visually resembling the women's own appearance and dress. Depictions of Mary on women's seals thus encouraged the onlooker visually to assimilate image and reality, and, by association, the authority of earthly and holy women.

---

[23] Rachel Meredith Davis, 'Material Evidence? Re-approaching Elite Women's Seals and Charters in Late Medieval Scotland', *PSAS*, 150 (2021), 301–26, at 303.

[24] *GMC*, pp. 143–4.

[25] Carol M. Meale, '"…alle the bokes that I haue of latyn, englisch, and frensch": Laywomen and their Books in Late Medieval England', in Carol M. Meale (ed.), *Women and Literature in Britain, 1150–1500* (Cambridge, 1996), pp. 128–58. An image of Margaret Hungerford's seal is reproduced at p. 129.

[26] Davis, 'Material Evidence?'.

[27] Davis, 'Material Evidence?', 309.

Ordering the Body and Household

For clerical writers and moralists, control over the household was achieved through control over the body.[28] It was by ordering her body and soul to God that the monastic superior and her lay counterpart were able to achieve the self-discipline praised by late medieval moralists, and their likeness to the mother of God. The exercise of bodily order and discipline found expression through the lay head of household's daily routines. Regardless of the order to which they belonged, most women's monastic houses followed the Benedictine Rule, which prescribed a fixed daily routine of praying the canonical hours, private meditation, mealtimes, recreation, reading, and sleep.[29] Accounts of the daily routines of Cecily Neville, duchess of York (†1495), and Margaret Beaufort suggest striking similarities in the daily activities practised by the monastic superior and high-status widows.[30] Both Cecily and Margaret are said to have arisen early to pray before going to breakfast, Cecily at 7:00am to hear low mass in her chamber, and Margaret between 6:00 and 7:00am to say the matins of the day in her chapel with one of her chaplains. According to her cupbearer, Henry Parker, Lord Morley, Margaret Beaufort continually engaged in masses until 11:00am. Following morning prayers, Cecily and Margaret went to dinner, during which time they were read to. In the afternoon the two women conducted business before attending evensong. Cecily is said to have then spent time in the company of her gentlewomen before saying nightly prayers in her closet. While in reality the women's daily routines were likely more varied than the prescriptive accounts suggest, they are nevertheless revealing of the ideal to which the women aspired, and of the close links between piety, idealised femininity, and exemplary household governance that permeated both lay and monastic settings.

The strict discipline exercised by the head of household extended to the members of her establishment, who formed an extension of her person. While noble houses differed from women's monastic communities in that they were

---

[28]   Sarah Salih, 'At Home Out of the House', in Caroline Dinshaw and David Wallace (eds), *The Cambridge Companion to Medieval Women's Writing* (Cambridge, 2003), pp. 124–40; Kim M. Phillips, 'Bodily Walls, Windows, and Doors: The Politics of Gesture in Late Fifteenth-Century English Books for Women', in J. Wogan-Browne, R. Voaden, A. Diamond et al. (eds), *Medieval Women: Texts and Contexts in Late Medieval Britain: Essays for Felicity Riddy* (Turnhout, 2000), pp. 185–98.

[29]   Oliva, *FMN*, p. 33.

[30]   Fisher, 'Mornynge Remembraunce'; Henry Parker, Lord Morley, 'The Account of the Miracles of the Sacrament'; 'A compendious recitation compiled of the order, rules and construction of the house of the right excellent Princess Cecily, late mother unto the right noble Prince, King Edward IV', in J. Nichols (ed.), *A Collection of Ordinances and Regulations for the Government of the Royal Household* (London, 1790), pp. 37–9.

predominantly staffed by men, the ladies and gentlewomen around the women's household made for a distinctive gendered grouping. The number of ladies and gentlewomen in the lady's service was not dissimilar to the average number of women religious found in most women's monastic communities, which rarely totalled more than twenty, except in the largest religious houses.[31] Margaret Pole had eleven women in her service, only one less than the 'usual twelve [women religious] under a prioress'.[32] Like their religious sisters, the women in lay households were bound together through ties of chastity, piety, and service. Of the good princess, de Pizan wrote that she 'will take upon herself the responsibility for the care of her women servants and companions, who she will ensure are all good and chaste, for she will not want any other sort of person around her […] The lady who is chaste will want all her women to be so too, on pain of being banished from her company'.[33]

Control over body was inextricably bound to control over space. Through the books she read, the head of the household was repeatedly exposed to images and words that couched her spiritual and sexual conduct in spatial terms. Conduct books written for lay audiences promoted the home as the place where the good, virtuous, and chaste woman could be found, in contrast to the harlot who freely roamed the streets.[34] The pages of women's prayer books were filled with images of the Virgin and women saints in enclosed, domestic spaces, such as chambers and walled gardens, which both contain and symbolise their chaste bodies. In women's monastic houses, *virgo inter virgines* imagery, in which the Virgin and Christ child are shown surrounded by virgin martyrs within an enclosed garden, enjoyed especial popularity, offering an idealised model of gendered kinship for the monastic superior and her sisters to identify with and emulate.[35]

The architecture of women's monastic communities and great households emphasised feminine chastity through enclosure and tightly regulated access. The close ties between women's bodies, chastity, and purity meant that enclosure was more frequently and more strictly applied to women monastics than their male counterparts.[36] The dormitories of the women religious occupied the innermost or 'deepest' space of the monastic complex, whereas in men's houses the deepest space was usually reserved for the chapter house.[37] The positioning of women's

[31] Erler, *Reading and Piety*, p. 30.
[32] Cited in Erler, *Reading and Piety*, p. 30.
[33] De Pizan, *Treasure*, p. 51.
[34] Salih, 'At Home', p. 125.
[35] Stanley E. Weed, 'My Sister, Bride, and Mother: Aspects of Female Piety in Some Images of the *Virgo inter Virgines*', *Magistra*, 4:1 (1998), 3–26.
[36] Lehfeldt, *Golden Age Spain*, p. 62.
[37] GMC, p. 164.

living quarters in the innermost reaches of the complex also occurred in noble residences where women's apartments and gardens occupied the inner sanctum of the household. Walled gardens were positioned so that they could only be viewed from the women's quarters, ensuring their control and regulation by the female gaze.[38]

The architecture of the monastic and noble houses facilitated surveillance in other ways. At Lacock, a strategically placed squint in the cloister enabled the monastic superior to observe the movements of the women religious while remaining hidden from view herself.[39] According to the Rule of St Francis, the monastic superior was supposed to occupy the common dormitory at night, to keep a watchful eye on the women in her charge. Similar expectations were placed on the secular head of household, who, according to Christine de Pizan, was to be 'in overall charge' and 'always watchful'.[40] In noble houses, the chambers of female servants were commonly located directly next to the mistress's bedchamber again to symbolise and protect (at least in theory) the chastity of the occupants.

Learned Piety

Learned piety was central to women's self-fashioning as exemplary household figureheads. A portrait of Avelina Cowdrey, who was the monastic superior of Wherwell (Hampshire) between 1518 and 1529, shows her dressed in her habit with a small bound book in her hands. A full body sculptural representation of Margaret Beaufort on the gatehouse of her foundation of Christ's College in Cambridge similarly depicts the countess in widows' weeds with a book clasped in both her hands (see Fig. 7.1).

The monastic superior and her lay counterpart exercised devout piety through their textual practices. Many larger monastic houses, such as Syon and Barking, had their own libraries, the contents of which was curated by the monastic superior. In 1404, eleven years after she had been elected monastic superior of Barking, Sibilla de Felton commissioned a manuscript containing the ordinal and customary of the house, which provided directions for the liturgy and the prescribed actions to be carried out during it. The ordinal and customary were intended for Sibilla's personal use, and for those who succeeded her as monastic superior. The Barking customary was also personalised in accordance with Sibilla's own interests, including detailed and specific directions on the annual distribution of books

---

[38]   Roberta Gilchrist, *Gender and Archaeology: Contesting the Past* (London, 1999), p. 137.
[39]   Spear, *Leadership*, p. 39.
[40]   De Pizan, *Treasure*, p. 146.

Fig. 7.1. Margaret Beaufort, as represented on the gatehouse of Christ's College, Cambridge. Image copyright of author, R. Delman.

among the women religious at Barking.[41] At Collyweston, Margaret Beaufort had a library containing numerous devotional works. The countess also translated the fourth book of Thomas à Kempis's *De Imitatione Christi* and the *Speculum Aureum Anime Peccatoris* from Latin into English. Both texts were intended to aid meditative devotion and could be found in monastic libraries. In the library catalogue of Syon, the *imitatio* is described as *solitariis et contemplativis utilis* ['useful for those of a solitary and contemplative nature'].[42] In 1502, the monastic superior of Syon, Elizabeth Gibbs, owned an English translation of the *imitatio*, which was inscribed with her name.[43]

The monastic superior and noble female head of household were assisted in their devotions by a chaplain or confessor. Rather than supplanting the authority of the women, the men aided them in their spiritual growth. In the sister-books, which were authored by Dutch and German women religious and were intended for communal use within the monastic community, obedience to a confessor or spiritual director shifted the locus of spiritual authority from the confessor to the penitent and the women religious.[44] Confessors also often acted as women's biographers after their deaths, therefore playing an important role in preserving their memory as exemplary housewives and in promoting them as models for future generations to follow. Confessors usually lived on site, where they could be available at regular intervals to provide spiritual guidance. The confessor at the monastic community of Sheppey occupied the chamber above the main gate-house. At Collyweston, the chamber reserved for Margaret Beaufort's confessor, John Fisher, was conveniently located close to her personal rooms.[45]

Fisher frequently aided Margaret in her private, meditative devotions, which took place in her prayer closet. Located within the innermost reaches of the residence, the closet was a site of devout interiority, where the devotee could clear their mind of other distractions and commune directly with God. In this respect, the closet might be regarded as a microcosm of monastic enclosure, affording the lay head of household the opportunity to engage in the type of meditative piety practised by the monastic superior and the women religious with their own confessors.

[41]   Dutton, 'Women's Use of Religious Literature', p. 237.
[42]   Brenda Hosington, 'Lady Margaret Beaufort's Translations as Mirrors of Practical Piety', in Micheline White (ed.), *English Women, Religion, and Textual Production, 1500–1625* (Burlington, 2011), pp. 185–203.
[43]   Power, *Nunneries*, p. 817.
[44]   Rabia Gregory, 'Penitence, Confession, and the Power of Submission in Late Medieval Women's Religious Communities', *Religions*, 3.3 (2012) , 646–61. For further discussion on this, see, Denissen, pp. 141–3.
[45]   SJC, D91.13, p. 42.

The lady's learned piety, as cultivated through her reading practices and her relationship with her confessor, had a direct bearing on the wider devotional culture of her household. As domestic figureheads, women were encouraged to foster and nurture reading communities.[46] That the members of monastic households looked to their superior to provide direction is attested by the sisters at Ankerwyke in Wraysbury, who in 1441 complained that they lacked a governess to teach them reading, song, and religious observance. In the preface to the *Nightingale*, a poem dedicated to Anne Stafford, duchess of Buckingham (†1480), Anne is posited as an authoritative teacher and is urged to call her household together as a reading community so that they might meditate upon the canonical hours.[47] Anne's daughter-in-law, Margaret Beaufort, actively directed the spiritual practices of her household, ordering multiple copies of her translation of the *Imitatio* and twelve masses, eight primers and ten books 'in nomine Jesu' for their use.[48]

The presence of multiple names in religious compilations further attests to the vibrancy of domestic devotional reading. An early printed edition of *The Chastising of God's Children*, for example, contains the names of four Bridgettine and two Augustinian women religious. Numerous devotional texts connected with Margaret Beaufort's household also contain the names of many of those in her service, including a primer in which there were two prayer cards from the Carthusian monastery at Sheen.

Communal reading was practised in both monastic and lay households.[49] Reading aloud at mealtimes was a requirement of the Benedictine Rule. According to the Rule, members of the monastic community were expected to develop signs for use during the meal so that they would not be interrupt the voice of the reader, who was to be a capable member of the community. Mealtime reading was so central to monastic life that when Katherine Pilly, the monastic superior of Flixton, stepped down from her role due to blindness in 1432, the bishop of Norwich tasked a woman religious named Cecilia Crayke to sit and read the divine service to her at mealtimes so that she would not be excluded from the experience.[50]

Mealtime reading was also practised in the households of devout widows. During dinner, Margaret Beaufort heard tales that became increasingly pious as the meal progressed, beginning with stories that were 'honest to make her

---

[46] Rebecca Krug, *Reading Families: Women's Literate Practice in Late Medieval England* (London, 2008), pp. 78–83.

[47] Krug, *Reading Families*, p. 93.

[48] Malcolm Underwood, 'Politics and Piety in the Household of Lady Margaret Beaufort', *JEH*, 38:1 (1987), 39–52, at 48.

[49] Oliva, *FMN*, p. 62.

[50] Power, *Nunneries*, pp. 57–8.

mery' and then moving on to virtuous tales of 'the life of Chryst or such like'. The countess would then converse with a bishop or other religious figure about 'some godly matter'.[51] Cecily Neville listened to readings from devotional texts, including Walter Hilton's *The Mixed Life* and the hagiographies of women saints, including Catherine and Bridget. She would then commit the tales to memory and recite them to those who joined her for supper that same evening.[52]

Gift Exchange

Gift exchange was a further means through which the monastic superior and her lay counterpart strengthened their ties to one another and fashioned themselves as spiritual figureheads of their respective households. Gifts distributed by women religious were usually handcrafted within the monastery; they included confections, devotional images and objects, embroideries, and fruit grown by the sisters within the gardens and orchards of the community. Larger monastic houses were equipped with production spaces such as still rooms or kitchens where women religious were able to produce medicines, perfumes, and comfits on a large scale.[53]

Gifts given by women religious commonly provided medicine for body and soul. For late medieval noblewomen, gifts of health were particularly important because they created significant opportunities for female agency and self-fashioning at a time when assisting the sick was both a Christian obligation and a household duty.[54] The women religious of the monastic community of Le Murate in Florence were particularly effective in cultivating women's kinship networks through the exchange of medical gifts, engaging in trans-national gift exchange with patrons such as Queen Leonor of Portugal (†1525). Following their receipt of Leonor's gifts of sugar and spices, both of which were highly prized for their medicinal uses, the Le Murate community reciprocated with small handmade gifts designed to 'benefit the queen's spiritual health and communicate a sense of shared religious identity'.[55]

Objects originating from monastic houses played an important role in defining the sacrality of laywomen's devotional spaces. Many of the counter-gifts given by the Le Murate community to Leonor of Portugal, among them a personalised prayer book, talismans, and garlands of silk flowers, were intended to equip the

[51] Parker, 'The Account of the Miracles', p. 263.
[52] The texts also appear in Cecily's last will and testament. See C. A. J. Armstrong, 'The Piety of Cecily, Duchess of York: A Study in Late Medieval Culture', in Douglas Woodruff (ed.), *For Hilaire Belloc: Essays in Honour of his 72nd Birthday* (London, 1942), pp. 73–94.
[53] Sharon T. Strocchia, *Forgotten Healers: Women and the Pursuit of Health in Late Renaissance Italy* (Harvard, 2019), p. 52.
[54] Strocchia, *Forgotten Healers*, p. 51.
[55] Strocchia, *Forgotten Healers*, p. 54.

space of the queen's own oratory or closet, where they shaped the queen's domestic space and defined her devotional practices.[56] When Margaret Beaufort was staying at Hatfield in Hertfordshire, several items were brought from the community of Syon for use within her closet.[57]

Like Leonor of Portugal, Margaret Beaufort regularly participated in the exchange of gifts of spiritual and bodily health with women religious. In the last six years of her life, Margaret frequently received gifts of rose water from friends and associates, including women religious from the community of minoresses, which stood on the peripheries of London.[58] Margaret's daughter-in-law, Elizabeth of York, also received a gift of rose water from the monastic superior at the minoresses in 1502–03.[59] It is probable that the women religious at the Minories were involved in the large-scale production of the water, as appears to have been the case for their neighbours at the community and hospital of St Mary Spital, where no less than three separate distilling workshops have been identified.[60]

Gifts of rose water were both practical and symbolic. The rose held a central place in the devotions of women religious, as 'nearly all the governing metaphors of late medieval piety can be distilled from the imagery of this single flower'.[61] In Germany, woodcuts from monastic houses frequently depict devotional scenes encased within roses. The imagery of Mary and the infant Christ in the rose garden also formed the origin of rosary beads, which were used by women religious and noblewomen in their daily devotions.

Rose water's healing properties were widely recognised due to the rose's associations with the Virgin Mary and Christ's Passion. Devotional texts likened Mary's tears to the soothing effects of rose water, which 'enhanced the efficacy of this precious liquid in the minds of the devout'.[62] In his *Le livre de seyntz medicines*, Henry of Lancaster drew on the rose's associations with both Mary and Christ, describing rose water 'as a liquid distilled from the rose petals of Christ's bleeding wounds into the Virgin's tears', which saved the patient from the heat of sin.[63] The

[56] Strocchia, *Forgotten Healers*, p. 65.

[57] SJC D91.21, p. 113.

[58] SJC D91.19, p. 20, 82, 83; D91.20, p. 42, 85; D91.21, p. 37.

[59] *Privy Purse Expenses of Elizabeth of York: Wardrobe Accounts of Edward the Fourth: with a Memoir of Elizabeth of York, and notes*, ed. Nicholas Harris Nicolas (London, 1830), p. 8.

[60] Chiz Harward, Nick Holder, Christopher Phillpotts, and Christopher Thomas (eds), *The Medieval Priory and Hospital of St Mary Spital and the Bishopsgate Suburb: Excavations at Spitalfields Market, London E1, 1991–2007* (London, 2019).

[61] Hamburger, *Nuns as Artists*, p. 63.

[62] Naoë K. Yoshikawa, 'Holy Medicine and Diseases of the Soul: Henry of Lancaster and Le Livre de Seyntz Medicines', *Medical History*, 53 (2009), 397–414, at 406.

[63] Yoshikawa, 'Holy Medicine', 406.

ingestion of rose water through recipes such as the expensive 'Manus Christi', a 'tasty cure-all' made from rose water, sugar and ground pearls, provided curative medicine for both body and soul. Gifts of rose water thus afforded monastic and lay women opportunities to demonstrate their piety and their roles as healers within their households and wider communities.

Conclusion

Architectural, social, and textual space combined to facilitate and uphold the lay head of household's performance of her devout authority in both monastic and secular residences. As the figureheads of domestic devotional communities, the monastic superior and her lay counterpart articulated their spiritual leadership through displays of bodily discipline and learned piety, which emanated from the personal to the communal. In the great residence, the closet was the epicentre of women's spirituality. Filled with texts and objects that were both common to and sourced from women's monastic communities, it provided a sacred space in which the noblewomen proved herself to be an exemplar comparable to the monastic superior. Through the exchange of gifts of health, women religious and laywomen shaped one another's lives and homes. Such gifts enabled them to cultivate their roles as spiritual and bodily healers and to demonstrate their proximity to the Virgin Mary, whom they both sought to represent and embody within their households.

Beyond the spiritual dimension of domestic governance considered here, future studies might usefully bring the more mundane or practical aspects of women's household management in lay and monastic settings – both of which have been written about separately – into comparative focus. Indeed, such an approach may help counter a historic tendency in scholarship to measure women's household management according to a default male standard, and instead allow for women's actions to be evaluated on their own terms. The ways in which laywomen's contact with women's monastic houses, especially spiritual powerhouses such as Syon Abbey, shaped the material and social fabric of their domestic space is another area deserving of more attention than the scope of this chapter has afforded. Future scholarship might also seek to bring temporally and geographically iso-lated perspectives into comparative focus, to consider how women religious and lay women interacted across time and space. Just as the borders between women's monastic communities and women's houses in the secular world were porous, so scholarship in the field must also strive to transcend boundaries and achieve con-nectivity across disciplinary, institutional, geographical, and period boundaries, as this volume seeks to do.

CHAPTER 8

Literacies, Learning, and Communal Reform: The Case of Alijt Bake

DIANA DENISSEN

WITH a few exceptions, medieval religious women have for a long time been perceived as unlearned. In recent decades, however, scholars such as Linda Olsson have argued that 'the complications surrounding past literacies highlight [...] the inadequate nature of our established terminology and paradigms'.[1] In other words: we need to think about women's literacies and learning in a different way, for instance by defining different levels of literacy. As the editors of the three volumes on *Nuns' Literacies in Medieval Europe* stated, it is important to use the plural 'literacies' instead of the singular 'literacy' to describe the engagement of religious women in medieval literate culture. The plural 'literacies' implies a range of variable literacy levels between different women religious and religious communities.[2]

Women's literacies ranged from practical or pragmatic literacy – the ability to read and/or write simple and everyday sentences – to the understanding of and/or ability to copy or compose more complex texts. Even if they could not read or write (well), medieval women could also be literate in the broader sense of the word by hearing texts that were read out to them: oral literacy. Literacy in the vernacular often differed from Latin literacy. Monica Hedlund stated that considering that Latin was used every day in the convent, most sisters must have learned (at least some) Latin, even though they were perhaps not full participants in Latin intellectual culture. We should, therefore, be aware of the 'intellectualis-ation of Latin' in our established terminologies.[3] This chapter discusses how late medieval northern European women religious engaged in literate culture, both in

---

[1] Linda Olson, 'Reading, Writing, and Relationships in Dialogue', in Linda Olson and Kathryn Kerby-Fulton (eds), *Voices in Dialogue: Reading Women in the Middle Ages* (Notre Dame, 2005), pp. 1–30, at p. 5.

[2] 'Introduction', *Nuns' Literacies: Antwerp*, p. xxv.

[3] Monica Hedlund, 'Nuns and Latin, with Special Reference to the Birgittines of Vadstena', *Nuns' Literacies: Hull*, pp. 97–114, at p. 105.

the vernacular and in Latin. A case study focuses on one woman in particular: the rebellious Dutch religious woman, Alijt Bake.[4]

Medieval Women's Literacies and Variations

Women's literacies varied across geographical regions.[5] In Vadstena Abbey in Sweden, for instance, schooling seems to have been going on in the community in the fifteenth century.[6] The Dutch house of Diepenveen near Deventer also had a convent school that was attended by postulants, novices, and initially possibly also by professed sisters who did not yet possess the required skills.[7] In writing, in 1922, of English women's religious communities Eileen Power argued that their standards of learning were not high: 'It is strange that in England there is no record of any house which can compare with Gandersheim, Hohenburg or Helfta; no record of any nun to compare with the learned women and great mystics'.[8] Three famous women religious of the German Helfta community, Mechtild of

---

[4]   This publication forms part of the early postdoc mobility project 'Raging Love: The Late Medieval Works and Lives of Margery Kempe (ca. 1373 – ca. 1440) and Alijt Bake (1415–1455)', funded by the Swiss National Research Foundation (2019–21).

[5]   This chapter focuses on northern Europe. For more on southern or eastern European contexts, see for instance: Alfred Thomas, 'Between Court and Cloister: Royal Patronage and Nuns' Literacy in Medieval East-Central Europe', in *Nuns' Literacies: Hull*, pp. 207–21; Blanca Garí, 'What Did Catalan Nuns Read? Women's Literacy in the Female Monasteries of Catalonia, Majorca, and Valencia', in *Nuns' Literacies: Antwerp*, pp. 125–48; Brian Richardson, 'Memorializing Living Saints in the Milanese Convent of Santa Marta in the Late Fifteenth and Early Sixteenth Century', in *Nuns' Literacies: Antwerp*, pp. 209–25; Viktória Hedvig Deák, 'The Legacy of St Margit: A Case-Study of a Dominican Monastery in Hungary', in *Nuns' Literacies: Antwerp*, pp. 229–49; Andrea Knox, 'Her Book-Lined Cell: Irish Nuns and the Development of Texts, Translation, and Literacy in Late Medieval Spain', in *Nuns' Literacies: Kansas*, pp. 67–86; Antonella Ambrosio, 'Literacy in Neapolitan Women's Convents: An Example of Female Handwriting in a Late Fifteenth-Century Accounts Ledger', in *Nuns' Literacies: Kansas*, pp. 89–108.

[6]   Jonas Carlquist, 'The Birgittine Sisters at Vadstena Abbey: Their Learning and Literacy, with Particular Reference to Table Reading', in *Nuns' Literacies: Hull*, pp. 239–51, at p. 250. There are several recent articles on Vadstena Abbey. See for instance also Hedlund, 'Nuns and Latin', pp. 97–118, Ingela Hedström, 'Vadstena Abbey and Female Literacy in Late Medieval Sweden', in *Nuns' Literacies: Hull*, pp. 253–72; Nils Dverstorp, 'Step by Step: The Process of Writing a Manuscript in the Female Convent of Vadstena', in *Nuns' Literacies: Kansas*, pp. 109–22.

[7]   For more on women's education in the Low Countries, see Wybren Scheepsma's standard work *Deemoed en devotie: De koorvrouwen van Windesheim en hun geschriften* (Amsterdam, 1997); Scheepsma, *MRW: Low Countries*, p. 44.

[8]   Power, *Nunneries*, p. 239.

Magdeburg (c. 1207–c. 1282/1294); St Gertrud the Great (1256–1301/2) and Mechtild von Hackeborn (1240/41–98), for instance, together produced over 1,200 pages of mystical writing.[9] Power, therefore, concludes that in comparison to this: 'The air of the English nunneries would seem to have been unfavourable to learning'.[10]

More recently, Veronica O'Mara has stated that English women religious indeed 'would seem to have been the poor relations in Europe' when it comes to more formalised forms of schooling and standards of education, but 'this is not to say that English nuns were routinely unlearned'.[11] In her quest for women's scribal activity in medieval English communities, O'Mara mentions Mary Nevel at Syon as 'one of the very few English nuns who can properly be labelled as a scribe'.[12] Contrary to this, there were numerous German women's communities that had a scriptorium with a group of active women scribes. Cynthia J. Cyrus identified no fewer than 416 women scribes who served German women's convents and evidence of forty-eight with scriptoria between the thirteenth and the early sixteenth century.[13] Again, the differences between Germany and England are striking. Overall, locational factors, therefore, significantly influenced medieval women literacies.

Another factor that affected the literacies of late medieval religious women was social status. As mentioned above, the fact that not all medieval women religious could read and/or write well did not necessarily mean that they did not engage with medieval literate culture at all. The lay sister Beli von Schalken from the Dominican convent of Töss, near Winterthur in Switzerland, liked to listen to table readings, a form of oral literacy, without having the same level of education as the choir sisters of the convent.[14] Jonas Carlquist asserts that 'table reading

---

[9]   Among these works are: *Das fliessendes Licht der Gottheit* (Mechtild of Magdeburg); *Liber specialis gratiae* (Mechtild von Hackeborn); *Legatus divinae pietatis* and *Exercitia spiritualia* (Gertrude the Great). For more on the late medieval religious landscape of northern Germany, see: Elizabeth Andersen, Henrike Lähnemann, and Anne Simon (eds), *A Companion to Mysticism and Devotion in Northern Germany and the Late Middle Ages* (Leiden, 2013). Mechtild of Magdeburg lived in a community of beguines in Magdeburg, Germany, before joining the Cistercian community at Helfta in the final years of her life. Women religious communities of beguines were especially popular in the medieval Low Countries. The well-known mystic and poet Hadewijch of Brabant is also associated with the beguine movement.

[10] Power, *Nunneries*, p. 239.

[11] Veronica O'Mara, 'The Late Medieval English Nun and her Scribal Activity: A Complicated Quest', in *Nuns' Literacies: Hull*, pp. 69–93, at p. 69.

[12] Veronica O'Mara, 'Scribal Engagement and the Late Medieval English Nun: The Quest Concludes?', in *Nuns' Literacies: Antwerp*, pp. 187–208, at p. 205.

[13] Cynthia J. Cyrus, *The Scribes for Women's Convents in Late Medieval Germany* (Toronto, 2009), p. 4.

[14] 'Von der seligen Schwester Beli von Schalken, der Laienschwester', in Elsbeth Stagel, *Deutsches Nonnenleben: Das Leben der schwestern zu Toss und der nonne von engeltal*

[...] may be perceived as a form of monastic reading that served to strengthen the individual sisters towards an integrated purpose'.[15] This form of community building might also have been the reason for the composition of the Middle English devotional compilation *The Chastising of God's Children*. This text was probably in the first instance written for a religious sister, who might have been from the Benedictine Barking Abbey and suggests an intimate knowledge of life in a convent and could have provided a daily table reading in English.[16]

Literacies, Latinate Culture, and Rise of the Vernacular

Oral literacy is also of central importance in *The Book of Margery Kempe*. Margery Kempe is in a different position to the religious women discussed earlier, because she was not enclosed in any way. She did not live in a convent, and neither was she an anchoress. In fact, quite the contrary: Margery Kempe travelled around England and the world. Kempe's level of literacy was not high, but her scribes read important texts to her: 'Hylton's boke' (Walter Hilton's book, probably his *Scale of Perfection*), 'Bridis boke' (the *Revelations* of St Bridget of Sweden), and *Incendium Amoris* by Richard Rolle, among others.[17] During her travels, Kempe is often confronted with her lack of literacy by the (male) figures of authority around her. In Leicester, when she was imprisoned and accused of Lollardy and unchaste behaviour, the steward of the city: 'spak Latyn unto hir. Many prestys stondyng abowtyn to here what sche schulde say, and other pepyl also. Sche seyd to the Stywarde: "Spekyth Englysch, yf yow lyketh, for I undyrstonde not what ye sey"'.[18] The steward speaks Latin to Margery Kempe to affirm his position as a member of the intellectual elite and Kempe's position as an outsider and uneducated woman. Yet, *The Book* stresses that Kempe, while 'not lettryd' had the 'witte and wisdom to answeryn so many lernyd men wythowtyn velani [shame, disgrace] or blame, thankyng be to God'.[19] *The Book* suggests that Kempe's personal relationship with Christ teaches her more than what she would be able to learn from books.

---

büchlein von der gnaden überlast. Eingeleitet und übertragen von Margarete Weinhandl (München, 1929), http://www.lexikus.de/bibliothek/Deutsches-Nonnenleben/Von-der-seligen-Schwester-Beli-von-Schalken-der-Laienschwester [accessed 16 March 2020].

[15] Carlquist, 'The Birgittine Sisters at Vadstena Abbey', p. 244.

[16] Joyce Bazire and Eric Colledge (eds), *The Chastising of God's Children and The Treatise of Perfection of the Sons of God* (Oxford, 1957), p. 44.

[17] Barry Windeatt (ed.), *The Book of Margery Kempe* (Cambridge, 2000), p. 115, lines 1257–8.

[18] Windeatt, *The Book*, p. 231, lines 3725–9.

[19] Windeatt, *The Book*, p. 257, lines 4290–1.

When Margery Kempe is confronted with the Latin of the intellectual elite, she does not understand it. This was the case for many women religious in the late medieval period, although women religious might very well have understood some Latin basics. Generally speaking, the way women engaged with Latinate culture goes through some important changes from about 1200 onwards.[20] Before this, men studied Latin to a far greater degree than women, but there were some key exceptions. The German Benedictine abbess Hildegard von Bingen can, for instance, be seen as one of the most influential authors and composers of the twelfth century.[21] Another important twelfth-century manuscript has a woman author, Herrad of Landsberg. Her *Hortus Delicarum* ('Garden of Delights'), an illuminated, encyclopaedic text, was written as a pedagogical tool for the novices of Hohenburg Abbey in the French region of Alsace. As Hedlund notes: 'Herrad stands out as a teacher who sees herself and her sisters as full participants in Latin intellectual culture'.[22] The *Hortus* 'does not depict Latin learning and theological discourse as unusual and inappropriate for a female audience', according to Fiona J. Griffiths, and the text 'suggests a richer intellectual culture for women than scholars have tended to allow'.[23] From about 1200 onwards, the monastic schools were declining and the new centres of learning that took their place, the cathedral schools and the universities, were excluding women from the Latin intellectual elite. Hedlund writes that this shift also marks the rise of women's interest in vernacular translations.[24]

The translators of Latin texts could, nevertheless, also be women. One of them was a sister of the Engelthal community in Germany, Cristin von Kornburg. In the fourteenth century, the community of Engelthal compiled a so-called 'sister book'. This text consists of two sections: the first contains the foundation story of the community, and the second is made up of biographical sketches of specific women religious, lay brothers, and priests. These biographical sketches were supposed to serve as models for the women religious who read them. They are fascinating examples of historiobiography mixed with a pinch of hagiography. The sister book of Engelthal tells us that Cristin von Kornburg 'grozze, swerew buch ze tisch deutet' ['interpreted or translated (*deuten*) large, difficult books at table'].[25]

---

[20] For more on this, see also Hedlund, 'Nuns and Latin', pp. 99–100.

[21] A good starting point to learn more about Hildegard von Bingen is Debra L. Stoudt et al. (eds), *A Companion to Hildegard of Bingen* (Leiden, 2014).

[22] Hedlund, 'Nuns and Latin', p. 99.

[23] Griffiths, *Garden of Delights*.

[24] Hedlund, 'Nuns and Latin', p. 100.

[25] Karl Schröder, *Der Nonne von Engelthal Büchlein von der Genaden Überlast*, Volumes *107–108* (Tübingen, 1871), p. 30. For more on the sister-book of Engelthal, see also

Cristin von Kornburg served her community by translating for the whole convent during the daily table reading and made 'large, difficult books' available to all.

The Dutch woman religious Truke van der Beeck from the Diepenveen community (near Deventer) did the same. Like the convent of Engelthal, the Diepenveen community also had a sister-book, in which lives of sixty women from this convent were compiled. This sister-book took shape roughly in the period between 1450 and 1525, so over the course of almost a century.[26] The Diepenveen sister-book narrates how, during table reading, she translated Latin texts into the Middle Dutch vernacular for her fellow sisters on the spot: 'Gherne studdierde sie ende zeer studioes was sie inden Latinschen bocken ende sie plach vake uten Latien in Duus toe reventer toe lesen' ['She studied eagerly and delved into the Latin books and translated from Latin into Dutch during refectory', DV, f. 329 r-v].[27] Cristin von Kornburg's and Truke van der Beeck's acts of live translation as a performative reinterpretation of a Latin text brought the women's monastic communities of Engelthal and Diepenveen together. Cyrus, therefore, proposes a 'bilingual and fundamentally bivalent model' of literacy in women's religious communities in which vernacular translations 'inform and are informed by Latin'.[28]

While the attitude of Truke van der Beeck towards Latin seems very practical, the motif that accompanies the theme of learning Latin in the Swiss sister-book of Töss is more spiritual and underlines that true knowledge is a gift of the Holy Spirit. The sister-book of Töss, which is now a part of Winterthur, consists of a chronicle and about forty entries about the different sisters of the Töss community. It has long been assumed that the Swiss mystic Elsbeth Stagel, who was known for her friendship and correspondence with Henry Suso, was the author of the sister-book, but now it is generally acknowledged that a collective of women from the Töss community were probably responsible for the work, completing the text around 1340.[29] As is described in the sister-book, during a liturgical service, one of the sisters in Töss miraculously understood all the Latin words.[30] This 'learning miracle' in the sister-book of Töss created some tension with the more pragmatic

Leonard P. Hindsley, *The Mystics of Engelthal: Writings from a Medieval Monastery* (New York, 1998).

[26]   Scheepsma, *MRW Low Countries*, pp. 25–6.

[27]   Scheepsma, *MRW Low Countries*, p. 71.

[28]   Cynthia J. Cyrus, 'Vernacular and Latinate Literacy in Viennese Women's Convents', in *Nuns' Literacies: Hull*, pp. 119–32, at p. 120.

[29]   Gertrud Jaron Lewis, *By Women, for Women, about Women: The Sister-Books of Fourteenth-Century Germany* (Toronto, 1996), p. 24.

[30]   Lewis, *By Women, for Women, about Women*, pp. 278–9.

attitude towards learning Latin in the sister-books of Engelthal and Diepenveen. However, the model of pragmatic literacy, strengthened by communal translation in Engelthal and Diepenveen, and the model of spiritual literacy created through affective experience in Töss, nevertheless, both underline an interest in learning and understanding Latin.

From this brief overview, it is clear women religious engaged with medieval literate culture in a variety of ways, depending on whether they were women religious or lay women like Margery Kempe, their geographical location, their class, and their social status. It is impossible to talk about just one form of medieval women's literacy. These literacies existed on a continuum, ranging from oral to written literacies and from the vernacular to Latin.

The Case of Alijt Bake

Literacy was central to the Dutch woman religious Alijt Bake's fifteenth-century programme of communal and spiritual reform in her convent in Ghent. Bake was born in Utrecht (now in the Netherlands) in 1413 or 1415 and she left this city in 1440 to go to the convent of Galilea in Ghent. Next to nothing is known about the first twenty-five years of her life.[31] One thing we do know about her, however, is that Bake lived together with an anchoress and dear friend in Utrecht before her departure. Possibly, Bake was the maidservant of this anchoress. Another one of Bake's friends was a nurse who probably lived and worked in the 'Saint Barbara and Saint Laurentius hospital' in Utrecht, founded by a community of beguines around 1359. Gradually, the group of women started forming a more official religious community with its own rule, but caring for the sick remained central to life in this community. Bake saw the different ways of life of her two friends, a secluded and contemplative life versus a more active life caring for the sick, both as holy and highly spiritual. Even though Bake wondered whether or not she should become an anchoress as well, she writes that she was advised to join a women's community instead. This illustrates that, even though this chapter focuses primarily on women religious who lived in convents, other and important forms of women's religious lives, such as the lives of anchoresses and beguines, existed alongside the lives of sisters in monastic communities, and these women read and produced texts too.

---

[31] In his new English translation of Bake's texts, John van Engen proposes 1413 rather than 1415 as Alijt Bake's year of birth. See John Van Engen, *The Writings of Alijt Bake: Teacher, Preacher, Prioress, and Spiritual Autobiographer* (forthcoming). Another recent publication that includes a chapter on Alijt Bake is Barbara Zimbalist, *Translating Christ in the Middle Ages: Gender, Authorship, and the Visionary Text in England, France, and the Low Countries* (Notre Dame, 2022). I would like to thank the author for allowing me to read an early version of this text.

Alijt Bake's community in Ghent was one of thirteen women's communities that belonged to the so-called Windesheim congregation, and part of the German-Dutch reform movement of the *Devotio moderna* that began in the late fourteenth century under the influence of the work of Geert Grote (1340–84).[32] The convent of Galilea, which was founded in 1430 or 1431, belonged to the last women's convents that joined the Windesheim congregation. The sisters in these places were called 'Sisters of the Common Life'. Salome Sticken's (1369–1449) *Vivendi Formula* ('Spiritual Guide of Common Life'), a normative rulebook that documents the experiences of Sticken as a spiritual leader, provides a good insight into the common life from the perspective of a woman author and teacher.[33] In this text, she recapitulates the daily rhythm of the sisters and the central importance of manual labour in the convent. Not only was manual labour important from a practical point of view – these women's monastic communities tried to be as self-sufficient as possible – but it was also seen as an exercise in humility, especially for the sisters who came from the higher classes in society. Furthermore, the *Vivendi Formula* tries to find a balance between 'the pursuit of a close personal relationship with God while at the same time fulfilling the obligations of communal living'.[34] To establish this personal relationship with God, writing and reading were important for the Sisters of the Common Life. However, books should be used in the right manner, which meant that writing and reading should only focus the attention on God. The way in which learning could (and could not) be used to reach spiritual perfection is also an important theme in Alijt Bake's texts.

LATIN LITERACY, RELUCTANCE, AND SCEPTICISM

Alijt Bake's multi-layered and at times paradoxical attitude towards reading, writing, and learning further illustrates the complexities of late medieval women's literacies. In a text called *Boexcken van mijn beghin ende voortganck* ('Book on my beginnings and progress'), which is characterised by Anne Bollmann as a 'spiritual handbook', Bake complains about the use of Latin in her convent in Ghent.[35] When Bake has to go to the choir with the other choir sisters, *Boexcken* describes how: 'She

[32] For an overview of the 'Modern Devotion' movement in English, see J. Van Engen, *Sisters and Brothers of the Common Life: The Devotio Moderna and the World of the Later Middle Ages* (Philadelphia, 2008).

[33] For more Salome Sticken's *Vivendi formula*, see A. Bollmann, 'Close Enough to Touch: Tension between Inner Devotion and Communal Piety in the Congregations of Sisters of the *Devotio Moderna*', in R. Hofman, C. Caspers, P. Nissen, M. van Dijk, and J. Oosterman (eds), *Inwardness, Individualization, and Religious Agency in the Late Medieval Low Countries* (Turnhout, 2020), pp. 137–58. This text had originally been written in the vernacular, but it is preserved only in a Latin translation.

[34] Bollmann, 'Close Enough', 141.

[35] Anne Bollman, '"Being a Woman of My Own": Alijt Bake (1415–1455) as Reformer of the

did not recite as loudly and quickly as they [the other nuns] wanted. Therefore she often had to endure a lot from them. [...] She read/sang badly, because she did not understand what she had read'.[36] Bake is convinced that her lack of understanding Latin impedes her spiritual progress. She reflects: 'Ik en verstaen die schrijfture niet ende daerom soo en can ick mijn herte niet behauden daerop' ['I do not understand the text of the lectures and therefore my heart cannot concentrate on it'].[37] In other words, the use of Latin in her late medieval convent had an exclusionary effect for the sister. Bake is explicit about the fact that the Latin echoes of learned church culture do not resonate with her. She says that 'her heart cannot concentrate on it', which I take to mean that she is not sufficiently moved by it: the Latin words do not evoke enough feelings in her heart.

Bake's lack of knowledge of the dominant church language Latin also contributed to her social exclusion in the convent. In addition to failing to understand the lectures and not being able to recite quickly in the choir, Bake does also not adapt well to other aspects of the communal life. Instead of focussing on the group, she often desires to be alone, which is not appreciated by her fellow sisters. In Bake's *Boexcken*, ideas about community and self are very much interconnected. Bake is supposed to show obedience to her community. She is expected to follow communal structures, whether she understands them or not. Her refusal to follow these communal structures leads to a form of socio-separation.

The importance of obedience to the communal structures in the convent, despite not understanding Latin, is illustrated in the sister-book of the Dominican community of women religious of Engelthal. Like Alijt Bake, Hedwig von Regensburg, who entered the order at a later age – she was 'ein vil alte schwester' – wanted to skip choir because she did not understand it: 'Die wolt sich dez chors ab tun: si verstund sin niht' ['She wanted to dispense with the choir: she did not understand it'].[38] Then, Hedwig hears a voice that tells her: 'Ge hintz chor: du verstest ez hie auzzen als wenig als dinen' ['Go to the choir: you understand it just as little out here as in there'].[39] This voice does not actually change Hedwig's ina-

---

Inner Self', in A. B. Mulder-Bakker (ed.), *Seeing and Knowing: Women and Learning in Medieval Europe, 1200–1550* (Turnhout, 2004), pp. 67–96, at p. 88.

[36] 'Sij en las niet soo luijde, noch soo ras als die menschen wel begeheert hadden. Ende hierom soo haddese dickwils soo veel te lijden. [...] Ende sy las veel qualicker, want sij wiest dan niet was sy las of ghelesen hadden': Bernard Spaapen (ed.), 'De autobiografie van Alijt Bake', *Ons Geestelijk Erf*, 41 (1967), at p. 277, lines 407–8 and pp. 278–9, lines 528–30. All translations from Alijt Bake's *Boexcken van mijn beghin ende voortganck* into English are my own.

[37] Spaapen (ed.), 'De autobiografie', 278–9, lines 528–30.

[38] Claire Taylor Jones, *Ruling the Spirit: Women, Liturgy, and Dominican Reform in Late Medieval Germany* (Philadelphia, 2007), p. 72.

[39] Taylor Jones, *Ruling the Spirit*, p. 72.

bility to understand Latin, but it attempts to change her attitude towards this lack of understanding. She will understand just as little inside as outside of the choir, but, nevertheless, she should participate in the choir. The need to follow the communal structures that are set in place in the convent of Engelthal, with an attitude of spiritual humility, will eventually lead to spiritual perfection. Indeed, Hedwig von Regensburg is rewarded. One day, during compline, 'da sahen sie alle daz ir ir hertz schain als die sunne durch ir gewant, reht als sie tut durch daz glaz' ['all saw that her heart shone like the sun through her robes, just as through glass'].[40] While Alijt Bake decides to go against the community by creating her own narrative, Hedwig shows obedience to communal structures and religious discipline.

In addition to Alijt Bake's negative view of Latin and her reluctance to follow communal structures, she is also sceptical about the things that can be learnt from books: 'Ghij sult weten vorwaer dat [ick] noijnt in boecken en studerede dan dat minnende open herte ons liefs Heeren Jesu Christi ofte sijne lieve noeder Maria' ['You have to know that [I] never studied in any other books than in the lovingly open heart of our dear lord Jesus Christ or that of his dear mother Mary'].[41] Bake is cautious about religious knowledge from books. Towards the end of her life, she repeats that Christ and his mother Mary are 'mijne boecken, mijn leeringhe en mijn studeeringhe ['my books, my schooling and what I study'].[42] The idea that reading should not be used to stir devotion was common for the Modern Devout, as Scheepsma notes.[43] Bake is convinced that the arguments of writers, teachers, and preachers will not bring people any closer to God: 'Jae, al deden sij oock mirakel met haer const, soo sijn sij blient ende doof ende onbekent in die ghewarighe weghen Godts' ['Even if they would perform miracles with their science, they are still blind and deaf and they do not know how to make progress on the paths of God's truth'].[44]

READING EXPERIENCE AND REFLECTION

Yet, somewhat paradoxically, reading and writing take a central place within the Modern Devotion movement and also in Bake's daily life. For instance, she describes how eager she is to read a book entitled *Van de neghen velden*, a Middle Dutch adaptation of *Neun-Felsen-Buch* by Rulman Merswin, but she does not know where to get it:

[40] Taylor Jones, *Ruling the Spirit*, p. 72–3.
[41] Spaapen (ed.), 'De autobiografie', p. 234, lines 427–9.
[42] Bernard Spaapen (ed.), 'De brief uit de ballingschap', *Ons Geestelijk Erf*, 41 (1967), 364, lines 259–60.
[43] W. F. Scheepsma (ed.), 'Van die memorie der passien ons Heren', *Ons Geestelijk Erf*, 68 (1994), 106–28, at p. 117.
[44] Spaapen (ed.), 'De autobiografie', p. 235, lines 419–21.

It happened that at a certain moment she very much longed to read a book that is called 'Of Nine Fields'. She had heard about it, but she did not know how to get hold of it. Finally she got it, as God wanted, on the Sunday before Christmas. She could not have it for a long time, so she read it all in one go. This did not take longer than about two hours. Then, the book had to be returned.[45]

Bake has to read the book in a rush, and she does not reflect on its contents until she has finished it:

Therefore she was in a big hurry and she read in a rushed manner, because she wanted to finish it. Then she would know the content of the book that attracted her so much. She read quickly until the eighth field. Then she felt encouragement deep inside her as if someone said: 'This is exactly what you are looking for. You miss this'. But she was in such a rush that she could not pay attention to it. She finished the book and gave it back, so that it could be returned to where it belonged.[46]

After she has read the text, Bake reflects on it in the days that follow. This form of reflection, or *ruminatio*, was important for the Modern Devout. It often consisted of a personal selection of important points from the text, so that the reader could deduce a spiritual meaning from it. *Ruminatio,* the 'chewing' of particular extracts of texts, often happened in the convent while doing household tasks such as spinning or sewing. During her reflections, Bake realises that the eighth field of the nine different fields that are described in *Van de neghen velden* especially moves her because it describes those souls that have surrendered themselves to

---

[45] 'Het gheviel dat haer herte seer ghetrocken wiert eenen tijt om te lesen een boexcken dat heet van de neghen velden, daer sij wat af ghehoort hadde. En sij wist niet waer dat sijt chrijghen saude. Ten lesten, alsoet Godt wilde, soo creecht sijt [dat] des sondach voor kerstdach. Ende het en mochte haer niet langhe blijven, al soo langhe dat sijt tot een sitten wt las, dat boven een hure of twee niet was, doen moeste dat weder wech': Spaapen (ed.), 'De autobiografie', p. 334, lines 306–12. It seems that *Fels* has been wrongly translated to 'veld' [field] in the Middle Dutch translation/adaptation.

[46] 'Hierom soo was sij seer haestich en las also haestelijck seer opdat sijt wt hebben saude, opdat sij weten mocht wat daerin stont, daer sij soo seer toe ghetrocken was. Alsoo last sijt haestelijck voort al tot het achtste velt toe. Daer ghevoelde sij een nope van binnen, recht oft segghen wilde: Dat ist dat ghij soeckt, daert u let. Maer sij was soo haestich dat sij daer niet op letten en cost. Sij last al deur tot dat wt was. Doen soo gaft sijt wederom thuijs te draghen daer<r>t behoorde': Spaapen (ed.), 'De autobiografie', pp. 334–5, lines 312–20. While *Van den neghen velden* did apparently not belong to the library of the convent of Galilea, it seems that certain books could be loaned, even for a couple of hours. Since Bake only has two hours to read the book, perhaps somebody took it with them while they visited the convent.

God in the basis but have not yet been able to completely let go of their deepest individual will. Bake recognises herself in this. When a soul would completely let go of its individuality, mystical union with the divine could possibly be achieved. Bake hopes to reach the ninth field of mystical union and one day find a place among the women mystics of her time. Many of these visionary women – Julian of Norwich, Hildegard of Bingen, and Angela of Foligno to name but a few – also wrote their visions down.

Bake's reading experience of *Van de neghen velden* has a profound influence on her. While Bake is sceptical about the intellectual arguments of writers, teachers and preachers, a book like *Van de neghen velden* is still instrumental for her spiritual development. Bake not only uses vernacular books to guide her on her spiritual path, but she also finds her voice through writing: 'dat schreef ick al op, dat ick niet vergheten en soude' ['I wrote it all down, so that I would not forget it'].[47] Writing helps Bake remember: by writing she makes the step from *ruminatio*, to *memoria*, the memorisation of important textual passages.[48] As Mertens states, texts that consisted of a selection of important sections from other texts were characterised by the Modern Devout as a particular text type: the *rapiarium*. The primary function of a *rapiarium* was to be a memory aid. These texts were not written with the aim to disseminate them.[49]

BAKE'S *BOEXCKEN*

Apart from a (probable) *rapiarium*, however, Bake eventually also started writing texts for her fellow sisters, with the explicit aim to disseminate them, including her autobiographical *Boexcken van mijn beghin ende voortganck*.[50] Bollman notes that the loose, 'patchwork' structure of *Boexcken*, which seems a reworking of some of Bake's earlier notes supplemented with memories, still reflects the method of successively compiling, contemplating, and rewriting that characterises the *rapiarium*.[51] The original copy of *Boexcken* has been lost, but we still have Bake's autograph in another manuscript, which is now at the

---

[47] Spaapen (ed.), 'De autobiografie', p. 259, lines 6–7.

[48] *Memoria* is one of the five divisions of ancient and medieval rhetoric. The other four divisions are: *inventio* (invention), *dispositio* (arrangement), *elocutio* (style), and *actio* (delivery). For more, see for instance: Mary Carruthers, *The Book of Memory: A Study of Memory in Medieval Culture* (Cambridge, 2011).

[49] Th. Mertens, 'Lezen met de pen. Ontwikkelingen in het laatmiddeleeuws geestelijk proza', in F. P. van Oostrom and Frank Willaert (eds), *De studie van de Middelnederlandse letterkunde: stand en toekomst* (Hilversum, 1989), pp. 187–200, at p. 197.

[50] A bibliographical and codicological overview of Alijt Bake's texts can be found in the appendix of Scheepsma's *Deemoed en Devotie*.

[51] Bollman, 'Being a Woman of My Own', p. 89.

Royal Library in Brussels. [52] Bake, who was elected as the new prioress in 1445, expresses an explicit wish for reform in her text. She describes herself as 'een moeder van onser oorder in reformatien des inwendighes levens' ['a mother of our religious order in reforming the inner life'].[53] In her *Boexcken,* Bake illustrates how her focus on the inner life took shape. She wants the sisters that read her text – she calls them 'mijn cleijne, crancke kinderen' ['my small, weak children'] – to follow her example.[54]

Although originally written around the year 1451, *Boexcken* was copied by sister Augustina Baert and by a later rector of Galilea, Jacobus Isabeels, in 1613. The copy of *Boexcken* in Ghent is the only extant version of the text.[55] The two scribes of *Boexcken* were telling the history of their convent and the place of this remarkable woman within it. It seems that especially Jacobus Isabeels had a profound influence on the text. The end of *Boexcken* includes a note stating:

> Hier eijndt het leven van Mater Aleyt Bake, priorinne van het clooster van Galileen binnen Ghende, overleden den 18en octobre 1455, beschreven door den Eerweerdighe Heer Fr. Jacobus Isabeels, rector int voornoemt clooster. 1613 den 12en octobre 1613 [Here ends the life of Mater Alijt Bake, prioress of the convent of Galilea in Ghent. She died on 18 October 1455. It (the text) was finished/adapted by Father Jacobus Isabeels, rector of the aforementioned convent. 12 October 1613].[56]

Boexcken is not only a medieval text, but it is of a hybrid nature, because next to Bake's life story as she (presumably) wrote it down, it contains the influences of at least two other copyists from different centuries. In the transmission of texts by medieval women, their voices often get intertwined with other (male) voices. We do not exactly know who is speaking at which point in Alijt Bake's text. *Boexcken,* therefore, blurs the boundaries between female and male authorship, as well as between individual and communal authorship. Communal authorship is also an important characteristic of the sister-books and of *The Book of Margery Kempe,* which was written with the help of her scribes.

In the first ten years that Bake was prioress of her convent of Galilea, her programme of inner reform took shape, but then, after a visitation by episcopal authorities in 1455, the Windesheim congregation put an end to it. In the same year, the sisters of Galilea were forbidden to write on visions or doctrine any

---

[52] Brussels, Royal Library, MSS 643–4.
[53] Spaapen (ed.), 'De autobiografie', p. 245, lines 655–6.
[54] Spaapen (ed.), 'De brief uit de ballingschap', p. 365, line 281.
[55] Ghent, University Library, MS 3854.
[56] Spaapen (ed.), 'De autobiografie', p. 350, lines 666–70.

longer or to translate any texts from Latin into the vernacular. The *Acta Capituli Windeschemensis* states:

> No nun or sister no matter what her status, may, either personally or through an intermediary, copy books which contain philosophical teachings or revelations, whether these originate in her own mind or that of her sisters, on penalty of imprisonment; henceforth should any such be discovered, it is the responsibility of all to ensure that they are immediately burned as soon as they are found or heard tell of; nor should any dare to translate such texts from Latin into Dutch.[57]

On top of this, the Windesheim congregation banished Alijt Bake to the Facons convent in Antwerp, away from her community, where she died not long after.

Conclusion

Medieval women religious were not routinely unlearned and the use of the plural 'literacies' allows for a broader interpretation of women's engagement with medieval literate culture. Late medieval northern European religious women often carved out their own spaces and created their own means of learning, whether through translation or by writing and reciting their own narratives in the vernacular. These narratives were transmitted in a polyvocal shape that blurred the edges between men, women, individual, and communal authorship. Future research on women's literacies could focus more on the complex relationship between male authors and diverse forms of women's writing, translating, and reading, as well as what Diane Watt has characterised in *Women, Writing and Religion in England and Beyond, 650–1000*, as the concept of 'male overwriting'.[58]

Writing and translation were not without risk for women religious. Clerical misogyny posed a significant threat for women who engaged in literary activities.

---

[57] 'Nulla monialis aut soror cuiuscunque status fuerit conscribat aliquos libros, doctrinas philosophicas aut revalationes continentes per se interpositamve personam ex sua propria mente vel aliarum sororum compositas sub poena carceris si qui inposterum reperti fuerint praecipitur omnibus quod statim illi ad quorum conspectum vel aures pervenerit eos igni tradere curent, similiter nec aliquem transferre praesumant de latino in theutonicum': S. Van der Woude, *Acta Capituli Windeshemense. Acta van de kapittelvergaderingen der Congregatie van Windesheim*, Kerkhistorische studiën VI (Den Haag, 1953); Zimbalist, *Translating Christ in the Middle Ages*.

[58] Diane Watt, *Women, Writing, and Religion in England and Beyond, 650–1000* (London, 2019).

For Alijt Bake and the sisters around her, writing could possibly lead to imprison-ment and book burning. Writing, in other words, could be dangerous for medie-val women. Despite this, women religious engaged with medieval literate culture in a variety of ways.

CHAPTER 9

Family and Friends: Gift-giving, Books, and Book Inscriptions in Women's Religious Communities

SARA CHARLES

G IFT-GIVING to women's religious communities in the form of books shows
strong relationships among women religious and their patrons, each other,
and families. Women religious were expected to renounce all worldly goods upon
entering a monastic community; however, individuals and communities would
have needed access to liturgical and sacred texts for both personal and communal
devotion. The physical comfort of an inherited book can be measured in terms of
emotional weight; the tactile relationship between holding a book in one's hand
that had also been cradled by a loved one creates a tangible connection. Moreover,
personal inscriptions in books are something that kept a vital link with the outside
world and served as a constant reminder of close relationships, even in an environment that endeavoured to limit contact. This chapter examines the importance
of gift giving, particularly books, in the later medieval period in England, and how
patrons, benefactors, and family ensured they were remembered both by individual women religious as well as the monastic community. It further explores the
importance of women and book networks, through the gift-giving of books within
a religious community, with examples of inscriptions between religious women.
Finally, inscriptions from family members are examined through the emotive
prism of gift-giving, and the palpable connections with loved ones through the
physical object of the book.

Family, Friends, and Connections

The medieval family is defined by David Herhily as a household unit, with kinship
at its core (that is, relationships defined by blood or marriage).[1] Families and

[1] David Herlihy, 'The Making of the Medieval Family: Symmetry, Structure, and
Sentiment', *Journal of Family History*, 8:2 (1983), 116–30, at p. 116.

wider kinship groups were significantly intertwined with women's monastic communities. These relationships were enhanced and solidified by patronage and benefaction, particularly when women entered a monastic community. Strong family links among patrons, benefactors, local communities, and women religious were to be expected as these ties – both secular and religious – were mutually beneficial. These connections were interwoven and these relationships between the outside community and the monastic house were constantly evolving. For example, every time members of the local community 'became involved in conventual affairs like the election of a new head of house, visited a house and received hospitality, became mixed up in a conflict over rights and privileges, or later became members of the religious house or sent women as new recruits', the relationship became more integral to the survival of both communities.[2]

From the period of the Christian conversion in England there were close family ties between women's monastic communities (which often housed both sexes) and the founding (often royal) families, created and maintained by the appointment of family members as superiors.[3] As the Middle Ages progressed, however, monastic houses became more socially diverse. Marilyn Oliva's research into women religious in the later medieval period, for example, found that within the diocese of Norwich 64 per cent came from the local parish gentry, with only 1 per cent from titled aristocracy.[4] This high proportion of parish gentry indicates how strong the links were between local religious houses and the community, with most venturing no further than ten miles away from their home parishes.

Many women entering a house would have come with fully formed networks already established with their local communities and natal families. By becoming a bride of Christ, a woman was expected to 'exchange' her immediate family for the universal family of Christianity, making a sacrifice on earth in return for the greater reward of the heavenly kingdom. Yet already established links in a community would not have been forgotten (by local community or women religious) and a move into a religious house would have further extended links and networks, rather than transposing them. This in turn would have benefited the religious community as their networks expanded through new members.

Patronage was a mutually beneficial exercise, as religious institutions gained extra support for their community and a voice in the outside world, and patrons could look forward to being rewarded in the afterlife for their earthly generosity. Karen Stöber's work on late medieval patronage demonstrates that lay patrons

---

2   Kimm Curran, 'Religious Women and their Communities in Late Medieval Scotland' (Unpublished Ph.D. dissertation, University of Glasgow, 2005), p. 19.
3   Yorke, *Anglo-Saxon*.
4   Oliva, *FMN*, pp. 53–4.

hoped to benefit from prayers for their soul and burial within the sacred grounds of the institution.[5] In return, they donated items to monastic communities, such as land and money as well as books. These gifts not only served as insurance against a prolonged time in purgatory, but also strengthened the relationship between community and religious house that would have been passed down through generations.

Gift-giving

Gift-giving was an intrinsic part of religious patronage. Although chapter 33 of the Rule of St Benedict prohibits the receipt of gifts by individuals without the consent of the superior, the ownership of personal belongings, gifts for the benefit of the whole community were warmly welcomed. It was not unusual for wealthy patrons to donate items to religious houses; for example, King Cnut and his consort Emma both gave luxury manuscripts, ornaments, and textiles to many institutions. In particular, Emma donated 'two cloaks, two copes with gold tassels, and a great gold chalice and a gospelbook similarly of gold' to the male community at Christ Church, Canterbury.[6] These ostentatious donations were largely political, designed to cement allegiances and to reassure an uncertain England of their piety.[7]

There is even evidence that craftsmen were employed and works commissioned for aesthetic and ceremonial purposes within a house. For example, in 1441 William Wenard left 80 marks to the community at Polsloe for the construction of a bell tower, and the community at Great Malvern had many of its windows commissioned by patrons of all social standing.[8] Other types of gift-giving also helped to furnish the houses, with necessary everyday items such as food, ornaments, clothing, and candles.

We also have many examples of books being given on a smaller scale, implying a more personal relationship with the receiving religious house. These were often given as gifts within families or handed down; allowing personal ownership of books within a religious house meant that women could keep hold of a real and tangible link with their previous life, and have a constant reminder of their natal bonds, particularly if the book had a personal inscription.

---

[5] Karen Stöber, *Late Medieval Monasteries and Their Patrons: England and Wales, c. 1300–1540* (Woodbridge, 2007).

[6] T. A. Heslop, 'The Production of de Luxe Manuscripts and the Patronage of King Cnut and Queen Emma', *Anglo-Saxon England*, 19 (1990), 151–95, at pp. 157–8.

[7] Heslop, 'de Luxe Manuscripts', pp. 157–8.

[8] Julian Luxford, *The Art and Architecture of English Benedictine Monasteries, 1300–1540* (Woodbridge, 2005), pp. 196–200.

Books can form familial and personal networks across different places. For example, Matilda de Lacy (1223–89), widow of Richard de Clare, fifth earl of Hertford, sixth earl of Gloucester (†1262) was a wealthy patroness who refounded Canonsleigh in Devon as a women's monastic community in 1284.[9] She gifted a copy of the *Ancrene Wisse*, writing at the beginning: 'Given to the abbey and community of [Canons]leigh by Dame Matilda de Clare'.[10] The *Ancrene Wisse* was a rule for anchoresses written in the early thirteenth century that became a popular text. It is not clear whether Matilda commissioned this manuscript specifically for the women's community, or whether she had obtained it from elsewhere, but her gifting of this particular book indicates she had an interest in the spiritual development of the community she founded. Also, by placing her name on the flyleaf of the manuscript, she ensured her name and generosity lived on throughout its time at the community, and that, ultimately, her gift on earth would work in her favour in the afterlife.

Another example is from Stonyhurst College, MS 9 where an inscription on fol. 1r reads: 'this is the psalter of the Blessed Mary at Tarrant, given by mistress Leticia Kaynes. Whoever shall remove it or otherwise tries to defraud, let them be accursed'.[11] Leticia Kaynes was a descendent of Ralph de Kaynes, the original founder of the house in 1186. It was refounded by Richard le Poor of Salisbury in 1228 (one of only two women's monastic communities in England to have been acknowledged by its General Chapter as Cistercian).[12] There is little information about Leticia Kaynes, but as a descendent of the original founder, she retained an interest in the community and vice versa. There are three surviving folios of the original calendar and psalter, including her obit, entered on 16 January (which is the same hand as the inscription). This would indicate that the gift was gratefully received by the community at Tarrant, and by entering her obit into the calendar it ensured that she would remain in the memory and prayers of the community.[13]

---

9   David N. Bell, *What Nuns Read: Books and Libraries in Medieval English Nunneries* (Kalamazoo, 1995), p. 126.

10 *Datum abbatie et conventui de Leghe per Dame M. de Clare*: London, BL, Cotton MS Cleopatra C VI, fol. 3r.

11 'Hoc est psalterium beate marie super Tharente de dono domine Leticie de Kaynes. Quicumque istude abstulerit siue defraudare studuerit anathema sit': Clitheroe, Stonyhurst College, Boardman Collection Catalogue, p.11, https://resources.finalsite.net/ images/v1628074077/stonyhurstacuk/nu9z3volpb9btoojrrss/CatalogueoftheBoardmanC ollectionofMediaevalMSSatStonyhurst-July2021final_1.pdf [accessed 19 Sept. 2021].

12 The other house was in Marham, Norfolk; see, Janet Burton, '*Moniales* and *ordo Cisterciensis* in Medieval England and Wales', in *Female vita religiosa*, pp. 375–89, at p. 377.

13 For community memory, see Mercedes Pérez Vidal, 'Female Aristocratic Networks: Books, Liturgy and Reform in Castilian Nunneries', in Emma O. Bérat, Rebecca Hardie,

Donors could also bequest multiple manuscripts and the will of Agnes Stapleton (*c.* 1360–1448) lists five separate women's monastic communities to receive her books: Arthington, Yorkshire (20s and my book called *Prick of Conscience*); Denney, Cambridgeshire (one crucifix and one French book); Esholt, Yorkshire (20s and my book called *The Chastising of God's Children*); Nun Monkton, Yorkshire (20s and my book called *Vice and Virtues*); and Sinningthwaite, Yorkshire (20s and my book called *Bonaventure*).[14] Agnes Stapleton's father was a member of parliament for Yorkshire (Sir John Godard of Bransholme, Yorkshire), as was her husband (Sir Brian Stapleton of Carlton, Yorkshire)[15] and both owned considerable land in the county – therefore it should come as no surprise she donated books to Yorkshire houses. Presumably they were places known to her. However, the donation to Denney in Cambridgeshire is more surprising. In her will, she specifically names the superior of Denney as recipient of one crucifix and one French book,[16] whereas the Yorkshire bequests are more generally to the *monialibus* (women religious of that house). This would suggest that Stapleton knew the superior at Denney (probably Katherine Sybyle), through a personal or familial relationship.

Interestingly, while Agnes leaves books to other members of her family in her will, she does not bequeath any books to male monastic communities. And while her donations to the women's religious houses were current devotional texts, she leaves her large psalter to William Plumpton (possibly her grandson). While it is encouraging to have evidence of literacy among women religious, the fact that Agnes chose such interesting, contemporary texts to give to women's monastic communities rather than just a standard liturgical book like a psalter, hints at a depth of knowledge and intellectual engagement among women religious at communities that had small numbers.[17]

and Irina Dumitrescu (eds), *Relations of Power: Women's Networks in the Middle Ages* (Göttingen, 2021), pp. 105–32.

[14] John William Clay (ed.), *North Country Wills* (Durham, 1908), pp. 48–9. The book Bonaventure was probably Nicholas Love's *Mirror of the Blessed Life of Christ*: see Bell, *What Nuns Read*, p. 168.

[15] *The History of Parliament: the House of Commons 1386–1421*, https://www.historyofpar-liamentonline.org/volume/1386-1421/member/godard-sir-john-1346-1392 and https://www.historyofparliamentonline.org/volume/1386-1421/member/stapleton-sir-brian-1417 [accessed 17 Sept. 2021].

[16] *Item ... Abbatisse de Denney, unum crucifixem et unum librum de Frensshe*: Clay, *North Country Wills*, p. 48.

[17] At the time of the dissolution most of these houses (except for Denney) had fewer than fifteen women religious in residence: Denney (35), Sinningthwaite (10), Arthington (10), Esholt (11), Nun Monkton (15). See Josiah Cox Russell, 'The Clerical Population of Medieval England', *Traditio*, 2 (1944), 177–212, p. 184; David Knowles and R. Neville

Books in a Monastic Environment

The written text was always a vital part of Christianity from the beginning, with the codex taking on a sacred role as the carrier of the word of God. The Rule of St Benedict places reading and meditating on spiritual texts as an intrinsic part of daily life (*lectio divina*). At Lent, members of the religious house were instructed to 'each receive a book from the library, to be read straight through in its entirety'.[18] However, many houses would not have had a dedicated library, or even many manuscripts, so a recess in the wall would have been more than adequate to store their collection, probably in the north eastern part of the cloister between the chapter house and the door into the monastic church, and examples of recesses can be found at Waverley Abbey, Surrey, and Dryburgh Abbey, Scotland.[19]

Early capitula of the Cistercian Order listed the books a house was expected to have in its possession to be fully functional: '*nec sine libris istis: psalterio, hymnario, collectane, antiphonario, gradali, regula, missali*'.[20] Extant medieval library catalogues and surviving inscriptions of monastic ownership, indicate this book list was adhered to but besides the required religious texts, houses owned medical, scientific and historical texts, indicating the wide reading matter available at the more wealthy monasteries.[21] Other practical items included deeds, account books, and annals, as well as books on husbandry.

The Rule of St Benedict gives clear instructions on when and where to read. Chapter 38 instructs that mealtimes were always to be accompanied by a reading from one of the members of the community. Regular readings also took place throughout the day when the community gathered for the daily offices. Private, silent reading was also encouraged, in the cloister or in the dormitory.[22] However, books

---

Hadcock, *Medieval Religious Houses: England and Wales*, 2nd edn (London, 1971), pp. 276, 270, 273, 263.

[18] E.g., *RSB*, Ch 38; Ch 42, and Ch 48.

[19] Sara Charles, 'The Martyrology of London, British Library, MS Cotton Claudius D III: A Textual and Palaeographic Analysis of the Manuscript to Determine its Origin' (Unpublished M.Res. dissertation, University of London, 2018), p. 135; John Clark, *The Care of Books* (Cambridge, 1901), p. 81; Kimm Curran, '"Through the Keyhole of the Monastic Library Door": Learning and Education in Scottish Medieval Monasteries', in Robert Anderson, Mark Freeman, and Lindsay Paterson (eds), *The Edinburgh History of Education in Scotland* (Edinburgh, 2015), pp. 25–38.

[20] Chrysogonus Waddell (ed.), *Twelfth-Century Statutes from the Cistercian General Chapter: Latin Text with English Notes and Commentary* (Brecht, 2002), p. 512.

[21] E.g., BL, Sloane MS 1975 (medical); British Library, Egerton MS 3314 (scientific) and Bury St Edmonds twelfth-century medieval catalogue (*Corpus of British Medieval Library Catalogues*, 16 vols (London, 1990), vol. 4, B13.253, B13.23a and B13.6.

[22] Curran, 'Monastic Library Door', pp. 27–9.

SARA CHARLES

given out at Lent were returned every night to the book cupboard,[23] indicating that books needed to be held communally, rather than individually.

Books and Networks of Women Religious

As inscriptions from manuscripts reveal relationships between patrons and religious houses, these can also show more subtle networks between women religious. An early example of the circulation of early Christian texts in England comes from Cuthswith, superior of Inkberrow, near Worcester, who inscribed her ownership (c. 700) in an Italian copy of Jerome's Commentary on Ecclesiastes. She wrote in an insular script 'Cuthsuuithae boec thaerae abbatissan' (a book of Cuthswith the abbess).[24] This manuscript is now in the library at Würzburg, providing an example of the geographical range of book traffic in this period – travelling from Italy, to England, to Germany.

The Book of Nunnaminster (London, British Library, MS Harley 2965) is a prayerbook written between 800 and 825, which was made in Mercia, featuring feminised Latin forms, indicating it was meant for female use.[25] It also contains, at the back of the manuscript, a record outlining boundaries of land belonging to Ealhswith, probably the same Ealhswith who married King Alfred and founded Nunnaminster, and the boundaries of these lands still correspond to archaeological evidence.[26] Evidence of later use is seen in the confession on a flyleaf (again using Latin female forms) sometime during the early tenth century, demonstrating the many owners and houses a medieval manuscript can pass through, cherished by its users and handed on through networks of women and women's monastic communities.[27]

Relationships and networks existed between men and women's communities too. Books may be lent or created for women's houses by male religious. For example, a thirteenth-century manuscript from the community of Wintney contains a martyrology and the Rule of St Benedict, copied for them by the monks at Waverley. Despite never acknowledging the nearby priory as a daughter house, Waverley clearly had a good relationship with Wintney during the early thirteenth

---

[23] Curran, 'Monastic Library Door', p. 28.
[24] Würzburg, University of Würtzburg, MS M.p.th.q.2, fol. 1r, http://vb.uni-wuerzburg.de/ub/mpthq2/pages/mpthq2/1.html [accessed 18 Sept. 2021]; Michelle P. Brown, 'Female Book-Ownership and Production in Anglo-Saxon England : The Evidence of the Ninth-Century Prayerbooks', in Christian J. Kay and Louise M. Sylvester (eds), *Lexis and Texts in Early English: Studies Presented to Jane Roberts* (Amsterdam, 2001), pp. 45–67, at p. 47.
[25] Brown, 'Female Book-Ownership', pp. 52–6.
[26] Brown, 'Female Book-Ownership', pp. 52–6.
[27] Brown, 'Female Book-Ownership', pp. 52–6.

century – going so far as to produce a good quality manuscript, with the entire text of the Rule of St Benedict specifically adapted for a female audience.[28]

An inscription on fol. 3v from a monk named Simon (probably from Waverley), also reveals the close relationship between the houses, since he wrote an Anglo-Norman verse on fol. 3v asking the head of the house and her community to receive him in the chapter as a brother and record his death 'in this book'.[29] Despite no other evidence of Waverley's involvement with the priory (Wintney seems to have had a closer relationship with Winchester), the physical evidence of a close relationship remains – the production of a manuscript is a serious investment and stands testament to an unofficial and unacknowledged relationship between the two communities.

Another example of an 'unofficial' connection comes from the commission or gifting of books to women religious communities. The Iona Psalter is a beautiful thirteenth-century manuscript that was intended as a gift to the women's community founded on Iona in *c.* 1203. It was founded by Ragnall mac Somairle, with his sister Bethóc installed as its superior. Although the psalter was produced in Oxford (as evidenced by the inclusion of the Oxford saint, Friðeswiðe, in the calendar), other saints, such as Columba and Adomnan, suggest a strong Ionian link.[30] It is very likely that Ragnall commissioned this book for his sister's community, and its ownership is verified by Bethóc's inscription on the flyleaf.[31] This again serves as an example of gifts to women's monastic communities, and the inclusion of an inscription that can provide much background knowledge to the history of a book.

Books were also lent or given between houses. A fifteenth-century inscription in a manuscript of assorted religious texts reads 'Be it remembered that Dame Maud Wade, prioress of Swine, has given this book to Dame Joan Hyltoft in Nun Cotham'.[32] However, there were sometimes disputes over books, as a visitation

---

[28] Sara Charles, 'The Literacy of English Nuns in the Early Thirteenth Century: Evidence from London, British Library, Cotton MS Claudius D. iii', *JMMS*, 6 (2017), 77–107.

[29] For a full transcription, see P. Meyer, 'Bribes de Littérature Anglo-Normande', in *Jahrbuch Für Romanische Und Englische Literatur*, ed. by A. Ebert (Leipzig, 1866), pp. 45–7.

[30] N. J. Morgan and J. J. G. Alexander, *Early Gothic Manuscripts I (1190–1250)* (London, 1982), pp. 76–7.

[31] See Tom Turpie, 'North-eastern Saints in the Aberdeen Breviary and the *Historia Gentis Scotorum* of Hector Boece: Liturgy, History and Religious Practice in Late Medieval Scotland', in Jane Geddes (ed.), *Medieval Art, Architecture and Archaeology in the Dioceses of Aberdeen and Moray* (Oxford, 2016), pp. 239–47, at p. 240; for the inscription of ownership of the psalter with Bethoc, NLS, MS 10000, f. 9r. I am grateful to Kimm Curran for the reference to the Iona Psalter.

[32] 'Be yt remembryd that dame mald Wade priorys of Swyne has gyven this boke to dame

to the community of Ankerwyke in 1441 reveals. William Alnwick, bishop of Lincoln, heard a list of grievances from Dame Margaret Kirkeby against the superior, Dame Clemence Medforde. Kirkeby accuses Medforde of 'carelessness and negligence', including giving away 'beautiful psalters kept in the house, ten in number'.[33] Medforde did confess to lending three of the psalters – one of them to the house of Bromhall and with the consent of the community. Although it is unclear whether Medforde was telling the truth here, the episode suggests that it was normal practice to lend books through the networks of women's communities. Also, Medforde's mention that the books were lent with the consent of the community does imply that a consultation process was established among the inhabitants on the lending books.

Several heads of houses bequeathed their personal books to their community on their deaths. For example, Edith Corf, superior at Tarrant, wrote in her psalter that after her death the book should be returned to the chantry at Tarrant.[34] However, it is book-giving between members of individual houses that can give an idea of networks and friendships. The community at Dartford, Kent, has a surviving manuscript inscription from the early sixteenth century that demonstrates the personal relationships that may have formed between sisters. Downside Abbey, MS 26542 has an inscription on fol. 3v that reads: 'This book is given to Betrice Chaumbir, and after her decease to sister Emme Wynter and to sister Denyse Caston, nuns of Dartford, and so to abide in the same house of the nuns of Dartford forever'.[35] Although there is little other information on the sisters mentioned (apart from Emme Wynter also owning two other surviving books),[36] the status of the women as sisters would suggest a genuine friendship among them.

Another fifteenth-century inscription from the Minories in London reads: 'Memorandum that Dame Annes Porter gave to Dame An Frenell, minoress without Aldgate of London, this book to give after her decease with the licence

---

joan hyltoft in nuncotom': see London, BL, MS Harley 2409, fol. 78v; also Bell, *What Nuns Read*, p. 171.

[33] A. Hamilton Thompson (ed.), *Visitations of Religious Houses in the Diocese of Lincoln, vol. 2: Records of Visitations held by William Alnwick, Bishop of Lincoln 1436–49, part 1* (Horncastle, 1918), p. 2.

[34] 'Istud psalterium constat Edithe Corf, prioresse; post decessum predicte Edithe reuertatur ad officium cantarie de Tarent': Bell, *What Nuns Read*, p. 211. See also Catherine Babington, sub-prioress at Campsey, who gifted her book to the community: Bell, *What Nuns Read*, p. 124.

[35] 'This boke is youe to Betryce Chaumbir', and aftir hir decese to sustir Emme Wynter and to sustir Denyse Caston', nonnes of Dertforthe, and so to abide in the saam hous of the nonnes of Dertforthe for euere': Bell, *What Nuns Read*, p. 130.

[36] Bell, *What Nuns Read*, pp. 130–3.

of her suffering to whom that she will. God safe, An'.[37] From the same house, a sixteenth-century psalter has the following inscription:

> Memorandum that this psalter was given by Beterice Carneburgh unto Dame Grace Centurio to have it for the term of her life, and after her decease to remain unto what sister of the Minoresses that it shall please the same grace to give it, never to be given away, sold, nor lent, but only to the Minoresses, they to pray perpetually for the souls named in this present psalter.[38]

These inscriptions reveal the deep connections between the women, and their loyalty to their community, with the insistence that the book remains there 'for euere'.

In an environment where personal possessions were supposed to be kept to a minimum, if not completely relinquished, a book represented valuable currency – either in status or emotion. Janika Bishop outlines the different values of books, economic and symbolic: 'The symbolic and abstract value associated with knowledge and learning, both firmly connected with books and literacy [means that] the actual monetary (that is, the *exchange*) value attributed to any single book or manuscript can easily surpass its mere production and material cost'.[39] The symbolic value is understood here as the gift of knowledge from the author to the reader.[40] Yet, apart from these economic and symbolic values of books, there is also an emotional value, bound up in its provenance.

The act of reading, or even just handling, a book, is tactile. Inheriting books from loved ones and touching the pages that they touched could invoke strong and tangible links with them. The known provenance of a book could also add weight of legacy and heritage, and passing on a book to a close friend in a religious community would have emotional resonance.[41] Many books within the monastic environment may have been with the community for a long time, with their

---

[37] 'Memorandum that dam Annes Porter gafe to dam An Frenell Meneres wythe owte Algate of Lundun this boke to gyfe aftur hur deses with the licens of hur sufferen to hom that she wull. God safe An': Bell, *What Nuns Read*, p. 150. There is some confusion over the word 'sufferin' here. Suffer could mean allow: the meaning would then be that the book would be given after her death, with the permission of her sisters, to whom she wishes.

[38] 'Memorandum that this Sawter was gevyn by Beterice Carneburgh unto Dame Grace Centurio to have it to her for terme of her lyfe, and aftir hir discesse to remayne unto what syster of the Meneres that it shall plese the seme grace to gyf it, never to be gevyn away, solde, nor lent, but onely to the Meneres, they to pray perpetually for the sawles named in this present Sawter': Bell, *What Nuns Read*, p. 150.

[39] Bishof, *Testaments, Donations, and the Values of Books as Gifts*, p. 59.

[40] Ann Astell, 'On the Usefulness and Use Value of Books: A Medieval and Modern Inquiry', in Scott D. Troyan (ed.), *Medieval Rhetoric* (London, 2004), pp. 41–62.

[41] On appointing women religious as memory-keepers of their community through their care of books and sacred objects, and their preservation of their foremothers, see Katie

history and memory enmeshed within the memory of the persons, donors, or community. The inscription records a moment in its life cycle, before being passed onto another owner or reader. All others thereafter would have the reminder of the writer of the inscription, thus adding to the book's longevity within the community and strengthening that sense of legacy and belonging. The books and inscriptions could almost act as a portal to accessing the community memory.

Books and Their Emotional Significance

If these inscriptions were written by a close family member, the emotional significance would have resonated even more deeply. Although some books may have been given as conspicuous symbols of a family's wealth and prestige, the inscriptions may tell a story of family connections, movement of women and family members to monastic institutions. The written words inside, combined with the book as a physical object, would have given it a greater weight.

For example, a psalter dating from the mid thirteenth century that belonged to Anne Felbrigge, a sister of Bruisyard Abbey, Suffolk, in the fourteenth century is inscribed by Anne herself: 'this is the book of sister Anne Felbrigge, which will become the property of the minoresses at Bruisyard after her death'.[42] This psalter is decorated with the family arms (a red lion rampant) painted on the fore-edge, and it also has obituary entries for Anne's mother and father written in the calendar.[43] Anne does not seem to have held a position of authority within the community, yet she clearly came from a wealthy family. Allowing this personal possession (which would have been used for personal devotion) may have been a source of comfort after the passing of her mother (†1416) and father (†1442). Although the dates for Anne's life are unknown, she was living at Bruisyard by the time of her father's death and chose proudly to commemorate him by adding his details to her psalter: 'Obitus venerabilis domini Simonis ffelbrygge militis' on fol. 7v. He in turn left provision for Anne and the abbey in his will: 'to Ann, his daughter, a nun at Brusyard in Suffolk, 13s. 4d. per ann. to be paid out of the manor of South Repps, for life, and after to the abbess and convent aforesaid, for ever'.[44] Here the family

---

A.-M. Bugyis, *The Care of Nuns: The Ministries of Benedictine Women in England during the Central Middle Ages* (New York, 2019), Chapter 1.

[42] 'Iste liber est sororis anne ffelbrygge ad terminum vite post cuius decessum pertinebit conventui minorissarum de Brusyerde': London, BL, Sloane MS 2400, fol. 2v.

[43] BL, Sloane MS 2400, fols 3r, 5v and 7v. For images, see http://www.bl.uk/catalogues/ illuminatedmanuscripts/record.asp?MSID=8811 [accessed 15 Dec. 2019].

[44] Francis Blomefield, 'North Erpingham Hundred: Felbrigg', in *An Essay Towards a Topographical History of the County of Norfolk*, vol. 8 (London, 1808), pp. 107–19, British History Online, http://www.british-history.ac.uk/topographical-hist-norfolk/ vol8/pp107-119 [accessed 15 Dec. 2019].

relationships were able to survive the move from the outside world to the cloister, and Anne's psalter would have been a constant reminder of her previous life with her family. The physical presence of her book may have also sparked memories of previous handlings of the manuscript, as memories become entwined with the senses and physical acts, such as the smell of lavender drifting in when turning a page, or even an accidental scorch mark on the parchment from a clumsily held candle. These memories may lie dormant, until suddenly revived by turning the same page, or rereading the same passage. By leaving this book to her community, Anne's mentions of her family could also have prompted those using it afterwards to retrieve their personal family memories, thereby creating a continuous mental connection between the religious women and their natal homes.

In an early fourteenth-century copy of the *Doctrine of the Heart* we find the following inscription:

> It is to wit that Dame Cristyne St Nicolas of the minoresses of London, daughter of Nicolas St Nycolas, squire, gives this book after her decease to the office of the [text erased] and to the office of the abbessry perpetually, thee which passed to god out of the world the year of our lord 1455, the ninth day of March, of whose soul god have mercy.[45]

The superior of the Minoresses in London, Christine St Nicolas, died on 9 March 1455, and gave this book to her community. It is interesting that her father, Nicholas St Nicolas, has been mentioned, and his status as squire. Again, this would have served as a reminder for others reading this book of close familial links, and perhaps sparked recollections of their own.

Another example is an inscription from a fifteenth-century manuscript containing works by Walter Hilton – *The Scale of Perfection*, *The Mixed Life* and *Bonum est*. It belonged to the superior of the London Minoresses, Dame Elizabeth Horwode, who obtained the book for her community sometime between 1460 and 1480. The inscription on fol. 94v reads:

> Dame Elizabeth Horwode, Abbess of the Minoresses of London, to her [spiritual] comfort bought this book, it to remain to the use of the sisters of the said place

---

[45] 'Hit ys to witt þt dame Cristyne seint nicolas of ye menoresse of london dowgh-tyr of nicolas Seint Nycolas squier geff þis boke aftyr hyr dysses to þe offyce of þe [text erased] and to þe offys of ye abbessry perpetually þe whyche passed to god out of þe worlde þe yere of owre lorde m.cccc.l.v þe ix day of marche of whoys soule god haue merci': Cambridge, Trinity College, MS B.14.15, fol. 78r, https://mss-cat.trin.cam.ac.uk/manuscripts/uv/view.php?n=B.14.15&n=B.14.15#?c=0&m=0&s=0&cv=80&xywh=1571%2C169%2C2522%2C1001.

to pray for thee ever and for the souls of her father and her mother, Thomas Horwode and Beatryxe, and the soul of master Robert Alderton.[46]

At the bottom of the page, in a different hand, the words 'thys bok longyth to the abbesry' ['this book belongs to the abbey'] were written. While this was not a personal possession of Elizabeth Horwode, and the inscription probably written by someone else, Mary Ehler describes this as 'doubly familial', invoking both the natal family and religious family.[47] Imploring the community to pray for the souls of Elizabeth's parents would not only recall personal family relationships, but could also allow those prayers to be in part for their own mothers and fathers.

The final example is a fifteenth-century Book of Hours from the community at Syon. This is a beautifully decorated manuscript, reflecting the high status of the women that entered Syon. On fol. 56v, the following inscription has been written: 'Of your charity pray for the souls of John Edwards and Margaret his wife and for Elizabeth their daughter, professed in Syon, for whose use this book was made'.[48] Underneath there is a symbol and the letter 'e', perhaps indicating a personal signature. Family relationships are cemented here, with Elizabeth being asked to remember her parents in her prayers after she enters the community. And despite the conspicuous consumption that came with high quality manuscripts, inscriptions are enclosed within a book, only visible to those leafing through the pages, making it a much more private interaction. That the inscription is tucked away on fol. 56v – hardly the ostentatious declaration it would have been had it appeared on the opening page – would imply that this was an intimate message to Elizabeth, for her to call to mind her parents and her life with them in a moment of personal prayer.

These family manuscripts demonstrate not only the importance of books in women's religious communities, but also how the personal could become part of the institutional through the inclusion of inscriptions. Books become a representation of the tangible link with the outside world, particularly if they came from their familial home, as in the case of Anne Felbrigge's book, which surely would have evoked memories of the placement of the book in domestic

---

[46] 'Dame Elizabeth horwode abbas of the menoresse off london to her gostle Comfforthe bowgtes thys boke hyt to Remayne to the Vse off þe Systerres of þe sayde place to pray for þe yeuer & For þe sowles off hyr Fader & her moder. Thomas horwode & beatryxe & þe sowle off mayster Robert Alderton': London, BL, Harley MS 2397, fol. 94v.

[47] Mary C. Erler, *Women, Reading and Piety in Late Medieval England* (Cambridge, 2002), pp. 27–8.

[48] 'Of your charite praye for the sowlys of John Edwarde and Margaret hys wyffe and for Elizabethe ther doughter professed yn Syon for whos use thy boke was made': London, BL, Cotton MS Appendix XIV, fol. 56v.

surroundings, possibly even being used by family members. But much more than that, these personal reminders of natal links, in books that were left to be shared by all, would have been internalised by the other female readers, who would have been able to draw on their own family memories. In some cases, these may not have been happy memories, but to many women religious these reminders of their previous domestic lives would have been a source of comfort and security.

Conclusion

Gift-giving and relationships between women religious and other female networks are areas that open up great possibilities for future research. This chapter has examined some of these relationships among patrons, women religious, their networks, and the natal family, through the practice of book-giving and inscriptions. The value that was imbued in inherited books – financial, spiritual, and emotional – served to cement firm links between women religious and their communities. Leaving behind a natal family meant that new connections were forged between women religious within their Christian family, and they could demonstrate this by passing on cherished books to each other. These books were often inscribed, and further investigation of the types of books that were inscribed, how gifts were given, to whom, and why certain books may have been more likely to be inscribed, may reveal much more about the lives of individual women religious, the monastic communities, and their networks. The consistent way that natal families were involved in religious communities demonstrates that it was also impossible completely to sever natal ties; and that a religious community was not just comprised of individual members, but that they brought with them a whole network of family relationships that could be woven into daily life, through the books that were such an essential part of their religious devotion, and the evocative book inscriptions contained within.

CHAPTER 10

Communities of Medieval Religious Women and Their Landscapes

YVONNE SEALE

W OMEN religious were embedded in the landscapes of the Middle Ages,
and studying how they engaged with those landscapes – through agricultural practices, building projects, and more – can help us better understand their
impact on the world around them.[1] Historians of landscape define their object of
study in various different ways, but the study of the historical landscape generally
involves the study of the interactions of geology, topography, cultural identities,
and human activities layered together in a given place over time.[2] At first glance,
it might not seem as if the study of the historical landscape could have much to
tell us about the history of women religious, and vice versa. After all, most women
religious in the Middle Ages would have spent much of their lives behind the
walls of their cloister, many communities of women religious had fewer financial
resources than did their male counterparts, and women generally were at a legal
disadvantage compared to men. How, then, could women religious influence the
landscape? Adopting a landscape approach to the study of women religious helps
us answer this question and prompts us to ask others. What kinds of relationships
existed between women religious and the natural world in the Middle Ages? How
did women religious manage both their resources and their relationships with the

---

[1] For a sense of the variety of approaches which historians and archaeologists have taken
   towards the history of the landscape, see Cornelius Holtorf and Howard Williams,
   'Landscapes and Memories', in Dan Hicks and Mary Beaudry (eds), *The Cambridge
   Companion to Historical Archaeology* (Cambridge, 2006), pp. 235–54; John S. Howe
   and Michael Wolfe, *Inventing Medieval Landscapes: Senses of Place in Western Europe*
   (Gainesville, 2002); Clare A. Lees and Gillian R. Overing, *A Place to Believe In: Locating
   Medieval Landscapes* (University Park, 2006).
[2] For a discussion of 'landscape' in medieval environmental history, see Richard C.
   Hoffman, *An Environmental History of Medieval Europe* (Cambridge, 2014), pp. 113–14;
   for definitions of landscape and landscape history more generally, see Richard Muir,
   'Conceptualising Landscape', *Landscapes*, 1:1 (2000), 4–21.

outside world? Were there differences between women religious and male religious in their use of the landscape?

This chapter focuses on how women religious helped to shape the landscapes they inhabited. First, it discusses the location of women's religious communities and the symbolic associations attached to those locations. Second, it considers the 'internal landscape' or layout of those communities, and how women religious organised the spaces in which they lived. It then turns to exploring the wider monastic estate – farmlands, water resources, woodlands, and more – and how women religious dealt with the challenges and disputes that arose from the landscape. Finally, it considers some of the legacies of monastic communities on the modern landscape and how new technologies can help us better to understand these places.

Locating Women's Monastic Communities within Sacred Landscapes

A particular place or landscape can have religious and affective meanings that are not purely topographical, but rather perpetuated through narratives as well as being framed by natural and built landmarks. Moving through and in a sacred landscape could take many forms for medieval Christians: crossing the boundaries of a parish or diocese, constructing a cross or shrine to commemorate the site of a miracle, visiting holy wells, going on pilgrimage, hearing church bells while labouring in the fields, or being aware of or seeing monasteries in the landscape. Houses of women religious formed part of, and were connected to, this wider sacred Christian landscape.

Choosing where to build a monastic community could be as much the result of religious aspirations as pragmatic considerations. Foundation narratives were generally keen to stress the 'monastic ideal' of settling in a wilderness, the taming of which was testament to piety and perseverance. For example, a tenth-century document from the community of Sant Joan de les Abadesses in Catalonia describes the events surrounding the community's foundation in 887. It states that the house was 'located in the waste or desert' and that the community was permitted to clear the lands 'from waste for cultivation'.[3] It is not clear how literally we should read this description, but it shows how important the idea of monastic settlements in wild places was for medieval Christians and their sense of the power of their faith.

A community could also deliberately choose its location to express the monastic ideals of asceticism and self-denial using the landscape around them. The

---

[3]   Jonathan Jarrett, 'Power over Past and Future: Abbess Emma and the Nunnery of Sant Joan de les Abadesses', *EME*, 12:3 (2003), 229–58, at pp. 242–3.

community of Coyroux in south central France was deliberately founded in an inhospitable location: a steep-sided valley whose floor was so rocky and narrow that a terrace had to be constructed to provide a sufficiently flat stretch of ground to build the monastery.[4] Shifting climactic conditions in the High Middle Ages resulting in higher sea levels made many of the northern islands of the Venetian lagoon unattractive for settlement. Yet in the late twelfth and thirteenth centuries, several women's monastic communities were established there.[5] These are not isolated cases. Roberta Gilchrist has argued that the tendency for communities of women religious in England to be located on more marginal and remote sites may have been a deliberate choice on the part of these women and their patrons, to stress their humility, poverty, and ascetic lifestyle.[6]

While many monastic institutions were founded in rural areas, partly out of a desire to imitate the scriptural 'voice crying out in the wilderness', a significant proportion of medieval religious institutions were established in towns and cities.[7] Communities of women religious would have been a visible part of the medieval urban landscape. Many houses were involved with the running of charitable establishments, such as hospitals and leper houses, and prosperous cities like late medieval Mainz could be home to many of them, all competing with one another for space and resources.[8] Given the location of many such institutions, the women religious who ran them would have been at the bustling heart of medieval urban expansion. They were perhaps drawn there because these were often marginal parts of the city and offered the most opportunity to tend to the poor and sick.[9]

---

[4]   Bernadette Barrière, 'The Cistercian Convent of Coyroux in the Twelfth and Thirteenth Centuries', *Gesta*, 31:2 (January 1992), 76–82.

[5]   Anna Maria Rapetti, 'Women and Monasticism in Venice in the Tenth to Twelfth Centuries', in *WMMW*, pp. 145–66, at p. 156.

[6]   See *GMC*, especially pp. 128–38.

[7]   See Isaiah 40. 3; John 1. 23; Mark 1. 3. However, as Elizabeth Freeman has pointed out, while narratives produced by male religious communities often referred to these scriptural passages or to others like Deuteronomy 32:10 in describing their communities as being sited in 'places of horror and vast solitude', narratives produced by or about communities of women tend not to place the same emphasis. Elizabeth Freeman, 'Cistercian Nuns in Medieval England: The Gendering of Geographic Marginalization', *Medieval Feminist Forum*, 43:2 (Dec. 2007), 26–39, at p. 26.

[8]   Lucy C. Barnhouse, 'Disordered Women? The Hospital Sisters of Mainz and Their Late Medieval Identities', *Medieval Feminist Forum*, 55:2 (2020), 60–97.

[9]   Núria Jornet Benito, 'Female Mendicant Spirituality in Catalan Territory: The Birth of the First Communities of Poor Clares', in *WMMW*, pp. 185–209, at pp. 200–1.

Internal Landscape of Women's Communities

The footprint of monastic houses – their internal layout – can tell us how the space would be used and the kinds of interactions that would take place within it. Looking at the precinct layouts of communities of medieval women religious allows us to see what Roberta Gilchrist has termed the set of 'collective spatial gestures' that were particular to each community or, in other words, how women religious could use architectural layout to create, reinforce, and demonstrate their identity as a group.[10] The size, location, and style of building could also indicate the expectations of a community's lay founders and patrons. For example, both the location of the community of Las Huelgas and its use as a dynastic burial site reflected the political aspirations of its founding patrons, the Castilian royal family, while its early adoption of Gothic architecture on the Iberian peninsula signalled the family's cultural sophistication.[11]

There was no single template for the layout of medieval monastic houses, although there were many similarities between communities and many common elements: a church, a cloister, a refectory (communal dining room), and a dormitory.[12] The cloister was perhaps the most evocative architectural element of a medieval monastery and generally took the form of covered walkways enclosing a quadrangle, which were themselves surrounded by the other main buildings of the monastery.[13] Medieval monasteries were constructed on scales large and small, depending on location, geography, and patronage. The community of Maubuisson, for example, was elaborate because of the patronage of its founder, Blanche of Castile, queen of France (†1252). The rare survival of the account books associated with Maubuisson's construction in the 1230s reveals payments made to craftspeople for fashioning the rafters and room beams for the chapel, the floor tiles for the community's dormitory, the 4,000 individual floorboards – even a fountain for the cloister.[14]

---

[10] *GMC*, p. 18.

[11] James D'Emilio, 'The Royal Convent of Las Huelgas: Dynastic Politics, Religious Reform and Artistic Change in Medieval Castile', in Meredith Parsons Lilich (ed.), *Cistercian Nuns and Their World* (Kalamazoo, 2005), pp. 191–282.

[12] This is a generalisation about monasteries in the high and Late Middle Ages. The houses of women religious in Ireland, for instance, often did not conform to the claustral plan. See Tracy E. Collins, 'An Archaeological Perspective on Female Monasticism in the Middle Ages in Ireland', in *WMMW*, pp. 229–51, at p. 239.

[13] For a discussion of the development of the monastic cloister, see Walter Horn, 'On the Origins of the Medieval Cloister', *Gesta*, 12:1/2 (1973), 13–52.

[14] Constance H. Berman (ed. and trans.), *Women and Monasticism in Medieval Europe: Sisters and Patrons of the Cistercian Reform*, TEAMS (Kalamazoo, 2002), p. 109; Lindy Grant, *Blanche of Castile: Queen of France* (New Haven, 2016), pp. 257–62.

However, most women's monastic houses were not built on such a lavish scale. The community of Beaupré-sur-la-Lys in northern France is more typical of what we find for medieval women religious. While nothing remains above ground of Beaupré, archaeological excavations at the site have provided a sense of what its east range looked like in the first half of the thirteenth century, with a sacristy on the northern end abutting the church, followed by a stairwell, which would have led upstairs to a dormitory, a chapter house, and a common room.[15]

Urban women's religious communities, like those of the beguines, were often spatially distinct from the towns around them without being cloistered. A four-teenth-century description of the beguinage of St Elizabeth in Ghent describes it as 'encircled by ditches and walls', with a central church, cemetery, and hospital. Several individual dwellings were constructed inside the beguinage for the beguines, each of which had its 'own garden, separated from the next by ditches or hedges.'[16] Such communities could be so large – the one at Liège was home to about 1,000 women in the mid-thirteenth century; the one at Mechelen home to some 1,500 by the late fifteenth century – that they were sometimes referred to as a *civitas beghinarum* ('city of beguines'), and it is impossible to imagine them as having anything other than a significant presence in the urban landscape.[17]

There can be challenges associated with looking at the inner landscape of medi-eval women's monastic communities. Whether ruined or intact, the extant struc-tures will only represent the last phase of a site's development. For example, the community of Almenêches, France, was founded in the sixth century, abandoned by the tenth, refounded about a century later, and subject to a series of major fires. Very little of its early medieval phase survives, and the visitor to Almenêches today will see a mostly sixteenth-century structure.[18] Even if a community's buildings have remained continuously in use by women religious since the Middle Ages, those buildings will almost certainly have been subject to damage, renovation, and redecoration over the centuries, and there may also be one or more phases of later building work overlaying or encompassing the initial medieval construction. For instance, the Munsterkerk at Roermond in the Netherlands was radically altered

---

[15]   Thomas Coomans, 'The Medieval Architecture of Cistercian Nunneries in the Low Countries', *Bulletin KNOB*, 103:3 (2004), 62–90, at p. 76.

[16]   Emilie Amt (ed.), *Women's Lives in Medieval Europe*, 2nd edn (Abingdon, 2010), p. 214. This beguinage is not to be confused with the later Groot Begijnhof Sint-Elisabeth, a replacement community built in a Ghent suburb in the 1870s.

[17]   Walter Simons, *Cities of Ladies: Beguine Communities in the Medieval Low Countries, 1200–1565* (Philadelphia, 2001), pp. 54–5.

[18]   Leonie V. Hicks, *Religious Life in Normandy, 1050–1300: Space, Gender, and Social Pressure* (Woodbridge, 2007), p. 193.

between 1844 and 1891, with towers added and medieval internal décor removed to better suit contemporary tastes.[19]

The Physical Landscape: The Wider Monastic Estate

Medieval women religious and their communities were expected to pray for the world and remain apart from it in 'this wilderness'. However, matters of the body – securing a sufficient supply of firewood for cooking and heating, managing water resources, and ensuring that a roof was kept in good repair – were important for the survival of the community. At a minimum, monasteries needed enough income to house, clothe, and feed their members. Most religious communities depended on the produce, in cash or in kind, of the lands that they held in order to do so. Whether acquired in the form of crops, timber, fuel, rental income, or something else, this generally required some form of intervention with the natural world, and so all but the most ephemeral of monasteries shaped the landscape around them. This was especially the case as, since monastic estates were not subject to subdivision or transition in the same manner as lay ones, religious institutions could maintain continuity of ownership over substantial tracts of land for centuries.

AGRICULTURE AND ANIMAL HUSBANDRY

Monastic gardens and orchards provided fruits, vegetables, and herbs, some of which had medicinal as well as culinary uses.[20] Such gardens and orchards were often enclosed by walls of stone, brick, or wattle, marking them out as sites of focused cultivation. However, many of the staples of the medieval diet were made from grains, and crops like wheat or oats were generally grown on a larger scale than that of a kitchen garden. Both the kinds of crops that could be planted, the yields that could be expected, and whether the crops were planted in open or enclosed field systems, varied greatly according to local climate, soil conditions, and customs.[21] The barns which were built to store the harvest were highly visible reminders in the landscape of the ownership that women religious had over their estates.[22] So too were the other built structures on their lands, as for example the circular dovecote and artificial fishpond at the monastery of St Catherine's at Shanagolden in south western Ireland; the ovens and mills operated

---

[19] Coomans, 'Medieval Architecture', 64.

[20] James Bond, 'Production and Consumption of Food and Drink in the Medieval Monastery', in Graham Keevill, Michael Aston, and Teresa Anne Hall (eds), *Monastic Archaeology: Papers on the Study of Medieval Monasteries* (Oxford, 2001), pp. 54–87.

[21] Bond, 'Production and Consumption', pp. 58–60.

[22] Berman, *White Nuns*, pp. 146–7.

by the women's community of Santo Domingo el Real in various neighbourhoods around Madrid; or the general use of ditches, fences, and walls to demarcate boundary lines, corral livestock, and keep out unwanted intruders.[23]

Many medieval women religious supported themselves through animal husbandry, such as raising sheep for their wool. While grain was one of the most land-efficient suppliers of calories available to people in the Middle Ages, intensive grain cultivation required a lot of ongoing manual labour—such as ploughing, sowing, weeding, harvesting, stacking, threshing, transporting, ditch digging, manure spreading, and the feeding and watering of draft animals – which could make sheep husbandry more lucrative in terms of comparative labour inputs and thus more attractive.[24] Although this may not have the immediately visible impact on the landscape of a ploughed field, generations of intensive grazing transform a landscape while transhumance brings human activity into often remote areas. The creation of sheep-runs could lead to a reduction in an area's human population, as former tenant farmers were dispossessed.[25] The Gilbertine house of Bullington in Lincolnshire, England, is an example of a community that shaped the landscape around it through its engagement in animal husbandry. Bullington supported itself in part by raising sheep on its several hundred acres. The priory's twelfth-century founder gave various woods, land, churches, a mill, and pasturage for 600 sheep to the fledgling community.[26] In the later twelfth century, William de Pontfoi granted the community two bovates of land, a dwelling and any associated outbuildings (a toft), and enough land to pasture 200 sheep at Ingham, some ten miles away, while Alexander de Crevequer gave the community 500 sheep and various pieces of land, including enough pasture to support 300 sheep.[27] By about 1300, the house exported about eighteen sacks of wool per year to Italy, with other

[23] Collins, 'Archaeological Perspective', p. 240; Francisco García-Serrano, 'Friars and Nuns: Dominican Economy and Religious Identity in Medieval Castile', in Francisco García-Serrano (ed.), *The Friars and Their Influence in Medieval Spain* (Amsterdam, 2018), pp. 159–74, at p. 173.

[24] David Stone, 'The Productivity and Management of Sheep in Late Medieval England', *The Agricultural History Review*, 51:1 (2003), pp. 1–22, at p. 1.

[25] The Welsh writer Walter Map (*c.* 1140–*c.* 1210) famously accused the Cistercian Order of causing new solitudes in the landscape and condemning the dispossessed poor to die of starvation. Walter Map, *De Nugis Curialium: Courtiers' Trifles*, ed. and trans. Montague R. James, rev. Christopher N. L. Brooke and Roger A. B. Mynors, OMT (Oxford, 1983), pp. 84–113.

[26] Golding, *Gilbert*, pp. 206–7, 297, 421.

[27] F. M. Stenton (ed.), *Documents Illustrative of the Social and Economic History of the Danelaw, from Various Collections, Records of the Social and Economic History of England and Wales*, 5 (London, 1920), pp. 41–2, 62–3. A bovate is a unit of land measurement based on the amount of land tillable by a single ox and is roughly equivalent to 15–20 acres/6–8 hectares.

Lincolnshire communities of women religious like Nun Ormsby and Stixwould exporting comparable amounts.[28]

Fish played a significant role in the monastic diet and many medieval monasteries constructed fishponds to help supplement their diet.[29] The fish is well-known as a Christian symbol, the rabbit perhaps less so. Yet the construction of so-called 'pillow mounds' (artificial earthwork rabbit warrens) at several British communities, such as at Nun Cotham, Lincolnshire, or Haddington, Scotland, may have been intended not only to ensure a steady supply of meat and fur, but also to provide a symbolic reminder to the women religious of the Christian hope for salvation.[30] The fish, meat, bread, and other foodstuffs that were shared around the refectory table were the produce of a landscape layered with practical and symbolic connotations.

WATER RESOURCES

Women's religious communities' control and use of water resources and access to them were not always visible. For instance, thanks to the gift of Geoffrey, son of Fulcradus, in 1116, the community of Fontevraud enjoyed a variety of rights over the ferry and tolls at the bustling nearby port of Rest, located near the confluence of the Vienne and Loire rivers.[31] The levying of tolls provided income to Fontevraud but also reinforced its importance in the regional landscape.

Other uses of water resources were more tangible. Access to water was obviously a necessity for a community. Conduits running from nearby springs provided water for drinking and sanitation purposes to the community of Barking near London.[32] Water had many other uses, as recognised in the bequests made

[28] Dorothy Mary Owen, *Church and Society in Medieval Lincolnshire* (Lincoln, 1971), p. 66.

[29] For a discussion of the role of fish in the monastic diet, see Caroline Polet and M. Anne Katzenberg, 'Reconstruction of the Diet in a Mediaeval Monastic Community from the Coast of Belgium', *Journal of Archaeological Science*, 30:5 (2003), 525–33.

[30] It is believed that rabbits were introduced to Britain and Ireland only during the High Middle Ages: David Stocker and Margarita Stocker, 'Sacred Profanity: The Theology of Rabbit Breeding and the Symbolic Landscape of the Warren', *World Archaeology*, 28:2 (Oct. 1996), 265–72, at pp. 268–70.

[31] Jean-Marc Bienvenu, Robert Favreau, and Georges Pon (eds), *Grand Cartulaire de Fontevraud*, vol. 1 (Poitiers, 2000), pp. 416–17.

[32] We know that these conduits existed because in 1462, the community lost their water supply when the owner of a nearby manor house dug up and broke the pipes of a conduit leading from springs on his land to the house and refused to remedy the situation until the community agreed to pay him an annual rent of 24 shillings. The community would later get their own back by finding a new water source on their own lands. James Bond, 'Monastic Water Management in Great Britain: A Review', in Keevill, Aston, and Hall (eds), *Monastic Archaeology*, pp. 88–136, at p. 93.

in 1247 by Isabelle, countess of Chartres, to the house of Lieu-Notre-Dame-lez-Romorantin. Isabelle specified that the community could use the ponds' waters 'according to their own needs, increasing or decreasing the size of those ponds as necessary'.[33] Isabelle's bequest was deliberately flexible, but we have many examples of the specific ways in which women religious used water resources. The houses of Humiliati sisters in Italy were often concentrated near water sources, to facilitate both the hospitals which they ran and their involvement in the textile industry.[34] Many of the famous hot springs in medieval Buda (now part of Budapest) were controlled by the community of Margit-sziget.[35] In the Late Middle Ages, the sisters of Moreaucourt took advantage of their location near the confluence of the Nièvre and Somme rivers to construct mills.[36] Such water mills could be used to grind grain or in textile fulling.

Other water resource projects were even more ambitious than mill construction. In the thirteenth century, several communities in Flanders undertook dyke and canal construction as part of a series of irrigation and land reclamation projects.[37] These projects helped to facilitate the speedy transport of wool to market by canal and created new land on which the communities' flocks could graze. The community of Saint-Georges was established on land between the city walls of Rennes and the banks of the river Vilaine. The ducal family of Brittany gave the house lucrative fishing, boating, and mill rights over the river, which was a major transportation artery. In the fifteenth century, construction work done to improve the city's defences inadvertently reversed the river's flow rate and reduced the efficiency of the water mills situated on it. In 1444, Abbess Perrine petitioned for redress, arguing that the works should be undone as they were harming the public good. While unsuccessful in this instance, the community would later succeed in obtaining a ducal order stopping the construction of earth and gravel enclosures and landfills (*barrières et comblement*), which had reduced the river's breadth.[38]

[33] Ernest Plat (ed.), *Cartulaire de l'abbaye royale du Lieu-Notre-Dame-lès-Romorantin* (Romorantin, 1892), pp. 7–10.

[34] Much of the work involved in processing wool is dependent on having access to a steady and abundant supply of water. Sally Mayall Brasher, *Women of the Humiliati: A Lay Religious Order in Medieval Civic Life* (New York, 2003), p. 37.

[35] András Végh, 'Buda-Pest 1300–Buda-Pest 1400. Two Topographical Snapshots', in Balász Nagy et al. (eds), *Medieval Buda in Context* (Leiden, 2016), pp. 169–203, at p. 191.

[36] Gérard Cahon, 'Le Prieuré de Moreaucourt', *Bulletin de la Société des Antiquaires de Picardie*, 629 (1993), 296–326, at p. 314.

[37] Erin Jordan, 'Transforming the Landscape: Cistercian Nuns and the Environment in the Medieval Low Countries', *JMH*, 44:2 (Mar. 2018), 187–201.

[38] Laura Mellinger, 'Environmentalist Nuns in Medieval Brittany? Saint-Georges and the River Vilaine', *Medieval Perspectives*, 10 (1995), 157–68, at pp. 160–2.

WOODLANDS AND OTHER RESOURCES

Medieval people understood that woodlands were a valuable natural resource. Many communities of women religious possessed the rights to collect firewood or cut timber in certain areas of woodlands, though often under very specific conditions. The community of Notre-Dame-aux-Nonnains in Troyes was given rights to collect firewood in the woods of Jeugny, but only 'a single wagonload [*biga*] of wood pulled by two horses per day'; the community was forbidden to take oak and beech except for any trees that had fallen 'as long as it is neither fit for lumber nor part of an ongoing sale'.[39]

The landscape provided other resources, such as salt and peat. The community of Notre-Dame de Saintes, near the western coast of France, enjoyed the rights to produce salt on its estates, as well as to send hunters into nearby woodlands to capture game.[40] The community at Westwood, Worcestershire, was not a wealthy house, but it had a *salinarium* (brine boiling place) at nearby Droitwich, together with rental income from a *puteum* (brine pit), which helped to support its sisters.[41]

The community of Marham in Norfolk was given rights to peat fields, with local tenants owing customary service of digging and carrying the peat. Over time, this peat extraction would have altered the landscape in very noticeable ways, creating ditches that would fill with water and that caused an increase in the size of the fenland around the community.[42] Uncontrolled peat extraction in the region to the north of Bruges and Ghent in the twelfth and thirteenth centuries caused subsidence and flooding, so that by the time donors made gifts of marsh to the community of Ravensberg in the late thirteenth century, it was on condition that only a small portion of the land could be used for peat extraction.[43]

SPIRITUAL RESOURCES

Women religious also derived an income from, and exerted an influence over, the spiritual landscape during the Middle Ages. One of the most prominent examples

---

[39] Richard Keyser, 'The Transformation of Traditional Woodland Management: Commercial Sylviculture in Medieval Champagne', *French Historical Studies*, 32:3 (Aug. 2009), 353–84, at p. 368.

[40] Hugh Feiss, 'Consecrated to Christ, Nuns of This Church Community: The Benedictines of Notre-Dame de Saintes, 1047–1792', *American Benedictine Review*, 45:3 (1994), 269–302, at pp. 271, 277; Theodore Grasilier (ed.), *Cartulaires inédits de la Saintonge*, vol. 2 (Niort, 1871), p. 4.

[41] Margaret Goodrich, 'Westwood: A Rural English Nunnery with its Local and French Connections', in Joan Greatrex (ed.), *The Vocation of Service to God and Neighbor: Essays on the Interests, Involvements and Problems of Religious Communities and their Members in Society* (Turnhout, 1998), pp. 43–57, at pp. 47–8.

[42] Freeman, 'Cistercian Nuns in Medieval England', pp. 33–4.

[43] Jordan, 'Transforming', p. 200.

of this was the control by religious women of certain churches, whether through their possession of a church's *ius patronatus* (the advowson, or right to nominate a candidate of their choice to be the priest of a vacant parish church), or through their appropriation of a church (a monastic community's acquisition of all a parish's tithes and endowments in return for financial support of a vicar or stipendiary chaplain for that parish). These rights could be highly lucrative: the community of Notre-Dame de Troyes received £70 annually thanks to its rights over just one church in the town.[44]

However, the possession of such rights may have required women to engage in a wide range of administrative and practical responsibilities.[45] For example, in 1325, the rights of presentation to a newly-established chapel in the cathedral of Florence were given to the sisters of Santa Clara, on the condition that they appoint chaplains of 'good comportment and fame'.[46] Women religious were also required to oversee the maintenance and repair of religious buildings, ensuring their continual presence in the landscape; in the late fifteenth and early sixteenth centuries the head of the community, Elizabeth Stephenson of Bungay in Suffolk, England, oversaw a rebuilding programme that included both her community's church and that of five other churches in Bungay's possession.[47] However, these responsibilities were not always clearly defined or wholeheartedly claimed: in 1308, there was confusion as to whether women religious or parishioners were responsible for the costs of repairing the church at Swine in Yorkshire.[48]

Managing Landscapes:
Disputes, Boundaries, and Forces of Nature

To manage their properties effectively, medieval women religious needed to develop administrative skills and to participate in technological and agricultural innovation.[49] The actions they took to preserve, develop, and harvest the

---

[44] Johnson, *Equal*, p. 185.

[45] Hedwig Röckelein, 'Die Frauenkonvente und ihre Pfarreien: Aufriss eines Problems', in Hedwig Röckelein (ed.), *Frauenstifte: Frauenklöster und ihre Pfarreien* (Essen, 2009), pp. 9–18.

[46] Samuel K. Cohn, *The Cult of Remembrance and the Black Death: Six Renaissance Cities in Central Italy* (Baltimore, 1997), p. 147.

[47] Oliva, *FMN*, p. 80.

[48] Ian Forrest, *Trustworthy Men: How Inequality and Faith Made the Medieval Church* (Princeton, 2020), p. 292.

[49] For a discussion of how the leaders of women's communities could do so, see Bruce L. Venarde, 'Praesidentes Negotiis: Abbesses as Managers in Twelfth-Century France', in Samuel K. Cohn and Steven A. Epstein (eds), *Portraits of Medieval and Renaissance Living: Essays in Memory of David Herlihy* (Ann Arbor, 1996), pp. 189–205.

resources to which they had access affected the wider landscape. This included, but was not limited to, consolidation or expansion of estates and farms as well as leasing out lands to local tenants. For example, the women's community of Port-Royal-des-Champs consolidated their holdings into unified granges, while the sisters of the house of di Paullo in Lodi, Italy, engaged in several sales or rental transactions in the second half of the thirteenth century – generally of small pieces of vineyards, orchards, or other arable land – which indicate a commitment to a process of consolidation and expansion.[50] The community of Timolin in Kildare, Ireland, mostly had consolidated estates near the community itself in south Kildare, Laois, and Wicklow. Tracy Collins has suggested that its holdings may have been a mixture of granges and lands let out to tenant farmers.[51] To the north of Timolin, the community of Lismullin, Meath, sublet 137 acres of land from the canons of Colp and placed their own tenants on the land to farm it.[52] This strategy only makes sense if it had the potential to turn a profit, and points to the flexibility of a community's estate management strategies. Medieval women religious could be accomplished stewards of the landscape.

BOUNDARIES AND DISPUTES

Boundaries were often precise and well understood in the Middle Ages, and many were clearly outlined in grants to monastic houses. For example, an 1197 charter preserved in the cartulary of the Hospitaller priory of Saint-Gilles describes the boundaries of a plot of land extending over land, meadows, and marshes and along a levee, 'with a similar straight line up to the cultivated land' of the women's community of Saint-Césaire of Arles, and from there 'by a right line up to the Rhône'.[53] This and other charters like it – some drawn up on the orders of or negotiated by the women themselves – use the presence of women religious to help impose a geographical order on the landscape.

Other records relating to women's religious communities and boundaries often tell of property disputes and their legal mediations and resolutions. When a group of friars arrived to settle in the Italian city of Treviso in the late 1260s, they found

---

[50]   Constance H. Berman, 'Cistercian Agriculture in Female Houses of Northern France, 1200–1300', in John Drendel (ed.), *Crisis in the Later Middle Ages: Beyond the Postan-Duby Paradigm* (Turnhout, 2015), pp. 339–63, at p. 350; Brasher, *Women of the Humiliati*, pp. 94–5.

[51]   Tracy Collins, 'Timolin: A Case Study of a Nunnery Estate in Later Medieval Ireland', *Anuario de Estudios Medievales*, 44:1 (2014), 51–80, at pp. 64, 72–3.

[52]   Hall, *Women and the Church*, pp. 137–40.

[53]   Daniel Le Blévec and Alain Venturini (eds), *Cartulaire du Prieuré de Saint-Gilles de l'Hôpital de Saint-Jean de Jérusalem: 1129–1210*, Documents, Études & Répertoires (IRHT), 49 (Paris, 1997), p. 63.

themselves at odds with the Dominican sisters of San Paolo. The women's community was in possession of an episcopal privilege that restricted the construction of new buildings near their cloister, although the friars wanted to build a church nearby. Following lengthy negotiations, the friars agreed to sell some of their land to the women's community, build their new church on a different plot of land a set distance from the sisters, and separate the two properties with hedges or walls.[54]

Other clashes over lands and boundaries could be brought about by local conflict or outbreaks of war. The sisters of Santa Monaca arrived in Florence seeking to flee unrest in the region around their original community at Castiglione.[55] The community began to construct a new complex for themselves in the city, but soon found themselves in dispute with the men's community of Santa Maria del Carmine. In 1447, the latter objected to the sisters' building work, citing a restriction on the construction of a religious institution within 140 rods (approximately 700 metres) of their community. The friars even went so far as to pull down the doorjambs of the sisters' new church. In 1449, the community of Santa Monaca obtained papal permission to finish the construction of their church, although on condition that they neither extend their monastery beyond its current block nor build a bell tower.

Medieval women religious could also find their communities uneasily located in the middle of the landscape of another's dispute. This seems to be the case with, for instance, the community of Ballymore in Westmeath, Ireland, which lay in the middle of a political buffer zone. Ballymore was likely founded by the powerful Anglo-Norman de Lacy family, given that it was located very near to the caput of their Westmeath manor. As political fortunes shifted in the Later Middle Ages, with Gaelic Irish lords resurgent, it became far more difficult for the community of Ballymore to manage its estates effectively, and the monastery went into decline.[56]

FORCES OF NATURE

The landscape could also resist attempts to control and work it, which could have disastrous consequences. When drought affected west central France in the late eleventh century, and 'the fiery ardor of the sun fiercely burnt up [...] cornfields, vineyards, and meadows, everything green', local people undertook a barefoot penitential pilgrimage to pray for relief.[57] When the pilgrimage stopped at the

54   Frances Andrews, *The Other Friars: The Carmelite, Augustinian, Sack, and Pied Friars in the Middle Ages* (Woodbridge, 2006), p. 110.
55   Andrews, *Other Friars*, pp. 139–40.
56   Yvonne Seale, 'De Monasterio Desolato: Patronage and Politics in a Frontier Irish Convent', *JMMS*, 4 (2015), 21–45.
57   Johnson, *Equal*, pp. 237–39.

priory of Saint-Julien, the head of the community, Lethoidis, played a key role in mediating an agreement with the local lord whose harsh rule was believed to have incited the drought as divine punishment. In 1381, the sisters of the normally prosperous Hungarian community of Margit-sziget, had to sell property 'due to the dearth, in order to buy food' and carry out urgent repairs to their monastery, likely because of the gruelling combination of a winter of heavy snowfall followed by a summer's drought.[58]

For all their construction of mills, dykes, and weirs, medieval people could also do little to prevent serious flooding. The sisters of Val-des-Vignes moved their community from a location next to a fording point of a river to higher ground after a serious flood in 1232.[59] The community of Santa Clara-a-Velha in Coimbra, Portugal, was founded on land near the banks of the Mondego River and it flooded so frequently that, on a number of occasions, the community felt it necessary to raise the interior floors of the monastery's buildings, constructing a kind of mezzanine level inside the church and relocating the altar there to escape the flood waters. Even such elaborate works were ultimately in vain, and the sisters had to abandon the site in 1677.[60]

Legacies

Every landscape is one made up of things left behind, the legacy of prior genera-tions. Even in locations where women religious have not been present for centuries, their impact can still be felt. Place name evidence is one example of this, showing us how women religious have a lingering presence in the historic memory of a landscape. In England, place names such as Nunburnholme, Yorkshire ('nuns' place at the springs'), Nuneaton, Warwickshire ('nuns' farmstead by a river'), and Nunthorpe, Yorkshire ('outlying farm held by nuns'), all clearly preserve the memory of women religious.[61] So too do the German Nonnweiler ('nuns' settle-ment') and the French villages of Beaumont-les-Nonains, Oise ('beautiful

[58] Andrea Kiss et al., 'Food Crisis in Fourteenth-Century Hungary: Indicators, Causes and Case Studies', in Martin Bauch and Gerrit Jasper Schenk (eds), *The Crisis of the 14th Century: Teleconnections Between Environmental and Societal Change?* (Berlin, 2020), pp. 100–29, at pp. 126–7.

[59] Anne E. Lester, 'Cares Beyond the Walls: Cistercian Nuns and the Care of Lepers in Twelfth- and Thirteenth-Century Northern France', in Emilia Jamroziak and Janet Burton (eds), *Religious and Laity in Western Europe, 1000–1400: Interaction, Negotiation, and Power* (Turnhout, 2006), pp. 197–224, at p. 211.

[60] Christopher M. Gerrard and David N. Petley, 'A Risk Society? Environmental Hazards, Risk and Resilience in the Later Middle Ages in Europe', *Natural Hazards*, 69:1 (Oct. 2013), 1051–79, at p. 1076.

[61] A. D. Mills, *A Dictionary of British Place Names* (Oxford, 2011), 350.

mountain of the nuns') or Rupt-aux-Nonains, Meuse ('nuns' river').[62] The monastic associations of other names may be less immediately obvious to English speakers, such as the Catalan Vallbona de les Monges ('Good Valley of the Nuns'), or the Irish place names Kilnagalliagh ('Nuns' Church', from the Old Irish *caillech*) in Clare or Corragunnagalliaghdoo ('Little Rock of the Black Nuns') Island off the coast of Mayo.[63] Place name evidence cannot be used uncritically, however. The name of the Parisian 'rue Trousse-Nonnain' ('Fuck-Nun Street') is a sarcastic reference to the street's association with prostitutes in the Middle Ages.[64]

Place name evidence is abstract, but there are more tangible if subtle ways that medieval women religious may continue to affect the landscape, even long after their communities have disappeared. For example, archaeobotanical investigations undertaken at the former Icelandic communities of Kirkjubæjarklaustur and Reynistaðaklaustur have suggested that the sites may still be home to distinctive 'medieval relict plants', the descendants of medicinally useful flora carried across the north Atlantic and introduced to Iceland to help stock monastic infirmaries.[65] In early modern Britain, local communities often 'read' the landscape around them in a way that emphasised continuities with their pre-Reformation past, and the ruins of monasteries helped to shape local understandings of and practices around space and place. For instance, women and children were buried at the site of the former community of women religious on the Scottish island of Iona well into the eighteenth century, suggesting lingering associations of gender and landscape.[66]

[62] Manfred Niemeyer (ed.), *Deutsches Ortsnamenbuch* (Berlin, 2012), p. 456; 'Beaumont-les-Nonains', *Dictionnaire topographique de la France*, https://dicotopo.cths.fr/ [accessed 1 Aug. 2021].

[63] Joan Coromines (ed.), *Onomasticon Cataloniae*, vol. 7 (Barcelona, 1997), p. 399, col. b; 'Cill na gCailleach/Kilnagalliagh', Logainm.ie: The Place-Names Database of Ireland, https://www.logainm.ie/en/7286 [accessed 1 Aug. 2021]; 'Carraigín na gCailleach Dubh/ Corragunnagalliaghdoo Island', *Logainm.ie: The Place-Names Database of Ireland*, https://www.logainm.ie/en/37391 [accessed 1 Aug. 2021]. While in modern Irish, *cailleach* has come to mean 'witch', in Old Irish the term meant 'veiled one' or woman religious. See Máirín Ní Dhonnchadha, '*Caillech* and Other Terms for Veiled Women in Medieval Irish Texts', *Éigse*, 28 (1995), 71–96.

[64] Today part of the rue Beaubourg. Jacques Hillairet, *Dictionnaire historique des rues de Paris*, vol. 1 (Paris, 1963), p. 162.

[65] Steinunn Kristjánsdóttir, Inger Larsson, and Per Arvid Åsen, 'The Icelandic Medieval Monastic Garden – Did It Exist?', *Scandinavian Journal of History*, 39:5 (Oct. 2014), 560–79.

[66] Roberta Gilchrist, *Sacred Heritage: Monastic Archaeology, Identities, Beliefs* (Cambridge, 2020), pp. 154–5.

Conclusion

The study of the roles played by women religious in the medieval landscape has the potential to bring new dimensions to a long-established field of historical study, and perhaps even to challenge the popular misconception of the Middle Ages as a time when women were passive, oppressed, and inconsequential. Landscape studies can show us how medieval women religious inhabited landscapes that changed – sometimes at their instigation – over time. Women religious could never operate outside of social or practical constraints. However, by viewing women's religious communities through the lens of landscape, we can better understand why they, their founders, or their patrons chose to locate their communities in certain places and how they laid them out, and how the particularities of their local landscape could provide both challenges and opportunities. Equally, new experiential approaches to landscape can allow us richer perspectives on the lives and afterlives of communities of women religious.[67] With new, less invasive, and less labour-intensive technologies such as global positioning systems (GPS), geographical information systems (GIS) modelling, and LiDAR increasingly available to researchers, new discoveries are being made that reveal in ever sharper detail the landscapes that medieval women religious knew and the horizons of their world.[68]

---

[67] Kimm Curran, '"Shadows of Ghosts": Rediscovering the Special Places of Medieval Female Monasteries through Experiential Approaches to Landscape', in Edel Bhreathnach, Malgorzara Kasnodębska D'Aughton, and Keith Smith (eds), *Monastic Europe: Medieval Communities, Landscapes, and Settlement* (Turnhout, 2019), pp. 523–44.

[68] LiDAR stands for light detection and ranging. It is a form of laser scanning capturing high-resolution 3D imaging, which uses light sensors to measure the distance between the sensor and the object. For GPS and GIS, see for example Henry P. Chapman and Helen Fenwick, 'Contextualising Previous Excavation: The Implications of Applying GPS Survey and GIS Modelling Techniques to Watton Priory, East Yorkshire', *MA*, 46:1 (June 2002), 81–9.

CHAPTER 11

Materiality and Archaeology of Women Religious

TRACY COLLINS

T HE discipline of archaeology is principally concerned with the study of past
societies through the physical and material remains and associated environmental material.[1] All remains, objects, and any other traces of humankind from
the past are considered elements of archaeological heritage and worthy of study.
Frequently, archaeological evidence can contradict written accounts, or bring
completely new evidence to bear, and so archaeology has its own unique contribution to make in the study of the past.[2] Medieval archaeology in particular –
perhaps because of its relatively later development as a discipline in comparison
to history – was once considered history's 'handmaiden', where archaeological
evidence complemented the supposedly already-known written evidence, and
thus merely reproduced 'another discipline's idea of the past'.[3] However, the use
of material culture and archaeology to discover women religious is a relatively
new approach in the study of women's monasticism and its importance is steadily
increasing as new archaeological discoveries are made.

This chapter focuses on how the use of archaeology can enhance our understanding of the variety of women religious and religious practice, as well as the distinctiveness in sites and standing remains. The first part provides a brief overview

---

[1] For introductions see Christopher Gerrard and Alejandra Gutiérrez (eds), *The Oxford
Handbook of Later Medieval Archaeology in Britain* (Oxford, 2018); Chris Gosden, Barry
Cunliffe, and Rosemary A. Joyce (eds), *The Oxford Handbook of Archaeology* (Oxford,
2009); Colin Renfrew and Paul Bahn, *Archaeology: Theories, Methods and Practice*, 4th
edn (London, 2004). For an overview of the archaeology of medieval life see, Roberta
Gilchrist, *Medieval Life: Archaeology and the Life Course* (Woodbridge, 2012).
[2] For example, *GMC*; Roberta Gilchrist and Barney Sloane, *Requiem: The Medieval
Monastic Cemetery in Britain* (London, 2005); Gilchrist, *Medieval Life*.
[3] *GMC*, pp. 8–15, at p. 9. Ivor Nöel Hume, 'Archaeology: Handmaiden to History', *The
North Carolina Historical Review*, 41:2 (1964), 214–25; Megan Perry, 'Is Bioarchaeology
a Handmaiden to History? Developing a Historical Bioarchaeology', *Journal of
Anthropological Archaeology*, 26 (2007), 486–515.

of the historiography of archaeological research and women religious, followed by a consideration of the archaeology and wider material culture of communities of women religious: their architecture, and artefactual evidence primarily from communities in England, Ireland, Scotland, and Germany. It continues with a discussion of the evidence derived from current archaeological excavation and investigation of material culture, as well as an archaeological landscape approach, particularly in relation to monastic estates.[4] The chapter concludes with suggestions for future interdisciplinary studies, which are critical to the development of the study of medieval women religious.

A Brief Historiography of Archaeological Research into Women's Religious Communities

It has been suggested that a predominantly male scholarship, in both history and archaeology, downplayed women's monasticism, although whether this was a deliberate act of misogyny or otherwise is perhaps a moot point.[5] Over the last three decades, historiography on women religious, however, has been affected by feminism and feminist approaches. The 'three waves' of feminism and other changing philosophical approaches, affected archaeological discourses across Europe and America.[6] Within an English context Roberta Gilchrist was the first archaeologist explicitly to employ a theoretical and gendered archaeological approach to a monument type in England, and indeed Europe, which created a watershed moment in the discipline of archaeology. Gilchrist's *Gender and Material Culture*, in particular, pioneered a new engendered agenda in medieval and monastic archaeology, and encouraged archaeologists and other scholars to perceive the archaeology of religious women in different ways.[7]

---

[4] For further discussion of monastic estates, see, above, Seale, pp. 171–8.

[5] For a critique see Judith Bennett, 'Medievalism and Feminism', in Nancy Partner (ed.), *Studying Medieval Women* (Cambridge, MA, 1993), pp. 7–29, at p. 23; *WMMW*, pp. 1–2; Margaret W. Conkey and Janet Spector, 'Archaeology and the Study of Gender', in Kelley Hays-Gilpin and David S. Whitley (eds), *Reader in Gender Archaeology* (London, 1998), pp. 12–45; Pamela L. Geller, 'Identity and Difference: Complicating Gender in Archaeology', *Annual Review of Anthropology*, 38 (2009), 65–81.

[6] For background see Matthew Johnson, *Archaeological Theory: An Introduction* (Chichester, 2010); Roberta Gilchrist, 'Medieval Archaeology and Theory: A Disciplinary Leap of Faith', in Roberta Gilchrist and Andrew Reynolds (eds), *Reflections: 50 Years of Medieval Archaeology 1957-2007* (Leeds, 2009), pp. 385–408; Tadhg O'Keeffe, 'Theory and Medieval Archaeology in Ireland and Beyond: The Narrative Tradition and the Archaeological Imagination', *Journal of Irish Archaeology*, XXVII (2018), 99–116.

[7] See for example *GMC*; Roberta Gilchrist, *Gender and Archaeology: Contesting the Past* (London, 1999).

Previously, archaeologists had paid little attention to women's religious communities, thinking they lacked documentary evidence and material culture, and were not worthy of investigation. For example, survival of later medieval Irish written sources is especially poor and there is no cartulary extant for a medieval community in Ireland.[8] There are relatively few surviving records for communities in England, and one surviving cartulary for a women's monastic community in Scotland.[9] The effects of the dissolution and reformation in England, Wales, Scotland, and Ireland in the sixteenth and seventeenth centuries, had dire consequences on each countries' later medieval material culture;[10] but perhaps more so for Ireland, where a process of plantation followed.[11] Religious buildings and traditional places of worship were abandoned, demolished or reused, and much of the portable material culture associated with later medieval religious and monastic practice was destroyed or lost for women religious, in a much more rigorous way than on the Continent. For example, in Ireland and Scotland, due to more turbulent histories in these regions, there is often little or no above ground trace of the remains of the structures used by these religious communities. Therefore, in these cases, secondary sources, such as seventeenth-and eighteenth-century lists,

[8] For a summary of historical sources and methodologies for Britain and Ireland see: Kimm Curran, 'Looking for Medieval Female Religious in Britain and Ireland: Sources, Methodologies and Pitfalls', in Karen Stöber, Julie Kerr, and Emilia Jamroziak (eds), *Monastic Life in the Medieval British Isles. Essays in Honour of Janet Burton* (Cardiff, 2018), pp. 161–72; Hall, *Women and the Church*, pp. 15–20; Christina Harrington, *Women in a Celtic Church Ireland 450–1150* (Oxford, 2002), pp. 1–19. Philomena Connolly, *Medieval Record Sources* (Dublin, 2002), pp. 45–9.

[9] Burton, *Monastic and Religious Orders*, pp. 85–108; Burton, 'Looking for Medieval Nuns', pp. 113–23. There is more continental documentary evidence. See Berman, *The White Nuns*; Emilia Jamroziak, *The Cistercian Order in Medieval Europe 1090–1500* (London, 2013), pp. 124–55; Cf. Curran, 'Religious Women'.

[10] David Crouch, *The Cambridge History of Britain: Medieval Britain c. 1000–1500* (Cambridge, 2017); John Miller, *The Cambridge History of Britain: Early Modern Britain 1450–1750* (Cambridge, 2017); Brendan Smith (ed.), *The Cambridge History of Ireland Volume I: 600–1550* (Cambridge, 2018); Jane Ohlmeyer (ed.), *The Cambridge History of Ireland Volume II: 1550–1730* (Cambridge, 2018). See also: Eamon Duffy, *The Stripping of the Altars: Traditional Religion in England c. 1400–c. 1580*, 2nd edn (London, 2005); David Gaimster and Roberta Gilchrist (eds), *The Archaeology of Reformation 1480–1580* (Leeds, 2003); Alexandra Walsham, *The Reformation of the Landscape: Religion, Identity, and Memory in Early Modern Britain and Ireland* (Oxford, 2011).

[11] Colm Donnelly, 'The Archaeology of the Ulster Planation', in Audrey Horning, Ruairí Ó Baoill, Colm Donnelly, and Paul Logue (eds), *The Post-Medieval Archaeology of Ireland 1550–1850* (Dublin, 2007), pp. 37–50; Denis Power, 'The Archaeology of the Munster Plantation', in Audrey Horning, Ruairí Ó Baoill, Colm Donnelly, and Paul Logue (eds), *The Post-Medieval Archaeology of Ireland 1550–1850* (Dublin, 2007), pp. 23–36.

Fig. 11.1. The Nuns' Church, Clonmacnoise, Co. Offaly. Image copyright of author, T. Collins.

may contain the only extant evidence of many communities of women religious and, in these cases, archaeology can make a significant contribution.[12]

Archaeological and architectural research have a similar progression with both disciplines developing from antiquarianism.[13] England had a research 'head-start' as several early publications emerged there – all undertaken by women – on women's monasticism,[14] double monasteries, hospitals, anchorites, and minoresses.[15] In the late nineteenth and early twentieth centuries, research on communities

---

[12] See for example early lists for Ireland, Louis Alemand, *Historie Monastique D'Irelande* (Paris, 1690); Mervyn Archdall, *Monasticum Hibernicum* (Dublin, 1786).

[13] For example, Bruce G. Trigger, 'The Coming of Age of the History of Archaeology', *Journal of Archaeological Research*, 2:1 (1994), 113–36; John Waddell, *Foundation Myths: The Beginnings of Irish Archaeology* (Dublin, 2005); Paul Bahn (ed.), *The History of Archaeology: An Introduction* (London, 2014).

[14] Lina Eckenstein, *Women Under Monasticism 500–1500* (Cambridge, 1896).

[15] Mary Bateson, 'The Origin and Early History of Early Double Monasteries', *TRHS*,

of women religious received attention only when their buildings were well-pre-served in the field.[16] The Nuns' Church, Clonmacnoise, Co. Offaly (see Fig. 11.1), restored in the 1860s, was the first example of monument conservation in Ireland, and Whitby, Yorkshire, an early example in England.[17]

These studies, however, looked at aspects of archaeology and architecture, rather than researching women's monasticism *per se*.[18] This approach acknowl-edged only the best architectural examples associated with women religious and did not explore the entire spectrum of the archaeology and architecture of that group. This has led to misconceptions about all women religious communities based on their associated architecture; for example, that they were usually poor, mismanaged, and inferior to contemporary male religious houses. These miscon-ceptions were not challenged until the work of historians and archaeologists in the 1970s and 1980s began to look at women religious communities in more depth.

Archaeology and Women Religious

There are almost 350 medieval women's monastic communities known from England, Ireland, Scotland, and Wales, many with an archaeological signature.[19]

13 (1899), 137–98; Rotha Mary Clay, *The Medieval Hospitals of England* (London, 1909); Rotha Mary Clay, *The Hermits and Anchorites of England* (London, 1914); Anne Bourdillon, *The Order of Minoresses in England* (Manchester, 1926).

[16] For example, Roy Gilyard-Beer, *Abbeys: An Introduction to the Religious Houses of England and Wales* (London, 1959); Harold J. Leask, *Irish Churches and Monastic Buildings*, 3 vols (Dundalk, 1955–60); Thomas J. Westropp, 'A Description of the Ancient Buildings and Crosses at Clonmacnois, King's County', *JRSAI*, 37 (1907), 277–306; Alison G. Reid and Doherty M. Lye, *Pitmiddle Village and Elcho Nunnery: Research and Excavation in Tayside* (Perth, 1988).

[17] Iona Priory in Scotland is another example of a women's religious house, where there has been architectural survey but little archaeological excavation, even with very good above ground register. See *Royal Commission on the Ancient and Historical Monuments of Scotland*, v. 4, Iona (Edinburgh, 1982).

[18] John Wardell, 'The History and Antiquities of St Catherine's Old Abbey, County Limerick (with a description of the conventual buildings by T. J. Westropp)', *JRSAI*, 14 (1904), 41–64.

[19] These date broadly from the Later Middle Ages and numbers are not definitive. Sixty-five have been identified on the island of Ireland; about 250 in England; up to fifteen in Scotland, and three in Wales. See *GMC*; Kimm Curran, 'Religious Women and their Communities in Late Medieval Scotland' (Unpublished PhD. dissertation, University of Glasgow, 2005); Jane Cartwright, *Feminine Sanctity and Spirituality in Medieval Wales* (Cardiff, 2008); Tracy Collins, 'An Archaeological Perspective on Female Monasticism in the Middle Ages in Ireland', in *WMMW*, pp. 229–51, at p. 235. Information on mon-uments, c.f. Sites and Monuments Records, Victoria County Histories, and national archives such as Historic Environment Scotland, thematic databases at Monastic Wales

Their material remains include – but are not limited to – structures, buildings (churches and domestic ranges),[20] and earthworks visible above the ground; deposits beneath the ground of foundations and layers related to the use of those buildings through time; burials, human remains, ecofacts,[21] and artefacts, for example devotional objects such as illuminated manuscripts, to much more mundane items like pottery and tools. For example, at the site of St Catherine's, Co. Limerick, excavations revealed medieval pottery of French imported ware and local wares were also recovered.[22]

Gilchrist's seminal publication on the archaeology and material culture of women religious, noted above, argued that women's monastic communities were not deviant to a male 'monastic standard'; these communities were inherently different and any direct comparison with male monasticism was therefore otiose.[23] This directly contradicted previous scholarship that characterised all women's religious communities as plain and poor in comparison to their male counterparts. Gilchrist created a fully-fledged concept of a gendered archaeology and rigorously applied it, changing paradigms in monastic archaeology. For example, high status communities and pre-Conquest foundations in England were once considered 'typical' foundations and used as a benchmark for all communities of women religious.[24] These foundations, however, were atypical, being wealthy and having royal associations from their beginnings.[25]

Most communities of women religious seem - with notable exceptions - to have been less well-connected (in terms of the social, political, and economic status of their founders) and therefore less wealthy than many of their male

https://www.monasticwales.org/ [accessed 25 May 2021] and Monastic Ireland https://monastic.ie [accessed 25 May 2021].

[20] For an introduction to monastic archaeology and architecture see Thomas Coomans, *Life Inside the Cloister: Understanding Monastic Architecture* (Leuven, 2018); Glyn Coppack, *Abbeys and Priories* (Stroud, 2006); Patrick J. Green, *Medieval Monasteries* (London, 2005); Mike Salter, *Medieval Nunneries* (Malvern, 2015).

[21] Ecofacts is a general term for organic material remains that have archaeological significance, such as animal bones, charcoal, plants, seeds, and pollen.

[22] Tracy Collins, 'Unveiling Female Monasticism in Later Medieval Ireland: Survey and Excavation at St Catherine's, Shanagolden, Co. Limerick', *Proceedings of the Royal Irish Academy*, 119C (2019), 103–71.

[23] *GMC*; Some historians had reached the same conclusion as Gilchrist; see, for example, Janet Burton, *The Yorkshire Nunneries in the Twelfth and Thirteenth Centuries* (York, 1979); Janet Burton, *Monastic and Religious Orders in Britain 1000–1300* (Cambridge, 1994); Janet Burton, 'Looking for Medieval Nuns', in Burton and Stöber, *Monasteries and Society*, pp. 113–23; *WMMW*, pp. 1–13, at p. 3.

[24] For example, Barking, Polesworth, Romsey, Shaftsbury, and Nunnaminster at Winchester, and perhaps, Kildare in Ireland, Yorke, *Anglo-Saxon*.

[25] For example, Foot, *Veiled Women*, pp. 145–98; *GMC*, pp. 25–36.

counterparts. This had an impact on the material remains such as the nature and layout of their buildings. While many developed a variety of claustral layouts more slowly than their male counterparts in England,[26] some in Ireland seem never to have built cloisters, rather using accommodation attached to churches, or free-standing structures, which may have been of stone, timber, cob, or indeed, a combination.[27] Women's monastic churches tended to be aisleless parallelograms, and only the most important and wealthy had transepts and side chapels, as at Romsey, Hampshire. There were various architectural solutions employed when churches were shared with a parish, such as galleries and screens.[28] Most medieval religious orders had women's religious communities officially or unofficially affiliated to them, but any categorisation of women religious by order is problematic and they are better studied as a distinct group in their own right.[29] The archaeology of women's religious communities is very diverse, and 'that lack of uniformity is itself their most distinctive characteristic'.[30]

In addition to the more traditional cloistered women religious, there are varieties of other types of women religious; these have been broadly termed 'The Other Monasticism'[31] and may include women religious such as nurses or 'sisters' in hospitals, anchorites, vowesses, canonesses, tertiaries, and beguines. Due to their chosen lifestyles – some following a religious life from their own private homes and others attached to a church or part of a community – they often did not leave a distinctive identifiable archaeological signature. Due to the nature of material evidence, the archaeology of these groups of women religious can be more challenging to detect. For example, hospitals were part of the wider group of medieval religious institutions, and many were managed by mixed religious communities.[32] Surviving evidence is often difficult to find because of the location of medieval

---

[26] James Bond, 'Medieval Nunneries in England and Wales: Buildings, Precincts and Estates', in Diana Wood (ed.), *Women and Religion in Medieval England* (Oxford, 2003), pp. 46–90, at pp. 68–70.

[27] Tracy Collins, *Female Monasticism in Medieval Ireland: An Archaeology* (Cork, 2021).

[28] Bond, 'Medieval Nunneries in England and Wales', pp. 55–62; Caroline Bruzelius, 'Hearing is Believing: Clarissan Architecture ca 1213–1340', *Gesta*, 31:2 (1992), 83–91; Collins, *Female Monasticism in Medieval Ireland*.

[29] For discussion see Burton, *Monastic and Religious Orders*, pp. 85–7.

[30] Bond, 'Medieval Nunneries in England and Wales', p. 86.

[31] Roberta Gilchrist, *Contemplation and Action: The Other Monasticism* (London, 1995). See also, Elizabeth Makowski, *"A Pernicious Sort of Woman": Quasi-Religious Women and Canon Lawyers in the Later Middle Ages* (Washington, DC, 2005); Alison More, *Fictive Orders and Feminine Religious Identities 1200–1600* (Oxford, 2018). See, above, More, pp. 61–75, Gunn, pp. 76–89, Richmond, pp. 90–104.

[32] Sheila Sweetinburgh, *The Role of the Hospital in Medieval England, Gift-giving and the Spiritual Economy* (Dublin, 2004).

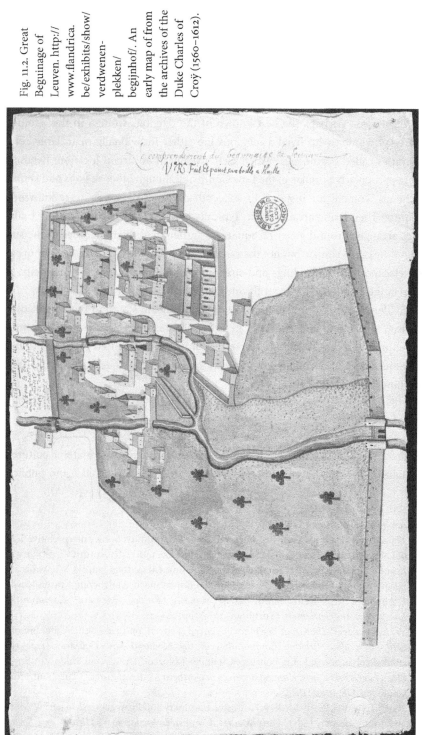

Fig. 11.2. Great Beguinage of Leuven. http://www.flandrica.be/exhibits/show/verdwenen-plekken/begijnhof/. An early map of from the archives of the Duke Charles of Croÿ (1560–1612).

hospitals, their later uses, the variety of charitable work undertaken there, and the links between women religious.[33] Those termed anchorites or recluses were individuals who chose to be enclosed in a single room attached to or near to a church – called an anchorhold – which they would never leave and where they would live a life of prayer and contemplation. Many of these are still standing, though none have been archaeologically investigated in any great depth or detail. [34]

Beguines – perhaps the best known of the religious women in this group – were lay women who lived a religious life either individually or in large communities called beguinages, which were usually in an urban location. Beguines were particularly popular in the Low Countries, though other regions had similar religious women; for instance in sixteenth-century Spain they were known as *beatas*.[35] Their living arrangements typically took one of two forms: either buildings arranged around a central square or garden, with blank façades to the surrounding city – similar but not the same as other religious institutions – or urban streetscapes where buildings and streets were walled off from the main city, as seen at the beguinage of Groot Begijnhof, Leuven, Belgium (see Fig. 11.2).[36]

Evidence of beguine communities is found in the standing remains of their houses, structures, and churches in urban locations across the Low Counties. Often many of these structures were reappropriated or reused for later beguine communities,[37] thus making investigations into the archaeology of medieval beguines more challenging.

Current Research

Earlier calls for research of medieval women's monasticism and material culture – including early medieval women religious – are being answered,[38] and publica-

[33] *GMC*, pp. 172–6.
[34] *Anchoritic Traditions*; *GMC*, pp. 177–81.
[35] María Del Mar Graña Cid, 'Beguines and Civic Community: Some Interpretative Keys of Late Medieval Urban Female Spirituality (Cordoba, 14th–15th centuries)', *Anuario De Estudios Medievales*, 42:2 (2012), 697–725; Nere Jone Intxaustegi Jauregi, 'Convents and Basque Familial Networks of Power', in Edel Bhreathnach, Małgorzata Krasnodębska-D'Aughton, and Keith Smith (eds), *Monastic Europe: Medieval Communities, Landscapes and Settlement* (Turnhout, 2019), pp. 503–21.
[36] W. A. Olyslager, *The Groot Begijnhof of Leuven* (Leuven, 1983); see also, Walter Simons, *Cities of Ladies: Beguine Communities in the Medieval Low Countries, 1200–1565* (Philadelphia, 2001); Letha Böhringer, Jennifer Kolpacoff Deane, and Hildo van Engen (eds), *Labels and Libels: Naming Beguines in Northern Medieval Europe* (Turnhout, 2014).
[37] Coomans, *Life Inside the Cloister*, pp. 61–2.
[38] Nancy Edwards, 'Early Medieval Munster: Summary and Prospect', in Michael A. Monk and John Sheehan (eds), *Early Medieval Munster, Archaeology, History and Society* (Cork, 1998), pp. 200–5, at p. 204; Roberta Gilchrist, 'The Archaeology of Medieval

tions are slowly but surely emerging in the discipline of archaeology.[39] Research into material culture has shown that medieval women and women's religious communities had significantly more agency in the patronage and manufacture of religious art and architecture than was previously acknowledged.[40] Due to the relative wealth of documentary sources in some regions and some extant contemporary medieval books as material culture, themes such as religious women's literacy, networks, manuscript and book production are being explored.[41] Studies of existing architectural remains have been and continue to be investigated, particularly those of the mendicant orders.[42] Mohn's work, which catalogues and discusses all known communities of women religious in Germany, is especially worthy of note as it provides analysis of structural designs of at least twenty-nine

---

English Nunneries: A Research Design', in Roberta Gilchrist and Harold Mytum (eds), *The Archaeology of Rural Monasteries*, BAR, 203 (Oxford, 1989), pp. 251–7.

[39] For example, Christy Cunniffe, 'The Canons and Canonesses of St Augustine at Clonfert', in Browne and Ó Clabaigh (eds), *Households of God*, pp. 103–23; Tracy Collins, 'Later Medieval Nunneries in Ireland: Form and Function', in Paul Barnwell (ed.), *Places of Worship in Britain and Ireland 1150–1350* (Donington, 2018), pp. 168–87; Conleth Manning, 'Finghin MacCarthaigh, King of Desmond, and the Mystery of the Second Nunnery at Clonmacnoise', in David Edwards (ed.), *Regions and Rulers in Ireland 1100–1650* (Dublin, 2004), pp. 20–6.

[40] Jenifer Ní Ghrádaigh, 'Mere Embroiderers? Women and Art in Early Medieval Ireland', in T. Martin (ed.), *Reassessing the Roles of Women as Makers in Medieval Art and Architecture* (Leiden, 2012), pp. 93–128; Hamburger, *Nuns as Artists*; Jeffrey Hamburger and Susan Marti (eds), *Crown and Veil. Female Monasticism from the Fifth to the Fifteenth Centuries* (New York, 2008); Corinne Schleif and Volker Schier, *Katerina's Windows: Donation and Devotion, Art and Music, as Heard and Seen through the Writings of a Birgittine Nun* (University Park, 2009). See, below, Vidal pp. 204–9.

[41] See Alison Beach, *Women and Scribes: Book Production and Monastic Reform in Twelfth-Century Bavaria* (Cambridge, 2004); David N. Bell, *What Nuns Read: Books and Libraries in Medieval English Nunneries* (Kalamazoo, 1995). For European context see: *Nuns' Literacies: Hull*; *Nuns' Literacies: Kansas*; *Nuns' Literacies: Antwerp*; Jennifer N. Brown and Donna Alfano Bussell (eds), *Barking Abbey and Medieval Literary Culture: Authorship and Authority in a Female Community* (York, 2012). See, above, Charles, pp. 154–62.

[42] For example, Caroline Bruzelius, 'Nuns in Space: Strict Enclosure and the Architecture of Clarisses in the Thirteenth Century', in I. Peterson (ed.), *Clare of Assisi: A Medieval and Modern Woman* (New York, 1996), pp. 53–74; Caroline Bruzelius, 'The Architecture of the Mendicant Orders in the Middle Ages: An Overview of Recent Literature', *Travaux*, 2 (2012), 365–86; Carola Jäggi, 'Eastern Choir or Western Gallery? The Problem of the Place of the Nuns' Choir in Koenigsfelden and Other Early Mendicant Nunneries', *Gesta*, 40:1 (2001), pp. 79–93; Margit Mersch, 'Programme, Pragmatism and Symbolism in Mendicant Architecture', in Anne Müller and Karen Stöber (eds), *Self-Representation of Medieval Religious Communities. The British Isles in Context* (Berlin, 2009), pp. 143–66.

houses, including ways in which architecture may have influenced how space was used.[43] The critical evaluation of space in women's monastic communities and its purpose in daily life and its change over time – showing the continued influence of Gilchrist's work – is emerging as an engaging topic.[44] For instance, Smith highlights the influence of female-specific *institutions* on enclosure, theoretical approaches to place and space, as well as how individual women religious defined their personal and communal contemplative life in Dominican communities. Wider European landscape studies and comparative studies with significant archaeological input are not yet common,[45] although a new ambitious agenda in the global archaeology of religion and monasticism has emerged, which may encourage such research.[46] Archaeological landscape studies have made significant contributions to the study of monastic precincts, granges, industry, and wider estates; these studies, are beginning to consider women's religious communities in monastic landscapes more broadly.[47]

---

[43] Claudia Mohn, *Mittelalterliche Klosteranlagen der Zisterzienserinnen: Architektur der Frauenkloster im mitteldeutschen Raum. Berliner Beitrage zu Bauforschung und Denkmalpflege 4* (Petersberg, 2006).

[44] For example, Constance H. Berman, 'How Much Space Did Medieval Nuns Have or Need?', in Sheila McNally (ed.), *Shaping Community: The Art and Archaeology of Monasticism*, BAR International Series, 941 (Oxford, 2001), pp. 100–16; Megan Cassidy-Welch, 'Space and Place in Medieval Contexts', *Parergon*, 27:2 (2010), 1–12; Megan Cassidy-Welch, *Imprisonment in the Medieval Religious Imagination, c. 1150–1400* (London, 2011), pp, 15–27; Anne Müller, 'Symbolic Meanings of Space in Female Monastic Tradition', in *WMMW*, pp. 299–326; Victoria C. Raguin and Sarah Stanbury (eds), *Women's Space. Patronage, Place and Gender in the Medieval Church* (New York, 2005); Julie A. Smith, '*Clausura Districta*: Conceiving Space and Community for Dominican Nuns in the Thirteenth Century', *Parergon*, 27.2, (2010), pp. 13–36.

[45] For an example of a historical study see Emilia Jamroziak and Karen Stöber (eds), *Monasteries on the Borders of Medieval Europe: Conflict and Cultural Interaction* (Turnhout, 2013).

[46] Historians, archaeologists, and those in other disciplines, such as geographical information systems (GIS), are beginning to engage in interdisciplinary studies to investigate monastic communities over time and across orders and regions. The potential for such studies has been set out recently; see Gabor Thomas, Aleks Pluskowshi, Roberta Gilchrist, Guillermo Garcia-Contreras Ruiz, Anders Andrén, Andrea Augenti, Grenville Astill, Jörn Staecker, and Heiki Valk, 'Religious Transformations in the Middle Ages: Towards a New Archaeological Agenda', *MA*, 61:2 (2017), 300–29.

[47] For example, see Derek Hall, *Scottish Monastic Landscapes* (Stroud, 2006), pp. 86–202 where women religious are included; Mick Aston, *Monasteries in the Landscape* (Stroud, 2000), pp. 125–57; Jemma Bezant, 'The Medieval Grants to Strata Florida Abbey: Mapping the Agency of Lordship', in Janet Burton and Karen Stöber (eds), *Monastic Wales: New Approaches* (Cardiff, 2013), pp. 73–87; Jemma Bezant, 'Revising the Monastic "Grange": Problems at the Edge of the Cistercian World', *JMMS*, 3 (2014), 51–70; Bond, 'Medieval Nunneries in England and Wales'; James Bond, *Monastic*

Archaeological excavation still remains the primary source of new data for women religious and Gilchrist synthesised the archaeological evidence up to the early 1990s.[48] Since then, further excavations have been published, for example, Chester,[49] Romsey Abbey,[50] Holywell Priory,[51] St Mary Clerkenwell,[52] and Grovebury Priory.[53] A significant research excavation of the Anglo-Saxon minster at Lyminge, Kent, which has early women religious associations, was concluded in 2015.[54] One of the few women's religious communities known in Wales, Llanllŷr, has been investigated,[55] and excavations in advance of development were completed at Littlemore Priory, Oxford.[56] The excavation of Littlemore

Landscapes (Stroud, 2004); Tracy Collins, 'Space and Place: Archaeologies of Female Monasticism in Later Medieval Ireland', in Victoria Blud, Diane Heath, and Einat Klafter (eds), *Gender in Medieval Places, Spaces and Thresholds* (London, 2019), pp. 25–43; Kimm Curran, '"Shadows of Ghosts": Rediscovering the Special Places of Medieval Female Monasteries through Experiential Approaches to Landscape', in Edel Bhreathnach, Malgorzara Kasnodębska-D'Aughton, and Keith Smith (eds), *Monastic Europe: Medieval Communities, Landscapes, and Settlement* (Turnhout, 2019), pp. 523–44; Stephen Moorhouse, 'Monastic Estates: Their Composition and Development', in Gilchrist and Mytum (eds), *The Archaeology of Rural Monasteries*, pp. 29–81. Also see, above, Seale, pp. 166–81.

[48] GMC.

[49] Simon Ward, *Excavations at Chester: The Lesser Medieval Religious Houses, Sites Investigated 1964–1983* (Chester, 1990).

[50] Ian Scott, 'Romsey Abbey: Benedictine Nunnery and Parish Church', in Graham Keevil, Mick Aston, and Teresa Hall (eds), *Monastic Archaeology* (Oxford, 2001), pp. 150–60.

[51] Raoul Bull, Simon Davis, Hana Lewis, and Christopher Phillpotts, with Aaron Birchenough, *Holywell Priory and the Development of Shoreditch to c. 1600. Archaeology from the London Overground East London Line* (London, 2011).

[52] Barney Sloane, 'Tenements in London's Monasteries c. 1450–1540', in Gaimster and Gilchrist (eds), *The Archaeology of Reformation*, pp. 290–8; Barney Sloane, *The Augustinian Nunnery of St Mary Clerkenwell, London* (London, 2012).

[53] Evelyn Baker, *La Grava Blair: The Archaeology and History of a Royal Manor and Alien Priory of Fontevrault* (York, 2013).

[54] See Lyminge Archaeological Project (2021), http://www.lymingearchaeology.org/ [25 May 2021]. Alex Knox and Gabor Thomas, 'Excavating Anglo-Saxon Lyminge', in D. Harrington and J. Carr (eds), *Lyminge: A History* (Lyminge, 2013); Gabor Thomas and Alex Knox (eds), *Early Medieval Monasticism in the North Sea Zone: Proceedings of a Conference Held to Celebrate the Conclusion of the Lyminge Excavations 2008–15. Anglo-Saxon Studies in Archaeology and History*, 20 (Oxford, 2017); Gabor Thomas, 'Life Before the Minster: The Social Dynamics of Monastic Foundation at Anglo-Saxon Lyminge, Kent', *Antiquaries Journal*, 93 (2013), 109–45.

[55] Jemma Bezant, *Medieval Welsh Settlement and Territory: Archaeological Evidence from a Teifi Landscape*, BAR British Series, 487 (Oxford, 2009), pp. 44–50; see also Dyfed Archaeological Trust, Llanllŷr Nunnery, Talsarn (2021), https://www.dyfedarchaeology.org.uk/wp/discovery/projects/llanllyr-nunnery-talsarn/ [accessed 25 May 2021].

[56] Paul Murray, 'Archaeological Excavations at Littlemore Priory Oxford' (Unpublished

Priory, for example, uncovered evidence of ceramic building materials including medieval coloured and patterned floor tiles, ridge tiles, quarry tiles and bricks. Also discovered were 176 metal objects, including a gold finger ring, shroud pins, iron nails, and a quantity of animal bone.[57] Recent excavations have produced some tantalising new evidence for beguines and beguinages, too; archaeological investigations of upstanding buildings associated with a community at Kempten, Germany, revealed an interesting assemblage of artefacts from the walls and 'dead spaces' between floors and ceilings, vaults, and attics, some of which related to the fourteenth-century beguines who lived there.[58]

Archaeological excavation has the potential to recover information on the things of everyday life and ritual practice.[59] The assemblage at Elcho Priory, Scotland is one exceptional example where book clasps may indicate literacy and book ownership within a monastic setting; an iron key, stained glass, pins, as well as a unique brass oil lamp could possibly tell us of economy and use in an everyday setting within the community.[60] Food, diet, and health in a women's monastic community can also be found through their material remains. A specialist analyses of human remains were undertaken on a medieval assemblage of 120 individuals from a beguine community at Breda, the Netherlands. The study concluded that the women of the beguinage were from the higher strata of society, 'when compared to contemporary assemblages from other medieval settlements, the overall health situation in the beguinage of Breda between 1296 and 1535 was very reasonable, which seemed only possible if the community was capable of sustaining themselves economically over time'.[61]

An important caveat in the consideration of women's human remains, however, is that it can be difficult to state definitively that a woman buried at the site was a woman religious. This is due to the nature of burial at women's monastic houses: women who were not part of the monastic community were also interred; burial places can be used over long time periods; burial is generally less segregated at women's monastic houses, either between men and

Report, John Moore Heritage Services, 2015). I am grateful to Paul Murray of John Moore Heritage Services for providing this.

[57] Murray, 'Littlemore Priory, Oxford', *passim*.

[58] Rainer Atzbach, 'The concealed finds from the Mühlberg-Ensemble in Kempten (southern Germany): Post-medieval archaeology on the second floor', *Post-Medieval Archaeology*, vol. 46, no. 2, 2012, 252–80.

[59] For examples of everyday life highlighted in the archaeological record see, Murray, 'Littlemore Priory, Oxford', *passim*; Barney Sloane, *The Augustinian Nunnery of St Mary Clerkenwell, London Excavations 1974–96* (London, 2012).

[60] Reid, *Elcho Nunnery*, pp. 48–84.

[61] F. E. Rijpma and G. J. R. Maat, *A Physical Anthropological Research of The Beguines of Breda 1267 to 1530 AD*, Barge's Anthropologica Nr. 11 (Leiden, 2005), p. 14.

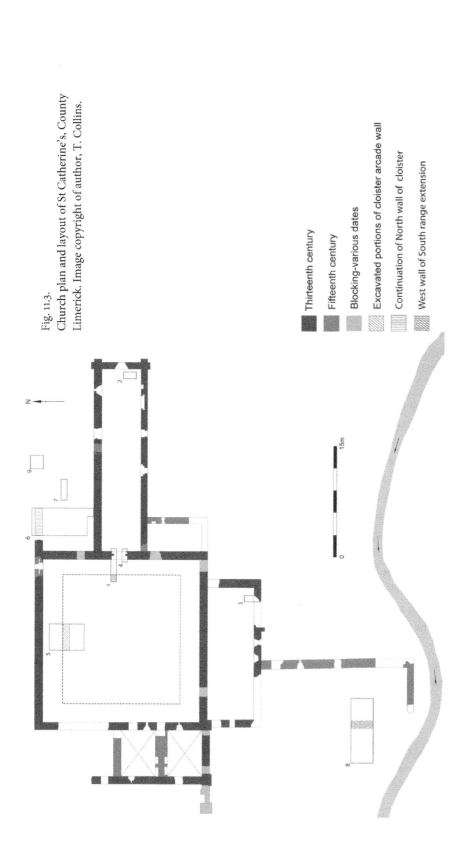

Fig. 11.3.
Church plan and layout of St Catherine's, County Limerick. Image copyright of author, T. Collins.

Thirteenth century
Fifteenth century
Blocking-various dates
Excavated portions of cloister arcade wall
Continuation of North wall of cloister
West wall of South range extension

N

15m

0

Fig. 11.4. View of the church's west doorway from the cloister at St Catherine's, County Limerick. Image copyright of author, T. Collins.

women, or religious and lay. Furthermore, grave goods that might indicate if the person was a woman religious – such as a special ring or perhaps a pater noster – are extremely rare and usually absent.[62] This must be borne in mind when considering human remains from women's monastic communities.

Excavations at the thirteenth-century community of St Catherine's, Co. Limerick, for example, revealed a change in the layout of the house at an early stage in its construction; the church was placed perpendicular to the west wall of the cloister, projecting from the cloister (see Fig. 11.3). It remains unclear why the church was arranged in such an unusual position, though it may have been to make use of an elaborate doorway which has been postulated was originally a putative chapter house doorway (see Fig. 11.4).[63]

This change meant that access to the church was through this single doorway in the west end and when the church was in use, the priest who was necessary for the celebration of daily mass (and sometimes more frequently), must have been permitted within the confines of the cloister. Later, in the fifteenth century when the church was made parochial, the structure was further altered to accommodate this sharing of space, when a door was inserted for the laity in the northern wall of

---

[62]   See Gilchrist and Sloane, *Requiem*, pp. 68–9.

[63]   For discussion of the ground plan at St Catherine's see Collins, 'Survey and Excavation at St Catherine's', *passim*.

the church, and the community's west doorway was made much smaller. Burials of women, children, and men were discovered in the church, cloister ambulatories, and outside the complex in an area that was likely a small graveyard. Nine burials were dated from the earliest phases of use in the thirteenth century through to the sixteenth century. Five of these individuals were considered women religious – currently the only assemblage from a women's monastic community in Ireland.[64]

Bioarchaeological analysis of thirty-five adult women from the medieval community of Littlemore, Oxford, showed that majority were over the age of forty-five years, and the excavations of the beguine community at Breda noted they were around the age of forty-three years.[65] Dental disease was normal for a medieval population and pathological conditions of the female group included healed blunt force trauma and various congenital defects. The most frequent condition was degenerative joint disease due to the unusually older age of the population.[66]

An extensive study of women's human remains from the monastic communities of Clementhorpe, York, and Elstow, Bedfordshire, showed lower death rates in the 20–49.9 years category than the 50+ years category, when compared to men's human remains from men's communities. While the men's monastic population was found to have higher dental caries (decay), both the populations of men and women showed similar levels of endocrine problems, osteoarthritis, spondylosis deformans, dental calculus (tartar), and periodontal disease. This suggested that both communities had a similar diet, oral hygiene, and similar types of physical activity. Interestingly, the southern women's religious community at Elstow had generally better health than those in the northern community of Clementhorpe.[67]

The recent discovery of lapis lazuli[68] in the dental calculus of a female skeleton dating to the late tenth to early twelfth centuries from a community of women

---

[64]   Collins, 'Survey and Excavation at St Catherine's', *passim*.

[65]   Rijpma and Maat, *Research of The Beguines of Breda*, p. 14.

[66]   Sharon Clough, 'Human Remains Report on Priory Hotel, Grenoble Road, Littlemore, Oxford' (Unpublished Report, John Moore Heritage Services Archaeological Burials Company, 2015), https://www.academia.edu/38006997/Human_Remains_Report_Priory_Hotel_Grenoble_Road_Littlemore_Oxford [accessed 25 May 2021]; see also Reid, *Elcho Nunnery*; Rijpma and Maat, *Research of The Beguines of Breda*, where tooth decay, healed fractures, infections (including two individuals suffering with tuberculosis), some dietary deficiencies, such as rickets, and changes in bone structure due to the ageing process were found among the Beguine population, pp. 1–14.

[67]   Diane Keeping, 'Life and Death in English Nunneries: A Biocultural Study of Variations in the Health of Women during the Later Medieval Period, 1066–1540' (Unpublished Ph.D dissertation, University of Bradford, 2000).

[68]   Lapis lazuli is a precious stone mined in what is now Afghanistan, which when processed produced a brilliant blue pigment called ultramarine, used in medieval manuscript illumination.

religious at Dalheim, Germany – interpreted as a woman religious working as a scribe or illuminator – is exciting new material proof of women's religious activity in areas more frequently associated with monks.[69] This study also highlights the potential for collaboration between archaeologists and scientists, as cutting-edge science can be applied to archaeological remains (in this case dental calculus) to produce exciting new evidence.

Future Directions

There has been a significant increase in the use of web-based databases, which greatly assist the sharing of data, both globally and across disciplines. Exciting developments are taking place, and many include archaeological and historical information on women's religious communities.[70] The benefit of such databases is that information can be updated, and links created to new projects in all disciplines interested in women's monasticism. Furthermore, there is a smaller number of primarily web-based groups that are dedicated to the study of women's monasticism, for example, The History of Women Religious of Britain and Ireland,[71] or medieval studies more generally, for example the Forum for Medieval and Renaissance Studies in Ireland.[72] Despite these new developments, linking up of data, and sharing resources, there remain gaps in scholarship.

It is somewhat surprising, that there continues to be a particular absence in the study of landscape archaeology and the monastic estates of women's religious communities, their site locations, and their remains.[73] For example, in Ireland, the first published discussion of the archaeology of early medieval ecclesiastical

---

[69]   Anita Radini, M. Tromp, A. Beach, E. Tong, C. Speller, M. McCormick, J. V. Dudgeon, M. J. Collins, F. Rühli, R. Kröger, and C. Warinner, 'Medieval Women's Early Involvement in Manuscript Production Suggested by Lapis Lazuli Identification in Dental Calculus', *Science Advances*, 5 (2019), 1–8.

[70]   Monastic Matrix, University of St Andrews (2021), https://arts.st-andrews.ac.uk/monasticmatrix/home; Monastic Ireland, The Discovery Programme (2014), http://monastic.ie/; Monastic Wales (2012), https://www.monasticwales.org/; FemMoData Female Monasticism's Database (2021), https://www.uni-goettingen.de/en/76297.html. [all accessed 25 May 2021].

[71]   History of Women Religious Britain and Ireland (2010), https://historyofwomenreligious.org/. [accessed 11 Jan. 2021].

[72]   Forum for Medieval and Renaissance Studies in Ireland (n.d.), https://fmrsi.wordpress.com. [accessed 11 Jan. 2021].

[73]   But for an important early study see Constance H. Berman, 'Medieval Agriculture, the Southern French Countryside and the Early Cistercians: A Study of Forty-Three Monasteries', *Transactions of the American Philosophical Society*, 76:5 (1986), 1–179; for a recent synthesis of ecclesiastical landscapes, cf. Jos C. Sanchez-Pardo et al., *Ecclesiastical Landscapes in Medieval Europe: An Archaeological Perspective* (Oxford, 2020).

estates, which included an estate related to a women's religious community, was only published in 2014.[74] Archaeologists in Ireland, unlike those in England,[75] have just begun to consider monastic and religious house precincts and granges,[76] such as at St John's Priory in Kilkenny,[77] St Mary's, Dublin,[78] and Bective, Co. Meath.[79] No archaeological attention had been paid to women's monasticism and their estates, prior to a desk-based consideration of the community estate of Timolin, Co. Kildare, for example.[80] The case in Scotland is equally lacking[81] with little or no attention given to the landscape archaeology of women's religious communities, with one exception.[82]

Essentially, more archaeological excavation is required – but it is an expensive and time-consuming process.[83] However, the results are promising and rewarding. Excavation can provide material culture and human remains for cutting-edge studies in past monastic life, health, diet, and work activities – as the identification

[74] Tomás Ó Carragáin, 'The Archaeology of Ecclesiastical Estates in Early Medieval Ireland: A Case Study of the Kingdom of Fir Maige', *Peritia*, 24–25 (2014), 266–312.

[75] For example, Aston, *Monasteries in the Landscape*; James Bond, 'The Estates of Evesham Abbey: A Preliminary Survey of their Medieval Topography', *Vale of Evesham Historical Society Research Papers*, 4 (1973), 1–62; James Bond, 'The Reconstruction of the Medieval Landscape: The Estates of Abingdon Abbey', *Landscape History*, 1 (1979), 59–75; Bond, 'Medieval Nunneries in England and Wales'; James Bond, *Monastic Landscapes* (Stroud, 2004); Glyn Coppack, 'Thornholme Priory: The Development of a Monastic Outer Court', in Gilchrist and Mytum (eds), *The Archaeology of Rural Monasteries*, pp. 185–222; Coppack, *Abbeys and Priories*; Glyn Coppack, 'How the Other Half Lived: Cistercian Nuns in Early Sixteenth Century Yorkshire', *Citeaux*, 59 (2008), 253–98.

[76] See, for example, Billy Colfer, *The Hook Peninsula, County Wexford* (Cork, 2004); Geraldine Stout, 'The Cistercian Grange: A Medieval Farming System', in Margaret Murphy and Matthew Stout (eds), *Agriculture and Settlement in Ireland* (Dublin, 2015), pp. 28–68.

[77] John Bradley, 'The Precinct of St John's Priory, Kilkenny at the Close of the Middle Ages', *Peritia*, 22–23 (2011–12), 317–45.

[78] Stout, 'The Cistercian Grange'.

[79] Geraldine Stout and Matthew Stout, *The Bective Abbey Project, Co. Meath Excavations 2009–12* (Dublin, 2016).

[80] Tracy Collins, 'Timolin: A Case Study of a Nunnery Estate in Later Medieval Ireland', *Anuario de Estudios Medievales*, 44:1 (2014) 51–80.

[81] See for example, Gilchrist, Roberta, 'Monastic Archaeology and National Identity: The Scottish Monastic Experience', in *Sacred Heritage: Monastic Archaeology, Identities, Beliefs* (Cambridge, 2020), pp. 37–70.

[82] Reid, *Elcho Nunnery*.

[83] For comparison, Spain, France, and Germany have completed more excavations than in England, Scotland, Wales, and Ireland combined. A more even spread of archaeological excavation across Europe would allow for more meaningful comparisons between regions and open new synergies.

of lapis lazuli at Dalheim has shown.[84] Isotopic analyses are beginning to shed light on the origins of monastics and whether they were native to the location of their burial.[85] For example, Elise Alonzi's work is investigating this theme by analysing a number of religious communities' human remains assemblages from Ireland.[86] Scientific analyses on environmental material from archaeological features such as cess pits and burials continue to change our views of medieval people in the past.[87] For example, female religious are commonly thought of as coming from the elite strata of society, but analysis of human remains suggests that this may not always have been the case, as several skeletons show evidence of manual work and nutritional deficiencies.[88] Field survey and geophysical survey can continue to assist in identification and preliminary recording of sites.[89] Geophysical survey is particularly exciting as it can reveal underground archaeology not visible above the ground's surface, showing that many sites may be much more extensive than previously thought. These activities are now complemented by high-resolution aerial photography and LiDAR imagery[90] of women's monastic landscapes, which will undoubtedly lead to further archaeological discoveries. Archaeological mapping and data interrogation has also been transformed using geographical information systems (GIS), where mapping imagery and various archaeological datasets can be consolidated, shared, and interrogated; its application will significantly progress the archaeological analyses of women's monastic landscapes and their communities into the future.[91]

---

[84] Radini et al., 'Medieval Women's Early Involvement in Manuscript Production'.

[85] Elise Alonzi, Niamh Daly, Gwyneth Gordon, Rachel Scott, and Kelly Knudson, 'Traveling Monastic Paths: Mobility and Religion at Medieval Irish Monasteries', *Journal of Anthropological Archaeology*, 55 (2019), article 101077; Elise Alonzi, 'Multi-Isotope Studies of Human Remains in Medieval Irish Archaeological Contexts', in Meriel McClatchie (ed.), *Approaches Towards Environmental Archaeology in Medieval Ireland* (Liverpool, forthcoming).

[86] For an overview of this work see the Newman Centre Lectures 20/21: Elise Alonzi, UCD, https://www.youtube.com/watch?v=ezzMTQKaLWU [accessed 26 June 2022].

[87] For example, Koen Deforce, Marie-Laure Van Hove, and Didier Willems, 'Analysis of Pollen and Intestinal Parasite Eggs from Medieval Graves from Nivelles, Belgium: Taphonomy of the Burial Ritual', *Journal of Archaeological Science: Reports*, 4 (2015), 596–604.

[88] For discussion see Collins, *Female Monasticism*, Chapter 8.

[89] Chris Gaffney and John Gater, *Revealing the Buried Past: Geophysics for Archaeologists* (Stroud, 2003).

[90] Simon Crutchley and Peter Crow, *Using Airborne Lidar in Archaeological Survey: The Light Fantastic HEAG179* (Swindon, 2018); see also, above, Seale, p. 181.

[91] Mark Gillings, Piraye Haciguzeller, and Gary Lock (eds), *Re-Mapping Archaeology: Critical Perspectives, Alternative Mappings* (London, 2020).

This leads to the potential to create synergies with scholars in other disciplines. Many archaeological excavation projects – due to the diverse nature of archaeological evidence itself comprising structures, artefacts, ecofacts, and human remains – can engage a wide variety of specialists: field archaeologists, historians, bioarchaeologists, zooarchaeologists, archaeobotantists, experimental archaeologists, metallurgists, pathologists, geneticists, and other scientists. For instance, a review of medieval Irish history at the end of the twentieth century highlighted the possibilities that interdisciplinary approaches might have.[92] The rejection of stereotypes in both history and archaeology was stressed, which could be achieved through micro-studies allowing women's monasticism, among others, to be considered actors with agency in narratives of the past. The movement away from the traditional single 'meta-narrative' of women religious towards a multi-narrative approach is slowly gaining momentum and is creating encouraging prospects for archaeology and other disciplines in revealing how these religious women may have lived their lives.

Furthermore, the study of women's monasticism – particularly in archaeology – can be artificially constrained by time periods. If the archaeology of women's monasticism can be considered thematically, across time periods, from the Middle Ages to the early modern period,[93] new dynamic synergies and research agendas will be established. The use of material culture and archaeology to reveal narratives of all types of women religious in the past is a relatively new approach in the broad study of women's monasticism. Archaeology coupled with other disciplines in truly interdisciplinary projects will undoubtedly produce exciting new avenues to knowledge about women's religious communities of the distant and more recent past.

---

[92] Edel Bhreathnach, 'Review: Medieval Irish History at the End of the Twentieth Century, Unfinished Work', *Irish Historical Studies*, 32 (2000), 260–71, at p. 266.

[93] See, for example, Bronagh Ann McShane, 'Negotiating Religious Change and Conflict: Female Religious Communities in Early Modern Ireland 1530–1641', *British Catholic History*, 33 (2017), 357–82; Bronagh-Ann McShane, 'Visualising the Reception and Circulation of Early Modern Nuns' Letters', *Journal of Historical Network Research*, 2 (2018), 1–25.

CHAPTER 12

Between Collective Memory and Individual Remembrance in Women's Religious Communities

MERCEDES PÉREZ VIDAL

WOMEN, especially women religious, created individual, collective, and historical memory and, over the last two decades, their roles have gained increasing scholarly attention. There has been a flourishing of studies analysing women
and the organisation of funerary memory, women commissioners and producers
of chronicles, liturgical and devotional books, and other narrative sources,[1] artefacts of material culture from memorial stones to sacred vessels,[2] and architecture.[3]
These studies demonstrate how women created, reinvented, or even erased the past
by consciously selecting some elements and concealing others, and also how men
and women collaborated in the memorial tradition of the Middle Ages.[4] Women
who acted as patrons self-consciously manipulated liturgy, artworks, buildings, and
spaces to shape their own, or their families', remembrance, and their dynastic identity. In the case of religious women, commemoration of their kin converged with

---

[1] Patrick Geary, *Phantoms of Remembrance: Memory and Oblivion at the End of the First Millennium* (Princeton, 1994); Elisabeth van Houts, *Memory and Gender in Medieval Europe 900–1200* (London, 1999); Gabriella Zarri and Nieves Baranda Leturio (eds), *Memoria e comunità femminili. Spagna e Italia, sec. XV–XVII. Memoria y comunidades femeninas. España e Italia, siglos XV–XVII* (Florence, 2011); Eva Butz and Alfons Zettler, 'The Making of the Carolingian *Libri Memoriales*: Exploring or Constructing the Past?', in Elma Brenner, Meredith Cohen, and Mary Franklin-Brown (eds), *Memory and Commemoration in Medieval Culture* (London, 2013), pp. 79–92.

[2] *GMC*; Van Houts argued for a gendered dimension to the process of remembering through the use of objects, which functioned as 'memory pegs': Van Houts, *Memory and Gender*, pp. 93–120. On books and memory see, above, Charles, pp. 154–62.

[3] Felipe Pereda, 'Liturgy as Women's Language: Two Noble Patrons Prepare for the End in Fifteenth-Century Spain', in Therese Martin (ed.), *Reassessing the Roles of Women as 'Makers' of Medieval Art and Architecture*, 2 vols (Leiden, 2012), vol. 2, pp. 937–88.

[4] Griffiths, *Garden of Delights*; Fiona J. Griffiths and Julie Hotchin (eds), *Partners in Spirit: Women, Men and Religious Life in Germany, 1100–1500* (Turnhout, 2014).

the memory of their communities.[5] Both of them were types of a collective and identity-oriented memorialisation developed since the Early Middle Ages, which coexisted with a later form of commemoration, a more individual one that entailed intercession, in the form of prayers, and donations, to shorten the time of the deceased in Purgatory.[6] These have to be studied together as women had an active role in the making 'multifaceted memory' that in some cases commemorated at the same time, a dynasty, a religious community, and an individual.[7]

The role of women as memory keepers of their families, through the foundation of monasteries, donations, and the institution of anniversaries for the deceased, has been explored in different territories, although further comparative analysis between diverse monastic landscapes by adopting a gender perspective is still necessary. Many 'elite' women's monastic communities worked as bastions of dynastic familial memory since the Early Middle Ages, and by the Central Middle Ages these foundations suffered significant changes as they passed from being 'family monasteries', closely ruled by members of the aristocracy, to being incorporated into the reforms based on the Rule of St Benedict and especially into the Cistercian Order.[8] However, their role as funerary memorials for the aristocracy or the royalty continued, and women collaborated with the new reformed orders in the commemoration of their lineage, as they would do later with the mendicants.[9]

[5]   Stefanie Seeberg, 'Women as Makers of Church Decoration: Illustrated Textiles at the Monasteries of Altenberg/Lahn, Ruperstberg, and Heiningen (13th–14th c.)', in Martin, *Reassessing the Roles*, vol. 1, pp. 355–92.

[6]   Michel Lauwers, *La mémoire des ancêtres, le souci des morts. Morts, rites et société au moyen âge (diocèse de Liège, XIe–XIIIe siècles)* (Paris, 1996); Jean Claude Schmidt, 'Images and the Work of Memory', in Brenner, Cohen, and Franklin-Brown (eds), *Memory and Commemoration*, pp. 13–32, at p. 18.

[7]   Cf. Ángela Múñoz Fernández, 'Memorias del coro: Constanza de Castilla y las políticas del recuerdo', in Zarri and Baranda Leturio (eds), *Memoria e Comunità Femminili*, pp. 27–48, at p. 36.

[8]   Michèle Gaillard, 'Female Monasteries of the Early Middle Ages (Seventh to Ninth Century) in Northern Gaul: Between Monastic Ideals and Aristocratic Powers', in *WMMW*, pp. 75–96; Gregoria Cavero Domínguez, 'Spanish Female Monasticism: "Family" Monasteries and their Transformation (Eleventh to Twelfth Centuries)', in *WMMW*, pp. 15–52. See, above, Vanderputten, pp. 22–42 and Sykes, pp. 43–60.

[9]   Thomas Coomans, 'Moniales cisterciennes et mémoire dynastique: églises funéraires princières et abbayes cisterciennes dans les anciens Pays-Bas médiévaux', *Cîteaux*, 56 (2005), 87–146. See also, Anne E. Lester, 'A Shared Imitation: Cistercian Convents and Crusader Families in Thirteenth-Century Champagne', *JMH*, 35 (2009), 353–70; Ghislain Baury, *Les religieuses de Castille. Patronage aristocratique et ordre cistercien, XIIe–XIIIe siècle* (Rennes, 2012); Anne-Hélène Allirot, 'Longchamp and Lourcine: The Role of Female Abbeys in the Construction of Capetian Memory (Late Thirteenth Century to Mid-Fourteenth Century)', in Brenner, Cohen, and Franklin-Brown (eds), *Memory and Commemoration*, pp. 243–60.

The gift-giving or donation of different artefacts of material culture – from luxurious garments, to relics, reliquaries, textiles, portable altars, liturgical books, or any other kind of *ornamenta ecclesiae* – made by women (either lay patronesses or monastic superiors) to religious institutions, has been subject to recent and increasing scrutiny. These studies show how women used these objects to express power over the religious foundations they protected, as well as showing their own identity and in the remembrance of their kin.[10] However, there is still potential for further development and the role of many of these objects, from reliquaries to liturgical books, has yet to be analysed and clarified, particularly for the Later Middle Ages. Other points requiring further study are the circulation of these artefacts through different networks, their placement and display within the liturgical space, and how this defined their role as 'objects of remembrance'.

Space and Memory

Space and materiality were indeed fundamental in the articulation and expression of individual, dynastic, or collective memory within religious foundations. The materials and the different position of tombs, memorials, or other commemorative artefacts, like shrines and reliquaries, within monastic spaces, helped to define their meaning in creating individual or collective memory. During the second half of the thirteenth century, as previous prohibitions were gradually abandoned, tombs moved progressively inside the church, to designated chapels, and later to areas of higher visibility: the choir, transept, and presbytery.[11] In addition to inhumation, the erection of tombs with a certain monumentality was allowed; later, chapels patronised by different families became frequent, with a 'privatisation' of some spaces.[12] However, some historians cling to the idea of a strict

---

[10]   Susan Marti, 'Königin Agnes und ihre geschenke. Zeugnisse, zuschreibungen und legenden', *Kunst und architektur in der Schweiz*, 47:2 (1996), 169–80; Therese Martin, 'Mujeres, hermanas e hijas: El mecenazgo femenino en la familia de Alfonso VI', *Anales de historia del arte*, 1 (2011), 147–79; Jitske Jasperse, 'Matilda, Leonor and Joanna: the Plantagenet Sisters and the Display of Dynastic Connections through Material Culture', *JMH*, 43:5 (2017), 523–47. These considerations can be extended to the liturgical books commissioned, donated, and used by these women: Mercedes Pérez Vidal, 'Female Aristocratic Networks: Books, Liturgy and Reform in Castilian Nunneries', in Emma O. Bérat, Rebecca Hardie, and Irina Dumitrescu (eds), *Relations of Power: Women's Networks in the Middle Ages* (Göttingen, 2021), pp. 105–32.

[11]   Caroline Bruzelius, 'The Dead Come to Town: Preaching, Burying, and Building in the Mendicant Orders', in Alexandra Gajewski and Zoë Opačić (eds), *The Year 1300 and the Creation of a New European Architecture* (Turnhout, 2008), pp. 209–30.

[12]   Official approval of the doctrine of Purgatory by the First (1245), and Second (1274) Councils of Lyon resulted in the increasing number of intercessory prayers, requests for inhumation, foundation of anniversaries and masses for the dead: Jacques Le Goff, *La*

gender division regarding liturgy and liturgical memory and argue that the lesser spiritual effectiveness of women's monasteries (as a consequence of the restrained liturgical responsibilities of women religious), and the stricter regulations over enclosure, would together have occasioned a lack of burial requests in women's monasteries.[13] This idea cannot be generalised as the implementation of enclosure varied significantly from place to place, even during the Later Middle Ages, and despite the limitations imposed on women's authority by conciliar legislation, there is evidence of women fulfilling ministerial roles during the Central and Later Middle Ages.[14] Thus, we encounter examples of women's monastic communities that received a significant number of burial requests: Santo Domingo de Madrid was authorised to receive lay burials in their monastery, a permission confirmed in 1285 by Sancho IV, and from then on the monastery received numerous requests for burial, as well as anniversaries and suffrages.[15] This situation only decayed in the fifteenth century when the superior of the community, Constanza de Castilla, promoted 'privatisation' of commemoration for the dead, by transforming the church's apse into a funerary chapel for her grandfather, King Pedro I, and other members of her lineage.[16] In this case, as well as in many other communities - Poissy, Unterlinden, Oetenbach, and Las Huelgas (Burgos) - enclosure was also permeable for the sake of the rituals of remembrance, as well as of other ceremonies (see Fig. 12.1).[17]

---

naissance du purgatoire (Paris, 1981); Philippe Ariès, 'Le purgatoire et la cosmologie de L'Au-delà', Annales. Histoire, Sciences Sociales, 38:1 (1983), 151–7.

[13] Valerie Garver argues sanctimoniales had a less visible and more domestic liturgical role, commemorating the deceased and reciting their names during the mass. Valerie L. Garver, Women and Aristocratic Culture in the Carolingian World (Ithaca, 2009), pp. 84–8.

[14] See, above, Vanderputten, pp. 22–42, Sykes, pp. 43–60, Lehfeldt, pp. 105–20.

[15] On burial and tomb locations within monastic topography see Carola Jäggi, 'Gräber und memoria in den Klarissen-und Dominikanerinnenklöstern des 13. und 14. Jahrhunderts', in Heidemarie Specht and Ralph Andraschek-Holzer (eds), Bettelorden in mitteleuropa: geschichte, kunst, spiritualität. Referate der gleichnamigen tagung vom 19. bis 22. März 2007 in St Pölten (St Pölten, 2008), pp. 689–705. For anniversaries and commemorations of the deceased at Santo Domingo de Madrid, see Archivo Histórico Nacional, Madrid, Clero, Libro 7338; The Archivo Histórico Nacional, Madrid, Clero, Pergaminos, 1357/11.

[16] Mercedes Pérez Vidal, Arte y liturgia en los monasterios de dominicas en Castilla. Desde los orígenes hasta la reforma observante (1218–1506) (Gijón, 2021), pp. 125–6.

[17] Alain Erlande Brandenburg, 'Art et politique sous Philippe le Bel. La priorale Saint-Louis de Poissy', Comptes-rendus des séances de l'Académie des Inscriptions et Belles Lettres, 131:3 (1987), 507–18; Carola Jäggi, 'Architecture et disposition liturgique des couvents féminins dans le Rhin supérieur aux XIIIe et XIVe siècles', in Madeleine Blondel, Jeffrey. F. Hamburger, and Catherine Leroy (eds), Les Dominicaines d'Unterlinden, 2 vols (Paris, 2000), vol. 1, pp. 89–107, at p. 95.

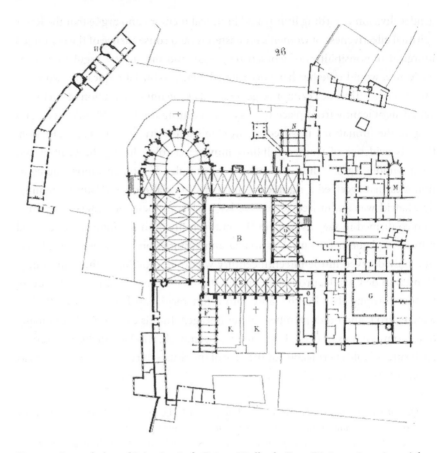

Fig. 12.1. Ground plan of Saint-Louis de Poissy. Viollet-le-Duc, *Dictionnaire raisonné de l'architecture française du XIe au XVIe siècle*, 1854–68, tome 1, p. 304.

Indeed, in some cases the choir for the women religious was a quasi-public space. From the mid-thirteenth in Las Huelgas, it was well documented that Pope Innocent IV offered indulgences to the faithful who visited the sepulchres of the monarchs in this choir on the anniversaries of their death.[18]

As friars entered the enclosure for the suffrages, women found innovative solutions to overcome enclosure limitations and to make themselves present in spaces often unavailable to them. The development of more precise and strict regulations on enclosure during the thirteenth century had far-reaching consequences on architecture, giving rise to a wide range of solutions for the position of

[18] Raquel Alonso Álvarez, 'La cabecera de las iglesias cistercienses femeninas en la corona de Castilla: clausura, *cura monialium* y representación aristocrática y regia', *Hortus artium medievalium*, 15:2 (2009), 341–53.

the choir for the women's community.[19] The location of the choir interfered with the memorialising of the dead, as the ideal placement of a tomb was in the presbytery, a restricted area for the women's community. As a consequence, women religious had restricted visibility of the monument, for instance, at the tomb of Maria of Hungary (c. 1257–1323) in Santa Maria donna Regina in Naples.[20] The double-sided funerary monument of Queen Elisenda de Montcada in the community of Pedralbes (c. 1340s) constituted an original solution to the problem of enclosure and the limiting of the sight of the women religious to view the tomb as part of the commemoration of the dead.[21] It offered the double possibility for her to be remembered as Montcada, queen of Aragon, crowned and dressed in regal robes, on the south wall of the presbytery, or as a widow or tertiary, veiled and crownless, on the cloister side, intended for the community of Pedralbes.

Although commemoration of founders, benefactors, or patrons constituted an essential part of liturgy, the individual commemoration of some exceptional women monastic superiors is also worthy of note. The tombs of male superiors and members of the ecclesiastical hierarchy have been studied showing how these weave a meaningful discourse on collective identity. This identity was more complex than the case of secular members of the aristocracy, as it combined their belonging to an order with their status as members of a family and lineage.[22] Sepulchres, located either in the choir for women's community or in the chapterhouse, were powerful reminders serving as *exempla* for the community who were sometimes depicted expressing their grief. A useful example is the procession of eleven women religious receiving the condolences of a male superior seen on the tomb of Urraca Díaz de Haro (r. 1222–62) in the community of Santa María de San Salvador de Cañas.

---

[19] Caroline Bruzelius, 'Hearing is Believing: Clarissan Architecture, ca.1213-1340', *Gesta*, 31 (1992), 83–91, and 'Nuns in Space: Architecture in the Thirteenth Century', in Ingrid J. Peterson (eds), *Clare of Assisi: A Medieval and Modern Woman* (New York, 1996), pp. 53–74; Mercedes Pérez Vidal, 'Estavan todas no coro e ben cantand' e eendo. Tipologie e funzioni dei cori nei monasteri delle domenicane dal XIII al XVI secolo, con particolare riferimento alla Castiglia', in Haude Morvan (ed.), *Spaces for Friars and Nuns: Mendicant Choirs and Church Interiors in Medieval and Early Modern Europe* (Rome, 2022), pp. 227–58.

[20] Tanja Michalsky, '*Mater serenissimi principis*: The Tomb of Maria of Hungary', in Janis Elliott and Cordelia Warr (eds), *The Church of Santa Maria Donna Regina: Art, Iconography, and Patronage in Fourteenth-century Naples* (Aldershot, 2004), pp. 61–78.

[21] Eileen McKiernan González, 'Reception, Gender and Memory: Elisenda de Montcada and her dual-effigy Tomb at Santa María de Pedralbes', in Martin (ed.), *Reassessing the Roles*, vol. 1, pp. 309–52.

[22] Alexandra Gajewski, 'Burial, Cult and Construction at Clairvaux', *Cîteaux*, 56, 1–4(2005), 47–85; Haude Morvan, 'Sépultures cardinalices et mémoire communautaire', in Fermín Miranda García and María Teresa López de Guereño Sanz (eds), *La muerte de los príncipes en la edad media* (Madrid, 2020), pp. 337–52.

Fig. 12.2. Tomb of Urraca Díaz de Haro, in San Salvador de Cañas. Photo: G. Freihalter with licence CC BY-SA 3.0.

Her monumental tomb was made some years after her death, showing the importance given by the community at this moment to the commemoration of her memory (see Fig. 12.2). Moreover, memory and identity were frequently re-elaborated to convey a particular message to the community. Thus, around the mid-fifteenth century, when the golden age marked by the ruling of Urraca as the superior had passed, the community remade her memory giving her a (new) fame of holiness.[23] In a similar way, Gerburg of Cappenberg (r. 1126–37), superior of St Servatius at Quedlinburg, also recreated the identity and story of the community, by likely commissioning a group of nearly identical effigial tomb-slabs commemorating the three eleventh-century superiors. According to Gerburg's interpretation, they would fit with the reforming ideals she was promoting.[24]

Commemoration of women superiors of monastic communities went in some cases far beyond the monastic walls, through different media, among which mortuary rolls stand out for their complexity. These were travelling artefacts that

[23] Ghislain Baury, 'Sainteté, mémoire et lignage des abbesses cisterciennes de Castille au XII: la comptesse Urraca de Cañas (Av.1207–1262)', Anuario de estudios medievales, 41:1 (2011), 151–82.

[24] Karen Blough, 'The Abbatial Effigies at Quedlinburg: A Convent's Identity Reconfigured', Gesta, 47:2 (2008), 147–69.

functioned as vehicles carrying individual memory in a collective act of remembrance. Their production is attested from the eighth to the sixteenth century, in different religious houses in France, Catalonia, Belgium, Germany, Austria, and England.[25] They consisted of a letter reporting the death, mainly of the superior, accompanied by a request of prayers for his or her soul, and they were carried by a roll-bearer (*breviator*) to many religious houses, where responses (*tituli*) to that request were added to the roll. The *tituli* included an exchange of prayers, a request and a promise, between the community who sent the roll and those who issued each *titulus*. Commemoration was thus articulated through a religious network that could involve a high number of religious communities, encompassing a vast territory. For instance, the roll of Matilda, the superior of Caen, (†1113), included *tituli* from 253 religious houses of both women and men, in France and England.[26] The functionality and materiality of a mortuary roll changed in the period between the announcement of a death, to its return to the monastery where it was stored or displayed. Its construction during the journey was completed at its return to the monastery and was therefore part of the performance.[27]

Ritual for the Dying and Liturgy for the Dead

Both the rituals of assistance to the dying and burial rites, and the weekly office for the dead, were at the roots of the collective identity and collective memory building. This was not only due to the insistence on the participation of all the members of the community, but also due to the character of the prayers, processions, and images used in them. All these rituals showed that the deceased were still members of the human community.[28] Liturgical processions together with visual reminders of the dead in the form of graveyards, tombs, painted and carved images, and manuscripts served to affirm collective notions of responsibility, community, and vocation. Apart from the tombs and other objects of remembrance, written sources are fundamental to our understanding of these performances that built collective memory and identity.

---

[25] Jean Dufour, *Recueil des rouleaux des morts (VIIIe siècle–vers 1536)*, dir. Jean Favier, 4 vols (Paris, 2008).

[26] Daniel Sheerin, 'Sisters in the Literary Agon: Texts from Communities of Women on the Mortuary Roll of the Abbess Matilda of La Trinité, Caen', in Laurie J. Churchill, Phyllis R. Brown, and Jane E. Jeffrey (eds), *Women Writing Latin: From Roman Antiquity to Early Modern Europe*, 3 vols (New York, 2002), vol. 2, pp. 93–131.

[27] Stacy Boldrick, 'Speculations on the Visibility and Display of a Mortuary Roll', in Jack Hartnell (ed.), *Continuous Page: Scrolls and Scrolling from Papyrus to Hypertext* (London, 2020), pp. 101–21.

[28] Patrick J. Geary, *Living with the Dead in the Middle Ages* (Ithaca, 1994), p. 2.

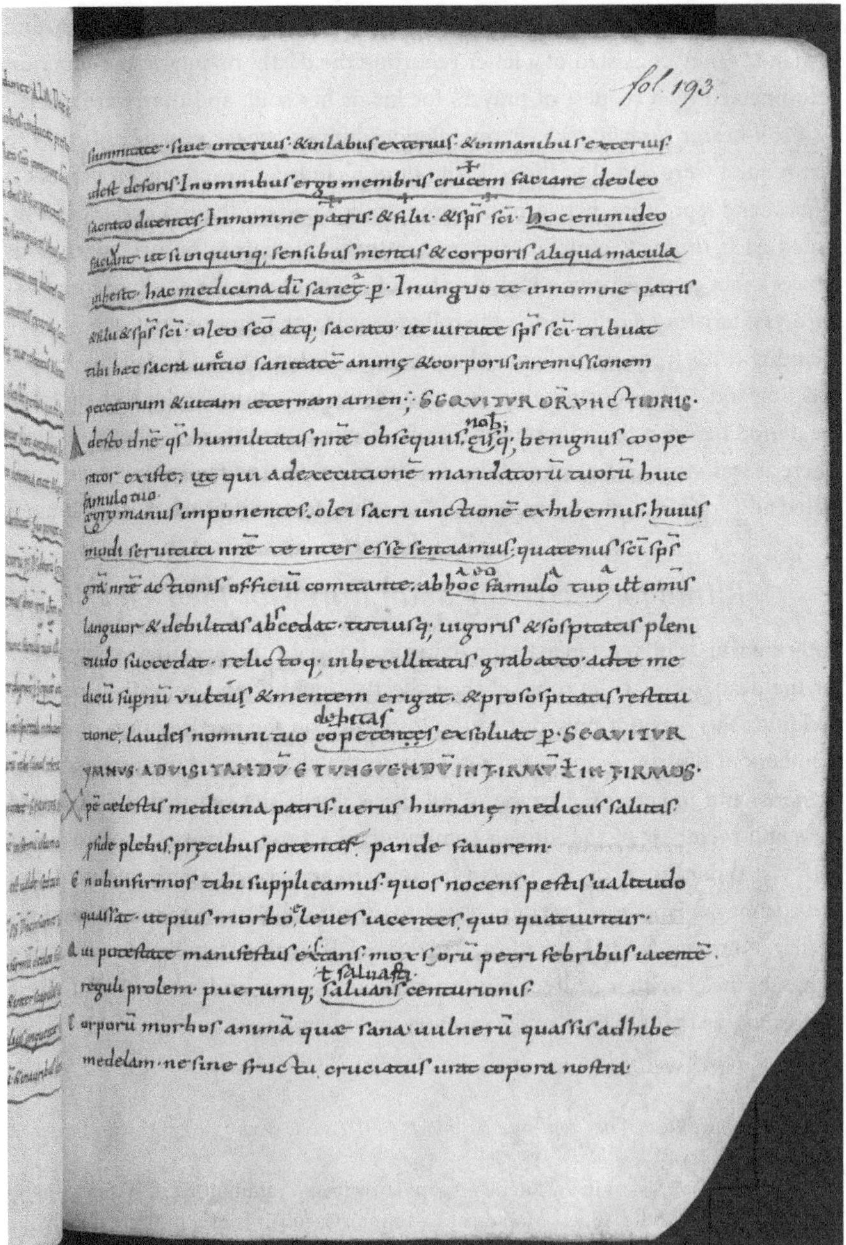

summitate siue interius & in labiis exterius & in manibus exterius
uel deforis In omnibus ergo membris crucem faciant de oleo
sancto dicentes Innomine patris & filii & spiritus sancti hoc enim deo
petente ut si inquinque sensibus mentis & corporis aliqua macula
inhesit hac medicina di sanetur p Inunguo te innomine patris
& filii & spiritus sancti oleo sancto atque sancto ut uirtute spiritus sancti tribuat
tibi hec sacri unctio sanitate anime & corporis inremissionem
peccatorum & uitam eternam amen SEQVITVR ORVHCTIDNIS
deseo dne qui humilitatis nostre obsequiis eisque benignus coope-
rator existe ut qui adexecutione mandatorum tuorum huic
famulo tuo
cum manus imponentes olei sacri unctione exhibemus huius
modi seruitutu nostre te intercessore sentiamus quatenus sancti spiritus
gratia nostre actionis officium comitante ab hoc famulo tuo ut amnis
languor & debilitas abscedat totusque uigoris & sospitatis pleni
tudo succedat relictoque inbecillitatis grabatto ad te me
dicum supnu uultus & mentem erigat & pro sospitatis restau
tione laudes nomini tuo competentes exsoluat p SEQVITVR
YMNVS ADVISITANDV ET TVNGVENDV INFIRMV ET IN FIRMOS
pe celestis medicina patris uerus humane medicus salutis
pfide plebis precibus potentis pande fauorem
e nu bus infirmos tibi supplicamus quos nocens pestis ualitudo
qualsat ut pius morbo leues iacentes quo quaerimur
d ui potestate manifestus extans mox soru petri febribus iacente
reguli prolem puerumque saluans centurionis
orporu morbos animam que sana uulneru quassis adhibe
medelam ne sine fructu cruciatus uite copora nostra

Fig. 12.3. *Sacramentarium,* Essen. Düsseldorf, ULB, MS-D-2, f. 193r. Photo: USL, Düsseldorf, urn: urn:nbn:de:hbz:061:1-174127, with licence CC BY-NC-ND 4.0.

TEXTS AND SPACES

The *libri vitae* or *libri memoriales* were the most evident commemorative text of the Carolingian world, produced by both men and women's communities. They combined liturgical texts with lists with the names of those to be commemorated, either living or dead, including members of the community, relatives, or individuals belonging to the social networks of the religious institution that produced them. They were deposited on altars with prayers offered for those named on their folios. In some cases, like the mid-ninth-century *Liber vitae* from San Salvatore and Santa Giulia in Brescia, entries recording the gifts to the house by the families of some women religious were also included.[29] Thus, these books embodied and shaped the collective memory and identity not only of these communities, but also of their social and political networks. Recent studies show the active role women played in the production of the *libri memoriales*, as well as their gendered use.[30]

This kind of analysis has also been done on other books, which had a similar function, transmitting practices relating to the remembrance of the dead, by the inclusion of some commemorative entries. A list naming both sisters and members of the laity to be commemorated was added in the tenth century to a ninth-century sacramentary from Essen, and a second sacramentary from the first half of the tenth century was used – and maybe written – by the sisters where they adapted liturgical material intended for male communities to reflect their own identity (see Fig. 12.3). For instance, the rituals for the sickness and the death in both, fit in with the Carolingian funerary liturgical culture that emphasised spiritual purification rather than physical recovery of the sick, but the ritual in the second sacramentary reflects a strong concern to prepare the soul for the Last Judgement, through confessions, penance, and anointing.[31]

A close examination of this and other liturgical sources highlights the participation and agency of women in the liturgy as they scripted, copied, and remade the memorial and liturgical books,[32] and they orchestrated and starred in various

---

[29] Rosamond McKitterick, *History and Memory in the Carolingian World* (Cambridge, 2004), p. 166.

[30] Rosamond McKitterick, *Books, Scribes and Learning in the Frankish Kingdoms, 6th–9th Centuries* (Aldershot, 1994), pp. 1–35; Grimard-Mongrain, *Genre, mémoire et histoire*.

[31] Jirki Thibaut, 'De ambigue observantie en heterogene identiteit van vrouwengemeenschappen in Saksen, ca. 800–1050' (Unpublished Ph.D. dissertation, Ghent University & KU Leuven, 2020), pp. 355–83.

[32] The close connections between illumination, liturgy, communal memory, and devotion have been explored by Jeffrey Hamburger, *The Visual and the Visionary: Art and Female Spirituality in Late Medieval Germany* (New York, 1988); Paula Cardoso, 'Art, Reform and Female Agency in the Portuguese Dominican Nunneries: Nuns as Producers and Patrons of Illuminated Manuscripts (ca. 1460–1560)' (Unpublished Ph.D. dissertation, Universidade Nova de Lisboa, 2019).

performances.[33] These examples - and others - confirm that women religious fulfilled ministerial roles, which had increasingly become exclusive to men since the post-Carolingian period, and particularly after the monastic and ecclesiastical reforms of the Central Middle Ages. The division of roles in liturgy was indeed organised, not on the basis of sex, but on office and, therefore, the superiors of a women's monastic communities could fill the role of the presider of the liturgy, as it is proved by several customaries and ordinals from these communities.[34]

Both customaries and ordinals provide a wealth of details on how men's and women's communities interacted within the liturgical spaces, on fluctuating spatial boundaries, changing uses of the different monastic spaces, and on the objects used in these ceremonies. Customaries appeared around the late eighth century and describe the daily customs (*consuetudines*) of a community, whether inside or outside the choir.[35] *Libri Ordinarii* provide a plan for the performance of liturgy throughout the calendar. They emerged in the eleventh century and are widespread from the following century.[36] The *consueta* from the women's monastic community of Las Huelgas is a unique source of information among Iberian *consuetudines* and *ordinales*, with specific allusions to the topography of the monastic complex.[37] Chapters 128–30, which describe funerary rituals and the celebration of anniversaries, are of striking importance for what they suggest of the role of the house as a dynastic pantheon. This was in the choir of the women's community, and clerics entered on special occasions.[38] Furthermore, Chapters

[33] Thibaut, *Rectamque regulam*, p. 352; Mary M. Schaefer, *Women in Pastoral Office: The Story of Santa Prassede, Rome* (Oxford, 2013); Katie A.-M. Bugyis, 'Women Priests at Barking Abbey in the Late Middle Ages', in Kathryn Kerby-Fulton, Katie A.-M. Bugyis, and John Van Engen (eds), *Women Intellectuals and Leaders in the Middle Ages* (Cambridge, 2020), pp. 319–34.

[34] Gisela Muschiol, 'Gender and Monastic Liturgy in the Latin West (High and Late Middle Ages)', *CHMM*, vol. 2, pp. 803–15.

[35] Isabelle Cochelin, 'Customaries as Inspirational Sources', in Carolyn Malone and Clark Maines (eds), *Consuetudines et Regulae: Sources for Monastic Life in the Middle Ages and the Early Modern Period* (Turnhout, 2014), pp. 27–55.

[36] Jürgen Bärsch, '*Liber ordinarius*: zur bedeutung eines liturgischen buchtyps für die erforschung des mittelalters', *Archa Verb: Yearbook for the Study of Medieval Theology*, 2 (2005), 10–58; Klaus Gereon Beuckers (ed.), *Liturgie in mittelalterlichen frauen-stiften. Forschungen zum 'liber ordinarius'* (Essen, 2012); Jeffrey Hamburger and Eva Schlotheuber (eds), *The Liber Ordinarius of Nivelles (Houghton Library, MS. Lat 422): Liturgy as Interdisciplinary Intersection* (Tübingen, 2020).

[37] David Catalunya, 'The Customary of the Royal Convent of Las Huelgas of Burgos: Female Liturgy, Female Scribes', *Medievalia*, 20: I (2017), 91–160, at p. 103.

[38] Raquel Alonso Álvarez, 'La cabecera de las iglesias cistercienses', 341–53; David Catalunya, 'Music, Space and Ritual in Medieval Castile, 1221–1350' (Unpublished Ph.D. dissertation, Universität Würzburg, 2016), p. 210.

111, 126, and 133 describe in great detail the rituals for the dying and the burial of sisters: chapter 133 states the nurse sister should touch the rattle (*tabula*) through the new cloister – *por la claustra nueva* – to announce the death of a sister. When this signal was heard, the community was to gather around the deceased.[39] This moment is depicted in a powerful and unusual image in a ritual from the Portuguese community in Aveiro, written in 1491 by sister of the house, Isabel Luís. The whole community gathers around the *tabula* and the instrument is used to illustrate the burial rite described in the text, symbolising the death of a member, and reinforcing the sense of community.[40] As stated in a fifteenth-century *breviarium* from Santo Domingo de Toledo, the rattle also had to be played in the cloister and other places when one of the sisters entered her final agony: 'soror penitus morti appropinquaverit, crebis ictibus pulsetur tabula in claustro et in aliis locis si necesse fuerit' (see Fig. 12.4).[41] Such rituals for the dying, and between the moment of death and the moment of burial, were also included in sacramentaries, as well as breviaries, psalters, processionals, and books of hours in the Later Middle Ages.[42]

The chapter house was also a burial place and a locus of memory, where the deceased were commemorated daily. It was a multi-functional space: a chapter of the rule was read daily there, and it served also to discuss all the affairs of the community; it was the place of confession of punishable acts (chapter of faults); and it was also a privileged burial place and a place of memory, where the deceased were commemorated daily. The book of the chapter, *Liber capituli*, was also called martyrology, although this was in fact a synecdoche, because besides the martyrology, it included the obituary-calendar with the anniversaries to be recited, the lessons of the gospels for the whole year, the rule and the constitutions, texts related to the history of the monastery or its mother house, and, in some cases, also rituals of profession.[43] If the ritual of the dying marked the end of a sister's life within a convent, its beginning was shaped by the rite of profession and, in some

---

[39] Ms. 6. Chapter 133, f 70v; Catalunya, 'The Customary', pp. 147–8.

[40] Museu de Aveiro, MAV-32/CD, fo. 29r. Paula Cardoso, 'Autonomy and the *Cura Monialium* in Female Monastic Art: The Fifteenth-Century Illuminated Manuscripts from the Dominican Monastery of Jesus of Aveiro', *JMH*, 44:4 (2018), 484–505, at p. 490.

[41] Bernardo Fueyo Suárez, *El breviario portátil de Santo Domingo el real de Toledo (ss. XIV–XV)* (Salamanca, 2014), p. 84.

[42] The difference between communal liturgy and some personal piety was not pronounced; see Susan Boynton, 'Prayer as Performance in Eleventh and Twelfth-Century Monastic Psalters', *Speculum*, 82 (2007), 895–931.

[43] As in the *Martirologium ad usum ordinis cisterciensis* (Las Huelgas, Ms. 1). Suárez determined it was made between 1236 and 1247 for Cîteaux, where marginal notes indicated it was used. It travelled to Burgos between 1240 and 1287, probably during the ruling of

communities, both took place in the chapter house.[44] The rituals of profession developed over the centuries, from the cutting of hair, to the changing of clothing, the presentation of a ring,[45] the *Altarsetzung* (altar setting) – a tradition that goes back at least to the High Middle Ages and to which from the tenth century was added the ceremony of coronation of women religious. Other ceremonies, such as the announcement of the Annunciation and Christmas or the Assumption of the Virgin, were also held in the chapter house, which was also one of the stations in many monastic processions.[46]

Texts from the lives of saints, the Virgin Mary, or even exegetical texts, intended to commemorate the history of the community or its religious identity might be read (*lectio publica*) in the chapter house or refectory, frequently during matins, or recited or sung.[47] These compositions were in many cases original and specific to the monastery or to the local religious context, and all these elements were arranged by religious communities to provide a place for the proclamation of monastic identity. Some of them were directly linked with specific, often miraculous, images venerated in the community, as for instance two Byzantine icons of the Virgin, worshipped respectively in Unterlinden, and in San Sisto in Rome. The Unterlinden legend associated with the icon was copied into the first part of the *Liber miraculorum*, which commemorated the history and memory of the community. At San Sisto it was copied in a lectionary in the early fourteenth century and was to be read at matins of the *Beatae Mariae Virginis in sabbato* office, between 22 and 28 April. This was in commemoration of the translation of the image, but it also followed the liturgical practice of Santa Maria in Tempulo, the community to which it had belonged.[48]

Abbess Eva (1261–2): Ana Suárez González, 'Un ex libris y algunas respuestas sobre el 'MS.1' de las Huelgas de Burgos', *Cistercium*, 245 (2006), 587–614.

[44] This was probably the case of Santo Spirito di Verona, whose *Liber capituli* also included also the ritual of profession, see Gian Maria Varanini, *Gli scaligeri, 1277–1387. Saggi e schede pubblicati in occasione della mostra storico-documentaria allestita dal museo di Castelvecchio di Verona (giugno-novembre 1988)* (Verona, 1988), p. 468.

[45] The *ordo romanus* specified that in their dedication as virgins, women religious should be presented with rings to symbolise marriage to Christ. Cf. Eva Schlotheuber, 'Best Clothes and Everyday Attire of Late Medieval Nuns', in Regula Schorta and Rainer Christoph Schwinges (eds), *Fashion and Clothing in Late Medieval Europe* (Riggisberg, 2010), pp. 139–54.

[46] The chapter houses of both Santo Domingo de Toledo and Jesús de Aveiro (Portugal) were decorated with a text of an antiphon from the office of the feast of the Assumption; see Cardoso, 'Autonomy and *cura monialium*', pp. 484–505; Pérez Vidal, *Arte y liturgia*.

[47] Hamburger, Schlotheuber, Marti, and Fassler (eds), *Liturgical Life*, vol. 1, pp. 211–80.

[48] See Joachim Joseph Berthier, *La vergine acheropita dei santi Domenico e Sisto a Roma* (Ferrara, 1889), Appendix, Doc. I; Vladimir. J. Koudelka, '"Le monasterium tempuli" et la fondation dominicaine de San Sisto', *AFP*, 31 (1961), 5–81.

Fig. 12.4. *Breviarium Portatile* from Santo Domingo de Toledo, Ms 06/508. Final section.
c. 1460–70. *Lectiones de beata Virgine in sabbatis* (ff. 343r–344v).
Image copyright of author, M. Pérez Vidal.

Some of these *interpolations* were also related to the commemoration of the deceased, as, for instance, were most likely the *historiae* included in the breviary from Santo Domingo de Toledo (*c.* 1460–70), mentioned above. One striking feature of this book is the inclusion of nine lessons taken from the treatise *De virginitate perpetua Sancte Marie* by Ildefonso, who was bishop of Toledo from 657 to 667, in the matins of the Office of the Virgin on Saturday (fols 343r–344v). *The Historiae de beata virginis in sabbatis,* were frequently interpolated in this part of the office in Dominican liturgical books, but the use of *De virginitate* is a peculiarity in a Dominican breviary.

This text was read in the office at matins in the Old Hispanic rite, and linked with *festum commemorationis annuntiationis beatissimae virginis,* whose celebration on 18 December was established by the Tenth Council of Toledo in 656.[49] Its presence in the breviary, apart from being clearly intended at the *cura monialium,* shows a continuation with this liturgical tradition.[50]

REMEMBRANCE AND MEMORY THROUGH DYNAMIC RITUALS AND PROCESSIONS

Both private and collective commemoration were linked to specific spaces and texts, but they were also expressed through dynamic rituals, moving from place to place, in which different kinds of material artefacts were involved. Liturgical space was not static but rather 'discursive', created to a large extent by liturgical performance,[51] in whose definition diverse notions of gender played an important role. It has already been discussed how during the Central and Later Middle Ages the progressive limitation of access to the altar and the sacraments by women religious found material articulation in the buildings using physical barriers. Thus, although the legislation on enclosure in women's communities has to be considered critically and in comparison, with the reality of each monastic community, there was a gender difference in the use of space.[52] As women religious had limited access to the church, some performances and processions

---

49   Margot Fassler, 'Mary in Seventh-Century Spain: the Mass Liturgy of Dec. 18', in Ismael Fernández de la Cuesta, Rosario Álvarez Martínez, and Ana Llorens Martín (eds), *El canto mozárabe y su entorno. Estudios sobre la música de la liturgia viejo hispánica* (Madrid, 2013), pp. 217–36; Kati Ihnat, 'Orígenes y desarrollo de la fiesta litúrgica de la Virgen María en Iberia', *Anuario de Estudios Medievales,* 49:2 (2019), 619–43 at p. 623.

50   A continuation also found in other books, see Office of the Blessed Virgin, Madrid, National Library, MS. 1566; Higinio Anglés and José Subirá, *Catálogo musical de la biblioteca nacional de Madrid* (Madrid, 1946), pp. 92–4, n. 31.

51   Susan Boynton, 'Cluniac Spaces of Performance', in Sulamith Brodbeck and Anne-Orange Poilpré (eds), *Visibilité et presence de l'image dans l'espace ecclesial. Byzance et moyen âge occidental* (Paris, 2019), pp. 63–91, at pp. 78–9.

52   Pérez Vidal, 'Estavan todas no coro', pp. 225–8.

were moved to other spaces: the cloister, inner oratories or chapels, specific places *ad caelebrandum officium*, as well as outside the convent.[53]

Since the Early Middle Ages, a specific commemorative day for the deceased had been set, although it varied from place to place. Odilo of Cluny chose All Souls Day (2 November) to institute the annual commemoration of all the faithful departed, with alms and prayers to relief the souls in Purgatory. The festivity was to be observed in all the monasteries dependent on Cluny, but it spread quickly beyond the Order to the whole western Church.[54] The procession on 2 November, *Commemoratio omnium fidelium defunctorum,* was also crucial in shaping collective memory through the monastic topography, as it had several stations in the different burial places in the convent: the church, choir for the sisters, cloisters, and chapter house, as well as in some images linked to funerary commemoration. In some cases, particularly among communities of Dominican women religious, there was a close relationship between the Marian devotions and the memory for the dead, influenced by the practices and customs of confraternities. For instance, in Santo Domingo de Lekeitio, a procession was held every Sunday and every feast day, after Compline, praying the Holy Rosary, and proceeding through different monastic spaces. This linked the commemoration of the deceased, both from the community, and lay people from the town of Lekeitio, among whom were probably some relatives of the women religious.[55] The community of the Alsatian monastery of Unterlinden used to pray the Rosary, especially at the time of their death.[56]

Together with the Marian feasts, Eucharistic piety and particular saints, the devotion to the passion of Christ took on added importance during the Late Middle Ages. Easter brought together the most remarkable moments of the liturgical year, starting with the procession held on Palm Sunday. This was followed by the liturgical celebration of the Sacred Triduum, from Maundy Thursday to Easter Sunday. During the Central and Later Middle Ages entire liturgical dramas might

[53] There is evidence for processions outside monastic communities and the participation of women religious in the *Corpus Christi* procession see, Gisela Muschiol, 'Time and Space', p. 198.

[54] The *Liber tramitis aevi Odilonis* is the oldest of the three preserved customaries from Cluny; see Isabelle Cochelin and Susan Boynton (eds), *From Dead of Night to End of Day: The Medieval Customs of Cluny: Du coeur de la nuit à la fin du jour: les coutumes clunisiennes au moyen âge* (Turnhout, 2005).

[55] Mercedes Pérez Vidal, 'La liturgia procesional de completas en el ámbito de los monasterios femeninos de la orden de predicadores en Castilla', *Hispania Sacra*, 69:139 (2017), 81–99.

[56] Jeffrey F. Hamburger, 'La Bibliothèque d'Unterlinden et l'art de la formation spirituelle', in Blondel, Hamburger, and Leroy (eds), *Les Dominicaines*, vol. 1, pp. 110–59, at p. 134.

be interpolated into the liturgy of these days, involving artworks and props, such as sepulchres, Christ's effigies, *sudaria*, or relics.[57]

The importance of liturgical performance, along with the associated images and objects, for building collective memory and strengthening the feeling of monastic community was particularly significant for the Observant reform movement during the fourteenth and fifteenth centuries.[58] The Observance promoted the return to a fundamental monastic value: obedience. In the case of women's religious communities, the application of this precept had a series of implications including strict enclosure, common life, the presence of friars-vicars, or the liturgical uniformity within a religious order,[59] although the implementation of all these measures varied from place to place. The attempt to restore enclosure determined the development of liturgies and para-liturgies and associated representations. For example, some processions originally performed outside the cloister, like the procession of the *Corpus Christi*, were moved inside and, in some cases, women religious re-created places they could not reach on a real pilgrimage inside the cloister. Topographic space was thus transformed by theological imagination and reconstructed as sacred locations through meditative exercises: the enactments of the Passion were performed by the communities of Wienhausen, of Augsburg, San Niccolò de Prato, and the Poor Clares of Madre Deus in Lisbon by way of 'virtual pilgrimage' to Jerusalem or Rome.[60]

[57] Tanjia Mattern, 'Liturgy and Performance in Northern Germany. Two Easter Plays from Wienhausen', in Elizabeth Andersen, Henrike Lähnemann, and Anne Simon (eds), *A Companion to Mysticism and Devotion in Northern Germany in the Late Middle Ages* (Leiden, 2013), pp. 285–316.

[58] See, above, More, pp. 72–3.

[59] Cf. Bert Roest and James D. Mixson, *A Companion to Observant Reform in Late Middle Ages and Beyond* (Leiden, 2015); Jürgen Bärsch, 'Liturgy and Reform: Northern German Convents in the late Middle Ages', in Elizabeth Andersen, Henrike Lähnemann, and Anne Simon (eds), *A Companion to Mysticism* (Leiden, 2013), pp. 21–46 at pp. 22–3.

[60] Muschiol, 'Time and Space', p. 198; June. L. Mecham, 'A Northern Jerusalem: Transforming the Spatial Geography of the Convent of Wienhausen', in Sarah M. Hamilton and Andrew Spicer (eds), *Defining the Holy: Sacred Space in Medieval and Early Modern Europe* (Aldershot, 2005), pp. 139–60; Marie Louise Ehrenschwendtner, 'Virtual Pilgrimages? Enclosure and the Practice of Piety at St Katherine's Convent, Augsburg', *JEH*, 60:1 (2009), 45–73; Kathryn Rudy, *Virtual Pilgrimages in the Convent: Imagining Jerusalem in the Late Middle Ages* (Turnhout, 2011); cf. Pérez Vidal, *Arte y liturgia*, pp. 282–91.

Conclusion

Both lay and religious women had a key role in the making of a 'multifaceted memory' that at the same time commemorated lineage, individuals, and religious communities: spaces, written sources, and different kind of artefacts from material culture were the material vehicles of remembrance. However, rather than being static, memory was mutable in time and space – both inside and outside the monastic walls – trespassing the borders of enclosure. Dead and living members of the social network where the community of women religious was settled were commemorated inside enclosure, whereas artefacts such as mortuary rolls travelled through a vast territory, carrying both the memory of a particular deceased superior and the collective memory of the religious community. The role the circulation, display, and performance of a great variety of 'objects of remembrance' – from reliquaries to liturgical books – had in building collective identity and individual remembrance has yet to be analysed and clarified. Moreover, moving from the particular to the general, the rituality of memory in women's religious communities should be studied in a comparative analysis between diverse monastic landscapes and territories.

To conclude: the analysis of the life and the afterlife of different kind of objects would constitute another area for future study related to collective memory building. The study of both continuities, similarities, or resignification in the functionality and materiality of many 'objects of remembrance' beyond the Middle Ages will be crucial to understand the past and the present of women's religious communities. This would include an exploration not only of the intention and purposes of these memorial images but, as well, of the sensorial affective response to them by the religious community and the devotees. Finally, in line with this long-term approach, a bigger challenge will be to offer a transversal and global perspective, overcoming Eurocentric accounts and periodisation.[61]

[61] The research for this chapter was conducted with the support of the Government of the Principality of Asturias through the FICYT, project SCPA–21–AYUD/2021/57166.

Select Bibliography

This volume ranges widely over a variety of subjects and chronologies and it is beyond the scope of this bibliography to list all works cited. Readers will find full references to primary sources (archival and published) in the notes to individual essays, as they will details of websites and electronic media used by our contributors. Here we confine ourselves to secondary works that specifically address aspects of religious women.

Secondary Sources

Affeldt, Werner (ed.), *Frauen in Spätantike und Frühmittelalter* (Sigmaringen, 1990).

Ahlers, Gerd, *Weibliches Zisterziensertum im Mittelalter und seine Klöster in Neidersachsen* (Berlin, 2002).

Alberzoni, Maria Pia, *Clare of Assisi and the Poor Sisters in the Thirteenth Century* (New York, 2004).

——, 'Jordan of Saxony and the Monastery of St Agnese in Bologna', *FS*, 68 (2010), 1–19.

Allirot, Anne-Hélène, 'Longchamp and Lourcine: The Role of Female Abbeys in the Construction of Capetian Memory (Late Thirteenth Century to Mid-Fourteenth Century)', in Elma Brenner, Meredith Cohen, and Mary Franklin-Brown (eds), *Memory and Commemoration in Medieval Culture* (London, 2013), pp. 243–60.

Alonso Álvarez, Raquel, 'La cabecera de las iglesias cistercienses femeninas en la corona de Castilla: clausura, *cura monialium* y representación aristocrática y regia', *Hortus Artium Medievalium*, 15:2 (2009), 341–53.

Alonzi, Elise, Niamh Daly, Gwyneth Gordon, Rachel Scott, and Kelly Knudson, 'Traveling Monastic Paths: Mobility and Religion at Medieval Irish Monasteries', *Journal of Anthropological Archaeology*, 55 (2019), Article no. 101077. https://doi.org/10.1016/j.jaa.2019.

Althoff, Gerd, 'Gandersheim und Quedlinburg: Ottonische Frauenkloster als Herrschafts- und Überlieferungszentren', *Frühmittelalterliche Studien*, 25 (1991), 123–44.

Andrews, Frances and Eleonora Rava (eds), *Ripensare le reclusione volontaria nell'Europa medievale*, 2 vols. Quaderni di storia religiosa medievale, 24:1–2 (2021).

Archer, Rowena E., '"How Ladies … Who Live on Their Manors Who Live on Their Manors Ought to Manage Their Households and Estates": Women as Landholders and Administrators in the Later Middle Ages', in P. J. P. Goldberg (ed.), *Women in Medieval English Society, c. 1200–1500* (Stroud, 1997), pp. 149–81.

Baker, Evelyn, *La Grava Blair: The Archaeology and History of a Royal Manor and Alien Priory of Fontevrault* (York, 2013).

Barrière, Bernadette, 'The Cistercian Convent of Coyroux in the Twelfth and Thirteenth Centuries', *Gesta*, 31:2 (Jan. 1992), 76–82.

Barrière, Bernadette, and Marie-Elizabeth Henneau (eds), *Cîteaux et les femmes* (Grane, 2001).

Bateson, Mary, 'The Origin and Early History of Early Double Monasteries', *TRHS*, 13 (1899), 137–98.

Baury, Ghislain, *Les religieuses de Castile: Patronage aristocratique et ordre cistercien XIIe–XIIIe siècles* (Rennes, 2012).

——, 'Sainteté, Mémoire et lignage des abbesses cisterciennes de Castille au XII: la comptesse Urraca de Cañas (Av.1207–1262)', *Anuario de Estudios Medievales*, 41:1 (2011), 151–82.

Beach, Alison I., *Women and Scribes: Book Production and Monastic Reform in Twelfth- Century Bavaria* (Cambridge, 2004).

Beach, Alison I., and Isabelle Cochelin (eds), *The Cambridge History of Medieval Monasticism in the Latin West*, Vols 1 and 2 (Cambridge, 2020).

Bell, David N., *What Nuns Read: Books and Libraries in Medieval English Nunneries* (Kalamazoo, 1995).

Benton, John F., 'The Paraclete and the Council of Rouen', in Thomas N. Bisson (ed.), *Culture, Power, and Personality in Medieval France* (London, 1991), pp. 411–16.

Berman, Constance H., 'Cistercian Agriculture in Female Houses of Northern France, 1200–1300', in John Drendel (ed.), *Crisis in the Later Middle Ages: Beyond the Postan-Duby Paradigm* (Turnhout, 2015), pp. 339–63.

——, *The Cistercian Evolution: The Invention of a Religious Order in Twelfth-Century Europe* (Philadelphia, 2000).

——, 'How Much Space Did Medieval Nuns Have or Need?', in Sheila McNally (ed.), *Shaping Community: The Art and Archaeology of Monasticism*, BAR International Series, 941 (Oxford, 2001), pp. 100–16.

——, 'Medieval Agriculture, the Southern French Countryside and the Early Cistercians: A Study of Forty-Three Monasteries', *Transactions of the American Philosophical Society*, 76:5 (1986), 1–179.

——, 'Were there Twelfth-Century Cistercian Nuns?', *CH*, 68:4 (1999), 824–64.

——, *The White Nuns: Cistercian Abbeys for Women in Medieval France* (Philadelphia, 2018).

——, *Women and Monasticism in Medieval Europe: Sisters and Patrons of the Cistercian Reform* (Kalamazoo, 2002).

Berthier, Joachim Joseph, *La Vergine acheropita dei Santi Domenico e Sisto a Roma* (Ferrara, 1889).

Beuckers, Klaus Gereon (ed.), *Liturgie in mittelalterlichen Frauenstiften. Forschungen zum 'Liber Ordinarius'* (Essen, 2012).

Bitel, Lisa M., *Landscape with Two Saints: How Genovefa of Paris and Brigit of Kildare Built Christianity in Barbarian Europe* (Oxford, 2009).

Blanton, V., V. O'Mara, and P. Stoop (eds), *Nuns' Literacies in Medieval Europe: The Antwerp Dialogue* (Turnhout, 2017).

——, *Nuns' Literacies in Medieval Europe: The Hull Dialogue* (Turnhout, 2013).

——, *Nuns' Literacies in Medieval Europe: The Kansas City Dialogue* (Turnhout, 2015).

Blennemann, Gordon, *Die Metzer Benediktinerinnen im Mittelalter. Studien zu den Handlungsspielräumen geistlicher Frauen* (Husum, 2011).

Blondel, Madeleine, Jeffrey F. Hamburger, and Catherine Leroy (eds), *Les dominicaines d'Unterlinden*, 2 vols (Paris, 2000).

Blough, Karen, 'The Abbatial Effigies at Quedlinburg: A Convent's Identity Reconfigured', *Gesta*, 47:2 (2008), 147–69.

Bodarwé, Katrinette, 'Ein Spinnennetz von Frauenklöstern: Kommunikation und Filiation zwischen sächsischen Frauenklöstern im Frühmittelalter', in G. Signori (ed.), *Lesen, Schreiben, Sticken und Erinnern: Beiträge zur Kultur- und Sozialgeschichte mittelalterlicher Frauenklöster* (Bielefeld, 2000), pp. 27–52.

——, *Sanctimoniales litteratae. Schriftlichkeit und Bildung in den ottonischen Frauenkommunitäten Gandersheim, Essen und Quedlinburg* (Münster, 2004).

Böhringer, Letha J., Jennifer Kolpacoff Deane, and H. van Engen (eds), *Labels and Libels: Naming Beguines in Northern Medieval Europe* (Turnhout, 2014).

Bollman, Anne, '"Being a Woman of My Own": Alijt Bake (1415–455) as Reformer of the Inner Self', in A. B. Mulder-Bakker (ed.), *Seeing and Knowing: Women and Learning in Medieval Europe, 1200–1550* (Turnhout, 2004), pp. 67–96.

Bolton, Brenda, 'Daughters of Rome: All One in Christ Jesus?', in W. J. Sheils and D. Wood (eds), *Women in the Church* (Oxford, 1990), pp. 101–15.

Bond, James, 'Medieval Nunneries in England and Wales: Buildings, Precincts and Estates', in Diana Wood (ed.), *Women and Religion in Medieval England* (Oxford, 2003), pp. 46–90.

Born, Myra M., *Women in the Military Orders of the Crusades* (New York, 2012).

Bornstein, Daniel, 'Relics, Ascetics, Living Saints', in Daniel Bornstein (ed.), *A People's History of Christianity* (Minneapolis, 2009), pp. 75–106.

Bourdillon, Anne, *The Order of Minoresses in England* (Manchester, 1926).

Bouter, N., *Unanimité et diversité cisterciennes: filiations – réseaux – relectures du XIIe au XVIIe siècle* (Sainte-Étienne, 2000).

Bouton, Jean de la Croix, *Les moniales cisterciennes*, 4 vols (Grignan, 1986–89).

Boynton, Susan, 'Cluniac Spaces of Performance', in Sulamith Brodbeck and Anne-Orange Poilpré (eds), *Visibilité et presence de l'image dans l'espace ecclesial. Byzance et Moyen Âge occidental* (Paris, 2019), pp. 63–91.

Brasher, Sally Mayall, *Women of the Humiliati: A Lay Religious Order in Medieval Civic Life* (New York, 2003).

Brown, Jennifer N., *Fruit of the Orchard: Reading Catherine of Siena in Late Medieval and Early Modern England* (Toronto, 2019).

Brown, Jennifer N., and Donna Alfano Bussell (eds), *Barking Abbey and*

Medieval Literary Culture: Authorship and Authority in a Female Community (York, 2012).

Brown, Michelle P., 'Female Book-Ownership and Production in Anglo-Saxon England: The Evidence of the Ninth-Century Prayerbooks', in Christian J. Kay and Louise M. Sylvester (eds), *Lexis and Texts in Early English: Studies Presented to Jane Roberts* (Amsterdam, 2001), pp. 45–67.

Bruzelius, Caroline, 'Hearing is Believing: Clarissan Architecture, *ca.* 1213–1340', *Gesta*, 31 (1992), 83–91.

——, 'Nuns in Space: Architecture in the thirteenth century', in Ingrid J. Peterson (ed.), *Clare of Assisi: A Medieval and Modern Woman* (New York, 1996), pp. 53–74.

Bugyis, Katie, A.-M. *The Care of Nuns: The Ministries of Benedictine Women in England During the Central Middle Ages* (Oxford, 2019).

——, 'Female Monastic Cantors and Sacristans in Central Medieval England: Four Sketches', in Katie A.-M. Bugyis, A. B. Kraebel, and Margot E. Fassler (eds), *Medieval Cantors and Their Craft: Music, Liturgy, and the Shaping of History, 800–1500* (York, 2017), pp. 151–69.

——, 'The Practice of Penance in Communities of Benedictine Women Religious in Central Medieval England', *Speculum*, 92:1 (2017), 36–84.

——, 'Women Priests at Barking Abbey in the Late Middle Ages', in Kathryn Kerby-Fulton, Katie A.-M. Bugyis, and John Van Engen (eds), *Women Intellectuals and Leaders in the Middle Ages* (Cambridge, 2020), pp. 319–34.

Bull, Raoul, Simon Davis, Hana Lewis, and Christopher Phillpotts, with Aaron Birchenough, *Holywell Priory and the Development of Shoreditch to c. 1600. Archaeology from the London Overground East London Line* (London, 2011).

Burns, Kathryn, *Colonial Habits: Convents and the Spiritual Economy of Cuzco, Peru* (Durham, NC, 1999).

——, '*Moniales* and *Ordo Cisterciensis* in Medieval England and Wales', in *Female vita religiosa*, pp. 375–89.

——, *The Yorkshire Nunneries in the Twelfth and Thirteenth Centuries* (York, 1979).

Burton, Janet, *Monastic and Religious Orders in Britain 1000–1300* (Cambridge, 1994).

——, 'Cloistered Women and Male Authority: Power and Authority in Yorkshire Nunneries in the Late Middle Ages', in Michael Prestwich, Richard Britnell, and Robin Frame (eds), *Thirteenth Century England*, X (Woodbridge, 2005), pp. 155–65.

Burton, Janet, and Karen Stöber (eds), *Monasteries and Society in the British Isles in the Later Middle Ages* (Woodbridge, 2008).

——, *Women in the Medieval Monastic World* (Turnhout, 2015).

Butz, Eva-Maria, and Alfons Zettler, 'Two Early Necrologies: The Examples of Remiremont (c. 820) and Verona (c. 810)', in J.-L. Dueffic (ed.), *Texte, liturgie et mémoire dans l'Eglise du Moyen Âge* (Turnhout, 2012), pp. 197–242.

Bynum, Caroline Walker, *Holy Feast and Holy Fast: The Religious Significance of Food to Medieval Women* (Berkeley, 1987).

Byrne, Philippa, 'Making Space for Leprous Nuns: Matthew Paris and the

Foundation of St Mary de Pré, St Albans', in Victoria Blud, Diane Heath, and Elnat Klafter (eds), *Gender in Medieval Places, Spaces, and Thresholds* (London, 2019), pp. 45–60.

Calvet-Marcadé, Gaëlle, 'L'abbé spoliateur de biens monastiques (Francie du Nord, IXe siècle)', in F. Bougard, P. Depreux, and R. Le Jan (eds), *Compétition et sacré au Haut moyen âge: Entre Médiation et Exclusion* (Turnhout, 2015), pp. 313–27.

Cardoso, Paula, 'Autonomy and the *cura monialium* in Female Monastic Art: The Fifteenth-Century Illuminated Manuscripts from the Dominican Monastery of Jesus of Aveiro', *JMH*, 44:4 (2018), 484–505.

Carrero Santamaría, Eduardo, 'Epigrafía y liturgia estacional entre el locutorio y el pasaje a la enfermería de la abadía de Santa María la Real de las Huelgas de Burgos', *Territorio, Sociedad y Poder*, 9 (2014), 115–32.

Cartwright, Jane, *Feminine Sanctity and Spirituality in Medieval Wales* (Cardiff, 2008).

Catalunya, David, 'The Customary of the Royal Convent of Las Huelgas of Burgos: Female Liturgy, Female Scribes', *Medievalia*, 20:1 (2017), 91–160.

Chapman, Henry P., and Helen Fenwick, 'Contextualising Previous Excavation: The Implications of Applying GPS Survey and GIS Modelling Techniques to Watton Priory, East Yorkshire', *Medieval Archaeology*, 46:1 (Jun. 2002), 81–9.

Charles, Sara, 'The Literacy of English Nuns in the Early Thirteenth Century: Evidence from London, British Library, Cotton MS Claudius D. iii', *JMMS*, 6 (2017), 77–107.

Clay, Rotha Mary, *The Hermits and Anchorites of England* (London, 1914).

Coakley, John, *Women, Men, and Spiritual Power* (New York, 2008).

Coldicott, Diana K., *Hampshire Nunneries* (Chichester, 1989).

Collins, Tracy, 'An Archaeology of Augustinian Nuns in Later Medieval Ireland', in Martin Browne and Colmán Ó Clabaigh (eds), *Households of God: The Regular Canons and Canonesses of Saint Augustine and of Prémontré in Medieval Ireland* (Dublin, 2019), pp. 87–102.

——, 'Space and Place: Archaeologies of Female Monasticism in Late Medieval Ireland', in Victoria Blud, Diane Heath, and Elnat Klafter (eds), *Gender in Medieval Places, Spaces, and Thresholds* (London, 2019), pp. 25–44.

——, *Female Monasticism in Medieval Ireland: An Archaeology* (Cork, 2021).

——, 'Later Medieval Nunneries in Ireland: Form and Function', in Paul Barnwell (ed.), *Places of Worship in Britain and Ireland 1150–1350* (Donington, 2018), pp. 168–87.

——, 'Timolin: A Case Study of a Nunnery Estate in Later Medieval Ireland', *Anuario de Estudios Medievales*, 44:1 (2014), 51–80.

——, 'Unveiling Female Monasticism in Later Medieval Ireland: Survey and Excavation at St Catherine's, Shanagolden, Co. Limerick', *Proceedings of the Royal Irish Academy*, 119:C (2019), 103–71.

Coomans, Thomas, *Life Inside the Cloister: Understanding Monastic Architecture* (Leuven, 2018).

——, 'The Medieval Architecture of Cistercian Nunneries in the Low Countries', *Bulletin KNOB*, 103:3 (2004), 62–90.

——, 'Moniales cisterciennes et mémoire dynastique: églises funéraires princières et abbayes cisterciennes dans les anciens Pays-Bas médiévaux', *Cîteaux*, 56 (2005), 87–146.

Coppack, Glyn, 'How the Other Half Lived: Cistercian Nuns in Early Sixteenth-Century Yorkshire', *Cîteaux*, 59 (2008), 253–98.

Creytens, Raymond, 'La Riforma del Monasteri Femminile dopo i Decreti Tridentini', in *Il Concilio de Trento e la Riforma Tridentina*, 2 vols (Rome, 1963), vol. 1, pp. 62–77.

Crick, Julia, 'The Wealth, Patronage, and Connections of Women's Houses in Late Anglo-Saxon England', *RB*, 109 (1999), pp. 154–84.

Cullum, Patricia, 'Vowesses and Veiled Widows: Medieval Female Piety in the Province of York', *Northern History*, 32 (1996), 21–41.

Cunniffe, Christy, 'The Canons and Canonesses of St Augustine at Clonfert', in Martin Browne and Colmán Ó Clabaigh (eds), *Households of God: The Regular Canons and Canonesses of Saint Augustine and of Prémontré in Medieval Ireland* (Dublin, 2019), pp. 103–23.

Curran, Kimm, 'Looking for Medieval Female Religious in Britain and Ireland: Sources, Methodologies, and Pitfalls', in Karen Stöber, Julie Kerr, and Emilia Jamroziak (eds), *Monastic Life in the Medieval British Isles. Essays in Honour of Janet Burton* (Cardiff, 2018), pp. 161–72.

——, Looking for Nuns: A Prosopographical Study of Scottish Nuns in the later Middle Ages', *Scottish Church History*, 35:1 (2005), 28–67.

——, '"Quhat say ye now, my lady priores? How have ye usit your office, can ye ges?": Politics, Power and Realities of the Office of a Prioress in her Community in Late Medieval Scotland', in Janet Burton and Karen Stöber (eds), *Monasteries and Society in the British Isles in the Later Middle Ages* (Woodbridge, 2008), pp. 124–41.

——, '"Shadows of Ghosts": Rediscovering the Special Places of Medieval Female Monasteries through Experiential Approaches to Landscape', in Edel Bhreathnach, Malgorzara Kasnodębska-D'Aughton, and Keith Smith (eds), *Monastic Europe: Medieval Communities, Landscapes, and Settlement* (Turnhout, 2019), pp. 523–44.

——, '"Through the Keyhole of the Monastic Library Door": Learning and Education in Scottish Medieval Monasteries', in Robert Anderson, Mark Freeman, and Lindsay Paterson (eds), *The Edinburgh History of Education in Scotland* (Edinburgh, 2015), pp. 25–38.

Cyrus, Cynthia J., *The Scribes for Women's Convents in Late Medieval Germany* (Toronto, 2009).

Dalarun, Jacques, *Robert d'Arbrissel: fondateur de Fontevraud* (Paris, 1986), trans. Bruce L. Venarde as *Robert of Arbrissel: Sex, Sin and Salvation in the Middle Ages* (Washington, DC, 2006).

——, 'Nouveaux aperçus sur Abélard, Héloïse et le Paraclet', *Francia*, 32 (2005), 19–66.

Dalarun, Jacques, (ed.), *Robert d'Arbrissel et la vie réligieuse dans l'Ouest de la France: Actes du colloque de Fontevraud, 13–16 décembre 2001* (Turnhout, 2004).

Davis, Rachel Meredith, 'Material Evidence? Re-approaching Elite Women's Seals and Charters in Late Medieval Scotland', *PSAS*, 150 (2021), 301–26.

Delman, Rachel M., 'The Vowesses, the Anchoresses, and the Aldermen's Wives: Lady Margaret Beaufort and the Devout Society of Late Medieval Stamford', *Urban History*, 48:1 (2021), 1–17.

Dereine, Charles, 'Les origines de Prémontré', *Revue d'Histoire Ecclésiastique*, 42 (1947), 352–78.

Doyno, Mary Harvey, 'The Creation of a Franciscan Lay Saint: Margaret of Cortona and her Legenda', *P & P*, 228 (2015), 57–91.

Driscoll, Michael Stephan, 'Reconstructing Liturgical History before the *libri ordinarii*. The Role of Medieval Women in Death and Burial Practices', in Charles Caspers and Louis van Tongeren (eds), *Unitas in pluralitate: Libri ordinarii als Quelle für die Kulturgeschichte; Libri ordinarii as sources for cultural history* (Münster, 2015), pp. 299–326.

Dunn, Marilyn, 'Convent Creativity', in Jane Couchman and Allyson M. Poska (eds), *The Ashgate Research Companion to Women and Gender in Early Modern Europe* (London, 2016), pp. 71–92.

Eckenstein, Lina, *Women Under Monasticism 500–1500* (Cambridge, 1896).

Edwards, Jennifer C., *Superior Women: Medieval Female Authority in Poitiers' Abbey of Sainte-Croix* (Oxford, 2019).

Edwards, Nancy, 'Early Medieval Munster: Summary and Prospect', in Michael A. Monk and John Sheehan (eds), *Early Medieval Munster, Archaeology, History and Society* (Cork, 1998), pp. 200–5.

Ehrenschwendtner, Marie Louise, 'Virtual Pilgrimages? Enclosure and the Practice of Piety at St Katherine's Convent, Augsburg', *JEH*, 60:1 (2009), 45–73.

Elkins, Sharon K., *Holy Women of Twelfth-Century England* (Chapel Hill, 1985).

Elm, Kaspar (ed.), *Norbert von Xanten: Adliger, Ordensstifter, Kirchenfürst* (Cologne, 1984).

Emerick, Keith, 'Whitby and Clonmacnoise', in H. King (ed.), *Clonmacnoise Studies, Volume 2* (Dublin, 2003), pp. 209–21.

Erens, A., 'Les soeurs dans l'Ordre de Prémontré, *Analecta Praemonstratensia*, 5 (1929), 5–26.

Erler, Mary C., 'English Vowed Women at the End of the Middle Ages', *Medieval Studies*, 57 (1995), 155–203.

——, 'Exchange of Books between Nuns and Laywomen: Three Surviving Examples', in *New Science out of Old Books: Studies in Manuscripts and Early Printed Books in Honour of A. I. Doyle* (Aldershot, 1995), pp. 360–73.

——, 'Syon's "Special Benefactors and Friends": Some Vowed Women', *Birgittiana*, 2 (1996), 209–22.

——, 'Three Fifteenth-Century Vowesses', in Caroline M. Barron and Anne F. Sutton (eds), *Medieval London Widows, 1300–1500* (London, 1994), pp. 165–84.

——, *Women, Reading, and Piety in Late Medieval England* (Cambridge, 2002).

Fassler Margot, 'Mary in Seventh-Century Spain: the Mass Liturgy of Dec. 18', in Ismael Fernández de la Cuesta, Rosario Álvarez Martínez, and Ana Llorens Martín (eds), *El canto mozárabe y su entorno. Estudios sobre la música de la liturgia viejo hispánica* (Madrid, 2013), pp. 217–36.

Feiss, Hugh, 'Consecrated to Christ, Nuns of This Church Community: The Benedictines of Notre-Dame de Saintes, 1047–1792', *American Benedictine Review*, 45:3 (1994), 269–302.

Felten, Franz J., 'Auf dem Weg zu Kanonissen und Kanonissenstift. Ordnungskonzepte der weiblichen vita religiosa bis ins 9. Jahrhundert', in I. Crusius (ed.), *Vita religiosa sanctimonialium: Norm und Praxis des weiblichen religiösen Lebens vom 6. bis zum 13. Jahrhundert* (Korb, 2005), pp. 71–92.

——, 'Verbandsbildung von Frauenklöstern: Le Paraclet, Prémy, Fontevraud mit einem Ausblick auf Cluny, Sempringham und Tart', in H. Keller and F. Neiske (eds), *Vom Kloster zum Klosterverband* (München, 1997), pp. 277–341.

——, 'What do we know about the life of Jutta and Hildegard at Disibodenberg and Rupertsberg?', in Debra Stoudt et al.(eds), *A Companion to Hildegard of Bingen* (Leiden, 2014), pp. 15–38.

Field, Sean L., *Isabelle of France: Capetian Sanctity and Franciscan Identity in the Thirteenth Century* (Notre Dame, 2006).

Flanagan, Sabine, *Hildegard of Bingen, 1098–1179: A Visionary Life* (London, 1998).

Flynn, William, 'Abelard and Rhetoric: Widows and Virgins at the Paraclete', in Babette Hellemans (ed.), *Rethinking Abelard: A Collection of Critical Essays* (Leiden, 2014), pp. 155–86.

de Fontette, Micheline, *Les religieuses à l'âge classique du droit canon* (Paris, 1967).

Foot, Sarah, *Veiled Women: Volume I: The Disappearance of Nuns from Anglo-Saxon England* (Aldershot, 2000).

——, *Veiled Women: Volume II: Female Religious Communities in England, 871–1066* (Aldershot, 2000).

Foxhall Forbes, Helen, 'Squabbling Siblings: Gender and Monastic Life in Late Anglo-Saxon Winchester', *GH*, 23:3 (2011), 653–84.

Freed, John, 'Urban Movements and the "*cura monialium*" in Thirteenth-Century Germany', *Viator*, 3 (1972), 311–27.

Freeman, Elizabeth, 'Cistercian Nuns in Medieval England: The Gendering of Geographic Marginalization', *Medieval Feminist Forum*, 43:2 (Dec. 2007), 26–39.

——, 'Houses of a Peculiar Order: Cistercian Nunneries in Medieval England, with special attention to the Fifteenth and Sixteenth Centuries', *Cîteaux*, 55 (2004), 245–87.

——, 'Nuns in the Public Sphere: Aelred of Rievaulx's *De Sanctimoniali de Wattun* and the Gendering of Authority', *Comitatus*, 27 (1996), 55–80.

——, 'Cistercian Nuns in Medieval England: Unofficial meets Official', *SCH*, 42 (2006), 110–19.

Frings, J., and J. Gerchow (eds), *Krone und Schleier. Kunst aus mittelalterlichen Frauenklöstern* (Bonn, 2005).

Fritz, Birgitta, 'The History and Spiritual Life of Vadstena Abbey', in Maria H. Oen (ed.), *A Companion to Birgitta of Sweden and her Legacy in the Later Middle Ages* (Leiden, 2019), pp. 132–58.

Fueyo Suárez, Bernardo, *El Breviario portátil de Santo Domingo el Real de Toledo (ss. XIV–XV)* (Salamanca, 2014).

Gaillard, Michèle, 'Les fondations d'abbayes féminines dans le Nord et l'Est de la Gaule à la fin du VIe siècle', *Revue d'histoire de l'église de France*, 76 (1990), 6–20.

——, *D'une réforme à l'autre (816–934): Les communautés religieuses en Lorraine à l'époque Carolingienne* (Paris, 2006).

Ganz, David, 'The Buildings of Godstow Nunnery', *Oxoniensia*, 37 (1972), 150–7.

García-Serrano, Francisco, 'Friars and Nuns: Dominican Economy and Religious Identity in Medieval Castile', in Francisco García-Serrano (ed.), *The Friars and Their Influence in Medieval Spain* (Amsterdam, 2018), pp. 159–74.

Garver, Valerie L., 'Learned Women? Liutberga and the Instruction of Carolingian Women', in J. L. Nelson and P. Wormald (eds), *Lay Intellectuals in the Carolingian World* (Cambridge, 2007), pp. 121–38.

——, *Women and Aristocratic Culture in the Carolingian World* (Ithaca, 2009).

Gilchrist, Roberta, 'The Archaeology of Medieval English Nunneries: A Research Design', in Roberta Gilchrist and Harold Mytum (eds), *The Archaeology of Rural Monasteries* (Oxford, 1989), pp. 251–60.

——, *Contemplation and Action, The Other Monasticism* (London, 1995).

——, *Gender and Material Culture. The Archaeology of Religious Women* (London, 1994).

——, *Sacred Heritage: Monastic Archaeology, Identities, Beliefs* (Cambridge, 2020).

Gilchrist, Roberta, and Marilyn Oliva, *Religious Women in Medieval East Anglia* (Norwich, 1993).

Gold, Penny S., 'The Charters of Le Ronceray d'Angers: Male/Female Interaction in Monastic Business', in Joel T. Rosenthal (ed.), *Medieval Women and the Sources of Medieval History* (Athens, 1990), pp. 122–32.

——, *The Lady and the Virgin: Image, Attitude and Experience in Twelfth-Century France* (Chicago, 1985).

Golding, Brian, 'Authority and Discipline at the Paraclete, Fontevraud and Sempringham', in Gert Melville and Anne Müller (eds), *Mittelalterliche Orden und Klöster im Vergleich: Methodische Ansätze und Perspektiven* (Munster, 2007), pp. 87–114.

——, *Gilbert of Sempringham and the Gilbertine Order c. 1130–c. 1300* (Oxford, 1995).

Goodrich, Margaret, 'Westwood: A Rural English Nunnery with its Local and French Connections', in Joan Greatrex (ed.), *The Vocation of Service to God and Neighbour: Essays on the Interests, Involvements, and Problems of Religious Communities and their Members in Society* (Turnhout, 1998), pp. 43–57.

Graham, Rose, *St Gilbert of Sempringham and the Gilbertines: A History of the only English Monastic Order* (London, 1901).

Graña Cid, María Del Mar, 'Beguines and Civic Community: Some Interpretative Keys of Late Medieval Urban Female Spirituality (Cordoba, 14th–15th centuries)', *Anuario De Estudios Medievales*, 42:2 (2012), 697–725.

Graves, Coburn V., 'English Cistercian Nunneries in Lincolnshire', *Speculum*, 54 (1979), 492–9.

——, 'The Organization of a Cistercian Nunnery in Lincolnshire', *Cîteaux*, 33 (1982), 333–50.

Gregory, Rabia, 'Penitence, Confession, and the Power of Submission in Late Medieval Women's Religious Communities', *Religions*, 3:3 (2012), 646–61.

Griffiths, Fiona J., 'Brides and *dominae*: Abelard's *cura monialium* at the Augustinian monastery of Marbach', *Viator*, 34 (2003), 57–88.

——, 'Men's Duty to Provide for Women's Needs: Abelard, Heloise, and their Negotiation of the *cura monialium*', *JMH*, 30 (2004), 1–24.

——, *Nuns' Priests' Tales: Men and Salvation in Medieval Women's Monastic Life* (Philadelphia, 2018).

Griffiths, Fiona J., and Julie Hotchin (eds), *Partners in Spirit: Women, Men and Religious Life in Germany, 1100–1500* (Turnhout, 2014).

Grollová, Jana, 'The "Clever Girls" of Prague: Beguines, Preachers, and Late Medieval Bohemian Religion', in Jennifer Kolpacoff Deane and Anne E. Lester (eds), *Between Orders and Heresy: Rethinking Medieval Religious Movements* (Toronto, 2022), pp. 307–36.

Grundmann, Herbert, *Religious Movements in the Middle Ages: The Historical Links Between Heresy, the Mendicant Orders, and the Women's Religious Movement in the Twelfth and Thirteenth Centuries*, Steven Rowan (trans.) (Notre Dame, 2005).

Guerra Medici, Maria Teresa, 'For a History of Women's Monastic Institutions. The Abbess: Role, Functions and Administration', *Bulletin of Medieval Canon Law*, 23 (1999), 30–55.

Gunn, Cate, *Ancrene Wisse: From Pastoral Literature to Vernacular Spirituality* (Cardiff, 2008).

——, '"Efter the measse-cos, hwen þe preost sacreð": When is the moment of ecstasy in Ancrene Wisse?', *NQ*, 246 (2001), 105–8.

——, 'Was there an Anchoress at Colne Priory?', *The Essex Society for Archaeology and History*, 2 (2011), 117–23.

Gunn, Cate, and Liz Herbert McAvoy (eds), *Medieval Anchorites in their Communities* (Cambridge, 2017).

Gunn, Cate, Liz Herbert McAvoy, and Naoë Kukita Yoshikawa (eds), *Women, Words and Devotional Literature in the Later Middle Ages* (Cambridge, forthcoming).

Hall, Dianne, *Women and the Church in Medieval Ireland, c. 1140–1540* (Dublin, 2003).

Hamburger, Jeffrey F., *Nuns as Artists: The Visual Culture of a Medieval Convent* (Berkeley, 1997).

——, *The Visual and the Visionary: Art and Female Spirituality in Late Medieval Germany* (New York, 1998).

Hamburger, Jeffrey, and Susan Marti (eds), *Crown and Veil: Female Monasticism from the Fifth to the Fifteenth Centuries* (New York, 2008).

Harrington, Christina, *Women in a Celtic Church Ireland: 450–1150* (Oxford, 2002).

Harrison, Anna, 'The Nuns of Helfta', in Julia A. Lamm (ed.), *The Wiley-Blackwell Companion to Christian Mysticism* (Oxford, 2013), pp. 297–310.

Hartmann, Sieglinde, 'Bridal Mysticism and the Politics of the Anchorhold: Dorothy of Montau', in Catherine Innes-Parker and Naoë Kukita Yoshikawa (eds), *Anchoritism in the Middle Ages: Texts and Traditions* (Cardiff, 2013), pp. 101–16.

Harward, Chiz, Nick Holder, Christopher Phillpotts, and Christopher Thomas (eds), *The Medieval Priory and Hospital of St Mary Spital and the Bishopsgate Suburb: Excavations at Spitalfields Market, London E1, 1991–2007* (London, 2019).

Healy-Varley, Margaret, 'Wounds Shall Be Worships: Anselm in Julian of Norwich's *Revelation of Love'*, *Journal of English and Germanic Philology*, 115 (2016), 186–212.

Heimmel, Jennifer P., *'God is our Mother': Julian of Norwich and the Medieval Image of Christian Feminine Divinity* (Salzburg, 1982).

Helvétius, Anne-Marie, 'L'abbatiat laïque comme relais du pouvoir royal aux frontières du royaume: Le cas du nord de la Neustrie au IXe siècle', in R. Le Jan (ed.), *La royauté et les élites dans l'Europe Carolingienne (du début du IXe aux environs de 920)* (Villeneuve d'Ascq, 1998), pp. 285–99.

——, 'Le monachisme féminin en Occident de l'Antiquité tardive au haut Moyen Age', in *Monachesimi d'oriente e d'occidente nell'alto medioevo: Spoleto, 31 marzo–6 aprile 2016*, vol. 2 (Spoleto, 2017), pp. 193–230.

——, 'La Passio de sainte Maxellende et la réforme d'une communauté féminine en Cambrésis', in M.-C. Isaïa and T. Garnier (eds), *Normes et hagiographie dans l'Occident (VIe–XVIe siècle)* (Turnhout, 2014), pp. 167–81.

——, 'Normes et pratiques de la vie monastique en Gaule avant 1050: Présentation des sources écrites', in O. Delouis and M. Mossakowska Gaubert (eds), *La vie quotidienne des moines en Orient et en Occident (IVe–Xe siècle). Vol. 1, L'état des sources* (Cairo, 2015), pp. 371–86.

Herzig, Tamar, *Savonarola's Women: Visions and Reforms in Renaissance Italy* (Chicago, 2007).

Hill, Carole, *Women and Religion in Late Medieval Norwich* (Woodbridge, 2010).

Hindsley, Leonard P., *The Mystics of Engelthal: Writings from a Medieval Monastery* (New York, 1998).

Hirbodian, Sigrid, 'Religious Women: Secular Canonesses and Beguines', in *OHCM*, pp. 285–99.

Hoernes, M., and H. Röckelein (eds), *Gandersheim und Essen: Vergleichende Untersuchungen zu sächsischen Frauenstiften* (Essen, 2006).

Hogg, James, 'The Carthusians. History and Heritage', in Krijn Pansters (ed.), *The Carthusians in the Low Countries: Studies in Monastic History and Heritage* (Leuven, 2014), pp. 31–56.

Hope, William St John, 'The Gilbertine Priory of Watton, in the East Riding of Yorkshire', *Yorkshire Archaeological Journal*, 58 (1901), 1–34.

Hosington, Brenda, 'Lady Margaret Beaufort's Translations as Mirrors of Practical Piety', in Micheline White (ed.), *English Women, Religion, and Textual Production, 1500–1625* (Burlington, 2011), pp. 185–203.

Hughes-Edwards, Mari, *Reading Medieval Anchoritism: Ideology and Spiritual Practices* (Cardiff, 2012).

Ihnat, Kati, 'Orígenes y desarrollo de la fiesta litúrgica de la Virgen María en Iberia', *Anuario de Estudios Medievales*, 49:2 (2019), 619–43.

Innes-Parker, Catherine, 'The Legacy of *Ancrene Wisse*', in Yoko Wada (ed.), *A Companion to Ancrene Wisse* (Cambridge, 2003), pp. 145–73.

——, 'Medieval Widowhood and Textual Guidance: The Corpus Revisions of *Ancrene Wisse* and the de Braose Anchoresses', *Florilegium*, 28 (2011), 95–124.

Intxaustegi, Nere Jone Jauregi, 'Convents and Basque Familial Networks of Power', in Edel Bhreathnach, Małgorzata Krasnodębska-D'Aughton, and Keith Smith (eds), *Monastic Europe: Medieval Communities, Landscapes, and Settlement* (Turnhout, 2019), pp. 503–21.

Iozzelli, Fortunato, 'I francescani ad Arezzo e a Cortona nel duocento', in *La presenza francescana nela Toscana del '200* (Florence, 1990), pp. 121–42.

Jäggi, Carola, 'Architecture et disposition liturgique des couvents féminins dans le Rhin supérieur aux XIIIe et XIVe siècles', in Madeleine Blondel, Jeffrey. F. Hamburger, and Catherine Leroy (eds), *Les Dominicaines d'Unterlinden*, 2 vols (Paris, 2000), vol. 1, pp. 89–107.

——, 'Eastern Choir or Western Gallery? The Problem of the Place of the Nuns' Choir in Koenigsfelden and Other Early Mendicant Nunneries', *Gesta*, 40:1 (2001), 79–93.

——, *Frauenklöster im Spätmittelalter: Die Kirchen der Klarissen und Dominikanerinnen im 13. und 14. Jahrhundert* (Petersberg, 2006).

——, 'Gräber und Memoria in den Klarissen-und Dominikanerinnenklöstern des 13. und 14. Jahrhunderts', in Heidemarie Specht and Ralph Andraschek-Holzer (eds), *Bettelorden in Mitteleuropa: Geschichte, Kunst, Spiritualität. Referate der gleichnamigen Tagung vom 19. bis 22. März 2007 in St Pölten* (St Pölten, 2008), pp. 689–705.

Jäggi, Carola, and Hans-Rudolf Meier, 'Eine Heilige zwischen Stadt und Konvent : das Euphrosynengrab im Kloster Klingental zu Basel', *Kunst + Architektur in der Schweiz = Art + architecture en Suisse = Arte + architettura in Svizzera*, 52 (2001), 16–26.

Jamroziak, Emilia, *The Cistercian Order in Medieval Europe, 1090–1500* (London, 2013).

Jamroziak, Emilia, and Karen Stöber (eds), *Monasteries on the Borders of Medieval Europe: Conflict and Cultural Interaction* (Turnhout, 2013).

Jaron Lewis, Gertrud, *By Women, for Women, about Women: The Sister-Books of Fourteenth-Century Germany* (Toronto, 1996).

Jarrett, Jonathan, 'Power over Past and Future: Abbess Emma and the Nunnery of Sant Joan de les Abadesses', *Early Medieval Europe*, 12:3 (2003), 229–58.

Johnson, Penelope D., *Equal in Monastic Profession: Religious Women in Medieval France* (Chicago, 1991).

Johnson, Sherri Franks, *Monastic Women and Religious Orders in Late Medieval Bologna* (Cambridge, 2014).

Jones, E. A., *Hermits and Anchorites in England* (Manchester, 2019).

Jones, E. A., and Alexandra Walsham (eds), *Syon Abbey and Its Books: Reading, Writing and Religion, c. 1400–1700* (Woodbridge, 2010).

Jordan, Erin, 'Gender Concerns: Monks, Nuns, and Patronage of the Cistercian Order in Thirteenth-Century Flanders and Hainault', *Speculum*, 87 (2012), 62–94.

——, 'Transforming the Landscape: Cistercian Nuns and the Environment in the Medieval Low Countries', *JMH*, 44:2 (Mar. 2018), 187–201.

——, *Women, Power and Religious Patronage in the Middle Ages* (New York, 2006).

Kaczynski, Berenice M. (ed.), *The Oxford Handbook of Christian Monasticism* (Oxford, 2020).

Kaelber, Lutz, *Schools of Asceticism: Ideology and Organisation in Medieval Religious Communities* (Philadelphia, 1998).

Kerr, Berenice M., *Religious Life for Women c. 1100–c. 1350: Fontevraud in England* (Oxford, 1999).

Kerr, Julie, *Monastic Hospitality: The Benedictines in England, c. 1070–c. 1250* (Woodbridge, 2007).

Knox, Alex, and Gabor Thomas, 'Excavating Anglo-Saxon Lyminge', in D. Harrington and J. Carr (eds), *Lyminge: A History: Part Four* (Lyminge, 2013), Ch. 20.

Knox, Lezlie, *Creating Clare of Assisi: Female Franciscan Identities in Later Medieval Italy* (Leiden, 2008).

Kottje, Raymund, 'Claustra sine armario?: Zum Unterschied von Kloster und Stift im Mittelalter', in J. F. Angerer and J. Lenzenweger (eds), *Consuetudines monasticae. Festgabe für Kassius Hallinger* (Rome, 1982), pp. 125–44.

Koudelka, Vladimir J., '"Le monasterium tempuli" et la fondation dominicaine de San Sisto', *AFP*, 31 (1961), 5–81.

Krings, Bruno, 'Zum Ordensrecht der Prämonstratenser bis zur Mitte de 12. Jahrhunderts', *Analecta Praemonstratensia*, 76 (2000), 9–28.

Kristjánsdóttir, Steinunn, Inger Larsson, and Per Arvid Åsen, 'The Icelandic Medieval Monastic Garden – Did It Exist?', *Scandinavian Journal of History*, 39:5 (Oct. 2014), 560–79.

Krug, Rebecca, *Reading Families: Women's Literate Practice in Late Medieval England* (London, 2008).

La Rocca, Cristina, 'Monachesimo femminile e poteri delle regine tra VIII e IX secolo', in G. Spinelli (ed.), *Il monachesimo italiano dall'età longobarda all'età ottoniana (secc. VIII–X)* (Cesena, 2006), pp. 119–43.

Lee, Paul, *Nunneries, Learning, and Spirituality in Late Medieval Society: The Dominican Priory of Dartford* (York, 2001).

Lehfeldt, Elizabeth A., 'Gender, the State, and Episcopal Authority: Hernando de Talavera and Richard Fox on Female Monastic Reform', *JMModS*, 42:3 (Fall, 2012), 615–34.

——, *Religious Women in Golden Age Spain: The Permeable Cloister* (Burlington, 2005).

——, 'Writing Religious Rules as an Interactive Process: Dominican Penitent Women and the Making of Their "Regula"', *Speculum*, 79 (2004), 660–87.

Lehmijoki-Gardner, Maiju, *Worldly Saints: Social Interaction of Dominican Penitent Women* (Helsinki, 1999).

Lester, Anne E., 'Cares Beyond the Walls: Cistercian Nuns and the Care of Lepers in Twelfth- and Thirteenth-Century Northern France', in Emilia Jamroziak and Janet Burton (eds), *Religious and Laity in Western Europe, 1000–1400: Interaction, Negotiation, and Power* (Turnhout, 2006), pp. 197–224.

——, *Creating Cistercian Nuns: The Women's Religious Movement and Its Reform in Thirteenth-Century Champagne* (Ithaca, 2011).

——, 'A Shared Imitation: Cistercian Convents and Crusader Families in Thirteenth-Century Champagne', *JMH*, 35 (2009), 353–70.

Licence, Tom, *Hermits and Recluses in English Society, 950–1200* (Oxford, 2011).

Lifshitz, Felice, 'Is Mother Superior? Towards a History of Feminine *Amtscharisma*', in John Carmi Parsons and Bonnie Wheeler (eds), *Medieval Mothering* (New York, 1996), pp. 117–38.

Lloyd, Joan Barclay, 'The Architectural Planning of Pope Innocent III's Nunnery of S. Sisto in Rome', in Andrea Sommerlechner (ed.), *Innocenzo III: Urbs et Orbis: atti del congresso internazionale, Roma, 9–15 settembre 1998* (Rome, 2003), pp. 1292–311.

——, *Dominicans and Franciscans in Medieval Rome: History, Architecture, and Art*, Medieval Monastic Studies, 6 (Turnhout, 2022).

——, 'Paintings for Dominican Nuns: A New Look at the Images of Saints, Scenes from the New Testament and Apocrypha, and Episodes from the Life of Saint Catherine of Siena in the Medieval Apse of San Sisto Vecchio in Rome', *Papers of the British School at Rome*, 80 (2012), 189–232.

Luongo, F. Thomas, *The Saintly Politics of Catherine of Siena* (Ithaca, 2006).

Luttrell A., and H. J. Nicolson (eds), *Hospitaller Women in the Middle Ages* (Aldershot, 2006).

Maclean, Simon, 'Queenship, Nunneries and Royal Widowhood in Carolingian Europe', *P & P*, 178 (2003), 3–38.

Makowski, Elizabeth, *Canon Law and Cloistered Women: Periculoso and Its Commentators, 1298–1545* (Washington, DC, 1997).

——, *English Nuns and the Law in the Middle Ages: Cloistered Nuns and Their Lawyers, 1293–1540* (Woodbridge, 2011).

——, *"A Pernicious Sort of Woman": Quasi-Religious Women and Canon Lawyers in the Later Middle Ages* (Washington, DC, 2005).

Manning, Conleth, 'Finghin MacCarthaigh, King of Desmond, and the Mystery of the Second Nunnery at Clonmacnoise', in David Edwards (ed.), *Regions and Rulers in Ireland 1100–1650* (Dublin, 2004), pp. 20–6.

Marti, Susan, *Malen, Schreiben un Beten: Die spätmittelalterliche Handschriftenproduktion im Doppelkloster Engelberg* (Zurich, 2002).

Martin, Therese, 'Mujeres, hermanas e hijas: El mecenazgo femenino en la familia de Alfonso VI', *Anales de historia del arte*, 1 (2011), 147–79.

Matter, E. Ann, 'Italian Holy Women: A Survey', in Alistair J. Minnis and Rosalynn Voaden (eds), *Medieval Holy Women in the Christian Tradition, c. 1100–c. 1500* (Turnhout, 2010), pp. 529–55.

Mazuela-Anguita, Ascensión, 'Confraternities as an Interface between Citizens and Convent: Musical Ceremonial in Sixteenth-Century Barcelona', *Confraternitas*, 31:2 (2020), 14–35.

McAvoy, Liz Herbert, *Medieval Anchoritisms: Gender, Space, and the Solitary Life* (Cambridge, 2011).

——, 'Uncovering the "Saintly Anchoress": Myths of Medieval Anchoritism and the Reclusion of Katharine de Audley', *Women's History Review*, 22:5 (2013), 801–19.

McAvoy, Liz Herbert (ed.), *Anchoritic Traditions of Medieval Europe* (Woodbridge, 2010).

——, *Rhetoric of the Anchorhold: Space, Place, and Body within the Discourses of Enclosure* (Cardiff, 2008).

McAvoy, Liz Herbert, and Mari Hughes-Edwards (eds), *Anchorites, Wombs and Tombs: Intersections of Gender and Enclosure in the Middle Ages* (Cardiff, 2005).

McKiernan González, Eileen, 'Reception, Gender, and Memory: Elisenda de Montcada and her Dual-Effigy Tomb at Santa María de Pedralbes', in Therese Martin (ed.), *Reassessing the Roles of Women as 'Makers' of Medieval Art and Architecture*, 2 vols (Leiden, 2012), Vol. 1, pp. 309–52.

McKitterick, Rosamund, 'Nuns' Scriptoria in England and Francia in the Eighth Century', *Francia*, 19:1 (1992), 1–35.

McNamara, Jo Ann K., 'The Herrenfrage: The Restructuring of the Gender System, 1050–1150', in Clare Lees (ed.), *Medieval Masculinities: Regarding Men in the Middle Ages* (Minneapolis, 1994), pp. 3–29.

——, *Sisters in Arms: Catholic Nuns through Two Millennia* (Cambridge, MA, 1996).

McShane, Bronagh Ann, 'Negotiating Religious Change and Conflict: Female Religious Communities in Early Modern Ireland 1530–1641', *British Catholic History*, 33 (2017) 357–82.

——, 'Visualising the Reception and Circulation of Early Modern Nuns' Letters', *Journal of Historical Network Research*, 2 (2018) 1–25.

Mecham, June L., 'A Northern Jerusalem: Transforming the Spatial Geography of the Convent of Wienhausen', in Sarah M. Hamilton and Andrew Spicer (eds), *Defining the Holy: Sacred Space in Medieval and Early Modern Europe* (Aldershot, 2005), pp. 139–60.

——, *Sacred Communities, Shared Devotions: Gender, Material Culture, and Monasticism in Late Medieval Germany* (Turnhout, 2014).

Mellinger, Laura, 'Environmentalist Nuns in Medieval Brittany? Saint-Georges and the River Vilaine', *Medieval Perspectives*, 10 (1995), 157–68.

——, 'Politics in the Convent: The Election of a Fifteenth-Century Abbess', *CH*, 63:4 (Dec. 1994), 529–40.

Melville, G., and A. Müller (eds), *Female Vita Religiosa Between Late Antiquity and the High Middle Ages* (Berlin, 2011).

Mersch, Margit, 'Programme, Pragmatism and Symbolism in Mendicant Architecture', in Anne Müller and Karen Stöber (eds), *Self-Representation of Medieval Religious Communities: The British Isles in Context* (Berlin, 2009), pp. 143–66.

Mews, Constant J., 'Hildegard of Bingen and the Hirsau Reform in Germany, 1080–1180', in Debra Stoudt et al. (eds), *A Companion to Hildegard of Bingen* (Leiden, 2014), pp. 57–83.

——, 'Imagining Heloise as Abbess of the Paraclete', *Journal of Religious History*, 44 (2020), 422–42.

——, 'Negotiating the Boundaries of Gender in Religious Life: Robert of Arbrissel and Hersende, Abelard and Heloise', *Viator*, 37 (2006), 113–48.

Miller, Tanya Stabler, *The Beguines of Medieval Paris: Gender, Patronage, and Spiritual Authority* (Philadelphia, 2014).

——, 'What's in a name? Clerical Representations of Parisian Beguines (1200–1328)', *JMH*, 33 (2007), 60–86.

Millett, Bella, '*Ancrene Wisse* and the Book of Hours', in Denis Renevey and Christiania Whitehead (eds), *Writing Religious Women: Female Spiritual and Textual Practices in Late Medieval England* (Cardiff, 2000), pp. 21–40.

——, '*Ancrene Wisse* and the Conditions of Confession', *English Studies*, 80 (1999), 193–215.

——, 'The Origins of *Ancrene Wisse*: New Answers, New Questions', *Medium Aevum*, 61 (1992), 206–28.

Minnis, Alastair, and Rosalynn Voaden (eds), *Medieval Holy Women in the Christian Tradition, c. 1100–c. 1500* (Turnhout, 2010).

Mohn, Claudia, *Mittelalterliche Klosteranlagen der Zisterzienserinnen: Architektur der Frauenkloster im mitteldeutschen Raum. Berliner Beitrage zu Bauforschung und Denkmalpflege*, 4 (Petersberg, 2006).

Montgomerie, Alexander, 'The Deathbed Dispositions of Elizabeth Prioress of The Abbey of Haddington, 1563', *TELAS*, 6 (Haddington, 1955), 1–5.

Mooney, Catherine M., *Clare of Assisi and the Thirteenth-Century Church: Religious Women, Rules, and Resistance* (Philadelphia, 2016).

More, Alison, 'Between Charity and Controversy: The Grey Sisters, Liminality, and the Religious Life', in Jennifer Kolpacoff Deane and Anne E. Lester (eds), *Between Orders and Heresy: Rethinking Medieval Religious Movements* (Toronto, 2022), pp. 242–62.

——, 'Dynamics of Regulation, Innovation, and Invention', in James Mixson and Bert Roest (eds), *Observant Reform in the Late Middle Ages and Beyond* (Leiden, 2015), pp. 85–110.

——, *Fictive Orders and Feminine Religious Identities, 1200–1600* (Oxford, 2018).

——, 'Institutionalizing Penitential Life in Later Medieval and Early Modern Europe: Third Orders, Rules, and Canonical Legitimacy', *CH*, 83 (2014), 297–323.

Morvan, Haude, 'Sépultures cardinalices et mémoire communautaire', in Fermín Miranda García and María Teresa López de Guereño Sanz (eds), *La muerte de los príncipes en la edad media* (Madrid, 2020), pp. 337–52.

Mueller, Joan, *A Companion to Clare of Assisi: Life, Writings, and Spirituality* (Leiden, 2010).

——, *The Privilege of Poverty: Clare of Assisi, Agnes of Prague, and the Struggle for a Franciscan Rule for Women* (Philadelphia, 2006).

Muessig, Carolyn, 'Catherine of Siena in late Medieval Sermons', in George

Ferzoco, Beverly Kienzle, and Carolyn Muessig (eds), *A Companion to Catherine of Siena* (Leiden, 2012), pp. 203–26.

——, 'Communities of Discourse: Religious Authority and the Role of Holy Women in the Later Middle Ages', in Anneke Mulder-Bakker (ed.), *Women and Experience in Later Medieval Writing* (New York, 2009), pp. 65–82.

Mulder-Bakker, Anneke, *Lives of the Anchoresses: The Rise of the Urban Recluse in Medieval Europe*, Myra Heerspink Scholz (trans.) (Philadelphia, 2005).

Muñoz Fernández, Ángela, 'Memorias del coro: Constanza de Castilla y las políticas del recuerdo', in Gabriella Zarri and Nieves Baranda Leturio (eds), *Memoria e Comunità Femminili* (Firenze, 2011), pp. 27–48.

Murray, Paul, *Archaeological Excavations at Littlemore Priory, Oxford* (Oxford, 2016).

Muschiol, Gisela, 'Time and Space. Liturgy and Rite in Female Monasteries of the Middle Ages', in Jeffrey. F. Hamburger and Susan Marti (eds), *Crown and Veil: Female Monasticism from the Fifth to the Fifteenth Centuries* (New York, 2008), pp. 191–206.

Newman, Barbara, *Voice of the Living Light: Hildegard of Bingen and Her World* (Berkeley, 1998).

Ní Dhonnchadha, Máirín, '*Caillech* and Other Terms for Veiled Women in Medieval Irish Texts', *Éigse*, 28 (1995), 71–96.

Nichols, John A., 'The Internal Organisation of English Cistercian Nunneries', *Citeaux*, 30 (1979), 23–40.

Nichols, John A., and Lillian T. Shank (eds), *Medieval Religious Women. Volume One: Distant Echoes* (Kalamazoo, 1984).

Nicolini, Ugolino, *Memoriale di Monteluce: cronaca del monastero delle clarisse di Perugia dal 1448 al 1838* (Porziuncola, 1983).

Nolan, Kathleen, 'The Queen's Choice: Eleanor of Aquitaine and the Tombs at Fontevraud', in Bonnie Wheeler and John C. Parson (eds), *Eleanor of Aquitaine: Lord and Lady* (New York, 2003), pp. 377–406.

Ó Carragáin, Tomás, 'The Archaeology of Ecclesiastical Estates in Early Medieval Ireland: A Case Study of the Kingdom of Fir Maige', *Peritia*, 24–25 (2014), 266–312.

Oliva, Marilyn, *The Convent and the Community in Late Medieval England: Female Monasteries in the Diocese of Norwich, 1350–1540* (Woodbridge, 1998).

——, 'Nuns at Home: The Domesticity of Sacred Space', in Maryanne Kowaleski and P. J. P. Goldberg (eds), *Medieval Domesticity: Home, Housing, and Household in Medieval England* (Cambridge, 2008), pp. 145–61.

Olson, Linda, 'Reading, Writing, and Relationships in Dialogue', in Linda Olson and Kathryn Kerby-Fulton (eds), *Voices in Dialogue: Reading Women in the Middle Ages* (Notre Dame, 2005), pp. 1–30.

Olyslager, W. A., *The Groot Begijnhof of Leuven* (Leuven, 1983).

Oschema, Klaus, 'Zur Gründung des Benediktinerinnenklosters Notre-Dame de Bouxières. Eine wiedergefundene Urkunde des 10. Jahrhunderts', *Mitteilungen des Instituts für Österreichische Geschichtsforschung*, 110 (2002), 182–90.

Parisse, Michel, 'Der Anteil der Lothringischen Benediktinerinnen an der monastischen Bewegung des 10. und 11. Jahrhunderts', in Peter Dinzelbacher (ed.), *Religiöse Frauenbewegung und mystische Frömmigkeit im Mittelalter* (Cologne, 1988), pp. 83–98.

——, 'Les monastères de femmes en Saxe des Carolingiens aux Saliens', in M. Parisse, *Religieux et religieuses en Empire du Xe au XIIe siècle* (Paris, 2011), pp. 141–72.

——, *Les nonnes au moyen âge* (Le Puy, 1983).

Pazienza, Annamaria, and Veronica West-Harling, 'Networking Nuns: Imperial Power and Family Alliances at S. Salvatore di Brescia (*c.* 837–61)', *JMMS*, 10 (2021), 9–39.

Pearson, Hilary, *The Recluse of Iftele: Annora de Briouze: The Life and Times of an Anchoress in Medieval England* (Iffley, 2019).

Pérez Vidal, Mercedes, *Arte y liturgia en los monasterios de dominicas en Castilla. Desde los orígenes hasta la reforma observante (1218–1506)* (Gijón, 2021).

——, 'Between the City and the Cloister. Saints, Liturgy and Devotion in the Dominican Nunneries in Late Medieval Castile', in Michele Ferrari (ed.), *Saints and the City: Beiträge zum Verständnis urbaner Sakralität in christlichen Gemeinschaften (5.–17. Jh.)* (Erlangen, 2015), pp. 233–67.

——, 'Estavan todas no coro e ben cantand' e Leendo Tipologie e funzioni dei cori nei monasteri delle Domenicane dal XIII al XVI secolo, con particolare riferimento alla Castiglia', in Haude Morvan (ed.), *Spaces for Friars and Nuns: Mendicant Choirs and Church Interiors in Medieval and Early Modern Europe* (Rome, 2021), pp. 227–58.

——, 'Female Aristocratic Networks: Books, Liturgy and Reform in Castilian Nunneries', in Emma O. Bérat, Rebecca Hardie, and Irina Dumitrescu (eds), *Relations of Power: Women's Networks in the Middle Ages* (Göttingen, 2021), pp. 105–32.

——, 'La liturgia procesional de Completas en el ámbito de los monasterios femeninos de la Orden de Predicadores en Castilla', *Hispania Sacra*, 69:139 (2017), 81–99.

——, 'Legislation, Architecture and Liturgy in the Dominican Nunneries in Castile during the Late Middle Ages. A world of *diversitas* and peculiarities', in Cornelia Linde (ed.), *Making and Breaking the Rules: Discussion, Implementation, and Consequences of Dominican Legislation* (Oxford, 2018), pp. 225–52.

Pernoud, Regine, 'The Preaching Peregrinations of a Twelfth-Century Nun, ca. 1158–70', in Audrey Davidson Ekdahl (ed.), *Wisdom Which Encircles Circles: Papers on Hildegard of Bingen* (Kalamazoo, 1996), pp. 15–26.

Petroff, Elizabeth A., 'Women and Mysticism in the Medieval World', in Nahir I. Otaño Gracia and Daniel Armenti (eds), *Women's Lives: Self-Representation, Reception and Appropriation in the Middle Ages* (Cardiff, 2022), pp. 13–33.

Phillips, Kim M., 'Bodily Walls, Windows, and Doors: The Politics of Gesture in Late Fifteenth-Century English Books for Women', in J. Wogan-Browne, R. Voaden, A. Diamond, et al. (eds), *Medieval Women: Texts and Contexts in Late Medieval Britain, Essays for Felicity Riddy* (Turnhout, 2000), pp. 185–98.

Polet, Caroline, and M. Anne Katzenberg, 'Reconstruction of the Diet in a Mediaeval Monastic Community from the Coast of Belgium', *Journal of Archaeological Science*, 30:5 (2003), 525–33.

Powell, Susan, *The Birgittines of Syon Abbey: Preaching and Print* (Turnhout, 2017).

Power, Eileen, *Medieval English Nunneries, c. 1275 to 1535* (Cambridge, 1922).

Radini, Anita, M. Tromp, A. Beach, E. Tong, C. Speller, M. McCormick, J. V. Dudgeon, M. J. Collins, F. Rühli, R. Kröger, and C. Warinner, 'Medieval Women's Early Involvement in Manuscript Production Suggested by Lapis Lazuli Identification in Dental Calculus', *Science Advances*, 5 (2019), 1–8.

Raguin, Victoria C., and Sarah Stanbury (eds), *Women's Space: Patronage, Place, and Gender in the Medieval Church* (New York, 2005).

Reid, Alison, G., and Doherty M. Lye, *Pitmiddle Village and Elcho Nunnery: Research and Excavation in Tayside* (Perth, 1988).

Richmond, Laura M., 'A Survey of Monumental Brasses of Late Medieval Vowesses', *Transactions of the Monumental Brass Society*, 23 (forthcoming, 2022).

Rijpma, F. E., and G. J. R. Maat, *A Physical Anthropological Research of The Beguines of Breda 1267 To 1530 AD*, Barge's Anthropologica Nr. 11 (Leiden, 2005), 1–14.

Roberts, Laura, 'The Spiritual Singularity of Syon Abbey and its Sisters', *Ezra's Archives*, 5:1 (Spring, 2015), 65–83.

Röckelein, Hedwig, 'Bairische, sächsische und mainfränkische Klostergründungen im Vergleich (8. Jahrhundert bis 1100)', in E. Schlotheuber (ed.), *Nonnen, Kanonissen und Mystikerinnen. Religiöse Frauengemeinschaften in Süddeutschland* (Göttingen, 2008), pp. 23–55.

——, 'Die Frauenkonvente und ihre Pfarreien: Aufriss eines Problems', in Hedwig Röckelein (ed.), *Frauenstifte: Frauenklöster und ihre Pfarreien* (Essen, 2009), pp. 9–18.

Roest, Bert, *Order and Disorder: The Poor Clares Between Foundation and Reform* (Leiden, 2013).

Roest, Bert, and James D. Mixson (eds), *A Companion to Observant Reform in Late Middle Ages and Beyond* (Leiden, 2015).

Rubin, Miri, 'An English anchorite: the making, unmaking and remaking of Christine Carpenter', in Rosemary Horrox and Sarah Rees Jones (eds), *Pragmatic Utopias: Ideals and Communities, 1200–1630* (Cambridge, 2001), pp. 204–23.

Rudy, Kathryn M., *Virtual Pilgrimages in the Convent: Imagining Jerusalem in the Late Middle Ages* (Turnhout, 2011).

Ruyman, Mallory A., 'Nuns as Gardeners: Using and Making Enclosed Gardens', *Athanor*, 35 (2017), 41–8.

Saetveit Miles, Laura, 'Queer Touch Between Holy Women: Julian of Norwich, Margery Kempe, Birgitta of Sweden, and the Visitation', in David Carrillo-Rangel, Delfi I. Nieto-Isabel, and Pablo Acosta-Garcia (eds), *Touching, Devotional Practices, and Visionary Experience in the Late Middle Ages* (Cambridge, 2019), pp. 203–35.

Sahli, Alejandra Concha, 'Habit Envy: Extra-Regular Religious Groups, Attire, and the Search for Legitimation Outside the Institutionalised Religious Orders', in Robin Netherton, Gale R. Owen-Crocker, and Monica L. Wright (eds), *Medieval Clothing and Textiles*, 15 (2019), pp. 137–56.

Salter, Mike, *Medieval Nunneries* (Malvern, 2015).

Schäfer, K. H., *Die Kanonissenstifter im deutschen Mittelalter* (Stuttgart, 1907).

Sauer, Michelle M., and Jenny C. Bledsoe (eds), *The Materiality of Middle English Anchoritic Devotion* (Leeds, 2001).

Schaefer, Mary M., *Women in Pastoral Office: The Story of Santa Prassede, Rome* (Oxford, 2013).

Scheck, Helene, 'Future Perfect: Reading Temporalities at the Royal Women's Monastery at Chelles, ca. 660–1050', *Mediaevalia*, 36–37 (2015/16), 9–50.

Scheepsma, Wybren, *Deemoed en devotie: De koorvrouwen van Windesheim en hun geschriften*, Nederlandse literatuur en cultuur in de Middeleeuwen 17 (Amsterdam, 1997); trans. David S. Johnson, *Medieval Religious Women in the Low Countries: The 'Modern Devotion', the Canonesses of Windesheim, and their Writings* (Woodbridge, 2004).

Schleif, Corinne, and Volker Schier, *Katerina's Windows: Donation and Devotion, Art and Music, as Heard and Seen through the Writings of a Birgittine Nun* (University Park, 2009).

Schlip, Thomas, *Frauen bauen Europa: Internationale Verflechtungen des Frauenstifts Essen* (Essen, 2011).

——, *Norm und Wirklichkeit religiöser Frauengemeinschaften im frühen Mittelalter* (Göttingen, 1998).

——, *Pro remedio et salute anime peragemus. Totengedenken am Frauenstift Essen im Mittelalter* (Essen, 2008).

Schlotheuber, Eva, 'Best Clothes and Everyday Attire of late Medieval Nuns', in Regula Schorta, Rainer C. Scwinges and Klaus Oschema (eds), *Fashion and Clothing in Late Medieval Europe* (Riggisberg, 2010), pp. 139–54.

——, 'Klostereintritt und übergangsriten. Die Bedeutung der Jungfräulichkeit für das Selbstverständnis der Nonnen der alten Orden', in Jeffrey Hamburger, Carola Jäggi, Susan Marti, and Hedwig Röckelein, (eds), *Frauen - Kloster - Kunst. Neue Forschungen zur Kulturgeschichte des Mittelalters. Beiträge zum Internationalen Kolloquium vom 13. bis 16. Mai 2005 anlässlich der Ausstellung 'Krone und Schleier'* (Turnhout, 2007), pp. 43–58.

Schulenberg, Jane T., *Forgetful of Their Sex: Female Sanctity and Society, ca. 500–1100* (Chicago, 1998).

——, 'Women's Monastic Communities, 500–1100: Patterns of Expansion and Decline', *Signs: Journal of Women in Culture and Society*, 14 (1989), 261–92.

Seale, Yvonne, '*De Monasterio Desolato*: Patronage and Politics in a Frontier Irish Convent', *JMMS*, 4 (2015), 21–45.

Seeberg, Stefanie, 'Women as Makers of Church Decoration: Illustrated Textiles at the Monasteries of Altenberg/Lahn, Ruperstberg, and Heiningen (13th–14th c.)', in Therese Martin (ed.), *Reassessing the Roles of Women as 'Makers' of Medieval Art and Architecture*, 2 vols (Leiden, 2012), vol. 1, pp. 355–92.

Sheerin, Daniel, 'Sisters in the Literary Agon: Texts from Communities of

Women on the Mortuary Roll of the Abbess Matilda of La Trinité, Caen',
in Laurie J. Churchill, Phyllis R. Brown, and Jane E. Jeffrey (eds), *Women
Writing Latin: From Roman Antiquity to Early Modern Europe*, 3 vols (New
York, 2002), vol. 2, pp. 93–131.

Sheils, W. J., and D. Wood (eds), *Women in the Church*, SCH, 27 (Oxford, 1990).

Simon, André, *L'Ordre des pénitentes de Ste Marie Madeleine en Allemagne au
XIIeme siècle* (Fribourg, 1918).

Simons, Walter, *Cities of Ladies: Beguine Communities in the Medieval Low
Countries, 1200–1550* (Philadelphia, 2003).

——, 'On the Margins of Religious Life: Hermits and Recluses, Penitents and
Tertiaries, Beguines and Beghards', in Miri Rubin and Walter Simons (eds),
The Cambridge History of Christianity, vol. 4: *Christianity in Western Europe,
c. 1110–c. 1500* (Cambridge, 2009), pp. 311–23.

Sloane, Barney, *The Augustinian Nunnery of St Mary Clerkenwell, London*
(London, 2012).

——, 'Tenements in London's Monasteries c. 1450–1540', in David Gaimster and
Roberta Gilchrist (eds), *The Archaeology of Reformation, 1480–1580* (Leeds,
2003), pp. 290–8.

Smith, Julie A., '*Clausura Districta*: Conceiving Space and Community for
Dominican Nuns in the Thirteenth Century', *Parergon*, 27:2 (2010), 13–36.

——, '*Debitum obedientie*: Heloise and Abelard on governance at the Paraclete',
Parergon, 25 (2008), 1–23.

——, *Ordering Women's Lives: Penitentials and Nunnery Rules in the Early
Medieval West* (Aldershot, 2001).

——, 'Prouille, Madrid, Rome: The Evolution of the Earliest Dominican *Instituta*
for Nuns', *JMH*, 35 (2009), 340–52.

Sorrentino, Janet, 'In Houses of Nuns, in Houses of Canons: A Liturgical
Dimension to Double Monasteries', *JMH*, 28 (2002), 361–72.

Spear, Valerie, *Leadership in Medieval English Nunneries* (Woodbridge, 2005).

Steuer, Susan, 'Identifying Chaste Widows: Documenting a Religious Vocation',
in L. E. Mitchell, K. L. French, and D. L. Biggs (eds), *The Ties that Bind: Essays
in Medieval British History in Honor of Barbara Hanawalt* (Burlington, 2011),
pp. 87–105.

Stöber, Karen, 'Female Patrons of Late Medieval English Monasteries', *Medieval
Prosopography*, 31 (2016), 115–36.

——, *Late Medieval Monasteries and Their Patrons: England and Wales, c.
1300–1540* (Woodbridge, 2007).

Stocker, Bärbel, 'Die Opfergeräte der heiligen Wiborada von St. Gallen – Eine
Frau als Zelebrantin der Eucharistie?', *Freiburger Diöcezan-Archiv*, 111 (1991),
405–19.

Stofferahn, Steven, 'Changing Views of Carolingian Women's Literary Culture:
The Evidence from Essen', *EME*, 8 (1999), 69–97.

Stoudt, Debra, George Ferzoco, and Beverly Keinzle (eds), *A Companion to
Hildegard of Bingen* (Leiden, 2014).

Stout, Geraldine, and Matthew Stout, *The Bective Abbey Project, Co. Meath
Excavations 2009–12* (Dublin, 2016).

Strocchia, Sharon T., *Nuns and Nunneries in Renaissance Florence* (Baltimore, 2009).

——, 'When the Bishop Married the Abbesss: Masculinity and Power in Florentine Episcopal Entry Rites, 1300-1600', *GH*, 19:2 (Aug. 2007), 346–68.

Stover, Justin A., 'Hildegard, the Schools and their Critics', in Stoudt et al. (eds), *A Companion to Hildegard* (Leiden, 2014), pp. 109–35.

Suárez González, Ana, 'Un ex libris y algunas respuestas sobre el 'MS.1' de las Huelgas de Burgos', *Cistercium*, 245 (2006), 587–614.

Sykes, Katherine, 'Canonici Albi et Moniales: Perceptions of the Twelfth-Century Double House', *JEH*, 60:2 (2009), 233–45.

——, *Inventing Sempringham: Gilbert of Sempringham and the Origins of the Role of Master* (Berlin, 2011).

——, 'Rewriting the Rules: Gender, Bodies and Monastic Legislation in the Twelfth and Thirteenth Centuries', *JMMS*, 9 (2020), 107–31.

Tarrant, Jacqueline, 'The Clementine Decrees on the Beguines: Conciliar and Papal Versions', *Archivum Historiae Pontificae*, 12 (1974), 300–8.

Taylor Jones, Claire, *Ruling the Spirit: Women, Liturgy, and Dominican Reform in Late Medieval Germany* (Philadelphia, 2007).

Temple, Liam Peter, 'Returning the English "Mystics" to their Medieval Milieu: Julian of Norwich, Margery Kempe, and Bridget of Sweden', *Women's Writing*, 23:2 (2016), 141–58.

Thibaut, Jirki, 'Female Abbatial Leadership and the Shaping of Communal Identity in Ninth-Century Saxony: The *Life* of Hathumoda of Gandesheim', *JMMS*, 7 (2018), 21–45.

——, 'Intermediary Leadership. The Agency of Abbesses in Ottonian Saxony', in Steven Vanderputten (ed.), *Abbots and Abbesses as a Human Resource in the Ninth- to Twelfth-Century West* (Zürich, 2018), pp. 39–56.

Thomas, Gabor, 'Life Before the Minster: The Social Dynamics of Monastic Foundation at Anglo-Saxon Lyminge, Kent', *Antiquaries Journal*, 93 (2013), 109–45.

Thomas, Gabor, and Alex Knox (eds), *Early Medieval Monasticism in the North Sea Zone: Proceedings of a Conference Held to Celebrate the Conclusion of the Lyminge Excavations 2008–15*. Anglo-Saxon Studies in Archaeology and History, 20 (Oxford, 2017).

Thompson, Augustine, 'The Origins of Religious Mendicancy in Medieval Europe', in Donald Prudlo (ed.), *The Origin, Development, and Refinement of Medieval Religious Mendicancies* (Leiden, 2011), pp. 3–30.

Thompson, Sally, *Women Religious: The Founding of English Nunneries After the Norman Conquest* (Oxford, 1991).

——, 'The Problem of Cistercian Nuns in the Twelfth and Thirteenth Centuries', in Derek Baker (ed.), *Medieval Women*, SCH Subsidia 1 (1978), pp. 227–52.

Tugwell, Simon, 'Were the Magdalen Nuns Really Turned into Dominicans in 1287?', *AFP*, 76 (2006), 39–77.

Vadas, András, 'Long-Term Perspectives on River Floods: The Dominican Nunnery on Margaret Island (Budapest) and the Danube River', *Interdisciplinaria Archaeologica*, 4 (2013), 73–82.

Vanderputten, Steven, '"Against the Custom": Hagiographical Rewriting and Female Abbatial Leadership at Mid-Eleventh-Century Remiremont', *JMMS*, 10 (2021), 41–66.

——, *Dark Age Nunneries: The Ambiguous Identity of Female Monasticism, 800–1050* (Ithaca, 2018).

——, 'Debating Reform in Tenth- and Early Eleventh-Century Female Monasticism', *Zeitschrift für Kirchengeschichte*, 125 (2014), 289–306.

——, 'The Dignity of Our Bodies and the Salvation of Our Souls. Scandal, Purity, and the Pursuit of Unity in Late Tenth-Century Monasticism', in Stefan Esders, Sarah Greer, and Alice Hicklin (eds), *Using and Not Using the Past after the Carolingian Empire, c. 900–c. 1050* (Abingdon, 2019), pp. 262–81.

——, *Dismantling the Medieval: Early Modern Perceptions of a Female Convent's Past* (Turnhout, 2021).

——, *Medieval Monasticisms: Forms and Experiences of the Monastic Life in the Latin West* (Munich, 2020).

Vanderputten, Steven, and Charles West, 'Inscribing Property, Rituals, and Royal Alliances: The "Theutberga Gospels" and the Abbey of Remiremont', *Mitteilungen des Instituts für Österreichische Geschichtsforschung*, 124 (2016), 296–321.

Venarde, Bruce L., 'Praesidentes Negotiis: Abbesses as Managers in Twelfth-Century France', in Samuel K. Cohn and Steven A. Epstein (eds), *Portraits of Medieval and Renaissance Living: Essays in Memory of David Herlihy* (Ann Arbor, 1996), pp. 189–205.

——, *Women's Monasticism and Medieval Society: Nunneries in France and England, 890–1215* (Ithaca, 1997).

Verdon, Jean, 'Notes sur le rôle économique des monastères féminins en France dans la seconde moitié du IXe et au début du Xe siècle', *RM*, 58 (1975), 329–44.

——, 'Recherches sur les monastères féminins dans la France du nord aux IXe–XIe siècles', *RM*, 59 (1976), 49–96.

Vernet, Felix, *Les ordres mendiants* (Paris, 1933).

Veyssière, Laurent, 'Cîteaux et Tart, fondations parallèles', in Bernadette Barrière and Marie-Elizabeth Henneau (eds), *Cîteaux et les femmes* (Grane, 2001), pp. 179–91.

Wada, Yoko (ed.), *A Companion to Ancrene Wisse* (Cambridge, 2003).

Wagner, Heinrich, 'Zur Notitia de servitio monasteriorum von 819', *Deutsches Archiv für Erforschung des Mittelalters*, 55 (1999), 417–38.

Ward, Simon, *Excavations at Chester: The Lesser Medieval Religious Houses, Sites Investigated 1964–1983* (Chester, 1990).

Wardell, John, 'The History and Antiquities of St Catherine's Old Abbey, County Limerick (with a description of the conventual buildings by T. J. Westropp)', *JRSAI*, 14 (1904), 41–64.

Warren, Ann K., *Anchorites and their Patrons in Medieval England* (Berkeley, 1985).

Warren, Nancy Bradley, *Spiritual Economies: Female Monasticism in Later Medieval England* (Philadelphia, 2001).

Weed, Stanley E., 'My Sister, Bride, and Mother: Aspects of Female Piety in Some Images of the *Virgo inter Virgines*', *Magistra*, 4:1 (1998), 3–26.

Wemple, Suzanne F., 'Female Monasticism in Italy and its Comparison with France and Germany From the Ninth Through the Eleventh Century', in U. Vorwerk and W. Affeldt (eds), *Frauen in Spätantike und Frühmittelalter. Lebensbedingungen – Lebensnormen – Lebensformen* (Sigmaringen, 1990), pp. 291–310.

——, *Women in Frankish Society: Marriage and the Cloister, 500 to 900* (Philadelphia, 1981).

West-Harling, Veronica, (ed.), *Female Monasticism in Italy in the Early Middle Ages: New Questions, New Debates* (Florence, 2019).

Wheeler, Bonnie (ed.), *Listening to Heloise: The Voice of a Twelfth-Century Woman* (New York, 2000).

Winston-Allen, Anne, *Convent Chronicles: Women Writing about Women and Reform in the Late Middle Ages* (Philadelphia, 2004).

Wischermann, Else M., *Marcigny-Sur-Loire. Gründungs- u. Frühgeschichte des 1. Cluniacenserinnenpriorates (1055–1150)* (Munich, 1986).

Wolbrink, Shelley, 'Women in the Premonstratensian Order of Northwestern Germany, 1120–1250', *Catholic Historical Review*, 89 (2003), 387–408.

Wolfram, Georg, 'Die Urkunde Ludwigs des Deutschen für das Glossindenkloster', *Mitteilungen des Instituts für Österreichische Geschichtsforschung*, 11 (1890), 1–27.

Wood, Charles Tuttle, 'Fontevraud, Dynasticism, and Eleanor of Aquitaine', in Bonnie Wheeler and John C. Parson (eds), *Eleanor of Aquitaine: Lord and Lady* (New York, 2003), pp. 407–22.

Wood, Laura M., 'In Search of the Mantle and Ring: Prosopographical Study of the Vowess in Late Medieval England', *Medieval Prosopography*, 34 (2019), 175–205.

Yorke, Barbara E., *Nunneries and the Anglo-Saxon Royal Houses* (London, 2003).

Zarri, Gabriella, 'Catherine of Siena and the Italian Public', in Jeffrey F. Hamburger and Gabriela Signori (eds), *Catherine of Siena: The Creation of a Cult* (Turnhout, 2013), pp. 69–79.

Zarri, Gabriella, and Nieves Baranda Leturio (eds), *Memoria e Comunità Femminili. Spagna e Italia, sec. XV–XVII. Memoria y comunidades femeninas. España e Italia, siglos XV–XVII* (Firenze, 2011).

Unpublished Theses

Beckers, Julie, 'Invisible Presence: The Poor Clares of Central Italy: Families, Veil, and Art Patronage, c. 1350–1550' (Unpublished Ph.D. dissertation, KU-Leuven, 2017).

Cardoso, Paula, 'Art, Reform and Female Agency in the Portuguese Dominican Nunneries: Nuns as Producers and Patrons of Illuminated Manuscripts (ca. 1460–1560)' (Unpublished Ph.D. dissertation, Universidade Nova de Lisboa, 2019).

Catalunya, David, 'Music, Space and Ritual in Medieval Castile, 1221–1350' (Unpublished Ph.D. dissertation, Universität Würzburg, 2016).

Curran, Kimm, 'Religious Women and their Communities in Late Medieval Scotland' (Unpublished Ph.D. dissertation, University of Glasgow, 2005).

Dutton, Anne Marie, 'Women's Use of Religious Literature in Late Medieval England' (Unpublished D.Phil. dissertation, University of York, 1995).

Grimard-Mongrain, Rosalie, 'Genre, mémoire et histoire dans le monastère San Salvatore/Santa Giulia à Brescia, VIIIe-IXe siècles' (Unpublished MA dissertation, Université de Montréal, 2018).

Keeping, Diane, 'Life and Death in English Nunneries: A Biocultural Study of Variations in the Health of Women During the Later Medieval Period, 1066–1540' (Unpublished Ph.D. dissertation, University of Bradford, 2000).

Martins, Nicole, 'Convento da Conceição de Beja: Arquitectura num período de transição (séculos XV e XVI)' (Unpublished Ph.D. dissertation, University of Lisbon, 2019).

Seale, Yvonne, '"Ten Thousand Women": Gender, Affinity, and the Development of the Premonstratensian Order in France' (Unpublished Ph.D. dissertation, University of Iowa, 2016).

Thibaut, Jirki, 'De ambigue observantie en heterogene identiteit van vrouwengemeenschappen in Saksen, ca. 800–1050' (Unpublished Ph.D. dissertation, Ghent University – KU Leuven, 2020).

Index

Note: places are located by their modern countries.

Studies in the History of Medieval Religion

ISSN 0955-2480

Founding Editor
Christopher Harper-Bill

Series Editor
Frances Andrews

Other volumes in
Studies in the History of Medieval Religion

Printed and bound by CPI Group (UK) Ltd, Croydon, CR0 4YY

03/06/2024

14509955-0001